The Socio-Economic Approach to Management Revisited

The Evolving Nature of SEAM in the 21st Century

A Volume in
Research in Management Consulting

Series Editor
Anthony F. Buono, *Bentley University*

Research in Management Consulting

Anthony F. Buono, Series Editor

The Socio-Economic Approach to Management Revisited

The Evolving Nature of SEAM in the 21st Century

Edited by

Anthony F. Buono
Bentley University

and

Henri Savall
University Jean Moulin Lyon 3 and ISEOR

INFORMATION AGE PUBLISHING, INC.
Charlotte, NC • www.infoagepub.com

Library of Congress Cataloging-in-Publication Data

A CIP record for this book is available from the Library of Congress
http://www.loc.gov

ISBN: 978-1-68123-161-7 (Paperback)
     978-1-68123-162-4 (Hardcover)
     978-1-68123-163-1 (ebook)

Printed in the United States of America

CONTENTS

INTRODUCTION

Anthony F. Buono

This book is part of an ongoing relationship with Henri Savall and his team of intervener-researchers at the Socio-Economic Institute for Firms and Organizations (ISEOR). It is the second volume in the Research in Management Consulting series that is based on an extended stay at ISEOR in Ecully, France, on the outskirts of Lyon, where I had another opportunity to work closely with the Center's consultant-scholars. One of the outcomes of my first sabbatical visit—*Socio-Economic Intervention in Organizations: The Intervener-Researcher and the SEAM Approach to Organizational Analysis*—a volume coedited with Savall, ISEOR's founder and director, attempted to capture the unique nature of this intervention framework with its tripartite focus on the qualitative, quantitative, and financial dimensions of organizational life (Buono & Savall, 2007). Working directly with ISEOR's intervener-researchers provided the opportunity to better understand the application of the socio-economic approach to management (SEAM) in a variety of organizational types (public and private, from traditional businesses to sports teams to the opera), societal cultures (Africa, Asia, France, Mexico, and the United States), and contexts (from supervisory roles and working with French notary publics and computer specialists to the unique challenges inherent in merger and acquisition integration).

The Socio-Economic Approach to Management Revisited: The Evolving Nature of SEAM in the 21st Century, pp. xi–xvi
Copyright © 2015 by Information Age Publishing

ISEOR can best be conceptualized as a hands-on learning laboratory, committed to the idea of evidence-based management and intervention —long before our current fascination with the concept (see, e.g., Pfeffer & Sutton, 2006; Rousseau & McCarthy, 2007). This evidence, as supported by ISEOR's extensive database—which draws on over 1,350 companies and organizations from 72 sectors and 39 countries on four continents collected over the past 40 years—captures the reality that the potential individuals bring to their organizations is vastly underutilized and underdeveloped. Highly critical of the classical scientific management approach to work organization, Savall and his colleagues also point to significant faults inherent in the traditional accounting model, noting how these approaches limit our ability to fully understand what is happening in our businesses and organizations. In the pages that follow, you will read about how a "virus" based on the early work by Frederick Taylor, Henri Fayol, and Max Weber—referred to as the "TFW virus"—has infiltrated our thinking about management and organization to the point where are falling well short of our own potential. The resultant *dysfunctions* this virus unleashes creates *hidden costs*—"hidden" because they are not captured by our accounting information systems—that lead to the *noncreation of potential*, readily destroying a firm's *value-added* possibilities.

This volume revisits the application of SEAM in the context of intervention challenges in the wake of the recent economic crisis and the disruptive change that has taken hold across the world. Reflecting on their work over the years, Savall and his partner Véronique Zardet (2013) have placed increased emphasis on the tensions created by the wider environment— what they refer to as *tetranormalization*—reflecting on how those tensions continually shape and influence practice in today's organizations. As Savall and Zardet argue, we are in the midst of profound upheaval that will play havoc with our economic and social lives for some time to come. If we are going to exert any influence on that reality, the challenges that we face moving forward must be conceptualized, constructed and dealt with today, for, as they argue, "the road to durable prosperity will be a long haul."

Thinking back to my initial stay at ISEOR in 2003, I observed a number of changes that have taken place within the SEAM model and ISEOR's intervention process. As I have noted in earlier volumes, one of the insights that has drawn me to Savall's and ISEOR's work over the years is their ongoing integrative and holistic focus on understanding the nuances and complexities of organizational life and then using that insight in crafting interventions. The basic foundation of SEAM—built on the idea of *strategic patience*, the need to undertake holistic intervention in organizations, and the challenge to get organizational members to listen to themselves (through what they refer to as the *mirror effect*)—has remained the same. In response to economic and organizational pressures in the current environment, however, there has been a concomitant emphasis on helping client organizations achieve short-term results while still maintaining focus on the long term. Many ideas that have become part of the current discourse within ISEOR were not as explicitly addressed during that first visit—from the destructive effect of the Taylorism-Fayolism-Weberism (TFW) virus, to the need to focus on ways to ensure the sustainability of a SEAM intervention, the growing importance of collaborative interactions between external and internal consultants (***intervener-researchers*** in SEAM parlance), and the growing importance of cocreating knowledge with client firms and organizations. Within this context, there was also much greater attention paid to ways of enhancing the role of internal change agents working in concert with external ISEOR intervener-researchers.

As I have become more immersed in the SEAM methodology over the years, I have become increasingly sensitive to the nuances associated with the framework. Given that, I was quite amused by the extent to which many of the tools and tactics that are captured in this volume as part of interventions with client organizations have also become part of the day to day operation in the ISEOR laboratory. At the end of one of my meetings with two of the contributors to the volume, for example, I was provided with my own PNAC—***periodically negotiable activity contract***—that captured our discussion and our sign off acknowledging the mutual commitments we had made. Developing our plan for the book, other intervener-researchers drew on ***resolution charts***—a tool filled out during meetings and distributed to participants immediately after that capture responsibility and noted action steps—to ensure continued and timely progress on the project. Even students at IAE Lyon, following some of my guest lectures at the university, used SEAM management tools, providing me with a PAP—***priority action plan***—that I would indeed follow-up on my promise to send them the PowerPoint slides that I used during our discussion. If a management tool has been successfully employed in intervention with hundreds of clients over the years, it makes perfect sense to draw on its promise within your own organization.

During my first sabbatical visit, one of the high points of my stay was a visit to the French bakery, Brioche Pasquier, to observe the ways in which SEAM had shaped the company's culture and operations. As I noted in that volume, Serge Pasquier, the bakery's chairman who spent the day with us touring the factory and talking about key practices, was a perfect example of what Davenport and Prusak (2003) referred to as the "idea practitioner," those key individuals who make new management ideas a reality within their companies. Pasquier explained how SEAM was "like a religion" at the bakery, one of the key reasons for the company's sustained level of high performance as one of the most successful bakery operations in France—

and since that time Brioche Pasquier has expanded to the United Kingdom and the United States.

During this past visit, I had the pleasure of interacting with another idea practitioner—Patrick Tabchoury, a senior hospital administrator, who was studying at ISEOR during my stay—who shared his experience piloting SEAM across three hospitals in Lebanon. His experience, which is captured in Chapter 14, further illustrates the power of the intervention framework—even in an environment characterized by high turbulence and severe financial stress—in meeting patient needs, enhancing quality while reducing costs. The opportunity to interact with ISEOR clients, to hear about the processes and outcomes in their own words, directly reinforces the potential of the method.

THE SOCIO-ECONOMIC APPROACH TO MANAGEMENT REVISITED

The volume contains 18 chapters that capture the essence of the intervention framework and how SEAM has evolved over the past decade. The first section begins with a chapter by Henri Savall and Véronique Zardet that presents an overview of the development of the socio-economic approach to management, and its guiding frameworks and methodology. The chapter's detailed explanation of how the underlying thinking, tools and techniques of socio-economic management have evolved serves as a primer for the remainder of the volume. The remaining chapters in that introductory section examine how our conventional wisdom about management and organization is challenged by findings in ISEOR's impressive database, the essence of sustaining SEAM interventions and its role in management control, and how SEAM contributes to true socially responsible practice. This section concludes with a detailed chapter on the *qualimetrics* methodology and the importance of integrating qualitative, quantitative, and financial data in any organizational diagnosis and intervention plan to ensure as complete an assessment of intervention impacts as possible.

The second section includes five chapters that focus on intra-organizational applications of SEAM in a variety of contexts. The chapters look at the challenge of true organizational reconstruction, short-term versus longer-term performance challenges, how the management of cultural institutions can be enhanced (the idea of developing the "artist-manager"), enterprise resource planning, and the application of SEAM in the transition of a family-owned Mexican firm from a small- to medium-sized business.

The volume concludes with seven chapters that examine the application of SEAM across various boundaries. This interorganization focus explores the way in which SEAM can be applied in: the architectural sector in France, focusing on its managerial, technical and environmental challenges; the strategy process in a global-local context; developing cooperative practices across hospitals in Lebanon; creating a collaborative environment to facilitate services for the disabled; working through crisis in a consortium of agricultural cooperatives; a network of environmental nongovernment organizations (NGOs); and modernizing public service organizations and enhancing their socio-economic performance.

As we did in the 2007 volume, the end of the book contains a combined glossary and chapter index that provides a definition of key terms in the SEAM framework and where they appear in the different chapters. As you might have already noticed in reading this introduction, these key terms are highlighted in ***bold italics*** throughout the volume, quickly drawing the reader's attention to their application in different contexts.

Reflecting on the changing nature of work and the workplace, the potential power of—and need for—***human potential*** has never been greater. Savall has always thought that the Western concept of *human resources* was misguided, that people are not a resource to use up but rather a source of potential to invest in, develop and nurture. As recent work on flourishing in organizations (Laszlow & Brown, 2014) and a conscious approach to business (Mackey & Sisodia, 2013) suggest, if we are to truly fulfill our aspiration that we can prosper in a healthful and vigorous way, experiencing mindfulness in our business interactions and experiences, we must develop that potential. Savall, Zardet and their team of intervener-researchers are to be commended for their long-term commitment to achieve these ideals, providing us with a valued framework for achieving sustainable social and economic performance in the world of organizations and businesses.

ACKNOWLEDGMENTS

Once again, I am indebted to many people and organizations in the creation of this volume. Bentley University, my academic home for the past 30 plus years, provided me with the opportunity to travel to Lyon during spring 2014 via my fourth sabbatical leave. ISEOR and IAE Lyon provided financial support to help make this experience a reality. Henri Savall and Véronique Zardet continued to be delightful hosts during my time at ISEOR, providing ample stimulation—intellectual, social, and culinary—that allowed me to enjoy all that ISEOR and Lyon have offer. For the second time, Amandine Savall was an outstanding project coordinator—in addition to sharing her intervention work in Chapter 13 of this volume, she was the key liaison with the host of intervener-research chapter contributors, and her detailed ***resolution charts*** kept us on track throughout the process. Marc Bonnet and Rickie Moore, long-time friends and colleagues, were also gracious with their time, insight and hospitality. This edited volume would not have been completed without the ongoing support and collaboration of all these individuals. My wife, Mary Alice, was also more than accommodating in allowing me to escape to France once again, though I'm sure the opportunity to join me in exploring the French Riviera was a definite motivating factor.

It is my hope that the framework, applications, and analyses in this volume will provide new insights into the evolving theory and practice of socio-economic management in today's VUCA world—our volatile, uncertain, complex and ambiguous environment. I would like to thank all the book's contributors—true intervener-researchers—for their good natured colleagueship and commitment to seeing the volume through completion. As with other volumes in the RMC series, it is my ultimate hope that this work will further enhance our understanding of the complexities of organizational life and the need to think of organizations as social *and* economic entities, with the concomitant need for truly integrative approaches to organizational diagnosis, analysis, intervention, and assessment.

REFERENCES

Buono, A. F., & Savall, H. (2007). *Socio-economic intervention in organizations: The intervener-researcher and the SEAM approach to organizational analysis.* Charlotte, NC: Information Age Publishing.

Davenport, T., & Prusak, L. (2003). *What's the big idea? Creating and capitalizing on the best management thinking.* Cambridge, MA: Harvard Business School Press.

Laszlow, C., & Brown, J. (2014). *Flourishing enterprise: The new spirit of business.* Palo Alto, CA: Stanford University Press.

Mackey, J., & Sisodia, R. (2013). *Conscious capitalism: Liberating the heroic spirit of business.* Cambridge, MA: Harvard University Press.

Pfeffer, J., & Sutton, R. I. (2006). *Hard facts, dangerous half-truths and total nonsense: Profiting from evidence-based management.* Cambridge, MA: Harvard Business School Press.

Rousseau, D. M., & McCarthy, S. (2007). Evidence-based management: Educating managers from an evidence-based perspective. *Academy of Management Learning & Education, 6*, 94-101.

Savall, H., & Zardet, V. (2013). *The dynamics and challenges of tetranormalization.* Charlotte, NC: Information Age Publishing.

PART I

THE SOCIO-ECONOMIC APPROACH TO MANAGEMENT: NEW INSIGHTS, NEW PERSPECTIVES

CHAPTER 1

REFLECTING ON SEAM IN THE 21ST CENTURY

New Ideas, New Advances[1]

Henri Savall and Véronique Zardet

For the past 10 years, micro-theories have been developed focusing in particular on human behavior in organizations. Emerging but dispersed concepts have been hatched. In the early 2010s, these micro-theories and concepts were integrated into a general model explaining the research results capitalized by ISEOR since the beginning of its work in 1973. What might be called today a "*meta socio-economic theory*," represented schematically in Figure 1.1, was the subject of previous publications in French and English (Savall & Zardet, 2004, 2005, 2012). A theory of knowledge has emerged, and the different scattered sub-models were built around the clover that symbolized the *socio-economic analysis model* (SEAM). This chapter is dedicated to presenting the new model of the *socio-economic theory* and to further developing the concept of *human potential*. Finally, the theoretical implications of the model, focused on the strategic management of companies and organizations, and on the sharing of *value-added* between stakeholders and the discovery of a new *hidden costs* factor

The Socio-Economic Approach to Management Revisited: The Evolving Nature of SEAM in the 21st Century, pp. 3–28

3

through tetranormalization are explained. The chapter concludes with a reflection on the contribution of the socio-economic model of businesses and organizations in meso- and macro-economic analysis.

The ISEOR's *research-interventions* for over 40 years in 1,350 companies and organizations from 72 sectors and 39 countries on four continents have led to the emergence of concepts and knowledge about the *functioning* of organizations and their performance. Our publications have attempted, over the past few years, to clarify the resulting knowledge, concepts and *tools* that have emerged from this work. This volume is dedicated to our ongoing re-*evaluation* of the SEAM process.

A NEW STATEMENT OF THE SOCIO-ECONOMIC THEORY OF ORGANIZATIONS AND TERRITORIES

The organizational informal production system (IPS) has a significant influence on individual and collective commitment at work. Its effect on individual and collective **conflict-cooperation** behavior can cause **dysfunctions** through organizational **structures**, acting as a moderator. These dysfunctions generate hidden costs, that is, **value-added destruction**, which negatively affects the firm's financial performance, for both **non-profit organizations** (e.g., a **balanced budget**) and the level of profit for businesses.

The Informal Production System

The informal production system consists of two performance factors— the *"Taylorism-Fayolism-Weberism virus"* infection level (referred to as the **TFW virus**; see Chapter 2) and the *activity piloting intensity* (Savall & Zardet, 2006, 2009a, 2009b). The organizational **activity piloting intensity**[2] variable is a key factor of success as regards the *improvement* in organizational performance. It consists of three levers: **actors stimulating information system**, **synchronization** and **cleaning up** of the informal production system. The *information* component can *stimulate* the receiver, individual or group, and incite the receiver to engage in decisive action, which implies the expenditure of human energy and competency. However, an organization also generates a large amount of *non*-stimulative information, which entails hidden costs and is not conducive to **economic performance**.

The *activity and actors synchronization* component, the second lever of activity piloting intensity is the development of **communication-concertation-cooperation (3C)** practices in real time of actors in activity processes. The synchronization deficiency has two effects. The first is failure to imagine and implement organizational innovations or operational improvements,

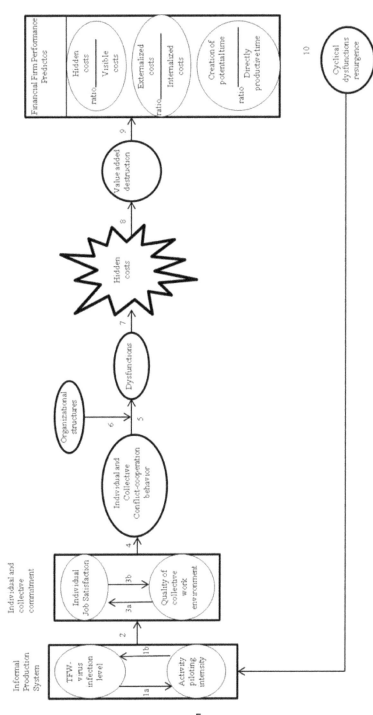

Figure 1.1. Modeling the socio-economic theory of hidden costs.

5

to negotiate the means and transverse arbitrations required for the implementation of action plans. This failure undermines **coordination** between the various departments of the company and any preventive actions, enabling dysfunction and hidden cost reduction. The second is failure in action priorities due to the instability of organizational behaviors, submitted to a new pressure from their private and public competitive environment.

The third **steering lever** is **periodically cleaning up** of dysfunctions. The organization is a living being that suffers from *natural pollution* as years go by, given structures, procedures and behaviors are subjected to inexorable deterioration over time, creating the organizational *entropy* phenomenon. This is the reason why regular re-examination of dysfunctions to check for recurrence is required – in essence, the *Informal Production System* loses part of its **efficiency** and efficacy if it is not periodically *cleaned up*.

Proposition 1a: *The level of TFW virus infection will have a negative effect on the activity piloting intensity (API) level.*

Proposition 1b: *The API level will have a negative effect on the level of TFW virus infection.*

Individual and Collective Commitment

The **individual and collective commitment** exists in the **interaction** between two factors: subjective *individual job satisfaction* and the objective *quality of collective work environment*. Many researchers refer to **commitment** theories. Sleesman, Conlon, McNamara, and Miles (2012), for example, link, through meta-analysis, decision-making issues and opportunity and sunk costs, showing the influence on **project management**, group identity, and responsibility.

Proposition 2: *Both interacting factors, the TFW and API, in the Informal Production System (IPS) influence the level of Individual and Collective Commitment (ICC).*

Individual job satisfaction depends on the dysfunctions level. Indeed, they are the consequence of dissatisfaction due to an insufficient level of *quality of life* in the workplace. Recent publications highlight the relationship between job satisfaction and job design or changes in work. Fahr (2011), for example, analyses the effect on job satisfaction of an *enriched job* design, which is characterized by a high degree of autonomy and multitasking. Wilkens and Nemerich (2011) explore individual rationalities in exchange relationships and show that *episodic changes* in work relationships are an usual and effective pattern for sustaining satisfaction at a high level.

The second component, **quality of collective work environment** includes the physical work environment and its dynamic. Dul, Ceylan, and Jaspers (2011) found that creative personality, social-organizational work environment, and physical work environment independently affect creative performance. The relative contribution of the physical work environment is smaller than that of the social-organizational work environment, and both contributions are smaller than that of creative personality.

Proposition 3a: *The quality of collective work environment affects individual job satisfaction and, therefore, individual and collective commitment.*

Proposition 3b: *Individual job satisfaction affects the quality of collective work environment perception and, therefore, the level of individual and collective commitment.*

Individual and Collective Conflict-Cooperation Behaviors

Individual and collective conflict-cooperation behaviors play a central role in the socio-economic theory. Behavior refers to the observed human action that has an impact on the physical and social environment. Behavior is characterized by its *conjunctural* and relatively *instable* nature, due to its ambivalent composition, with one part conflicting and another part cooperating.

The actors' strategies and sets also play an important role in the behavior's dynamic. All actors have *informal powers* which they can use, either to contribute to or to detract from the organization's economic performance. The mainstream management and economics literature *underestimates the recurrent state of conflict* within the organization. Denying conflict subsequently impacts human behavior and individual and collective economic performance.

Proposition 4: *Individual and collective commitment level influences the level of individual and collective conflict-cooperation behavior.*

Dysfunctions are gaps compared to **orthofunctioning**, which refers to the accurate **functioning** desired by the organization's internal and external **stakeholders**. Dysfunctions cause dissatisfaction and damage. They can be tacit or expressed in the form of claims by stakeholders. Analysis highlights that dysfunctions lead to a *double and interactive responsibility* both individually and collectively. It is extremely rare that dysfunctions account for the actions of a single individual, contrary to preconceived ideas. They are the result, in particular, of the theories and practices of classical school management, under the influence of the **TFW virus** (Savall, 2010; Savall & Zardet, 2006; Savall, Zardet, & Bonnet, 2010).

> **Proposition 5:** *The individual and collective conflict-cooperation system generates organizational dysfunctions classified in six categories: working* **conditions**, **work organization**, **time management**, *communication-co-ordination-cooperation*, **integrated training** *and strategy implementation.*

Organizational Structures

Organizational **structures** are made of a set of elements in the organization that exhibit properties of relative stability (Savall, 2007; Savall & Zardet, 1987, 2010). They can be classified into five categories: physical, technological, organizational, demographic and mental structures.

> **Proposition 6:** *Organizational structures are a moderating variable in the process of generating dysfunctions.*

Hidden Costs

Hidden costs are those costs that are not detected by the organization's financial information system, which includes budgets, profit and loss account, balance sheet, general and management accounting, and **piloting logbooks** (Savall, 1974, 1975; Savall & Zardet, 1987, 2010). Hidden costs include *overcharges*, *non-products* and opportunity costs. Visible costs are all cost categories that appear on the company information system. They can measure the evolution and the use of financial **resources**, but do not have the power to analyze the overall causes of **productivity**. On the contrary, hidden costs are phenomenological in nature can explain the quality defects of the organization's operation.

> **Proposition 7:** *Organizational* **dysfunctions** *generate hidden costs, which are not considered, either in accounting information systems or in decision making models.*

Value-Added Destruction

Hidden costs consist of the **destruction of value-added**, which is partly or completely left out of the organization's accounting system. This loss consists of both surplus expenditures and opportunity costs that affect the capacity of organizational s**urvival-development**. The waste of economic resources is due to useless expenditures as well as the *non-creation* of value-added by **internal actors**. The destruction of value-added can be measured at different levels of the economic and geopolitical space: individual, organizational, sectorial, regional and national.

The **hourly contribution to value added on variable cost (HCVAVC)** *ratio* is an accurate indicator of the organizational **sustainable global economic performance**.

> **Proposition 8:** *Organizational hidden costs generate value added destruction, in two forms: excessive actual operating costs and opportunity costs.*

Financial Firm Performance

Sustainable economic organizational performance comes from short- and long-term rational utilization of the organization's resources, and takes into account psycho-sociological and anthropological criteria in defining its economic action. Two components form sustainable **economic performance**: **immediate results** and **creation of potential**. *Immediate results* are the results under the heading of visible costs and visible performance that are identified and assessed by the **actors**. These outcomes are often referred to as short-term economic results, such as they appear in the company's yearly profit and loss statement. *Creation of potential* refers to self-finance investment, which will have a positive impact on future economic performance. There are three synthetic ratios that serve as predictors, which constitute noted performance variances but can also anticipate the future performance: hidden costs/visible costs; **externalized costs /internalized costs**; and creation of potential time/ **directly productive time**. These *three strategic ratios* explain the level of organizational performance through financial quantitative variables. The three predictors represent the health status of the organization and are sustainable global performance indicators.

> **Proposition 9:** *Value added destruction engendered by dysfunctions cuts down the global and sustainable economic performance and bottom line, the* **internal structure** *of which is represented by three strategic performance indicators: hidden costs/visible costs ratios; externalized costs/ internalized costs(EC/IC); creation of potential time/ directly productive time (CPT/DPT).*

Cyclical Dysfunctions Resurgence

Dysfunctions have a spontaneous propensity to develop and follow life cycle logic. Remedying a dysfunction at a specific point in time (p_i) temporarily reduces its negative effects. However, the dysfunction then re-appears at period (p_{i+1}) and, once again, produces two kinds of negative effects: (1) dissatisfaction of some stakeholders, and (2) destruction of value-added.

Dysfunctions are therefore cyclical phenomena, as organizational activity shows **periodic resurgence** of dysfunctions that generate *recurrent hidden costs*. Thus, human behavior and skills have to be monitored, due to the dysfunctions linked to repeated absences, work quality, person's management, working atmosphere in the teams, the social climate in the company, and the quality of **communication** by management and staff members.

> **Proposition 10:** *The current structure, at period (pi), organizational economic performance structure, through its three strategic indicators, has an impact on cyclical dysfunction resurgence and are predictors of next period (p + 1) organizational performance. The lower HD/HV and EC/IC ratios and the higher CPT/DPT ratio, the higher the organizational economic performance, all things being equal.*

> **Proposition 11:** *Cyclical dysfunctions resurgence trend induces the level of informal production system (IPS), that is, TFW virus infection and* **activity piloting intensity** *(API) level and generates a new cycle of hidden costs which influences organizational economic performance. Continue until resurgence trend induces new cycles (p + 2..., p + i..., p + n) of both dysfunctions and value-added destruction.*

From the perspective of organizational theory, hidden costs can be sustainably recycled into **value added creation**, by improving the individual and collective **commitment** level of staff members. From a scientific perspective, it is also important to examine the variance of hidden costs. The concept of hidden costs becomes solidly justified when their variance is fully demonstrated; otherwise we would come back to the organization slack theory of Anglo-Saxon origin (Cyert & March, 1956; March & Simon, 1958; Näslund, 1964; Reder, 1947). This theory has largely been utilized by theorists and practitioners to justify the ideology that dysfunctions are a necessary part of organizational life. In diametric opposition to this theory, we consider that hidden costs measured at a given moment correspond to hypertrophied slack due to organizational entropy. This slack can be divided into two elements: *physiological*, as a necessary part of the enterprise's life, and *pathological*. Incompressible hidden costs are seen as part of the enterprise's physiology, while compressible hidden costs, that is, costs reduced by the enterprise's **socio-economic development actions**, are declared *pathological*, since their elimination improves the enterprise's state of health and wealth.

Contrary to some organizational theories that oppose human development approaches, instead favoring qualitative advantages as inducement (e.g., work content, working conditions, recognition, promotion) to approaches that emphasize quantitative monetary benefits (e.g., wages developments, performance related bonuses, employee shareholding), socio-economic management considers that these two advantages are inseparable.

Another implication of hidden costs theory refers us to the limits of the managerial subordination paradigm, which is founded on rationalism, individualism, work depersonalization, static job definition, exclusive hierarchy, and elitism. This paradigm underpins classical organization theory, whose leading proponents, Taylor, Fayol and Weber, have had a significant and lasting influence on organization and management practices.

From an academic viewpoint, *socio-economic theory* helps to clarify the unexplained elements in value creation factors at a macroeconomic or societal level. The hidden costs concept is a *tool* for valuing economic performance at different levels of value creation: individual, team, organizational and societal, thanks to the isomorphism principle. The *hourly contribution to value added on variable cost* (HCVAVC) indicator measures the performance of an individual, as a "*nano-GDP*." This value is then aggregated at team, organizational, regional levels, until national GDP is captured.

Corporate social responsibility (CSR) is an intrinsic component of socio-economic theory, although the term is not used profusely. Indeed, the organization is an active unit, which has many levers at its disposal to increase individual job satisfaction and the quality of the collective work environment, so that the actors are better taken into account in terms of their human and social dimensions. With more attention to their individual and collective behavior, they generate less dysfunction and fewer hidden costs, increasing the company's economic performance as well as its contribution to value creation within its territory at the national level. Socio-economic theory proposes a representation of the performance links between the levels of the individual, the organization of its territory, and more generally in society, based on the development of a sustainably bearable social responsibility policy.

HUMAN POTENTIAL AND ITS THREE MAJOR COMPONENTS

The *human potential* concept plays a central role in socio-economic theory. One of the fundamental assumptions is that the *qualitative development* of human potential, that is., the quality of behaviors and skills development, is a primordial *intangible investment* (IIQDHP). It generates a high level of value-added and competitive advantage for the company that is hard to imitate on the market. The human potential level and intensity in an organization is based on three main components: human energy, the actors' behavior in the workplace, and their skills.

The Individual and Collective Energy

We can draw an analogy to the theory of the active units as designed by François Perroux (1975). He stated that individuals, as members of an organization bear an endogenous energy they more or less activate in their professional sphere. The energy level that is used depends on the degree of compatibility between the *project* of each individual and the collective strategy of the organization (Savall, 1978, 1979; Savall & Zardet, 1995). The higher the compatibility, the greater the individual's commitment to business practices that create value-added. This value-added is then distributed among the organization stakeholders. Conversely, when compatibility is low, individuals are less involved in their professional activity and generate, in *interaction* with their business partners, more *dysfunctions* and *hidden costs* by searching how to apply their excess energy in extra-professional sphere. The role of management and leadership is to stimulate actors – individually and in teams—to in the deployment of their creative energy. One of the issues concerning the *commitment* of organizational members arises because of the current complexity of the environment. Due to the financial crisis and pressures associated with globalization, there are two kinds of human energy in conflict. *Recurrent energy* allows for recurring activities with a certain stability of methods, procedures, processes, and skills. However, the *change energy* required by growth in complexity, *competitive pressure* and speed of innovation, is inadequate in most companies and their members.

Behaviors

Professional behaviors play a central role in the socio-economic theory. The ISEOR *intervention-research* shows that observable human behaviors have major impacts on the social and economic performance of the organization. They also showed that the needs of organizational members in a professional situation are multifaceted—physiological, psychological, sociological, and economic. The activation of professional behaviors depends on a number of factors such as recognition, development, career development, and qualitative and monetary remuneration. The analysis of *conflict-cooperation* is central in socio-economic theory, with an emphasis on such observed behavioral dialectics as involvement versus avoidance, commitment versus disobedience, *creation versus value destruction*, and teamwork versus selfish competition. Especially in the current climate, professional behavior criteria tend to be more discriminating in the management of **human potential** than the professional skills criteria. Indeed, changing professional skills seems easier than changing behaviors, although professional skills are actually used *only if* the **actors** have the will to and adopt pro-active behaviors.

Professional Skills

The professional skills level results from knowledge mobilization focused on helping to complete company activities. The socio-economic theory differentiates two types of knowledge: the current and reactive **living knowledge** activated by individuals, in thought and action, versus **inert knowledge**, issued from the past, preserved, formalized and represented by symbols and signs on written *memory supports*. This knowledge is mobilized through the **cognitive interactivity** mechanism, notably due to interpersonal exchange between one or more individuals. It can also happen in inert knowledge animation, when reading a text or viewing an image inspires an actor or group to develop ideas, opinions, feelings or acts. Professional skills are used when cognitive interactivity produces its effects—such as when activities are assigned to individuals who then mobilize their knowledge acquired through *experience*. We understand the negative impact of the **TFW virus (Taylorism-Fayolism-Weberism)**, which severely limits the range of activities that a person is asked to perform (Savall & Zardet, 2010). The latter quickly loses the acquired knowledge that returns to an inert state if not implemented in his or her current occupation. The obsolescence of knowledge and skills, that we had frequently observed, is a major source of chronic dysfunctions within organizations.

Temporal Evolution of Human Potential Components

Organization observation has underscored that human potential undergoes a life cycle phenomenon. Thus, over time energy has a propensity to wear away. It requires **maintenance**; otherwise it deteriorates over time through the **entropy** phenomenon. Behaviors change very frequently according to how things go with professional and non-professional events. It requires a significant amount of managerial attention to keep listening, promoting dialogue, and very frequently contracting performance with employees. Skills are also subject to erosion and deterioration. This phenomenon requires preventive and maintenance actions with regard to skills potential in order to ensure their availability for the organization activities.

The Socio-Economic Theory of Power

The existence of hidden costs at all levels of the company (top management, middle management, line employees) led the socio-economic theory to balance the concept of power used by many theories of organizations. It highlights the high level of individual and group informal power in the organization, approximately measured through hidden costs. The *socio-economic theory* of power states that no actor, regardless of his or her place in the organization, is devoid of powers and responsibilities. Formal powers are organized and prioritized, while informal powers are spread throughout the company and present even in low-skilled positions.

Human Potential and the Diversity of Organizations

The *socio-economic qualimetric diagnoses methodology* to collect and analyze data, designed by the ISEOR team (Savall & Zardet, 1987, 2004, 2011; Savall, Zardet, & Bonnet, 2000-2008), has an ethical and *democratic* dimension. Indeed, dysfunctions and *productivity* losses are witnessed by company employees who are suffering from or generating dysfunctions in interaction with their collaborators. The desire for increased well-being encourages these actors to reveal the dysfunctions that disrupt their activity and deteriorate their *life conditions at work*. They express legitimately their perception of these dysfunctions and their impacts through semi-structured interviews.

Following the principle of *generic contingency* (Savall & Zardet, 1996), we selected a subset of 45 socio-economic diagnoses made in different departments, agencies and workshops from ISEOR's 1,350 case database. These companies employ 3,268 persons in total (directors, managers, employees & workers). They are located in 5 countries, on 3 continents, and represent 9 major sectors and 40 different fields of activity (see Figure 1.2).

The 9,300 *fieldnote quotes* resulting from interviews of these diagnoses were the subject of a *content analysis* (Savall et al., 2000–2008), using a qualitative analysis software called SEGESE® (created by ISEOR: Krief & Zardet, 2013; Savall & Zardet, 1987; Zardet & Harbi, 2007). The analysis identified 890 *key ideas* expressing *generic dysfunctions*. After validation by all interviewees—a process referred to as the *mirror-effect*—these key ideas were submitted to a second content analysis, which helped to summarize the 447 *main ideas* into 89 *dysfunctions baskets*. A third content analysis was then used to state the nature of the issues and sub-issues related to human potential.

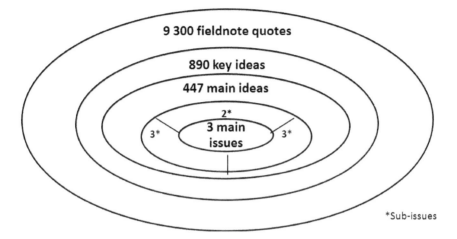

Figure 1.2.   Summary of the content analysis of the interviews (45 organizations employing 3,268 persons).

Three major categories of issues were highlighted:

- *Management of Human Potential* focusing on: (1) the *failures and difficulties of management quality,* related to decision and management systems, information systems, ***synchronization*** practices in the company, and especially the practices of management and supervision; and (2) *the difficulties of skills and human potential management,* related to ***training,*** a lack of internal skills, the formalization of knowledge and energy of the actors.
- *Organization, Methods and Working Conditions* encompassing: (1) the *methods of work and* ***time management,*** including standards, rules and procedures as well as planning and programming of activities; (2) *the physical work conditions,* relating to the premises, the workload, the atmosphere and the schedule; and (3) ***work organization*** *and* ***delegation,*** concerning the organizational structure, the allocation of tasks, functions and missions as well as the resources allocated for the activity.
- *Communication, involvement and cooperation* emphasizing: (1) *communication-concertation-cooperation;* (2) *cooperation and transversality,* affecting difficulties of ***internal customer-supplier*** relationships, boundaries, and lack of synergy; and (3) *involvement and* ***cohesion*** *of the actors,* relating to the differences in involvement and its consequences on cohesion, the difficulties in obtaining consensus among basic personnel or teams of directors and managers

Table 1.1 indicates the weighting of different common issues to organizations studied.

Table 1.1.   Typology of Issues Related to Human Potential

Main Issues	Main Ideas of Dysfunctions		Sub-issues	Main Ideas of Dysfunctions	
	Number	*%*		*Number*	*%*
Human potential management	169	38%	Management quality	95	21%
			Skills' management	74	17%
Organization, methods and working conditions	143	32%	Methods of work and time management	57	13%
			Working conditions	46	10%
			Work organization and delegation	40	9%
Communication, involvement and cooperation	135	30%	Communication-concertation-cooperation	50	11%
			Cooperation and transversality	48	11%
			Involvement and cohesion	37	8%
Total	**447**	**100%**		447	100%

Hidden Costs Linked to Human Potential

The research conducted in compliance with the socio-economic theory demonstrates that the diversity of the companies and organizations does not significantly impact the nature of the ***dysfunctions*** that affect ***human potential***. Regardless of the country, sector or industry, size, legal status (public, private, associative), purpose (profit or non-profit) or financial situation (prosperity or difficulty), the 45 observed organizations show similar organizational issues. These problems affect the individual and collective energy, behaviors, and skills that are the primary components of human potential within companies and organizations.

These dysfunctions impact employee satisfaction at work and the performance of the company. Indeed, the ***value-added destruction*** average order of magnitude is 29,100 euros of *hidden costs* per person and per year. It represents a 60% evaporation of ***resources*** of the company's payroll and

95 billion euros for 3,268 persons. Other studies have shown than 35 to 55 percent of these hidden costs are recoverable into value added (Savall & Zardet, 2008b; see also Chapter 2), through change processes such as *SEAM interventions*.

The quasi-universality of human potential issues, in spite of the cultural, ethical and geopolitical diversity of the organizations can be astonishing. However, the organizational biology metaphor considers dysfunctions as non-specific *organizational pathologies*. In the human biology area, beyond the obvious diversity of individuals, the universality of pathologies has allowed significant progresses in curative and preventive medicine. It is what we can wish for, by analogy, for improving companies, the health of organizations, and the preservation of employment.

STRATEGIC BEDROCK THEORY

Through research at ISEOR, we have also discovered (strategic bedrock theory) that the success of the *external strategy* of a company depends on its degree of *internal cohesion*. This finding allows more or less high *strategic ambitions*. Conversely, delays or *strategic failures* are due to cracks in internal cohesion. More than the relevance of strategic choices, it is the internal strategic strength of an organization (skills, proactive behavior, internal cohesion between hierarchical levels, cooperation between sectors) that contributes to its *strategic performance*.

The level of the TFW virus infection degrades the level of team cohesion and organization, and tends to reduce the level of *activity piloting intensity*. However, team cohesion and organization constitute a key factor in piloting intensity and decision making. Similarly, the level of activity piloting intensity affects the level of team cohesion and organization, and tends to reduce the level of virus infection. In fact, the level of team cohesion and organization has an impact on the *sustainable socio-economic performance* level of the organization (Savall & Zardet, 2009a, 2009b; Savall, Zardet, & Bonnet, 2010).

The process of transformation simultaneously developing cohesion and sustainable *economic performance* was practiced and evaluated in over one thousand cases of companies and organizations (Savall & Zardet, 2008a, 2014). Six steps structure this process of change (Savall & Zardet, 1987, 1995, 2008b; Savall et al., 2008):

1. awareness of a sustainable external threat to a proactive strategy;
2. decision of a proactive strategy of integral innovation to promote *competitiveness*;

3. awareness of internal cohesion deficiency, making it difficult or impossible to achieve the decided upon proactive strategy;
4. decision of an internal strategy of transformation oriented towards human potential of the company or organization, and based on IIQDHP to increase the degree of cohesion necessary for the success of the external strategy;
5. engagement of a *metamorphosis* action, by the *socio-economic intervention* method; and
6. *evaluation* of the change in economic performance obtained, taking into account the intensity of the change energy measured by the total annual amortization and individual of IIQDHP.

The *qualitative, quantitative, and financial analysis* of 35 cases of companies and organizations that have implemented this process has helped to trace the dissatisfaction due to cohesion deficiency caused by the TFW virus (Savall, 2011) on different categories of actors, from top management to basic personnel and the destruction of value added leading to hidden costs of €29,000 per person and per year on average. The analysis of 13 of these cases led us to characterize the actions to improve social and economic performance, whose common element was increased cohesion. The resultant intervention, which constituted an *intangible investment in qualitative development of human potential* (IIQDHP), was very profitable (210% to 4014%). A leverage effect of intangible investment in cohesion has been highlighted with a multiplier of 2 to 20, except for one case where the multiplier is close to 1, which corresponds to a repayment period of one year. The return on investment is much lower than one year in other cases (1 to 6 months). It is clear from this analysis that improving internal cohesion—the organizational base—enhances the *sustainable strategic performance* of the organization.

SUSTAINABLE SOCIO-ECONOMIC PRODUCTIVITY: VALUE SHARING BETWEEN STAKEHOLDERS

The notion of *productivity* is still often influenced by that of volume yield —Taylorism. The notion of *socio-economic productivity* refers to the ability of humans to produce value, useful to themselves and to others, by implementing their *human potential. Socio-economic productivity* takes into account the hidden costs that reduce the level of *economic performance* and dissatisfaction that cause dysfunctions by affecting *social performance*.

Any professional or extra-professional organization has a spontaneous tendency to produce hidden cost-performance, resulting from endogenous or exogenous dysfunctions and their fluctuations. Individual and collective human productivity has a high potential elasticity that corresponds to a level (more or less) of high hidden costs. It follows that an organization is likely to increase its production at constant *effectiveness*, without increasing weekly working time, if it is able to reduce its dysfunctions. This ability is acquired through an organizational *learning* process, focused on the behavior of actors and their *interactions* with the organization's structures.

The *intervention-research* carried out by ISEOR illustrate, through the recycling of hidden costs into value added, that it is possible to increase the level of human productivity without degrading working conditions—in fact, on the contrary, improving them. More spectacular is the observation over a long period—more than 10 years of continuous improvement in the global human productivity—that reveals the immense resources that humans have within themselves, with the ability to transform their organizations through their involvement in *socio-economic measurable performance*. A few of our oldest cases provide inspiring testimonials—including Brioche Pasquier, General Protection, Technord, CCI of Morbihan—that are supported by our global database (see Buono & Savall, 2007; ISEOR, 2009).

The substantial deposits of hidden costs are recyclable resources to finance innovative actions, free resources and time, in order to affect them to endogenous proactive strategies. Thus, any company or organization may, without additional external resources, self-finance its *intangible investment in qualitative development of human potential (IIQDHP)* and consolidate its internal *cohesion*, *a source of* sustainable performance. The improvement of the latter, thanks to a more *innovative* and better negotiated strategy with its key internal and external *stakeholders*, allows the organization to more effectively and efficiently integrate sets of standards that are compatible, multiple, and varied. The emerging development of hybrid partnerships, between companies, organizations and public and private institutions, is effective and efficient; it creates value-added for stakeholders and the territories over which they exercise their economic and social activities and complex competitive games.

The *conflict-cooperation* dialectic demonstrated by Perroux (1973) in the economic universe is at the heart of socio-economic theory, in the interactions between individuals, groups, and companies. The hidden costs are also an expression of conflicting relationships. As a recycling of these hidden costs shows, periodically renewed negotiating strategies provide more benefit than tax strategies embedded in economic performance—increases that can be shared between the various stakeholders.

DISCOVERY OF NEW HIDDEN COST FACTORS:
TETRANORMALIZATION

Part of the *macro-economy*, socio-economic theory went deeper inside organizations, down to the work team level. Then the fields of application
of our work, with companies up to 30,000 organizational members and
cross-organizational issues led us to go back to the macro-economic level.
We then identified an *isomorphism* with respect to dysfunctions and hidden
costs, delineating **macro-dysfunctions** such as wastes of pharmaceuticals
purchased but not consumed and **macro-hidden costs**, estimated at 3 billion
euros per year in France. This path led to a new research program focused
on **tetranormalization,** developed at ISEOR, since 2003, with an international network of **intervener-researchers** from the United States, Mexico,
Canada, Argentina, Lebanon, Spain, Portugal, and France (see Savall &
Zardet, 2013).

Emergence of the Concept

Over the long-term (between 10 and 30 years), we followed the evolution of approximately 15 companies and institutions—in France, Belgium,
and Mexico—by observing from the inside, through a dialogue with actors
(managers, executives, personnel). We attempted to measure the most
important aspects of organizational life, focusing on their increasing
difficulties in such areas as understanding, making decisions, enacting
and monitoring, each in its place within the organization, in an increasingly complex, multifaceted, fluctuating, and confusing environment. We
observed how risky the navigation became between business, family and
individual life in this environment, which was often perceived as hostile
with scattered pitfalls both in daily operations and long-term **projects**.

We observed the phenomena of **entrepreneurial and economic abstention**
—increasing delays in decision making, hypertrophy of the precautionary
principle, and a discouragement of the most active players at all levels of
the companies and institutions. When we looked outside the companies,
we observed—through the media, associative and cultural lives, and lit-
erary criticism (especially in the United States)—a growing number of
exchanges and articles that brought to light the proliferation of standards
and norms, their contradictions and instabilities. The dynamic interactions
between these factors drew out and exposed scandals, which were occurring
on local, regional and national levels. Guided by the structural theory of
Bernácer (1922, 1945; Savall, 1975, 2012) on recurrent crises, we watched
more closely the concerns of stakeholders in businesses and organizations,
and their helplessness in action.

A rudimentary *qualitative model* emerged in our minds (Savall & Zardet, 2005, 2013), based on the idea that this avalanche of standards and norms could be classified in four areas with relatively stable attraction and repulsion forces. Two poles partition the social dimension of the universe: (1) social and quality, and (2) safety and environment standards and norms. The two other poles partition the economic dimension: (1) trade standards and (2) accounting and financial standards.

Intervention-research projects conducted within companies uncovered an exogenous factor that *exacerbated hidden costs*—the tetranormalized environment, that is to say, the proliferation of conflicting standards and norms that affect all areas of company life (Savall & Zardet, 2005, 2013), in a context of increasing globalization and aggravated crises. The 1990 and 2007–2008 housing crises, running through the new economy in the early 2000s, were precursors to the global financial crisis of 2008. The discovery of this *tetranormalized universe* reactivated the original objective of the socio-economic theory—to consolidate *entrepreneurship and intrapreneurship capitalism*, by dissociating it from speculative financial capitalism, in line with our research on macroeconomics (Savall, 1973, 1975, 2012; see also Chapter 3). Moreover, two conferences on globalization were organized by the Association of François Perroux (in 2002 and 2008), chaired by Henri Savall.

Tetranormalization designates four divisions of standards that daily plague organizations, the standard to be understood in a broad sense of *economic and social rules of the game*. This standard can be applied to an intra- or inter-organizational level, intra- or inter-territorial. The standards include trade and exchanges trade (e.g., WTO), finance and accounting (e.g., IAS-IFRS), social relationships (e.g., ILO) and the triptych quality-safety-environment (e.g., ISO).

Companies engaged in *socio-economic management* discovered barriers to the progress of their performance because of the avalanche of conflicting standards and norms. Tetranormalization was first studied from the perspective of the entrepreneur, highlighting the fundamental *dialectics*—conflict/cooperation, constraint-threat/opportunity-innovation. New standards and norms create constraints in business operations, and some standards and norms reflect protectionism characteristics or constitute barriers to entry. However, tetranormalization can also be a source of innovation and proactive business strategies when the chief executive officer agrees to be the real monitor of the *integration of standards* and norms that affect the business operations. When tetranormalization is poorly integrated into the company, it causes extra dysfunctions and hidden costs incurred by the company and its stakeholders. When it is carefully integrated, it is a source of performance—economic, social, and societal progress—because it allows companies to recover the real and potential value-added. Therefore, the level of *global sustainable business performance* depends on the quality of integration of standards and their compatibility application. Funding for *development policies of social responsibility* is rooted in potential **resources** of the company, formed by its deposit of hidden costs.

Strategies that better incorporate tetranormalized environmental standards are advantageous for the company and its stakeholders, provided that their convergence is organized—partly outside the organization, partly within the company. This convergence requires the development of skills as regard of periodic **negotiations** between stakeholders.

The Hidden Side of Tetranormalization: Social Responsibility

A close observation of the **tetranormalization** phenomenon shows the intensification of production of all kinds of standards and norms, labels, certifications, and identifiers. These standards and norms emanate from an increasing multiplicity of institutions and organizations operating in the *market of standards and norms*, as producers, trainers, auditors, certifiers, experts, and so forth. Thus, conflict and competition between standards and norms accumulate. Indeed, in spite of often worthwhile and "well-intentioned" ideas that standards and norms convey, they exert a protectionist function at the national and/or industry level. An example is the tough negotiations between France and the United States to lift the ban on Roquefort cheese in the name of so-called safety standards. The controversies on scientific knowledge increase, as reflected in the controversies about the resistance of bacteria to antibiotics or on the ambivalent effects of hormonal treatments during menopause.

Besides the problem of production standards and norms, questions arise about their effective implementation, the reality of sanctions, and deliberate frauds and falsifications. Fraud is an infringement of rules and seriously distorts the economic and social game. Besides its moral dimension, it causes unfair competition between economic partners. Espionage and piracy constitute infringements of intellectual and industrial property, and they have a moral and criminal aspect—an aspect of disruption of the mechanisms that ensure economic and social system equilibrium. Indeed, investors are denied the return on investment they expect, while the predators do not assume the real cost of the innovation of which they unduly benefit. Tax havens constitute another kind of fraud by playing on territorial contradictions between standards and norms.

Who would really benefits from these standards, among the various stakeholders? Behind the "good" practices suggested by the standards, a lucid analysis reveals the existence of *powerful business assets*. Standards are an intangible product issued by producers that generate new business developments such as audits, inspections, the need for expertise, consulting, control, legal and judicial litigation, **training**, and so forth. Multiple intermediary agents between producers and users appear, all the more numerous as the normative texts become blurred. Many industries are growing, such as compensation, grants, sports, humanitarian, and creditors to small- and medium-sized (**SME**) firms. Within health markets, for example, depression is now a growing disease that calls for advertising **communication**, medical consultations, pharmacopoeia, prevention products, and a restructuring of psychiatry.

The corporate social responsibility (CSR) of public and private organizations, as well as public authorities, is increasingly questioned, jeopardizing its funding. The concept of *sustainable social responsibility* emphasizes the dual nature—economic and social—of these issues, ranging from public health, food safety, and **regulation** of the labor market, to unemployment and welfare, as well as political responsibility in inequality and poverty. Within this context, poverty has two aspects—moral and socio-economic —and it creates hidden costs of lost **development opportunity** for both the poor and rich populations. As a result, the transfer of wealth cannot be a development solution and constitutes a *macro-hidden cost*. Further work on the tetranormalization phenomenon will help us better understand how companies are taking advantage of the emerging dynamics that are intensifying.

RETURN TO THE MESO- AND MACRO-ENVIRONMENT

The model we have designed to explain the generation of the socio-economic value within an organization has an isomorphism character if one tries to understand how the value created within a company or organization contributes to the value creation of an area (territory), such as a country. The economic value generated by one hour of work, which we refer to as HCVAVC, constitutes a "nano GDP": it is the *socio-economic performance* of all companies in an industry or a territory that feeds GDP of this economic meso-perimeter, and subsequently the GDP of a region in a state. This represents a return to joint work between management science and economics. Indeed, in 1973, Henri Savall, trained in macro-economics, decided to focus his research on the company level, considering that economic science was unable to explain and understand how to generate economic value in a country or industry. Furthermore, this work is currently moving towards research on a macroscopic institutional framework, placing these dynamics in the context of socio-economic organizational theory. The chapter on socially responsible capitalism presents this new research (see Chapter 5 in this volume).

DISSEMINATION OF THE RESEARCH: MOVING FORWARD

Reflecting on our research over the past 40 years, our findings have an innovative character that challenges many established principles of the strategy and management of organizations (see Chapter 2). ISEOR is committed to accelerating the dissemination of this work, reaching out to scholarly practitioners and practical scholars who work in and consult with companies. For the past five years we have created a number of inter-enterprises courses on new *socio-economic management control* practices (e.g., self-financing the company through hidden resources), the need to develop *new sales management* practices (e.g., sales in a turbulent environment), the importance of behavior management in organizations (managing behavior in workplace), the need for leaders as "number one" in their organization to develop their managerial skills and share their problems out of their company (e.g., our "Number One" course), and finally the importance of deploying a proactive business intelligence system (e.g., business intelligence systems).

Forty years of research-interventions in companies and organizations have allowed us to formalize fundamental epistemological research findings. Three epistemological pillars were designed in 1995 (Savall & Zardet, 1996) then developed and structured to explain some deep mechanisms of *knowledge creation*, whether it is scientific knowledge published by researchers, or "ordinary" knowledge expressed within companies and organizations. Works on the analogy between medical research and *intervention-research* performed by ISEOR's team were published, demonstrating the power of the biological metaphor between the company and the human body, despite its limitations.

The new scientific program of ISEOR concerns the conditions for the sustainability of *socio-economic performance* within organizations. Indeed, thanks to very long longitudinal *intervention-research projects* with companies and organizations (beginning 5, 12, 18, and even 30 years), we benefit from research that has allowed us to identify the various conditions and at what level of growth is socio-economic performance sustainable over time. This volume is dedicated to enhancing our understanding of this evolving knowledge and insight.

NOTES

1. The research for this chapter has been influenced by a number of works that are not directly referred to in the text, including Aristote (2014a, 2014b),

Bernácer (1955), Boje & Rosile (2003), Gephart (2009), Péron & Bonnet (2008), Perroux (1935/1965, 1974 1979), and Zardet and Voyant (2003).

2. Through the volume terms that are highlighted in **bold italics** are defined in the SEAM Glossary, with reference to their inclusion in the different chapters in the volume.

REFERENCES

Aristote. (2014a). Éthique à Nicomaque [Ethics to Nicomaque]. In P. Pellegrin (Ed.), *Aristote, œuvres complètes* [Aristote, integral work]. (pp. 1975–2226). Paris, France: Flammarion.

Aristote. (2014b). Les politiques [Politics]. In P. Pellegrin (Ed.), *Aristote, oeuvres complètes* [Aristote, integral work] (pp. 2321–2536). Paris, France: Flammarion.

Bernácer, G. (1922). La teoría de las disponibilidades como interpretación de las crisis y del problema social [The theory of availability and interpretation of the crisis and the social problema]. *Revista Nacional de Economía, 40*, 128–158.

Bernácer, G. (1925). *El interés del capital: El problema de sus orígenes* [The interest of capital: The problem of its origin]. Alicante, Spain: Ed. Lucentum.

Bernácer, G. (1945). *La teoría funcional del dinero* [The functional theory of money]. Madrid, Spain: Consejo Superior de Investigaciones Científicas.

Bernácer, G. (1955). *Una economía libre, sin crisis y sin paro* [A free economy without crisis and without unemployment]. Madrid, Spain: Aguilar.

Boje, D., & Rosile, G.-A. (2003). Comparison of socio-economic and other trans-organizational development methods. *Journal of Change Organizational Management, 16*(1), 10–20.

Buono, A. F., & Savall, H. (Eds.) (2007). *Socio-economic intervention in organizations: The intervener-researcher and the SEAM approach to organizational analysis.* Charlotte, NC: Information Age Publishing.

Cyert, R. M., & March, J. G (1956). Organizational factors in the theory of oligopoly. *Quarterly Journal of Economics, 70*, 44–64.

Dul, J., Ceylan, C., & Jaspers, F. (2011). Knowledge worker's creativity and the role of the physical work environment. *Human Resource Management, 50*(6), 715–734.

Fahr, R. (2011). Job design and job satisfaction: Empirical evidence for Germany. *Management Revue, 22*(1), 28–46.

Gephart, R. P. (2009). An invitation to ethnostatistics. *Revue Sciences de gestion– Management Sciences–Ciencias de Gestión, 70*, 85.

ISEOR. (2009). *Management socio-économique: une approche innovante.* [Socio-economic approach to management: An innovative approach]. Actes du Colloque d'Automne organisé par l'ISEOR sous la direction d'Henri Savall, Véronique Zardet et Marc Bonnet. Paris, France: Economica.

Krief, N., & Zardet, V. (2013). Analyse de données qualitatives et recherche-intervention [Qualitative data analysis and intervention-research]. *Recherches en Sciences de Gestion–Management Sciences–Ciencias de Gestión, 95*, 211– 237

March, J. G., & Simon, H. A. (1958). *Organizations.* Boston, MA: Harvard Book List.

Näslund, B. (1964). Organizational slack. *Ekonomisk Tidskrift, 1*, 26–31.

Péron, M., & Bonnet, M. (2008). CSR in intervention-research: Example of an implementation of the SEAM model. *Revue Sciences de Gestion–Management Sciences–Ciencias de Gestión.*

Perroux, F. (1965). La *pensée économique de Joseph Schumpeter. Les dynamiques du capitalisme* [The economic thought of Joseph Schumpeter: Dynamics of capitalism]. Geneva, Switzerland: Droz. (Orginal work published 1935).

Perroux, F. (1973). *Pouvoir et économie* [Power and economy]. Paris, France: Bordas.

Perroux, F. (1974). Économie de la ressource humaine [Economics of human resources]. *Revue Mondes en développement.* ISMEA, 15–81.

Perroux (1975). Unités actives et mathématiques nouvelles. Révision de la théorie de l'équilibre économique général [Active unities and new mathematics. General equilibrium theory revision]. Paris, France: Dunod

Perroux, F. (1979). L'entreprise, l'équilibre rénové et les coûts « cachés » [The enterprise, the renovated balance and the 'hidden' costs]. Preface in H. Savall. *Reconstruire l'entreprise* [Reconstructing the enterprise] Paris, France: Dunod.

Reder, M. W. (1947). A reconsideration of marginal productivity theory. *Journal of Political Economy, 55,* 450–458.

Savall, H. (1973). *G. Bernácer: L'hétérodoxie en science économique* [G. Bernácer: Heterodoxy in economics]. Col. Les grands Économistes, Paris, France: Dalloz.

Savall, H. (1974–1975–1977). *Enrichir le travail humain dans les entreprises et les organisations* [An economic evaluation of job enrichment]. Paris: Dunod.

Savall, H. (1975). *G. Bernácer. L'hétérodoxieen science économique* [Germán Bernácer. Heterodoxy in economics]. Paris, France: Dalloz

Savall, H. (1978). Propos d'étape sur la régulation socio-économique de l'entreprise par la recherche de la comptabilité de l'efficience économique et du développement humain [Remarks for a new stage in the socio-economic regulation of the enterprise by research on accountability of economic efficiency and human development], *Economie Appliquée, 4,* 965–998.

Savall, H. (1979). *Reconstruire l'entreprise: Analyse socio-économique des conditions de travail* [Reconstructing the enterprise: Socio-economic analysis of working conditions]. Paris, France: Dunod.

Savall, H. (1981–2010). *Work and people: An economic evaluation of job enrichment.* 1st ed. New-York: Oxford University Press; 2nd ed. Charlotte, NC: Information Age Publishing

Savall, H. (2007). ISEOR's socio-economic method: A case of scientific consultancy. In A. F. Buono & H. Savall (Eds.), *Socio-economic intervention in organization: The intervener researcher and the SEAM approach to organizational analysis* (pp. 1–31). Charlotte, NC: Information Age Publishing.

Savall, H. (2011), Keynote speaker, Petite lecture épistemologique sans prétention de la responsabilité sociale de l'entreprise [Little epistemological reading without arrogance of corporate social responsibility]; ADERSE 2011 Conference proceedings, on CSR and global governance, March, published in Le Flanchec, Uzan, & Doucin (Eds.), *RSE et gouvernance mondiale* [CSR and global governance], pp. 3-22.

Savall, H. (2012). *Origine radicale des crises économiques: Germán Bernácer, précurseur visionnaire* [Root origin of crises: Germán Bernácer, a visionary forerunner]. Charlotte, NC: Information Age Publishing.

Savall, H., & Zardet, V. (1987). *Maîtriser les coûts et les performances cachés : Le contrat d'activité périodiquement négociables* [Mastering hidden costs and performance: The periodically negotiable activity contract]. Paris, France: Economica.

Savall, H., & Zardet, V. (1992). *Le nouveau contrôle de gestion: Méthode des coûts-performances cachés* [New management control: The hidden cost-performance method]. Paris: Éditions Comptables Malesherbes-Eyrolles

Savall, H., & Zardet, V. (1995-2005). *Ingénierie stratégique du roseau, souple et enracinée* [Strategic engineering of the reed, flexible and rooted]. Paris: Economica.

Savall, H., & Zardet, V. (1996) La dimension cognitive de la recherche-intervention: la production de connaissances par interactivité cognitive [The cognitive dimension of intervention-research: The production of knowledge through cognivitive interactivity]. *Revue Internationale de Systémique, 10*(1-2), 157–189.

Savall, H., & Zardet, V. (2004–2011). *Recherche en sciences de gestion : Approche qualimétrique. Observer l'objet complexe.* [Research in management sciences: The qualimetric approach: Observing the complex object]. Paris, France: Economica.

Savall, H., & Zardet, V. (2005). *Tétranormalisation: Défis et dynamiques* [Competitive challenges and dynamics of tetra-normalization]. Paris, France: Economica

Savall, H., & Zardet, V. (2006). Théorie socio-économique des organisations : impacts sur quelques concepts dominants dans les théories et pratiques managériales [Socio-economic theory: Impacts on some mainstream concepts in management theories and pratices] *Academy of Management (ODC Division) & ISEOR Conference*, pp. 267–302.

Savall, H., & Zardet, V. (2008a). *Mastering hidden costs and performance.* Charlotte, NC: Information Age Publishing.

Savall, H., & Zardet, V. (2008b) Le concept de coût-valeur des activités. Contribution de la théorie socio-économique des organisations [The concept of cost-value of activities. Contribution of socio-economic theory of organizations]. *Recherches en Sciences de Gestion–Management Sciences–Ciencias de Gestión, 64,* 61–90

Savall, H., & Zardet, V. (2009a). Mesure et pilotage de la responsabilité sociale et sociétale de l'entreprise: Résultats de recherches longitudinales [Measuring and piloting corporate social responsibility : results from longitudinal research]. *International conference proceedings and doctoral consortium,* partnership between the Academy of Management (AOM) and ISEOR, Lyon, June, pp. 25-53.

Savall, H., & Zardet, V. (2009b), Responsabilidad social y societal de la empresa: indicadores para dialogar con las partes interesadas [The corporate social responsibility: Indicators to converse with stakeholders]. *ACACIA's Conference proceedings,* July, UAM–México, pp. 31-59.

Savall, H., & Zardet, V. (2010), Le non-dit dans la théorie socio-économique des organisations: Situations de management et pièces de théâtre [Unvoiced comment in the socio-economic theory of organizations: Management situations and theatrics], In R. Ocler (Ed.), *Fantasmes, mythes, non-dits et quiproquo: Analyse de discours et organisation* [Fantasy, myths, unvoiced and misunderstanding: Analysis of speech and organization] (pp. 9–35) Paris: L'Harmattan.

Savall, H., & Zardet, V. (2011) *The qualimetrics approach: Observing the complex object*. Charlotte, NC: Information Age Publishing.

Savall, H., & Zardet, V. (2012, October) *Nouvel énoncé de la théorie socio-économique des organisations et des territoires* [New statements of the socio-economic theory of organizations and territory]. Lyon, France: Cahier de recherche ISEOR.

Savall, H., & Zardet, V. (2013). *The dynamics and challenges of tetranormalization*. Charlotte, NC: Information Age Publishing.

Savall, H., & Zardet, V. (2014). *La théorie du socle stratégique et l'effet de levier de la cohésion* [The strategic bedrock theory and the cohesion leverage effect]. 5è colloque et séminaire doctoral international de l'ISEOR – AOM, June 2014, France, pp. 27–56.

Savall, H., Zardet, V., & Bonnet, M. (2000-2008). *Releasing the untapped potential of enterprises through socio-economic management*. Geneva: Éditions IOT-BIT.

Savall, H., Zardet, V., & Bonnet, M. (2010), RSE et développement durable, fondements de la théorie socio-économique des organisations [CSR and sustainable development, basis of socio-economic theory] ; paper, ADERSE Conference proceedings, march, La Rochelle, published in Nicole Barthe & J.-Jacques Rosé (Eds.), *RSE et développement durable* [CSR between globalization and sustainable development] (pp. 3-36, 239-268. Brussels: De Boeck.

Sleesman, D.J., Conlon D.E., McNamara G. and Miles J.E. (2012). Cleaning Up the Big Muddy: A Meta-Analytic Review of the Determinants of the Escalation of Commitment, *Academy of Management Journal*, 55 (3): 541-562.

Wilkens, U., & Nemerich, D. (2011). Love it, change it, or leave it: Understanding highly-skilled flexible workers' job satisfaction from a psychological contract perspective. *Management Revue*, 22(1), 65–83.

Zardet, V., & Harbi, N. (2007). SEAMES®. A professional knowledge management software program. In A. F. Buono & H. Savall (Eds.), *Socio-economic interventions in organizations: The intervener-researcher and the SEAM approach to organizational analysis* (pp. 33–42). Charlotte NC: Information Age Publishing.

Zardet, V., & Voyant, O. (2003). Organizational transformation through the socio-economic approach in an industrial context. *Journal of Organizational Change Management*, 16(1), 56–71.

CHAPTER 2

REFLECTING ON CONVENTIONAL WISDOM

Learning From the Database[1]

Henri Savall and Véronique Zardet

Over the past decade, socio-economic theory has received significant exposure throughout the United States (Boje & Rosile, 2003a; Buono & Savall, 2007; Conbere & Heorhiadi, 2011; Cummings & Worley, 2014; Gephart, 2013; Sorensen et al., 2010). This work was built it based on the idea that ***human potential*** is badly treated (mistreated) by economic and management theories (Savall, 1974, 1979). This research reflects the three basic assumptions of ***socio-economic theory***: the primary place of human potential; the limitations of the classic accounting model; and the criticism of the scientific management of ***work organizations***.

REFLECTIONS ON MANAGEMENT AND ORGANIZATION THEORY

The first assumption comes from the *macro-economic theory of the two production factors*, in its various versions—classical, which is Marxist in nature, and

The Socio-Economic Approach to Management Revisited: The Evolving Nature of SEAM in the 21st Century, pp. 29–53
29

neo-classical or Keynesian. According to this theory, two factors account for the creation of economic value: capital and labor. However, the work of econometricians dealing with the most developed theory, named the *production function* (Carré, Dubois, & Malinvaud, 1972; Perroux, 1973), demonstrates that these two quantified factors account for only a small part of economic value. Indeed, the unexplained residual factor accounts for half of the measured value in terms of GDP. The socio-economic theory was built on the belief that this residual factor could be analyzed by assessing the **hidden costs and performances**, in essence, what the *theory of two natural equivalent factors* cannot measure. The hidden costs concept allows us to understand why two organizations with the same capitalistic intensity and human resources, in terms of workforce and skills, can have significantly different economic performance, to the point where eventually, one is growing and the other disappears or loses its autonomy.

According to the second assumption, the limitations of the "classic" accounting model (Savall, 1974, 1975, 1977, 2010; Savall & Zardet, 1987, 1992, 2008) can be reduced, which enhances its relevance in decision making. The basic accounting model recognizes input and output, but without registering creation, destruction or non-creation of value mechanisms. This system posts expenses, incomes, and revenues, but it cannot identify the part of **hidden costs** linked to **dysfunctions**, inexorably created by the organization. Indeed, these costs are, in part, composed of financial costs, which are diffused in the costs accounts and partly by **non-production** or loss of earnings. These are clearly ignored by general accounts or cost accounting (Cappelletti & Hoarau, 2013; Savall & Zardet, 1992). The hidden costs-performances are an important contributing factor of value creation. It is also, as an *actionable* concept, a descriptive factor. When a company implements a strategy to recycle part of its hidden costs into **value-added**, it leads to an increase in its **sustainable economic performance**.

The third assumption states that classic organizational models (e.g., **TFW virus**) are the main reason for the **ineffectiveness and inefficiency** of economic activity (Savall & Zardet, 2006, 2010). This hypothesis reflects traditional organization and management theory, whose founding fathers were Taylor, Fayol and Weber. Although it was created more than a century ago, this model is still the basis of major practices we have seen in the companies and organizations we have studied—1,350 organizations in 39 countries, on 4 continents (Savall & Zardet, 2013). In fact, the principles of the TFW virus—the maximal division of labor, dichotomy between conception, decision and realization of activities (Fayol, 1916; Taylor, 1911), the depersonalization of jobs and the prominence of impersonal rules (Weber, 1924)—are still thriving in contemporary organizations (Savall & Zardet, 2006, 2010).

Two Production Factors Theory

At the macro-economic level, economists and management strategists have focused on capital growth as a key performance factor. Researchers in organizational behavior and industrial psychology think that changing work content is a key variable of this performance, trying to predict individual performance. Unfortunately, these theories fall well short of helping us to actually predict individual or organizational performance.

The theory of organizational performance is present in macro-economic theory, as proposed by the classical (Adam Smith, 1776), Marxist (Marx, 1848, 1862), neo-classical (Pareto, 1927; Walras, 1877), and Keynesian (Keynes, 1936) economists and their successors. However, these old works as well as recent ones show the existence of a major "residual factor" that cannot explain half of the level of growth in national economies (Carré, Dubois, & Malinvaud, 1972; De Boeck & Denison, 1967; Pascale, 2011; Perroux, 1973; Solow, 1956; Stoléru 1969). As a result, critical analysis of the neoclassical model of economic growth led to the proposal to include the human capital variable (Becker, 1964; Becker, Murphy, & Tamura, 1990 Brunetti, 1997; Beine & Docquier, 2000; Corsi & Guarini, 2007). The recent literature highlights a theory of endogenous growth (Lucas, 1988; Romer, 1986), whose models have inspired many works and comments (see Darreau, 2002; Heertje, Pieretti, & Bartholomew, 2003).

Refuting the equivalence of the two production factors marks the starting point of socio-economic theory construction. It proposes to consider that the residual factor in the production function could be made clearer by the concept of hidden cost-performance in order to better understand the "black hole" of the performance theories. We have remedied this conceptual error by differentiating factors related to the *superstructure*, that is, the *visible* part of economic phenomena (e.g., capital, labor, technological innovation), and the intangible and *hidden infrastructure* based on human potential and its ability to spend energy and creativity to drive innovative *projects*. The many *intervention-research* projects we have engaged in over the past decades have allowed us to build a socio-economic theory that demonstrates the two factors capital and labor are not equivalent. Capital is an *inert* factor, based on objects, equipment, immobilizations and/or cash, whereas labor, which we name *human potential*, is the only *active* factor of economic value creation.

Observing professional practices within organizations shows that only human activity is intelligent and pro-active—adapting to its environment, creating products (goods or services, commercial and noncommercial), and detecting new and innovative needs. Indeed, men and women, individually and collectively, *activate* (or not) their energy and related behavioral dynamics, choosing whether to implement their professional expertise to produce economic value, using equipment and tools, a valuable but *inert* factor.

The so-called intelligent machines were designed, used, and maintained by humans who have incorporated some of the knowledge that only humans are able to create, produce, reproduce, disseminate, transform, improve, and question. The variable, financial, and material capital is therefore a valuable tool developed—built up or destroyed, used or wasted —by them. Thus, these factors are highly complementary and not systematically interchangeable, unlike what some brutal downsizing decisions would like to show.

The TFW Virus

The TFW virus metaphor refers to the anachronistic survival of organization principles of the classical schools, put forward by Taylor (1911), Fayol (1916), and Weber (1924), (Savall, 2011; Savall & Zardet, 2006, 2009a, 2009b, 2010; Savall, Zardet, & Bonnet, 2010). These principles readily contributed to the economic and social progress in their time, and the combined models of these three theorists have generated an extensive literature on job analysis, recruitment and organization theory.

It is regrettable, however, that a century later, theorists, experts, and practitioners continue to propagate three obsolete principles: the *maximal division* of labor, the *dichotomy* between conception, decision and realization of activities, and the *depersonalization* of jobs, organization charts, processes, methods, and rules (Lussato, 1977; De Montmollin, 1981). These factors no longer contribute to sustainable overall performance, considering the evolution of behavior, skills, social environment, and national and international policies (Savall, 1974, 1981, 2010). Our intervention-research database highlights the counter-productive effects of these principles. These three theorists have in common the *submission* paradigm, considering that a person, in a legal subordination relationship due to a contract, must spontaneously follow his or her manager's guidelines. However, observations of organizations clearly demonstrate that this is *not* how it works.

The **socio-economic theory**, in contrast, is based on an alternative paradigm—*contracting*. Rather than trying to force a professional conduct model upon **actors** (organizational members), it is more effective to explain beforehand—to speak or negotiate—to get expected results according to a pedagogical logic of quasi-democratic essence. Hidden costs are, in essence, markers of spontaneous individual and collective insubordination of actors.

A virus is defined as a small infectious agent, formed by a group of submicroscopic entities reproducing themselves inside animal, human, or plant cells. Most viruses are pathogenic. The degree of TFW virus infection on organizational modes and dominant managerial practices refers to a more or less important *cooperation deficiency* between participants in an activity – between individuals on a team or between the same organization sites, subsidiaries or departments (Savall & Zardet, 2009a, 2009b; Savall, Zardet, & Bonnet, 2010). A well-advised criticism is not aimed at Taylor, Fayol, or Weber themselves, but rather at their successors—the theorists, experts, and practitioners who continue to be agents of obsoletes theories in an environment that has gone through numerous, in-depth mutations. Indeed, the human, social, and geopolitical context as well as the level of education of the labor force has considerably evolved over the past century.

VALUE-ADDED GROWTH
STRATEGY VERSUS COST REDUCTION

One of the central tenets of socio-economic theory is a focus on growth rather than *cost reduction* per se. By measuring the *hidden costs and performances*, a company fosters on the value-added growth and performance.

Pilot Performance Developing Value Versus Reducing Costs

Implementation of management control based on value development replaces progressively a traditional management control orientation based on *turnover* maximization and, sometimes false, compression of costs. That is to choose a *recycling of hidden costs into value-added* strategy that consists of producing and selling added volumes, at reduced prices, without reducing margins because of the decrease of cost price: improving product quality, increasing the **creation of potential** through developing participative internal strategic action, training, technological and competitive intelligence, maintaining and developing the workforce, and enhancing employee loyalty and employability. This combines to increase returns for stakeholders—shareholders, directors, managers and employees, social and financial institutions—developing highly profitable *intangible investment* (return on investment of IIQDHP).

Periodic Assessment of HCVAVC: Economic Creation Source

To implement an adaptive organization strategy based on the development of *internal cohesion* and significant investment in the qualitative development of **human potential** simultaneously requires implementing a **periodical evaluation of such a change** and its *economic impacts*. We have implemented, in a large number of companies and organizations that drove these strategies, a permanent evaluation method of economic performance based on the assessment of the evolution of the **hourly contribution to value-added on variable costs (HCVAVC)**, calculated by the ratio: value-added on variable costs/number of hours paid. This ratio includes labor costs, structural costs, and a share of the benefits. This indicator measures the overall result of multiple actions on the *external and internal performance factors*. So when a company deals with **external factors**, for example, by better trading its purchases of raw materials or by increasing its sales thanks to improvements of product quality, the HCVAVC increases. When an organization deals with its internal factors, for example, by leading a training action to reduce quality defects or by improving the **work organization** and the **integration process** of new recruits to reduce **absenteeism** and **staff turnover**, HCVAVC also increases.

The ratio is a capacity indicator of the **survival and development** of organizations and **strategic warning**, based on a calculation that can be provisional or real, monthly, biannual, or annual. The strategic warning sounds when the HCVAVC decreases. Three major scenarios are possible to address the company's economic situation: development, stagnation, or recession. In each of these scenarios, the action lever is the same—human potential, measured by the required number of worked hours to create the expected amount of value-added.

The HCVAVC is a very useful indicator to assess *organizational dynamics* and can also be calculated at the national, regional or sectoral levels based on existing statistics on hours worked. The national GDP measures the value-added created in a territory, over a given period, divided into three areas of income (wages, taxes, remuneration of capita). The HCVAVC that represents the average value-added created by any organization member in one hour, in cooperation with other actors, is *"nano-GDP."* If this indicator was generalized to all companies as a **piloting tool** of their economic performance, it would focus more attention on creating value-added rather than **reducing costs** or increasing shareholder dividends. This concept essentially connects macro-economies and organization management, a relevant link in this current crisis.

Developing Intangible Investment

SEAM implementation in numerous cases (1,315 organizations) shows that the increase of **effectiveness, efficiency** and company **competitiveness** mainly depends on the increase of *intangible investment in the qualitative devel-*

opment of human potential (***IIQDHP***). This investment consists of enhancing the entire company's employee ***competencies***, energy, ***synchronization*** and employability. It includes leaders, executives, supervisors, technicians, employees, and shop-floor workers.

IIQDHP Composition and Integrated Training

Our concept of ***integrated training*** corresponds to an internal and external adaptation of training as it seeks to respond correctly to the assessment of both the company's business and new market needs. This focus is not systematically offered by vocational training, which fails to capitalize on the expertise gained through experience. We therefore do not equate our integrated training with some form of on-the-job training (learning by doing). It is not limited to the acquisition of technical knowledge, but is based on a transformative approach that involves the active participation of employees within the evolution of their field.

Integrated training is, in this sense, a real development factor for both the individual and the organization. It leads to a more participatory form of management, with support for a ***manual of integrated training*** that capitalizes on learning knowledge. This last point is at the root of our conception of learning, which we define as a "structured assimilation of learning knowledge in the real execution of professional activity and reusable later." It reflects the development of human potential and a method of enrichment of this potential at both the individual and group level.

High Level of Profitability of IIQDHP

Drawing on ISEOR's database, we extracted 40 case studies, half of which are ***SME***s and the other half are large companies and organizations, where ISEOR led intervention-research of pro-active endogenous strategies (Savall & Zardet, 1995, 2005). The methodology consists of analyzing ***dysfunctions*** and measuring their ***hidden costs***, then supporting the organization to create and implement a ***socio-economic innovation project***. A subsequent evaluation measured the intangible investment amount and the value-added increase obtained through the decrease of the dysfunctions. Intangible investments included *exogenous investment*, corresponding to the sum paid to external partners (e.g., fees and travel expenses of ***intervener-researcher***, study, training) and *endogenous investment*, corresponding to the time spent by the organization staff to participate to project groups (e.g., studies, training implementation, new products and services development). The overall rate of return of the intangible investment was calculated as the rate of return on investment and intangible investment rate per person.

The socio-economic change dynamics in these organizations led to hidden-costs recycling into value-added creation. This process allowed the companies and organizations to increase their ***sustainable economic perfor-***

mance. The ISEOR database shows that the rate of hidden costs recycling into value-added, that is, the ratio of hidden costs recouped either through lower *charges* or, as is often the case, in revenue increases (in an accounting sense), hovers between 35% and 55% of the hidden cost amount calculated throughout the *diagnosis phase*. The intangible investment cost for obtaining those results has a high profitability rate hovering between 210% and 4,014%. Each euro or dollar invested in developing human potential in a *SEAM intervention process* can thus be said to yield between 2 and 40 euros or dollars in investment return (ROI). No material investment has such investment return rate (Savall & Zardet, 2008).

The intangible investment in human potential qualitative development is more profitable compared to material investment. The counterparts have a hybrid characteristic and consist of improving work conditions (health, satisfaction) and increasing purchasing power. Sustainable economic performance has two components: (1) short-term measurable immediate results, and (2) creation of potential, consisting of material and intangible investment. The creation of potential is self-financed by the organization and will positively impact its future economic performance.

Thus, qualitative development, that is, the quality of behaviors and skills development of the human potential, is a primordial intangible investment (IIQDHP). It generates a high level of value-added and a competitive advantage for the company that is hard to imitate on the market since it is conceived by the company itself with its *internal resources*.

Socio-economic intervention-research demonstrates that organizations, regardless of their size, sector, legal status, or location, have the capacity to self-finance a significant part of their survival and development without depending on outside financing. Indeed, the sizeable hidden-cost pool constitutes resources that can be re-used for financing innovative actions, releasing time and resources that can be focused on endogenous proactive strategy. Thus, any company can, without added external funding, self-finance its investments in developing human potential and its internal cohesion, a tangible source of sustainable performance.

Decentralizing Control

The ways to improve the effectiveness and efficiency of management control go through a transformation of relationships and *respective roles* of management controllers and operational managers to enable a better anchored function in the company through the development of *self-management control* by managers (Ennajem, 2011). Furthermore, management control indicators should be reconsidered, to further encourage developing value-added on variable costs of the organization, as well as sanctions-reward systems that stimulate the economic responsibility of leaders, managers and staff. Thus, the relevance and reliability of management control depend on the degree of **cooperation** between management controllers and operational managers. It also requires more systematic qualitative and quantitative information gathering of non-financial performance (see Chapter 6).

As an example, in a European company, a subsidiary of a world group listed on the New York Stock Exchange, proactive strategy deployment was facilitated by the implementation of **socio-economic management tools** in the headquarters' various divisions and department—a biannual **priority action plan** per team and **periodically negotiable activity contracts** (**PNAC**) for each employee were created. In addition, an important decision with regard to *management control decentralization* was to position controllers, not anymore in the financial department at headquarters but with the Divisions directors, to develop their activities. Previously their activity was entirely dedicated to reporting to headquarters. One of the first effects was compliance with the deadline to send the monthly reports to the world headquarters, which was not ensured in the past. This result was made possible due to the collaboration between operational directors in the divisions and the controllers, which led them to rationalize and actively pilot the monthly reporting process.

An **evaluation** demonstrated that the amount of endogenous and exogenous **intangible investments** made in 2012 by the organization showed a record surplus. Since 2013 this investment has produced a 10% increase in **hourly contribution to value-added on variable costs** (**HCVAVC**) up from 62 € to 68 €. It represents a return on investment of 2,000%, with each invested euro gaining an average of 20 €. The company has created a surplus of 7 million euro of value added and 48% higher net profit on a 12% declining market.

The performance from this strategy can be explained by the combination of different factors (Datry & Savall, 2014). First, there was a proactive chief executive officer who was able to make acceptable decisions that were provisionally "unpopular" but prevented drastic downsizing decisions. Second, there was increased economic pressure for **immediate results** in the short term, which played a role of stimulator for managers and supervisors. The group required a rapid increase of economic performance and **productivity** by acting on purchases (target of −2.5 million €) and **turnover** (target of 1.5 million €). The obtained results were beyond the group's expectations, because the increase in value added was 7 million euro instead of 5 as requested by the group.

COMPARATIVE ABILITY BETWEEN
SMEs AND LARGE COMPANIES

The idea that large and small- and medium-sized enterprises (SMEs) have different characteristics is widely accepted by practitioners and the literature. However, the ISEOR database shows that the nature of dysfunctions and the level of hidden costs are not significantly different. The use of **SEAMES® software (SEGESE®):** created by ISEOR for the treatment of diagnosis interviews (used in more than 1,000 companies and organizations) enabled us to create a dysfunctions inventory that was identified during the many research-interventions led by nearly 600 ISEOR researchers. Similarly, the level of hidden costs for SMEs and large organizations was in the same range, varying from 20,000 euro to 60,000 euro per person per year. Thus, in three-quarters of SMEs, the hidden costs reduction rate fluctuated between 33% and 66% compared to the original amount, which is a result quite similar to that of large companies (see Table 2.1).

Table 2.1.   Comparison Between Return on Investment Delay of IIQDHP in SMEs Versus Large Companies

	SMEs (20)		Large Organizations (20)	
Repayment period of intangible investment in human potential	Number of organizations	%	Number of organizations	%
Less than 1 month	12	60%	9	45%
Between 1 to 2 months	6	30%	6	30%
Between 2 to 3 months	1	5%	1	5%
Between 4 to 6 months	1	5%	4	20%

The significant difference is the time necessary to achieve these results. In SMEs, a 6 or 8 month time period, with a time investment of approximately one day per month on the part of executive officers was sufficient for this improved performance (see Figure 2.1). In large companies, this period was between one and two years (see Figure 2.2). Size does play a role, because in SMEs the decision between a **project group** and a director is short and the implementation follows quickly after, so much so that from one month to another, significant change can be measured. In large organizations, the **project phase** is more severed from the implementation stage, which starts usually after the four months required for the **development** stage of the **socio-economic innovation project**.

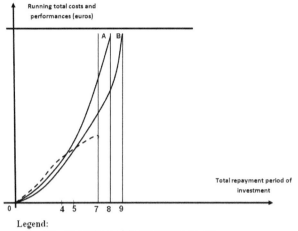

Figure 2.1. Cash flow rhythms of intangible *investment in qualitative development of human potential (IIQDHP*)* in 20 SMEs.

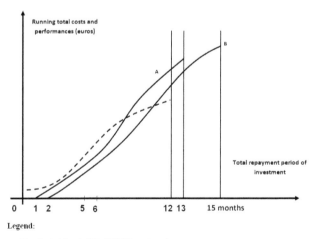

Figure 2.2. Cash flow rhythms of intangible investment in qualitative development in human potential (IIQDHP*) in 20 Large organizations.

We can retain the profitability criterion and return on investment as one of the agility indicators of organization (or at least its resistance to change). The comparative study of a sample of 40 organizations—20 SMEs and 20 large companies—points to some differences in the observed results. The repayment period for *intangible investment in qualitative development of human potential* (***IIQDHP***) is a bit longer in large organizations than in smaller ones. In the study sample, 90% of SMEs had less than a two month repayment period, compared to 75% for large companies.

The cost of IIQDHP results from concurrent costs that are incremented during the change process: bills of external consultant fees that range throughout the process, structures costs that are settled monthly to different suppliers, the cost of time spent, and the salaries and employee benefits by all the ***actors*** involved. Zero based, at the beginning of process, the IIQDHP cost culminates at the end of the process. In profitability calculation, the breakdown of the repayment period begins from this very moment. Therefore, it takes less than one month to recover the outlay in 75% of cases and between 1 and 2 months in 90%. This is the simplified reasoning that we have chosen in the presentation of our results.

The profitability of investment (IIQDHP), however, starts earlier. For SMEs, results begin sometimes before the middle of the process. Indeed, improvement of the actors' ***time management*** practices and the reduction of ***dysfunctions***, whose main ***hidden cost*** is assessed in terms of ***regulation time*** and is reallocated to create value-added, eliminates 30 to 60% of ***overtime*** and ***non-production***. Thus, as soon as the third or fourth month, the incremental cost of IIQDHP becomes negative, because the recovery of value-added is bigger than the cost of time spent in the improvement action (IIQDHP). So in our simplified approach when we consider that the return on investment occurs only at the end of the change process, we overvalue the repayment period of IIQDHP and we consequently undervalue its profitability.

Proposal to Solve Financial Issues of SMEs

Excessive dependence, facing main customers or shippers and external funders (e.g., banks) is a major reason for SME and ***VSE (very small enterprise)*** fragility. While it is true that in most countries in the world they appear as an economic prosperity incubator, their creation should be encouraged and their ability of ***survival and development*** consolidated. Studies converge to denounce the fragility of SMEs, as measured by their early death rate, the many failures of companies' transmission and their demise. A ***strategic management*** approach for SMEs enables them to increase their cash flow by recycling hidden costs, limiting their need for bank financing at a reasonable threshold. It will stimulate economic vitality of the SME network in their own interest and for territories where they are set up, whether municipality, region, or nation. Major customers or shippers, the external funders and banks have guarantees against excessive *risk* of SMEs sinking.

Our proposal is to recommend a *mixed financing of SMEs* based on a more balanced distribution of their cash flow and debt. It implies that these firms should acquire some expertise in **recycling hidden costs in value added creation**. This expertise would improve the SMEs' power in economic **negotiation** in a constraining and highly competitive environment. It would also balance the customer's power in negotiating terms and mitigate this recurring problem of unequal exchanges that expects the legislator to regulate.

The banking system could develop new SME financing products by drawing its inspiration from based on our concept of **mixed funding agreements**. The assessment model of the survival and development capacity of SMEs by their bank would no longer be based on the traditional good results chronicle of the last three years, but on a *new ratio* that consists of past profitability and IIQDHP *level mix*. Indeed, this ratio measures **effectiveness** and **efficiency** of organization practices in recent years to reach a consisting level of IIQDHP with very high profitability. The latter would become a company's robustness prognostic indicator, which is more relevant than their current level of technological investment. The SME's bank would become a real consultant in strategic management, creating a new trust relationship that has recently been undermined by speculative practices and value-added predation widespread among financing specialists. Bank credit will not only depend on a favorable chronic of past results in the classic sense of immediate results but on companies' ability to invest in their **human potential**. Mixed financing of SMEs increases their autonomy, stimulates their **strategic ambition**, and decreases their dependency.

PRIVATE COMPANIES AND PUBLIC SERVICE ORGANIZATIONS (PSO)

An Organization for Economic Co-operation and Development (OECD) study shows that public service organizations in its 32 member's countries face difficulties unifying public services quality and coping with budgetary constraints. OECD presents mixed results and underlines the importance of management quality and management skills in public organizations, and notes a delay in the public service modernization process (PSO).

Public management *values*, related to the public service notion, are also being criticized, focusing on the need to find a balance between **competitiveness** and solidarity, between economic effectiveness and social equity, and between performance and **cohesion**.

Socio-Economic Management as a Public Service Modernization Model

Based on **collaborative initiatives** with the Mexican federal government, which has used **socio-economic management** as a method of modernizing public services and developing human resources management practices in the public services, ISEOR was invited to present its method during the OECD annual meeting in Paris (November, 2011), in which delegates, ministers, state secretaries and senior officials of member countries attended. The authors of this chapter presented the results of **pilot projects** carried out in public administrations and organizations in Mexico, Belgium, and France. The Secretary of State for Public Service of Mexico and the Federal High Officer in charge of human resources followed up by presenting the SEAM experiment carried out in Mexico.

Sustainable Innovation Strategies in Public Services

The **intervention-research** presented in this section is drawn from 27 cases of French, Belgian, and Mexican PSOs that implemented socio-economic management. Despite the current budgetary constraints endured by these organizations, the results assessed by ISEOR confirm that PSOs are potentially competitive and that jobs in this sector can be attractive, including for the younger generation provided that there is **pro-active** human resources management. Moreover, we could observe a behavioral modification of users in the way that they use the word customer also courted out by the literature. The notion of customer, an actor feeling a need and asking for a product or service to satisfy it, is integrated in **socio-economic theory** (Savall, 1974; Savall & Zardet, 1987), whatever the organization status. The intervention-research carried out showed that this definition illustrates customer satisfaction (Méan & Ombelets, 2008; Pigaglio, 2009; Savall & Zardet, 2007).

Self-Financing Public Service Modernization

As companies, PSOs create chronic dysfunctions sources of hidden costs ranging from 15,000 euro to 58,000 euro per person per year. These hidden costs represent an economic resource deposit that evaporates continuously, causing an inflation of public service costs. The existence of these unmeasured and unsuspected reserves suggests that any PSO can ensure its **survival and development**, despite budgetary constraints due to debt and state and local authorities' deficits, if they learn how to recycle hidden costs into value-added. This loss in value, particularly, comes from archaic procedures and organizations explained earlier as the **TFW virus** (Savall &

Zardet, 2006, 2009a, 2009b; Savall, Zardet, & Bonnet, 2010). The resultant conception of organization and management curbs potential *multi-skills* because it is no longer adapted to the levels of staff education, skills and aspiration, nor to the new demands of citizen-users.

Hourly Contribution to Value-Added on Variable Costs (HCVAVC)

Socio-economic indicators help to measure the evolution of organizational efficiency. The HCVAVC pinpoints the progress of the overall *socio-economic performance* of the organization. It reflects the *economic value* of one worked hour in PSO. This indicator, calculated in France, Belgium and Mexico, assess whether overall socio-economic performance has improved. If it increases, it is a sign of significantly better *effectiveness and efficiency*, with controlled use of public *resources* allotted to a PSO and *social performance* for users and staff.

Contrary to generally accepted ideas, *productivity* reserves in the public sector are in the same order of magnitude as in the private sector. As our research has underscored classic *piloting methods*, transposed into public service organizations—such as classical cost accounting, superficial ABC method, and dashboards limited to reporting—are a scarcely effective. Wanting to apply outdated methods to public service organizations is a strategic error that can readily delay their modernization. However, these experiments of socio-economic modernization show that when PSO are more efficient, they spread value in their *external environment*, with a multiplier effect of economic and social prosperity. The notion of efficiency is often associated with economic individualism, whereas PSO can be both more efficient and generate *positive externalities* for users and staff. As an example, the Ministry of the State of Yucatan has made many improvements in its operations and was able to self-finance the implementation of a digital system of procedures for users (Savall & Zardet, 2007).

Representative Pilot Actions in the Public Sector

In France, the case of the Social Security Contribution Collection Office (URSSAF) is particularly illuminating. This Public Service Organization (PSO) has been applying socio-economic management since 1996 and has significantly improved its efficiency, which was recognized by the Central Agency (ACCOSS) for major national accounts, which were reserved to the Paris's agency. Rhône URSSAF currently pilots the merger of eight URSSAFs of the Rhône-Alpes region. In this PSO of 400 employees, hidden costs during socio-economic management implementation amounted to 20,000 euros per person per year, that is, a reserve of 8 million euros partially convertible into *creation of value-added*. However, 35 to 55% of these hidden costs could be converted into resources, recovered to finance the public program (between 2.8 million and 4.4 million euros).

Other ISEOR interventions in the public sector were used to measure **hidden costs**. As examples, intervention carried out in a pilot region, employing 30,000 people of La Poste (whose overall workforce amounted to 290,000 people), with 22,000 euro per person per year or a Chamber of Commerce and Industry concessionary of a commercial port and airport, with 26,000 euro per person per year. In Mexico, ISEOR carried out an intervention following the request of the Government of the State of Yucatan and the federal government, identifying 164,000 pesos per person per year in hidden costs. In Belgium, **implementation of socio-economic management** since 2000 in the Public Employment Agency and Training in Wallonia (FOREM) stimulated the agents' mobilization around the new tasks of the Agency. Hidden costs amounted to 27,600 euros per person per year, which were recycled into value-added through **integrated training**, improvement of **working conditions**, and development of an organization that was more interesting for the staff. It allowed a steady increase of efficiency and a better use of public funds.

Socio-economic management has also been applied in some dozens of PSOs. It simultaneously meets the employer's productivity wish and demands for improved work conditions and a purchasing power increase despite the crisis, as expressed by unions and staff at all levels of responsibility.

Improving Social and Economic Performance

In the mainstream literature, theories in public administration and political science point out that there are significant and stable differences between public and private organizations in terms of motivation, staff selection, organizational procedures, and **bureaucracy** (Rainey, Backoff, & Levine, 1976; Rainey & Chun, 2005; Rainey, Pandey, & Bozeman, 1995). The *differentialist* paradigm asserts that private and public companies should work with different practices and logic. However, it comes down to tautological reasoning where the compilation of academic representations will not lead to another vision. Indeed, only comparative scientific observation allows mitigating the widespread *differentialist theory*. Thus, close observation of private companies and public organizations shows that both categories, faced with globalization and the financial crisis, are looking for tools to help them combine **sustainable economic performance** and social performance. It is important to remember that the method is based on the involvement of all levels of **actors**, placing the entire human potential at the core of **socio-economic intervention device** (**Horivert**).

Among the observed results in PSO from different countries, all have implemented **management tools—internal-external strategic action** (**IESAP**) and the **Priority Action Plan** (**PAP**)—that break down concrete actions of the strategy to the last agent of the organization. In the case of social security administration in France, actors, starting from the national strategy defined by the State, declined this strategy at the department level. The implementation rate of priority actions increased significantly, which has enabled this agency to improve its efficiency. Similarly in the case of a public administration of professional training and employment in Belgium that employed 4,400 officers, the general manager formalized an IESAP from the strategy of the Walloon Government (Méan & Ombelets, 2008). This plan was then translated by the involved echelons in priority actions over a six month period. All the managers reduced their PSO's PAP to their appropriate level.

It is also essential that modernization of management practices should not be limited to contracted collective annual objectives and means provided by law, but that there should be a true individual and team *communication* scheme focused on developing increased **commitment** among organizational members. The goal is to enhance work-related content and working conditions, and to establish a dialogue between teams and between agents and their managers. The principles of subsidiarity and proximity are factors of efficiency and sustainable efficiency in PSO.

In addition, the results of socio-economic management are very positive in developing and emerging countries. It could be adopted in upgrading intervention methods of these countries, as recommended by the World Bank, the IMF, and the OCD. It could allow better use of precious resources distributed by these international organizations. In sum, some legal differences between the two types of organizations and their organizational impacts do not justify *differentialist* theory of specific sectors, whether public or private.

COMPARING LEAN AND SOCIO-ECONOMIC MANAGEMENT

If companies and organizations ask for management methods, it is especially important to meet their needs. A major difference between LEAN and socio-economic management is the grasp of this need—the underlying goals of these tools are different. LEAN provides tools focused on improving productivity, whereas socio-economic management focuses on stimulating creativity, increasing staff skills, and improving individual and group performance. In addition, LEAN is characterized by a multitude of specialized methods, while the socio-economic management has an interconnected tools system, which is shared across the enterprise, a *cohesion* factor. Within SEAM, the employees' role is to develop their skills and become a source of improvement ideas. Both approaches, however, are oriented to customers, although LEAN focuses on external customers and SEAM focuses on both external customers and staff, who are considered *internal customers*.

Table 2.2.   Comparison of LEAN and SEAM

	Divergent Objectives	
Themes	*SEAM*	*LEAN*
Objectives	• Approach based on human • Sustainable overall performance • TFW Anti-virus (fight excessive specialization)	• Approach looking at external environment (customer) • Improve performance • Reduce visible costs
Origins	• Man is disobedient, intelligent, an actor and strategic → work with strangers • Work attractiveness	• Taylorism • Industrial methods (Lean manufacturing) ⇒ Sequencing
Means	Negotiation to build a cohesion	Assumption : Default cohesion and respect
Field of application	• Tools • According to a process • Policy ⇒ Creation of a pro-active strategy	• Work organization • Procedures ⇒ Do not influence strategy
Diagnosis	Dysfunctional according 6 themes, participative including each hierarchical level, valorization of dysfunctions → awareness	No diagnosis Standard implementation
Tools	Articulated system for person and team → encourage negotiation between actors, empower them and de-compartmentalize departments → overall cohesion	Process orientation, standardization, costs reduction → possible alienation
Training	Internal interveners and every manager	Lean manager et specialized training according to sector
Improvement	Custom-made by actors according to their problems	Standard methods to plan and reduce loss of time

(Table continues on next page)

Table 2.2.   (Continues)

	Divergent Objectives	
Themes	SEAM	LEAN
Work conditions	Include in the approach	Hyper-specialization: Human-machine
Wages	Individual according to collective and individual objectives	Undefined

Despite divergent objectives (see Table 2.2), both methods have some points of convergence. Indeed, their implementation is done gradually through actions that mobilize internal stakeholders. However, the **project manager** in socio-economic management is, in any case, the chief executive officer, and people who ensure an internal relay, referred to as "**internal interveners**," provide methodological assistance to all managers at any organization level. Employee training is exclusively internal in LEAN, while in socio-economic management it is carried out concomitantly in with intra-company and inter-company training teams. The dissemination of LEAN is implemented through localized working groups and does not concern the entire organization in a common dynamic.

The results of both methods are also different. Perhaps most interesting is that more than 40 years later, there have not been any adverse effects of SEAM reported on organizations and their members—something that cannot be stated for LEAN. LEAN management has developed a negative reputation, especially in terms of the deterioration of work conditions. In the LEAN system, following a sometimes forced implementation and search for **immediate results**, people suffer from an increase of stress and anxiety at work. Staff often notices an impoverishment of their work because it is more specialized and they are isolated in their jobs. Our observations have also witnessed a decline in creativity and in the actors' innovation capacity, as well as the development of musculoskeletal disorders (MSDs) due to the endless repetition of some tasks.

CONCLUSION: SUSTAINING SOCIO-ECONOMIC PERFORMANCE

The raison d'être of management is organizational performance. It is an important conceptual challenge that consists of articulating three performance levels: individual, organizational and societal, in a "multi-level" model while trying to link macro and micro dimensions (Rousseau, 2011). Socio-economic theory has its roots in macro-economic research (Savall,

1974, 1975), especially the theory of crises and underemployment. Yet, a main conclusion is that macro-economic analysis is not adequate to understand value creation. An approach that alternates macro- and micro-economic analyses was needed, using an "elevator" (bottom-up/top-down) for observing how different levels of activities contribute to the creation of economic value—individual, team, company, sector, local, regional, national, and international territories. Linking these different levels allows us to understand how value is generated through the *interactions* between these different levels of analysis.

The multilevel model we propose is based on an assumption of isomorphism in value creation from the societal to the individual levels, through the organization and the working team. The quasi-universality of human potential, in spite of the cultural, ethical and geopolitical diversity of organizations, can astonish. The *organizational biology metaphor* considers dysfunctions as non-specific *organizational pathologies*. In the human biology area, beyond the obvious diversity of the individuals, the universality of pathologies has allowed significant progresses in curative and preventive medicine. It is what we can wish for, by analogy, in order to improve companies and organizational health and to preserve employment. Thus, socio-economic theory has attempted to create more relevant decision- making tools that take dysfunctions and their hidden costs into account. Moreover, socio-economic theory can be applied on a number of different levels—organization or company, territory as a tangled organization, companies or groups of institutions. While this volume is focused on organization, the proposed concepts and assumptions also have implications for the territory level, as outsourced costs for instance.

NOTE

1. The research for this chapter has been influenced by a number of works that are not directly referred to in the text, including Aristote (2014), Barth and Martin (2014), Boje (2007, 2008, 2009), Boje and Rosile (2003a), Caghassi (2009), Gephart (2009), Pasquier, P. (2009), Pasquier, S. (1995), Péron and Péron (2003), Perroux (1979), Savall (2012), Savall and Zardet (2011), and Savall, Zardet, and Bonnet (2000, 2008).

REFERENCES

Aristote. (2014). Réfutations sophistiques [Sophistical Refutations]. In P. Pellergin (Ed.), *Aristote, œuvres complètes* [Aristote, integral work] (pp. 453–506). Paris, France: Flammarion.

Barth, I., & Martin, Y.-H. (2014). *Le manager et le philosophe* [The manager and the philosopher]. Paris, France: Le Passeur Éditeur.

Becker, G. S. (1964). *Human capital*. Chicago, IL: University of Chicago Press.

Becker, G., Murphy, K., & Tamura, R. (1990). Economic growth, human capital and population growth. *Journal of Political Economy, 98* (5), S12–S137.

Beine, M., & Docquier, F. (2000). *Croissance et convergence économiques* [Economic growth and convergence]. Louvain-la-Neuve, France: De Boeck.

Boje, D. M. (2007). Globalization antenarratives. In A. Mills, J. C. Helms-Mills, & C. Forshaw (Eds.), *Organizational behavior in a global context* (pp. 505–549). Toronto, Ontario, Canada: Garamond.

Boje, D. M. (2008). *Critical theory ethics for business and public administration*. Charlotte, NC: Information Age Publishing.

Boje, D. M. (2009). *Storytelling, appreciative inquiry, and tetranormalization*. Paper presented at the international conference organized in partnership with the ISEOR and Divisions of the Academy of Management, Lyon, France.

Boje, D., & Rosile, G.-A. (2003a). Comparison of socio-economic and other transorganizational development methods. *Journal of Change Organizational Management, 16*(1), 10–20.

Boje, D. M., & Rosile, G. A. (2003b). Theatrics of SEAM. *Journal of Organizational Change Management, 16*(1), 21–32.

Brunetti, A. (1997). *Politique et croissance économique : comparaison de données internationales* [Politic and economic growth: Comparison of international data]. Paris, France: OECD.

Buono, A. F., & Savall, H. (Eds.). (2007). *Socio-economic intervention in organizations: The intervener-researcher and the SEAM approach to organizational analysis*. Charlotte, NC: Information Age Publishing.

Caghassi, J. (2009). Articulation gouvernance / management [Governance/management articulation]. In H. Savall, V. Zardet, & M. Bonnet (Eds.), *Management socio-économique, une approche innovante* [Socio-economic approach to management. An innovative approach]. Paris, France: Economica.

Cappelletti, L., & Hoarau, C. (2013) *Finance et contrôle au quotidien* [Finance and control in the day-to-day]. Paris: Dunod

Carré, J.-J., Dubois, P., & Malinvaud, E. (1972). *La croissance française: Un essai d'analyse causale de l'après-guerre* [French growth: A causal analysis test of the post-war]. Paris, France: Édition du Seuil.

Conbere, J., & Heorhiadi, A. (2011). Socio-economic approach to management. *Organization Development Practitioner, 43*(1), 6–10.

Corsi, M., & Guarini, G., (2007). La fonction de productivité de Sylos Labini: Aspects théoriques et empiriques [The productivity function of Sylos Labini : Theoretical and empirical aspects]. *Revue d'économie industrielle, 118*, 1–25.

Cummings, T., & Worley, C. (2014). *Organization development and change*. Independence, KY: Cengage Learning.

Darreau, P. (2002,). *Croissance et politique économique* [Growth and economic policy].

Datry, F., & Savall, A. (2014, May). *Seeking economic resources: SEAM intervention-research Case in a Belgian subsidiary of a NYSE listed American group*. SEAM Conference in North America. Minneapolis, MN.

De Boeck, P., & E. Denison (1967). *Why growth rates differ*. New York, NY: The Brookings Institution.

De Montmollin, M. (1981). *Le Taylorisme à visage humain* [Human face of Taylorism]. Paris, France: L'Harmattan.

Ennajem, C. (2011). *Évolution du rôle du contrôleur de gestion* [Evolution of the management controller role]. Sarrebruck, Deutchland: Éditions Universitaires Européennes.

Fayol, H. (1916). *Administration industrielle et générale* [Industrial and global administration]. Paris, France: Dunod.

Gephart, R. P. (2009). An Invitation to Ethnostatistics. *Revue Sciences de gestion–Management Sciences–Ciencias de Gestión, 70,* 85.

Gephart, R. P. (2013). Doing research with words: Qualitative methodologies and industrial/organizational psychology. In J. M. Cortina & R. S. Landis (Eds.), *Modern research methods for the study of behavior in organizations*, (pp. 265–318). New York, NY: Routledge.

Heertje, A., Pieretti, P., & Barthélémy, P. (2003). *Principes d'économie politique* [Principles of economic policy]. Louvain-la-Neuve, France: De Boeck.

Keynes, J. M. (1936). *The general theory of employment, interest, and money*. Cambridge, UK: Cambridge University Press.

Lucas, R. (1988). On the mechanics of economic development. *Journal of Monetary Economics, 22,* 3–42.

Lussato, B. (1977). *Introduction critique aux théories d'organisation* [Critical introduction to organizational theories]. Paris, France: Bordas.

Marx, K. (1848). *Critique de l'économie politique: Contribution à la critique de l'économie politique* [The critique of political economy: Contribution to the critique of political economy]. Paris, France : Éditions Sociales.

Marx, K. (1862). *Le Capital* [*The Capital*]. Paris, France: M. Lachâtre.

Méan, J. P., & Ombelets, N., in ISEOR. (2008) *Modernisation des services publics, fécondité des partenariats publics-privés* [Public services modernization: Public-private partnerships fecondity]. Paris, France: Economica.

Pareto, V. (1927). *Manual of Political economy*. London, UK: Macmillan.

Pascale, R. (2011). La empresa en tiempos de la economía del conocimiento. Desafíos estrategia, costos e interdisciplinaridad [The enterprise in time of knowledge economy: Challenges strategy, costs and interdisciplinary]. *XII Congrès International des Coûts,* Punta del Este, Uruguay.

Pasquier, S. (1995). Préface [Preface]. In *Ingénierie stratégique du roseau, souple et enracinée* [Strategic engineering of the reed, flexible and rooted]. Paris, France: Economica.

Pasquier, P. (2009). Deux cas emblématiques de développement économique durable des entreprises [Two emblematic cases of sustainable economic development of enterprises]. In H. Savall, V. Zardet, & M. Bonnet (Eds.), *Management socio-économique, une approche innovante* [Socio-economic approach to management: An innovative approach]. Paris, France: Economica.

Péron, M., & Péron, M. (2003). Postmodernism and the socio-economic approach to organizations. *Journal of Organizational Change Management, 16*(1), 49–55.

Perroux, F. (1973). *Pouvoir et économie* [Power and economy]. Paris, France: Bordas.

Perroux, F. (1979). L'entreprise, l'équilibre rénové et les coûts "caches" [The enterprise, the renovated balance and the "hidden" costs]. Preface. In H. Savall. *Reconstruire l'entreprise* [Reconstructing the enterprise] Paris, France: Dunod.

Pigaglio, G. (2009). *Les mutations stratégiques d'un organisme public: Cas de l'ISE à l'URSSAF de Lyon* [Strategic mutations of a public company: Case of socio-economic intervention-research at URSSAF Lyon]. In H. Savall, V. Zardet, & M. Bonnet (Eds.), *Management socio-économique, une approche innovante* [SEAM, an innovative approach]. Paris, France: Economica

Rainey, H. G., & Chun, Y. H. (2005). Public and private management compared. *The Oxford handbook of public management, 72,* 102.

Rainey, H. G., Backoff, R. W., & Levine, C. H. (1976). Comparing public and private organizations. *Public Administration Review, 36* (2), 233–244.

Rainey, H. G., Pandey, S., & Bozeman, B. (1995). Research note: Public and private managers' perceptions of red tape. *Public Administration Review, 55*(6), 567–574.

Romer, P. (1986). Increasing returns and long run growth. *Journal of Political Economy, 94*(5), 1002–1037.

Rousseau, D. (2011). Reinforcing the micro/macro bridge: organizational thinking and pluralistic vehicles. *Journal of Management, 37*(2), 429–442.

Savall, H. (1974–1975–1977). *Enrichir le travail humain dans les entreprises et les organisations* [An economic evaluation of job enrichment]. Paris: Dunod.

Savall, H. (1981–2010). *Work and people: An economic evaluation of job enrichment.* 1st ed. New York: Oxford University Press ; 2nd ed. Charlotte, NC: Information Age Publishing

Savall, H. (2011), Keynote speaker, Petite lecture épistemologique sans prétention de la responsabilité sociale de l'entreprise [Little epistemological reading without arrogance of corporate social responsibility]; ADERSE 2011 Conference proceedings, on CSR and global governance, march, published in Le Flanchec, Uzan & Doucin (editors), *RSE et gouvernance mondiale* [CSR and global governance] p. 3–22.

Savall, H. (2012). *Origine radicale des crises économiques: Germán Bernácer, précurseur visionnaire* [Root origin of crises: Germán Bernácer, a visionary forerunner]. Charlotte, NC: Information Age Publishing.

Savall, H., & Zardet, V. (1987). *Maîtriser les coûts et les performances cachés : Le contrat d'activité périodiquement négociables* [Mastering hidden costs and performances: The periodically negotiable activity contract]. Paris, France: Economica.

Savall, H.. & Zardet, V. (1992). *Le nouveau contrôle de gestion: Méthode des coûts-per-formances cachés* [New management control: The hidden cost-performance method]. Paris: Éditions Comptables Malesherbes-Eyrolles

Savall, H., & Zardet, V. (1995–2005). *Ingénierie stratégique du roseau, souple et enra-cinée* [Strategic engineering of the reed, flexible and rooted]. Paris, France: Economica.

Savall, H., & Zardet, V. (2005). *Tétranormalisation: Défis et dynamiques* [Competitive challenges and dynamics of tetra-normalization]. Paris, France: Economica.

Savall, H., & Zardet, V. (2006). Théorie socio-économique des organisations: Impacts sur quelques concepts dominants dans les théories et pratiques managériales [Socio-economic theory: Impacts on some mainstream concepts in management theories and pratices]. *Academy of Management (ODC Division) & ISEOR Conference*, pp. 267–302.

Savall, H., & Zardet, V. (2007, June). *L'importance stratégique de l'investissement incorporel: résultats qualimétriques de cas d'entreprises* [The strategic importance of intangible investment: Qualimetric results of company cases]. In Colloque *IIC-ISEOR-American Accounting Association*, Lyon, France.

Savall, H., & Zardet, V. (2008*). Mastering hidden costs and performance*. Charlotte, NC: Information Age Publishing.

Savall, H., & Zardet, V. (2009a), Mesure et pilotage de la responsabilité sociale et sociétale de l'entreprise: Résultats de recherches longitudinales [Measuring and piloting corporate social responsibility: Results from longitudinal research]; paper, *International conference proceedings and doctoral consortium, partnership between the Academy Of Management (AOM) and ISEOR*, Lyon, June, pp. 25–53.

Savall, H., & Zardet, V. (2009b). Responsabilidad social y societal de la empresa: indicadores para dialogar con las partes interesadas [The corporate social responsibility: Indicators to converse with stakeholders]; paper, *ACACIA's Conference proceedings*, July, UAM – México, pp. 31-59.

Savall, H., & Zardet, V. (2010), Le non-dit dans la théorie socio-économique des organisations : situations de management et pièces de théâtre [Unvoiced comment in the socio-economic theory of organizations: Management situations and theatrics] In R. Ocler (Ed.), *Fantasmes, mythes, non-dits et quiproquo: Analyse de discours et organisation* [Fantasy, myths, unvoiced and misunderstanding: Analysis of speech and organization] (pp. 9–35). Paris: L'Harmattan.

Savall, H., & Zardet, V. (2011). *The qualimetrics approach: Observing the complex object*. Charlotte, NC: Information Age Publishing.

Savall, H., & Zardet, V. (2013). The *dynamics and challenges of tetranormalization*. Charlotte, NC: Information Age Publishing

Savall, H., Zardet, V., & Bonnet, M. (2000–2008). *Releasing the untapped potential of enterprises through socio-economic management*. Geneva: Éditions IOT-BIT.

Savall, H., Zardet, V., & Bonnet, M. (2010), RSE et développement durable, fondements de la théorie socio-économique des organisations [CSR and sustainable development, basis of socio-economic theory]; paper, ADERSE Conference proceedings, march, La Rochelle, published in Nicole Barthe & J.-Jacques Rosé (Eds.), *RSE et développement durable* [CSR between globalization and sustainable development] (pp. 3–36, 239–268) Brussels: De Boeck.

Smith, A. (1776). *Inquiry into the nature and causes of the wealth of nations*. London, UK: W. Strahan & T. Cadell.

Solow, R. M. (1956). A contribution to the theory of economic growth. *The Quarterly Journal of Economics, 70*(1), 65–94.

Sorensen, P. F., Yaeger, T. F., Savall, H., Zardet, V., Bonnet, M., & Peron, M. (2010). A review of two major global and international approaches to organizational change: SEAM and appreciative inquiry. *Organization Development Journal, 28*(4), 31–39.

Stoléru, L. (1969). *L'équilibre et la croissance économique* [Balance and economic growth]. Paris, France: Dunod.

Taylor, F. W. (1911). *The principles of scientific management*. New York, NY: Harpers and Brothers.

Walras, L. (1877). *Eléments d'économie politique pure ou théorie de la richesse sociale* [Elements of pure economic policy or social wealth theory]. Lausanne, Switzerland: Imprimerie L. Corbaz.

Weber, M. (1924–1964). *The theory of social and economic organization*. New York, NY: Free Press.

CHAPTER 3

IN SEARCH OF SUSTAINABLE FIRM PERFORMANCE

The Socio-Economic Approach to Management Interventions[1]

Gérard Desmaison and Rickie Moore

Sustainable prosperity is a key to the success of companies of the 21st century. In their quest for sustained *economic performance*, firms are challenged to identify the endogenous drivers of their performance, notably the performance measurement system, the stakeholder economic value creation processes, and appropriate management methods and practices, and to validate the coherence among them. Among these many factors, the sustainability of the methods of management plays a critical role in helping to achieve the overall performance of the firm. The question therefore is how to develop and practice sustainable methods of management in companies in order to improve the overall performance of the *actors* and reconcile organizational change with high levels of satisfaction. Given the fact that the concept of sustainability is multi-faceted, however, we will

The Socio-Economic Approach to Management Revisited: The Evolving Nature of SEAM in the 21st Century, pp. 55–74
Copyright © 2015 by Information Age Publishing
All rights of reproduction in any form reserved.

first outline our approach to the concept in utilizing it as an illustration of overall economic performance.

SUSTAINABILITY AS THE DRIVER OF ECONOMIC PERFORMANCE

The practice of management traces its roots back to the science of mathematics and the administration of the military establishment. Over time, the more mainstream approach to the economic performance of firms has increasingly been biased towards their financial performance (Cameron, 1967; Goldsmith, 1969; Mc Kinnon, 1973; Schumpeter, 1911) and this trend has clearly influenced the management methods, techniques, and practices that have been developed and used in firms. Over time, the prevalence of this bias has led to a "normatization" of finance being considered first and foremost, as the essential element of importance for the performance of the firm.

As with all biases, the cause-effect relationship is often problematic and subject to debate. In one major contribution to the topic, Hansen and Wernerfelt (1989) illustrated that the economic and organizational factors were both determinants of firm performance, and they argued that the organizational ones were twice as influential in firm performance compared to economic factors. While firms are required to incorporate the dynamics of their *external environments*, their performance is primarily a reflection and outcome of their *internal organization* and operations. In essence, their external performance is determined and driven by their *internal performance*.

Sustainability, Economic Performance, and Corporate Social Responsibility

The question driving this chapter concerns how firms can develop more sustainable management practices and ensure they endure over time, while simultaneously integrating organizational change and creating the conditions for employees to gain satisfaction from their work environments. Sustainability, as a concept, advocates the maintenance of production systems without degrading or destroying their surrounding environment. The philosophy of the concept is that an entity in its normal operation should be careful not to destroy the underlying ecosystem, which is necessary for the very existence of the entity.

Since their inception, firms have always grappled with the *interaction* and *integration* of people, strategy, *structure*, systems, and processes, and their impact on the performance and results of the firm. However, the notion of firm performance has largely been dominated by quantitative and especially financial dimensions (the "bottom line"). The balance sheet and the profit and loss statements were considered the leading indicators of firm performance. However, several theorists, researchers, sociologists, and other observers have been arguing that this biased view of reality is destructive and undermines the sustainability of the firm's performance, as the other dimensions of the performance are ignored or underrated. This view has consistently argued for the *development* of a more balanced approach, which would facilitate performance sustainability.

For several years, the concept of *overall economic performance* has been gaining in recognition and importance in the management landscape. In the early 1990s, the term "triple bottom line" was introduced by John Elkington, a British advocate for social and environmental responsibility of individuals and firms, as a means on repositioning and enlarging the narrow spectrum that had come to characterize firm performance (see Elkington, 1997). A longtime member of the corporate responsibility movement for over four decades, Elkington (1997) argued for the integration of three key domains in the performance of the firm—people, planet, and profit. Elkington's proposal quickly gained relevance as it was widely considered as a practical evolution of the sustainable development concept that had been introduced in the United Nations debates on the future of society and business in the mid-80s.

Within firms, the manner in which employees, strategy, structure, systems, and processes interact and are integrated and managed directly impact the performance and results of the firm. The resultant interaction also determines the extent to which the performance is sustainable. Increasingly, a growing number of firms are embracing the notion of *sustainable economic performance* and are expressing their interests in developing more sustainable methods. However, subject to the exogenous pressures of the market and competitive business environment, many business leaders tend to opt for quick fix remedies as opposed to developing more enduring approaches. If quick fixes provide fast results, they seldom create long-lasting solutions. Cutting costs and downsizing the workforce may be effective in reducing expenditures, but they do not provide for nor sustain the performance of the firm. On the contrary, once firms embark on the quick fix journey, they rapidly find themselves locked in the quick fix spiral. Consequently, they will most likely be condemned to staying the course, substituting and replacing one quick fix with another. Fundamentally, they are transformed into riders on the quick fix roller coaster, caught in the quest for a miracle and dazed by the mirage of the quick result.

Undoubtedly, many business leaders are extremely apprehensive about the complexity involved in achieving firm performance. Some leaders are uncomfortable and insecure when they are exposed to situations within their firms that they are unable to fully control—such as dealing with employee behavior. Integrating such variability can prove to be daunting and time consuming, carrying significant personal *risk* for leaders and managers—from identifying and understanding the various points of view within a firm and exposure to the risk of being wrong, to the risk of being confronted and challenged on unpopular decisions.

The notion of the sustainable economic performance of the firm that we advocate in our research requires that firms identify the key endogenous drivers of their economic performance and improve the coherence between them. The focus should be on the firm's performance measurement system, stakeholder-based economic value creation processes, and the management methods and practices used within the firm in order to create the conditions for the sustainability of their performance and to obtain their objectives.

In the mainstream economic literature, economists have compiled a set of indicators that they use to describe the economic performance of a country: interest rates, gross domestic product (GDP) and GDP growth rate, consumer price index (CPI), producer price index (PPI), housing starts, durable goods, and so forth. These indicators have also been compiled into a composite index of leading economic indicators (LEI) that is used to predict the future economic activity of a country average workweek (manufacturing), initial unemployment claims, new orders for consumer goods, vendor performance, plant and equipment orders, building permits, change in unfilled durable orders, sensitive material prices, stock price (S&P 500), real money, index of consumer expectations, and so forth.[2] As opposed to predicting the outcome or evolution of any particular segment in a national economy, the leading indicators index, through the analysis and *evaluation* of periodical measures, can be used to indicate the likely direction of the economy. Economists argue that in improving these structural dimensions the economic well-being of a country can be assured and developed, and citizens will be able to enjoy greater *socio-economic prosperity*.

The fundamental issue about sustaining the development of the *economic performance* of firms has its parallel in the efforts to sustain the economic performance of a country. A structural approach provides for greater sustainability. In organizational economics, the development of the performance of a firm is anchored in the reflection on how it develops its competitive advantage. Why do some firms, within the same sector and employing similar means in responding to the identical problem as their competitors, achieve superior performance and others fail miserably?

Within the *socio-economic approach to management (**SEAM**)* (Savall, 2010; Savall & Zardet, 1987) provide a useful basis for our focus on the sustainable economic performance of firm. As reflected in Table 3.1, they argue that the economic performance of the firm is comprised of both its *immediate results* and the development of its potential. Integrating the short-term actions of the firm with its medium- and long-term strategy, Savall and Zardet emphasize that the *social performance* of the firm and the economic performance of a firm are inseparable and in dissociable from each other. These *performances are integrated* and constitute an inseparable duo vis-à-vis all stakeholders.

Table 3.1.   Economic Performance in SEAM

Economic Performance	
=	
+	
Immediate Results	**Creation of Potential**
– Productivity	– Creating new products and services
– Efficiency	– Adopting new technologies
– Competitive Advantage	– Developing long-term competitiveness
– Profitability	– Improving employee competencies
– Short-term self financing	– Ongoing – behavioral training

Sharing Savall and Zardet's (1987) view that the economic and social performances of a firm are integrated and inclusive, and that together they form a whole that should not be considered as separate, incompatible and antagonistic objectives, we argue that all corporate transformation efforts that fail to integrate the *creation of economic value* for all its stakeholders, in particular its employees, would in essence undermine or impede the sustainability of the effort.

Numerous eminent scholars that share the satisfaction-service-performance paradigm have sought to demonstrate the direct correlation between employee satisfaction, customer satisfaction and the financial performance of the firm (see, e.g., Hallowell, Schlesinger, & Zornitsky, 1996; Schuler & Jackson, 1987; Pfeffer, 1994). Even though we embrace this paradigm, we are conscious of the cooptation of the term economic performance as being considered as just the financial performance of the firm. Many CEOs and managers have understood the importance and necessity of sustaining the economic performance of their firms, but few are successful in effectively combining the creation of economic value for all its stakeholders while simultaneously pursuing its economic existence and objectives. They know what should be done but are incapable or unwilling to do so, even at the detrimental risk of the firm. While *infrastructure*, technology, finances, and market opportunity can provide for the creation of competitive advantage, Walker (2001, p. 4) noted that:

> Executives increasingly indicate that they believe people make a critical difference in an organization's ability to achieve its objectives. Distinctive organizational and human capabilities enable an enterprise to pursue growth opportunities by leveraging its strengths and create a competitive advantage.

Reporting on a survey by Accenture of 500 executives who were desirous of having a high-performance workforce, Walker (2001) recalled that while it was largely recognized that "people issues" have gained importance, one-third of the executives felt that not enough was being done and only one in four had made significant changes in their approach.

According to SEAM there is a direct correlation between client satisfaction, employee satisfaction, and the economic performance of the firm. Many CEOs and managers have understood both the importance and the necessity to adopt this comprehensive view of their firms, but few have really implemented the appropriate and *sustainable* management practices in order to maintain the firm's performance. Savall and Zardet (2013) argue that sustainable global corporate performance requires that firms and organizations identify the endogenous drivers of their performance and verify that the degree of internal coherence among them is high. They also advocate that sustainable management methods contribute to *economic performance* by enabling them to effectively reconcile the financial and human dimensions within them.

More reflection on the economic performance of firms and its sustainability takes place in the applied and practitioner literature. If politically the notion of sustainability has become a major issue (e.g., *sustainable development*), it is increasingly being introduced in business school curricula and the mainstream academic literature. According to the Global Reporting Initiative (GRI) *Guidelines* framework,[3] the economic performance of the firm is considered as the assessment of the direct and indirect economic impacts of a firm—positive and negative—on its stakeholders. The "scope and purpose" of the GRI index of economic indicators, as articulated in the Guidelines, extend beyond traditional financial indicators. For the GRI, the concept of economic performance "encompasses all aspects of the organization's economic *interactions*, including the traditional measures used in financial accounting, as well as intangible assets that do not systematically appear in financial statements."[4]

The chapter now turns to a corollary concept – the sustainability (the long-lastingness or durability) of management methods through the longitudinal application of the SEAM process. The discussion will draw on interventions in several organizations. The guiding question is how to develop and practice sustainable methods of management in companies in order to improve the *overall performance* of organizational members.

SUSTAINABILITY OF MANAGEMENT METHODS IN ORGANIZATIONS: THE STUDY

By *sustainability*, we mean continuity, durability, permanence, persistence, and stability. In this section, we consider *management methods* to be the set of rational and organized efforts to pilot, plan, develop, and control an organization in all areas of its activity. These methods include such frameworks as the McKinsey matrix, BCG matrix, Balanced Score Card (Kaplan & Norton, 1992), and the *socio-economic approach to management (SEAM)*.

Observations and Problems

Our research is the result of numerous observations during our extensive corporate career as C-suite executives and analysis of the academic literature, focusing on the evolution of management methods and its destabilizing effect on organizations and their members.

Management Methods are Numerous, Evolving Over Time
In 1995, Alain Chauvet identified 132 different management methods. Some have disappeared or gone out of fashion (e.g., S-curve, OPT, Waenier, Sweet cherry), while others have emerged, becoming the latest management fad (e.g., the Balanced Scorecard, 6 Sigma, Lean Management). These different methods seem to have a flexible duration of life in companies.

Changes in Management Methods Contribute to the Destabilization of Organizations
We frequently noticed that the implementation of new management methods generally involves organizational changes, which often includes the blocking of ongoing *projects*, pending new guidelines, withdrawal of *actors*, and a period of learning that could ultimately lead to a waste of time in the *development* of the organization. Work is a place where everyone plays an identity (Enriquez, 2002), reflecting their self-esteem (Lenhardt,1992). Some changes in *poorly managed management methods* can lead to serious organizational disasters and failures.

Scope of the Research

Based on these observations, it seems both interesting and relevant to investigate the sustainability of management methods in organizations. We were guided by a number of questions in our investigation:

- Are there appropriate management methods that are sustainable?
- Which factors impact or explain the sustainability of these methods?
- How do the actors (managers, employees, *interveners-researchers*, consultants) react to the change of methods?
- How can the sustainability of projects be improved to avoid *psychosocial risks* for the actors?

Our methodology draws on the **qualimetrics** approach (Savall & Zardet, 2004, 2011). The research is based on an action-research project with a comprehensive interactive approach to sense making between the researchers and the multiple actors to produce additional knowledge (principles of **cognitive interactivity** and **contradictory intersubjectivity**).

Design of the Study

Our study has been lead in two steps: (1) first we observe a unique method of management (SEAM) in the organizations, then (2) we explore the generalization of the findings about SEAM to others methods of management (see Table 3.2).

Table 3.2.   Conditions of Sustainability of SEAM Interventions

		Interviews		
Leaders and managers		**Intervener– researchers**		**Employees**
16 mirror effects + 8 new interviews + analysis				
		SEGESE		
552 field-note quotes >>> 54 key ideas >>>> 22 main ideas				
Conditions of sustainability of SEAM				
				Specificities of SEAM
	Generalizable conditions of sustainability to other managment method			
Well known method (Six sigma)	<———————— Check with ————————>			Emergent methods
Conditions of sustainability of management methods				

Our experimental materials consist mainly of cross-interviews of three populations:

- *Leaders and managers* who have implemented or using SEAM, between 1985 and 2011, in their organizations, representing 35 interventions representative of the wide range interventions by ISEOR (size, branch, activity, public, and private).
- *ISEOR intervener-researchers* at the senior level (with at least 10 years of experience) as experts of the problem, representing in total more than 100 years of SEAM experience.
- *Employees* who worked directly with the authors during **socio-economic interventions**, experiencing the same situations at the same time even though they may have evolved differently.

Overall, 552 field-note quotes from the interviewees were classified into themes and sub-themes and imputed to a key idea, with the related frequency of the item. The project utilized **SEAMES® software (SEGESE®):** as a database to structure the treatment of the verbatim quotes in the form of key ideas (see Table 3.2 for an example). We completed the crossed interviews of persons using SEAM with other interviews of leaders and managers practicing different management methods popular (such as Six Sigma) or emerging.

Our **key ideas** were checked by 16 restitutions to interviewees (**mirror effect**) and presentations to other leaders and managers utilizing SEAM in order to define the conditions of the sustainability of SEAM interventions.

Generalization to Other Management Methods

The findings concerning SEAM are interesting but not representative of the global context of a study on sustainability in management. In order to generalize our findings to other methods of management:

- We started from the findings about the sustainability of SEAM interventions.
- Then, we determined which of these findings were specific to SEAM. We were obliged to define how SEAM is different from other methods of management (e.g., an academic research center involves conditions of sustainability not applicable to other methods).
- We extracted the findings generalizable to other methods.
- We checked our generalization through interviews of leaders and managers utilizing other management methods (three managing with SIX SIGMA and two with emergent methods).

As final result, we developed the conditions of sustainability of methods in management, including SEAM. We have balanced these results with our experience with leadership in organization and the academic literature.

Before presenting the condition of sustainability of management methods, it seems interesting to explain how SEAM is different from other methods. Although these items are presented in other chapters, they are captured here as an overview of the specificities of SEAM. After this step, we can examine how SEAM compares to other methods of management.

The Sustainability of SEAM Interventions

Based on the main results of the field experiment, the sustainability of *socio-economic management interventions* is mainly linked to four basic factors. We focused on the characteristics for SEAM illustrated by some quotes expressed by the interviewees.

Meeting Expectations about Economic Results

Based on the SEAM database, economic results are measurable from the first months of intervention. As Savall and Zardet (2007, 2008) have demonstrated, the speed of return on investment (at least from 1 month to 6 months maximum) interventions. The failure to achieve these expected economic outcomes from the intervention leads to doubts about the *effectiveness and efficiency* of the method. If these expectations are not met, it can lead to a depreciation of the image of the leader or manager who chose the intervention.

- "That stops if the economic promises are not kept."
- "Nevertheless, we were always in loss the second year. It [(implementation of SEAM] is the cause of the stop."
- "Evaluation of the intervention on the qualitative, quantitative and financial aspects and conversion of the hidden costs."

It is thus important to have good *communication* (internal and external) about the initial results as early as possible to reinforce the effectiveness of the implementation.

- "Sell the results of what was made."
- "Communicate on examples of companies having succeeded without pressure."
- "Internally, communicate on our quick wins and successes."

The Leader's Relationship With the Interveners

The perception of a ***strategic threat*** by a leader generates the choice of a method to respond to that threat, and it is expected to be implemented as long as it responds to that threat.

- "The perception of a threat for the future of the company … it is different from objective threats which are not conscious."
- "The success depends on the interiorization and the perception of a threat."

The intervention is therefore not a ***project*** per se, which by definition has a beginning and an end and is non-recurring in nature. The sustainability of a management method in an organization also depends on the leader who decided its implementation, according to his conviction, performance, and personal qualities.

- "What matters, it is the personal conviction of the leader."
- "It is bound to the implication of the boss."
- "A leader decision-maker and decided."
- "Courage, conviction, constancy. Perseverance."
- "An iron fist in a velvet glove."

Given the long-term nature of SEAM, there is a period of adaptation necessary to acquire the trust between the leader and the intervener before the kick-off (generally between 6 and 9 months).

- "Six months of reflection/maturation/motivation and signature after 9 months of the agreement."
- "That needs a phase of apprenticeship of mutual trust."
- "The freedom to act between us and ISEOR entailed a deep mutual trust."
- "Stoppings in the course of intervention are rare, because the process of negotiation is long and there is signature of a research contract."
- "The non-signature of a project is not a problem: it is the non-success which would be one; thus, the negotiation is long."

We found relatively few stoppages of SEAM interventions in our interviews, and those that did typically were based on exogenous causes (e.g., merger, reorganization).

- "It is often connected to the people ... drift is accepted from the starting up, but not from the interveners."
- "It is due to people ... a new leader with a consultant with whom he has already worked."
- "There is a permanent risk of being a subsidiary with a group which already has HR policies and management control, but that pushes us to the compulsory success."

The departure of the key manager is the most likely factor as the intervention is closely identified with the individual who introduces it.

- "If I leave, I am not sure that the project continues."
- "The failures which I knew are owed to direct or indirect departures of leaders"
- "As soon as CEOs left, it was finished."

The Extent to Which the Method is Embedded in the Organization

The setting-up of any method of management typically entails tensions and frictions between behaviors of the **actors** and structures, which can create **hidden costs** for the organization. The introduction of a new management method questions the interrelationship between the actors and requires them to learn to work differently together. For instance, SEAM has normative tools oriented to integrate individuals in a new way of working together: 3C process, Dynamic Integrated Functional and Operational Resource Integrated System, PNAC; Six Sigma, in contrast, leans on a range of functions of increasing know-how (e.g., Levels of Belts).

In every organizational change, actors have to find an agreement based on a dynamic understanding of all their individual strategies (Crozier & Friedberg, 1981), not only through the official rules but also a zone of indecision due to a relative freedom of individuals or groups. The introduction of an organizational change questions this balance and recreates a zone of uncertainty where actors need to find a new way to work together or to build new conventions.

A convention is a system of mutual expectations on the skills and behaviors designed as being obvious. Boltanski and Thevenot (1987) explain how much a convention is imaginary to unifying managerial ideologies submitted to quickly renewed fashions.

Figure 3.1 illustrates the components of embedding a management method. The sustainability of the approach depends on the extent to which the method is truly embedded throughout the organization. The embedding of a method depends on knowledge and mastery across the organization, including:

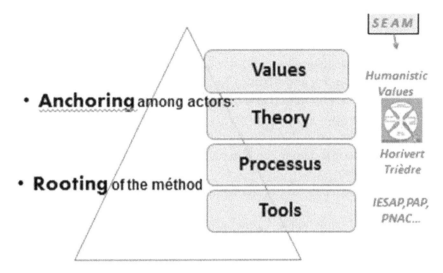

Figure 3.1.   Embedding a management method.

- The *values* related to the method and the *theory* of the method, which allow anchoring among actors. In particular, for SEAM, the underlying foundation of humanist values combined with the knowledge and understanding of the concept of the ISEOR clover contribute strongly to commitment to the method by organizational members:

  - "The human approach of the general and understandable management."
  - "The important thing in my life, it is the human factor, the value of people, I always wanted to make people progress."
  - "What pleases me it is the philosophy, the ethical embodiment of the human being within the company in whom I believe:
  - "The leader has to have a conception of the management which grants a place to the human being, in the economy of the company."

- *Processes* **and** *tools* that facilitate the ***rooting*** of the method in the organization. In particular for SEAM, the process of setting-up ***HORIVERT***, the ***SEAM Star***, the three axes of the ***Trihedral*** enable the sustainability of the method. These processes are supported by an array of ***management tools*** (e.g., ***competency grid, internal and external strategic action plan, PAP, time management, strategic piloting indicators, PNAC***):

- "The quality and the fast training of the internal interveners insure the sustainability of the method in the company…. Attention to that needed rigor in the methodology. "
- "The integration of SEAM by internal training (swarming, autonomy and sharing)."
- "The ISEOR and external consultants were contributions of energy."
- "Change nothing the method."
- "Do not change the system, the tools, because they are very effective."
- "Especially do not change the tools, all the tools."

The degree of embedding is generally stronger among leaders who have mastered these four elements, while it is sufficient for the majority of employees to only know the tools.

Embedding a management method is further influenced by a process of continuous *maintenance* and control driven by leaders and in support of the actors:

- "It would be necessary to make audits of tools (CPNA)."
- "To improve: a compulsory diagnosis after some years, compulsory training of the new employees."
- "There is sustainability where there is maintenance (Examples of 3 projects by the interviewee)."

When the management method stops and according the degree of embedding:

- The decision-making (leaders) try to go on and immortalize the acquired management method (*hidden life*) in the organization or in another one. Concerning SEAM, we met several leaders having continued to manage their entity with SEAM or implanting SEAM in another company after an official decision to stop) the method:
  - "SEAM had become a way of functioning, a reflex."
  - "Later I joined the CEO, who manages with SEAM"
  - "I retry without ISEOR, because I have the values inside me."
  - "We kept the spirit and some tools. The spirit, it is the success by the people."
  - "When I was promoted to CEO in Austria, I implemented SEAMBIS, the equivalent of SEAM in B."

Table 3.3.   An Example of the Interview Structure and Process

TOPIC: THE ACTORS OF THE SEAM PROJECT

Main Idea: THE ROLE OF LEADER

Key ideas:

PERSONAL BELIEF OF THE LEADER CONDITIONING THE SUCCESS OF INTERVENTION

   Verbatim (examples)

   "Firm and final decision of the CEO"

   "What matters is the personal conviction of the leader"

   "Requires the willingness of management change"

   "The concern of the leader is to save his project"

NEXT KEY IDEA

- "My past as an internal trainer allowed me to integrate well all the tools."

- The non-decision-making actors (employees) adapt in one way or another one to the new method of dominant management. It is thus their **survival** in the organizations that motivates them (managerial resilience):

  - "The HQ did not believe in it, my new boss either, and we followed."
  - "That was fast forgotten because that disturbed us a lot."
  - "SEAM lasted 3 years only, later I had full of bosses with different methods."
  - "Then, we moved on. To do and to undo is still to work."

Development of Human Potential

Human potential can be defined as the intelligent and active every human activity devotes to adapt to its environment, to create goods and services, identify new and innovative needs. The human potential is inalienable contrary to the human capital (Savall, 1974; Savall & Zardet, 1987, 2005).

The individual human potential has different powers of adaptation to a collective and normative method. At each change of a management method, the creative *energy* of each actor or human potential investment is questioned, and thus the motivation, involvement. Each is shared between submission and resistance, and the cards are reshuffled and actors must establish new agreements (or convention as defined by Boltanski, a time space necessary for the understanding and support of actors). Between every convention, there is a questioning of the **human potential** and thus the motivation of and the implication for every actor is shared between submission and resistance. The implementation of human potential based management prepares actors to changes in management methods and to become *agile* managers:

- "I always needed HR support, a support of the teams, because we move inside of people. Why not to integrate them into the method?"
- "The positive factors before setting-up… locations of the underlying memberships, the sensibility in dashboards and in managers."
- "I especially approached the knowledge and self-control in the team's management."
- "What was the most difficult, they are brakes bound to the introduction of a new culture."

EVALUATION OF THE SUSTAINABILITY OF A MANAGEMENT METHOD

From these results and in order to help the leaders and managers to find solutions facilitating the changes of management methods, we developed a 22 item that helps to evaluate the sustainability of the management method. The completed template allows for the assessment of the sustainability of a management method with a profile, a sustainability score, and 3 concrete actions to set up.

This self-diagnosis was tested with 12 leaders and managers and was led as a session of coaching. Its purpose was to make the leaders aware of the **risks** for the sustainability of the method of management and to set up appropriate actions plan (proactive and preventive) and to explain why a management method was not **sustainable** (curative feedback). Its purpose was not to show how a management method is more sustainable than another. The 12 self-diagnoses, based on different methods of management, small or large organizations, in process or stopped, seem to show than SEAM has a good sustainability potential. As noted by a senior CEO in our study:

Table 3.4.   Example for the 3 First Questions

QUESTIONS	0	1	2	3	Evaluation
1 At what level do you estimate the credibility of your business-plan linking the arrival of the method of management to a recovery-improvement of the results/profits/performance?		X			Full credibility = 3
2 What is the key performance indicators (KPI) that allow you to say that your method of management contributes to the development of your company?			X		No KPI = 0
3 Calculation of the potential earnings which you expect with this method?				X	Precise calculation with follow-up = 3

Table 3.5.   Leaders and Managers Self-Diagnosis

	TOTAL	3	5	6	8	SCORE 55%
Further to this self-diagnosis, what are the 3 actions you decide to implement in your organization? *(Examples of answers)*						When? With who?
1. *Implement KPI to follow the success of the method.*						*Asap, Controller*
2. *Introduce a process of maintenance of the tools (audit).*						*Asap, HR*
3. *To have a face to face meeting with X (opponent).*						*Next week , X*

I looked and I look for another method which would be more effective than SEAM. I have already made the tour of Six Sigma, BSC, reengineering ... costs killers. They are less effective. The advantage of SEAM is the engineering of the change and the high success rate.

For the leaders, the added value lies more in the additional prodding aroused by these questions than in the precise answers to these questions. The discussion that followed was more useful than the obtained profile of durability. The leaders appropriate the actions plan to make a method of management sustainable. This support acts as an auto-activation of the human potential of the main actors that allows them to find for themselves the answers to their problems.

CONCLUSION

For the economic period which we live at this beginning of 21st century (crisis, pushed neo-liberal, pressure of the short term), the global and sustainable performance of companies is based, at the same time, on the achievement of *immediate results* and in the *creation of development potentials*.

A part of the success of the global and sustainable performance relies on the *creation of economic value* of which the human potential is the only active and creative factor. The generation of performance requires a contractualization between the stakeholders (Savall & Zardet, 2005, 2013). One of the levers of the global and sustainable performance is the *piloting* of people and the activities which we can group under the term of "management methods." There are many ways to perpetuate a method of management in a company in particular by trying to influence the degree of embedding of this method in the organization and the duration of the missions of the leaders.

Our longitudinal research on SEAM interventions shows that this method had strengths and advantages to be a sustainable method in organizations. Furthermore, once implanted, it seems to be a curative (auto diagnostic of *dysfunctions*, *hidden costs*) and preventive (*creation of potential*) therapeutics to accompany a global and sustainable performance. We highlighted the essential role of the human potential and its *development* which leads to the membership of the actors in a new method of management and contributes to their agility.

NOTES

1. The research for this chapter has been influenced by a number of works that are not directly referred to in the text, including Boje and Rosile (2003), Buono and Savall (2007), Gephart (2009), Perroux (1979), Savall (1981, 2010, 2012), Savall and Zardet (1992, 1995, 2005, 2008, 2009), and Savall, Zardet, and Bonnet (2000, 2008).
2. See http://pages.stern.nyu.edu/~nroubini/bci/IndexLeadingEconomicInd.htm
3. See http://www.globalreporting.org/index.asp
4. For more information on the Global Reporting Guidelines, go to: http://www.globalreporting.org/guidelines/2002/c45.asp

REFERENCES

Boje, D., & Rosile, G.-A. (2003). Comparison of socio-economic and other transorganizational development methods. *Journal of Change Organizational Management*, *16*(1), 10–20.

Boltanski, L., & Chiapello, E. (1999). *Le nouvel esprit du capitalisme* [The new spirit of capitalism]. Paris, France: Gallimard.

Boltanski, L., & Thevenot, L. (1987). *Les économies de la Grandeur: Cahier du centre d'étude pour l'emploi* [The economies of the immensity: Journal of Employment Study Center]. Paris, France: Presses Universitaires de France.

Buono, A. F., & Savall, H. (Eds.). (2007). *Socio-economic intervention in organizations: The intervener-researcher and the SEAM approach to organizational analysis.* Charlotte, NC: Information Age Publishing.

Cameron, R. (1967). *Banking in the early stages of industrialization.* New York, NY: Oxford University Press

Crozier, M., & Friedberg, E. (1981). *L'acteur et le système: Les contraintes de l'action collective* [The actor and the system: Collective action constraints]. Paris, France: Seuil.

Elkington, J. (1997). *Cannibals with forks: Triple bottom line of 21st century business.* Oxford, UK: Capstone.

Enriquez, E. (2002). *L'organisation en analyse* [The organization in analysis]. Paris, France: Presses Universitaires de France.

Gephart, R. P. (2009). An invitation to ethnostatistics. *Revue Sciences de gestion–Management Sciences–Ciencias de Gestión, 70,* 85.

Goldsmith, R. (1969). *Financial structure and development,* New Haven, CT: Yale University Press.

Hallowell, R., Schlesinger, L. A., & Zornitsky, J. (1996). Internal service quality, customer and job satisfaction: Linkages and implications for management. *Human Resource Planning, 19,* 20–31.

Hansen, G. S., & Wernerfelt, B. (1989). Determinants of firm performance: The relative importance of economic and organizational factors. *Strategic Management Journal, 10*(5), 399–411.

Kaplan, R. S., & Norton, D. P. (1992). The balanced scored card: Measures that drive performances. *Harvard Business Review, 70*(1), 71–79.

Lenhardt, V. (1992). *Les responsables porteurs de sens: Culture et pratique du coaching et du team-building* [Coaching for meaning: The culture and practice of coaching and team building] (2nd Ed.). Paris, France: INSEP.

Mc Kinnon, R. (1973). *Money and capital in economic development,* Washington, DC: Brookings Institution

Perroux, F. (1979). L'entreprise, l'équilibre rénové et les coûts cachés [The enterprise, the renovated balance and the "hidden" costs]. Preface. In H. Savall. *Reconstruire l'entreprise* [Reconstructing the enterprise] Paris, France: Dunod.

Pfeffer, J. (1994). *Competitive advantage through people: Unleashing the power of the work force.* Boston, MA: Harvard Business School Press.

Savall, H. (1974–1975–1977). *Enrichir le travail humain dans les entreprises et les organisations* [An economic evaluation of job enrichment]. Paris: Dunod.

Savall, H. (1981–2010). *Work and people: An economic evaluation of job enrichment.* 1st ed. New-York: Oxford University Press ; 2nd ed. Charlotte, NC: Information Age Publishing.

Savall, H., & Zardet, V. (2007). *L'importance stratégique de l'investissement incorporel: Résultats qualimétriques de cas d'entreprises* [Intangible investment strategic relevance: Qualimetrics results of company cases]. Paper presented at the Colloque IIC-ISEOR-American Accounting Association, Lyon, France.

Savall, H. (2012). *Origine radicale des crises économiques: Germán Bernácer, précurseur visionnaire* [Root origin of crises: Germán Bernácer, a visionary forerunner]. Charlotte, NC: Information Age Publishing.

Savall, H., & Zardet, V. (1987). Les coûts caches et l'analyse socio-économique des organizations [Hidden costs and the socio-economic analysis of organizations] *Encyclopédie du Management*. Paris, France: Economica

Savall, H., & Zardet, V. (1987). *Maîtriser les coûts et les performances cachés : Le contrat d'activité périodiquement négociables* [Mastering hidden costs and performance: The periodically negotiable activity contract]. Paris: Economica.

Savall, H., & Zardet, V. (1992). *Le nouveau contrôle de gestion: Méthode des coûts-performances cachés* [New management control: The hidden cost-performance method]. Paris: Éditions Comptables Malesherbes-Eyrolles

Savall, H. & Zardet, V. (1995–2005–2009). *Ingénierie stratégique du roseau, souple et enracinée* [Strategic engineering of the reed, flexible and rooted]. Paris: Economica.

Savall, H., & Zardet, V. (2004). *Recherche en sciences de gestion : Approche qualimétrique. Observer l'objet complexe.* [Research in management sciences: The qualimetric approach: Observing the complex object]. Paris, France: Economica.

Savall, H., & Zardet, V. (2005). Tétranormalisation: Défis et dynamiques [Competitive challenges and dynamics of tetra-normalization]. Paris, France: Economica.

Savall, H., & Zardet, V. (2008). *Mastering hidden costs and performance*. Charlotte, NC: Information Age Publishing.

Savall, H., & Zardet, V. (2011). *The qualimetrics approach: Observing the complex object*. Charlotte, NC: Information Age Publishing.

Savall, H., & Zardet, V. (2013). *The dynamics and challenges of tetranormalization*. Charlotte, NC: Information Age Publishing.

Savall, H., Zardet, V., & Bonnet, M. (2000-2008). *Releasing the untapped potential of enterprises through socio-economic management*. Geneva: Éditions IOT-BIT.

Schuler, R., & Jackson, S. (1987). Linking competitive strategies and human resource management practices. *Academy of Management Executive*, *1*(3), 207–219.

Schumpeter, J. A. (1911). *A theory of economic development*. Cambridge, MA: Harvard University Press.

Van de Ven, A., & Johnson, P. (2006). Knowledge for theory and practice. *Academy of Management*, *31*(4), 802–821.

Walker, J. W. (2001). Human capital: Beyond HR? *Human Resources Planning*, *24*(2), 4–5.

CHAPTER 4

THE SOCIO-ECONOMIC APPROACH TO MANAGEMENT CONTROL[1]

Laurent Cappelletti, Murray Lindsay, and Cécile Ennajem

The chapter sheds light on the ability of SEAM to develop an innovative management control system for improving change and human potential management as well as creating tangible value. We have called this ability the *socio-economic approach to management control* (SEAMC). The first part of the chapter focuses on how SEAMC may appear as an innovative platform for change and human potential *development*. The next two sections then explain how SEAMC, through its change and tools axes, fosters *economic performance*.

SEAM AS AN INNOVATIVE PLATFORM

In this first section we look at the other side of the strategy coin dealing with how management control systems can facilitate organizational adaptation to change occurring in both the *internal and external environments*. In this regard, the empirical record is not good. Organizational transformation

The Socio-Economic Approach to Management Revisited: The Evolving Nature of SEAM in the 21st Century, pp. 75–102
Copyright © 2015 by Information Age Publishing

initiatives often fail (Kotter, 1996) and the vast majority of firms, including large firms, survive relatively short periods (Stubbart & Knight, 2006). In fact, it is now conventional wisdom that attackers from the outside are considered to have an advantage when a new business model threatens an existing market or technological regime (Schoemaker, 2008).

Hamel and Zanini (2014) write that the modern organization was not designed for deep and proactive change, a view that has led to change being considered in exceptional rather than normal terms. For example, until relatively recently, strategy continued to be viewed as static based on the assumptions of stability and continuity (Montgomery, 2008; Schoemaker, 2008). This led to management control being defined predominantly in terms of the process management uses to implement or execute the firm's planned strategy (Anthony, 1988; Anthony & Govindarajan, 2007; Merchant & Van der Stede, 2012). With the strategy in place, the role of the well-documented failure of periodic strategic planning sessions was simply to program and fine tune the strategy as well as to take steps to defend the company's established position (Mintzberg, 1994). Thus, when the need for change became apparent—often in response to a crisis, perceived threat or opportunity, or *implementation* of "best practice"—the change effort reflected an episodic interruption to the status quo that was initiated, scripted, and steered from the top (Hamel & Zanini, 2014). And the result was that all too often such top-down solutions were too late and cast in the wrong terms, lacking employee buy-in.

In examining this situation, Hamel and Zanini (2014) write that what is required is "a real-time, socially constructed approach to change, so that the leader's job isn't to design a change program but to build a *change platform*—one that allows anyone to initiate change, recruit confederates, suggest solutions, and launch experiments" across the entire organization. SEAM would seem to represent such a platform. Hamel and Zanini's analysis provides a useful vantage point in which to examine the efficacy of the SEAM model of change, because it provides considerable insight into the problems and addresses—if only conceptually—how change needs to be reconsidered. Consequently, the remainder of this chapter examines Hamel and Zanini's analysis, illustrating how SEAM incorporates their recommendations in its essential logic along with providing a more complete rationale for the prescriptions. A summary and roadmap of the discussion appears in Table 4.1.

A second purpose of this section is to study the conditions under which an innovative approach to management control such as SEAM may contribute to sustainable *development* of **human potential** through the changes involved. *Human potential* is defined here as the factors that create value, which are embedded in individuals (e.g., skills, competencies, commitment) and the **interactions** among them. The results of the study indicate that the value of *human potential* can be measured effectively through an indicator of SEAM called the **hourly contribution to value-added on variable costs** (HCVAVC).

Table 4.1.   How SEAM Addresses the Issues and the Proposed Solutions Facilitating Change in Organizations

Problem	Issue	Redress	SEAM
Change is framed in terms of an episodic interruption to the status quo	Organizations need to continuously adapt to their evolving external and internal environments; however, the ability to stimulate the need for and effectively orchestrate change is not reflected in companies' core management systems and processes	The role of the chief executive must change from change agent in chief to change enabler Need to abandon Kurt Lewin's "unfreeze-change-freeze" model of change and replace it with a view that more closely resembles "permanent slush" A *change platform* that permits anyone to initiate change, recruit confederates, suggest solutions, and launch experiments across the entire organization is needed	Higher levels of management steer and energize the process HORIVERT diagnostic (Axis A) and application of the various management tools (Axis B) allow the process to be self-managed and "solutions" are socially constructed Twice yearly process of diagnostic and tools make change a continuous feature
Change is initiated and managed from the top	Senior management is not close enough to the action (periphery). Cultural lock-in following from fixed mental models and risk-averse executives lead to perpetuation of the status quo. By the time the need for change becomes apparent it is often too late and cast in the wrong terms	Information from the periphery must be obtained and amplified requiring regular information conduits from both inside and outside the company The *responsibility* for amplifying the need for change needs to be syndicated across the organization as part of everyone's duties.	HISOFIS, including strategic vigilance Strategic piloting indicators Diagnostic (HORIVERT)

(Table continues on next page)

Table 4.1.   (Continued)

Problem	Issue	Redress	SEAM
	Lack of employee buy-in	People have to be *involved* to harness their discretionary creativity and energy and to minimize cynicism and resistance.	Employee responsibility and involvement is a fundamental principle HORIVERT, diagnostic projects, priority action plans, PNAC, strategic vigilance
"Breakthrough" solutions cannot be predetermined in advance	Leads to solutions being limited by what people at the top can imagine which is inconsistent with how innovation works	Solutions need to *emerge* based on a process of *social construction* that gives everyone the right to set priorities, diagnose barriers and generate options	Principles of cognitive interactivity and contradictory intersubjectivity and putting an idea into action leads to progressive convergence towards a common view

The calculation of **HCVAVC** is derived from the Profit and Loss Statement of the company:

- Profit or Loss = Sales – Variable Costs – Fixed Costs.
- Sales-Variable Costs = Contribution to Value-Added on Variable Costs (CVAVC).
- *HCVAVC* = (CVAVC / Total number of hours worked per year).

HCVAVC measures the hourly average of employees' value added to the firm. The indicator does not determine the cost of personnel but rather the average value they produce, which allows a determination of the *human potential* of the firm (Buono & Savall, 2007). Thus, *HCVAVC* is a more relevant indicator of the value of *human potential* than the variable cost of salaried or hourly employees, which is often used in studies focusing on the *competitiveness* of companies.

KEY ELEMENTS FOR BUILDING CHANGE INTO THE ORGANIZATION'S DNA

Hamel and Zanini (2014) discuss three main issues that need to be resolved if change efforts, particularly those transformational in nature, are going to be more successful.

From Episodic to Continuous Change

Hamel and Zanini (2014) write that change can no longer be constructed in terms of an episodic event but rather needs to be viewed as an ongoing activity—one that is facilitated by constructing a change platform permitting *self-organization* of the process that does not need to be initiated and managed from the top. This recommendation reflects that a relentlessly evolving business world requires organizations to keep pace. However, SEAM goes a step further in providing a more complete explanation, one whose omission explains why change efforts have historically encountered so much failure.

SEAM teaches that an inherent conflict exists within organizations because of the dynamic friction occurring between organizational **structures** and employee behavior that leads to **dysfunctions** and subsequent **hidden cost**s impairing the organization's sustainable socio-*economic performance*. Reasons underlying this conflict include the use of imperfect information, the complexity of organizations' interconnected component parts, different logics in use among **actors** and departments, the use of mental models that always oversimplify and neglect important aspects of the situation, and the instability of the **external environment** that amplifies the negative consequences of these factors. For this reason, SEAM challenges the belief that an optimal or total solution exists that remains valid over time because, left untended, organizational **cohesion** decays as the component parts gradually revert to their natural parochial tendencies. The result is that an organization's capacity to negotiate its survival and prosperity becomes impaired, which in turn increases the level of *dysfunctions*.

As a consequence of this natural and inevitable process of entropy, SEAM includes the **integration** and periodic irrigation of *dysfunctions* as a continuous and key management process. These activities serve to create and maintain the internal *cohesion* SEAM assumes to be essential in providing the necessary foundation supporting strategic adaptation and the activation of the unused potential of employees—a view that that has only been recently emphasized by Savall and Zardet (2014). Thus an ongoing organizational change process is seen as being crucial to sustained performance, leading to the fundamental importance SEAM places on the ability of top management to "pilot" or steer this process (Savall, 2003, p. 37). This view is also consistent with Hamel and Zanini (2014) recommendation that (1) the role of the chief executive must change from change agent-in-chief to change enabler and (2) why Kurt Lewin's "unfreeze-change-freeze" model of change needs to be replaced with one that more closely resembles "permanent slush."

As reflected in Figure 4.1, SEAM builds change into the management systems and processes as an ongoing and normal organizational rhythm based on cycling around three axes: process (a), **management tools** (b), and political and strategy (c) (Buono & Savall, 2007).

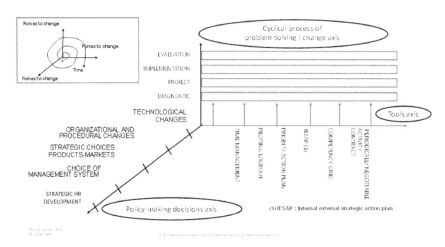

Figure 4.1.   The three axes of the SEAM HORIVERT model.

The *change axis* is put into operation twice a year and involves top and middle managers along with lower-level employees. The initial ***diagnosis*** stage reveals *dysfunctions* based on in-depth semi-structured interviewers by internal or **external interveners** that focus on *dysfunctions* across horizontal and vertical slices (***HORIVERT***) of the organization. These interviews are conducted for every member of the managerial team and with 30 to 50 percent of the remaining personnel. Once all interviews are completed a *diagnosis* is presented to the entire group of interviewees using a technique called the **mirror effect**. The purpose of these presentations is to allow participants to hear the dysfunctions raised and validate them in a consensual manner. As this occurs, the change process begins to get energized as people begin to see that their concerns are being taken seriously.

The next stage entails formalizing a project to reduce the identified *dysfunctions*, improve working conditions and/or create (human) potential that is currently not being realized, as revealed in the *diagnosis*. This project is broken down into "baskets" based on particular themes. Figure 4.2 illustrates the basic process, one that is replicated over and over again as part of the general method. A *project leader* is chosen who is appropriately placed to lead the various facets of the project. This leader collaborates with direct reports as well as with his or her supervisor in establishing the terms of the project and to select *focus groups* leaders tasked with pursuing in-depth research to obtain a cooperative solution for each basket. The *focus group* leader selects a team comprised of people bringing direct knowledge to the problem (i.e., experts) as well as "naïve" members who work in other functions to provide an outside, integrative perspective. This person interacts with other members of the full group to discuss plans and progress as well to coordinate and seek advice and, if necessary, obtain authorization for expenditures to collect information or conduct experiments. The outer ring and the focus groups depicted in Figure 4.2 illustrate how this process facilitates **integration** (**cooperation**) and participation (involvement) of people at different levels.

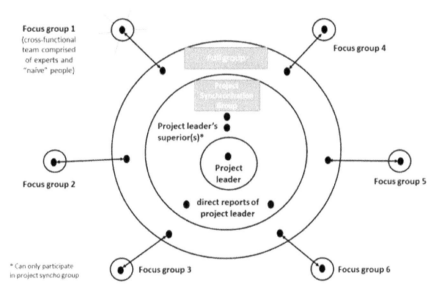

Figure 4.2.   An example of the process of integration and involvement in change.

Following that phase, proposed steps are implemented using the *management tool*s in Axis B illustrated in Figure 4.1. Key to this *implementation* is where the selected actions are broken down and distributed into the *priority action plans* of all the departments concerned, with certain actions becoming targets for specific objectives stipulated in the *periodically negotiated contracts* of employees responsible for their *implementation*. Results are then evaluated in a participative manner to enable the determination of next steps.

Additionally, as part of what SEAM calls **HISOFIS** (humanly integrated and stimulating operational and functional information system), various *management tools* are used to *stimulate* continuous change (and human growth). One way this occurs is by augmenting employees' skills for developing *human potential* and keeping up with the objectives of the company strategy (**competency grid** map). Another is the requirement of building time into one's schedule for balancing execution activities along with taking actions aimed at creating long-term value (time management). In seeking to pursue the goal of sustainable performance rather than profit maximization, SEAM seeks to balance the short and long terms by taking action today to create potential for the future. While striving for such a balance is "inefficient" in the short term, it reflects the necessary tradeoff in achieving durable, long run performance (de Geus 1997).

Achieving such balance is further enabled by the preparation of **internal and external strategic action plans**. These plans take into account both external objectives (e.g., market share, customer satisfaction, quality of suppliers) as well as internal objectives regarding such things as technology, fixed and **intangible investments**, and training programs. This plan is re-evaluated every year to delineate organizational focus in the coming three to five years based on the **evaluation** of specific projects, progress reported by the **strategic piloting indicators**, and incorporating the intelligence gained from the company's **strategic vigilance**. Finally, the **strategic piloting logbook** evaluates progress in qualitative, quantitative and financial terms, which adds more nuances of the environment and the organization's *interaction* with it for decision making. These indicators are used by members of the management team to direct staff and activities in their respective zones of responsibility in terms of the daily management of operational activities and the creation of potential activities, in terms of short-term, medium-term and long-term results.

This section can be summarized by stating that the *socio-economic approach to management* is based on using a variety of different types of information (**HISOFIS**) to *stimulate* staff and management to take action that creates energy towards developing human and organizational potential (in terms of the leaders' strategic ambition) while at the same time attaining short, medium and long-term economic objectives. This creates the conditions for establishing a dynamic tension between stability and change.

Everyone Must be Responsible For and Involved With Change

Conventional thinking is based on the idea that strategy is something that should only occur at the top, far removed from the day-to-day, frontline operations of the organization. However, the reality is that people who carry out strategy must also be actively involved in creating it because they are the ones in touch with the competition, customers, markets, products, employees and technology (Mintzberg, 1987). Moreover, individuals view issues or problems in self-limiting ways whereas true innovation focuses on connecting already existing ideas in novel ways (Duggan, 2007). Therefore, generating innovative ideas is facilitated by a group of people possessing a diversity of knowledge and experiences utilizing integrative and divergent thinking (Lindsay, 2015). Such diversity introduces different mental models reflecting salient factors and interpretations of causal relationships at work that permits more alternatives to be considered within the decision-making process (Martin, 2009).

SEAM promotes this requirement in two ways. First, divergent thinking is facilitated by the numerous integrative and decentralized decision-making processes of SEAM (Figure 4.1 is an example). Second, SEAM eschews divisions fostered by the virus of hierarchy and believes everyone has a responsibility and the ability to contribute to innovation. Engaging employees not only creates the energy unleashing their creativity, it also serves to reduce the use of informal powers that can be used to resistant change (Savall & Zardet, 2008a). As Hamel and Zanini (2014) state, "genuine buy-in is the product of involvement." SEAM fosters such involvement in the identification of *dysfunctions* and participating in developing solutions to overcome them, proposing ideas for the creation of potential, and being involved in *strategic vigilance* and the *implementation* of continuous improvement projects.

The Social Construction of Change

There are two key reasons underlying Hamel and Zanini's (2014) recommendation that transformational change needs to be socially constructed. First, as the authors state, change that breaks new ground cannot be programed in advance; otherwise, the solution space is limited to what a handful of people located at the top can imagine and this is unlikely to be successful. Instead, truly innovative ideas need to be considered in *emergent* terms. For example, Bhide (2000) found that in 90% of all successful new businesses, the strategy that ultimately led to success was not the founder's original, intended strategy. Instead, the successful strategy emerged based on *learning* what worked. Hammel and Zanini explain this point using the example of the social web. They write: "no single individual or entity invented the social web. It emerged, in all its weird and wonderful variety, because the Internet is a powerful platform for making connections and because thousands of entrepreneurs were free to develop new business models to harness that power."

The upshot is that organizations need to attempt to replicate what SEAM calls a **heuristic** process, from taking small steps that allows ideas to emerge based on a process of experimentation that is akin to what McGrath and MacMillan (1995) have called "discovery based planning." This process incorporates creativity, financial discipline, **risk** management, and, most importantly, the ability to learn from past action through formal evaluation. This view is based on the belief within SEAM that the power of putting an idea into action is more important than deriving the idea itself—even if derived collaboratively—because the complexity of a transformative idea portends that there will not necessarily be initial agreement in its meaning and/or implications. Instead, progressive convergence towards a common view occurs by putting an idea into action (Lafley, Martin, Rivkin, & Sigglekow, 2012).

The second reason underlying the social construction of change is to counter the powerful forces impeding strategic adaptation. Foster and Kaplan (2001) have coined these collective forces as "cultural lock-in." As a company grows and expands, it deals with the increased complexity of its operations by developing processes, increasing the level of formality and establishing a **structure** that bests fit its chosen strategy. These decisions are optimized for the existing market in the sense they reflect the current strategy and mental models of senior management. Over time the value system inherent in these decisions becomes self-reinforcing and self-sustaining because of the cognitive, organizational and political biases underlying cultural lock-in. While cultural lock-in facilitates implementing the current strategy, it impedes adapting to significant market shifts, serving to explain the downfall of once highly successful companies.

The way to counter cultural lock-in is to "move from the individual to the collective, from the decision maker to the decision-making process, and from the executive to the organization" (Kahneman, Lovallo, & Sibony 2011, p. 52). This recommendation has two implications for our discussion. One is that the stimulus for change requires a process aimed at seeking and amplifying signals from the periphery—the place where new companies or existing companies are attempting to explore unmet customer needs and/or to develop new capabilities, new technologies or new ways of doing business (Foster & Kaplan, 2001). However, this information possesses what Mintzberg (1987) calls a "soft underbelly": it reflects ambiguous signals that must be decoded and interpreted in a way that does not succumb to cultural lock-in.

SEAM reflects these considerations in several ways. First, it employs elements of what Gephart (2014) calls "deliberative democracy" that is connected with valid **communication**. This occurs through the **qualimetric** principles of ***cognitive interactivity*** and ***contradictory intersubjectivity***. The former reflects the view that the value of information can be increased and, ultimately, mindsets changed over successive feedback loops if people are prepared to honestly and regularly communicate with one another and allow a diversity of ideas to flourish and be considered, regardless of their origin. The latter is based on accepting the complexity of organizational reality and the fact that organizational *actors* will have diverse perceptions of this reality. The goal is to transform these different views of the world into a shared and more "objective" view for collective work, one that leads to increased commitment and buy-in. Thus the former is necessary to achieve the latter, and the latter is achieved by taking steps connected with the *heuristic* process of progressive convergence described above.

Second, as stated earlier, stimulating information needs to be produced that incites the receiver to engage in decisive action that energizes the organization's capacity for adaptation. In this connection, SEAM's approach to *strategic vigilance* is noteworthy. Across the organization certain people are appointed as the "captors" or amplifiers of strategic information located on the periphery of the organization concerning such things as markets, technology, and products along with considerations of internal organization and human potential. Periodically, meetings are held between these captors and members of the organization's strategic group consisting of high level management to discuss the significance of this intelligence. This intelligence along with the other information provided by the *management tool*s feeds into the political and strategic decisions axis, the place where senior leaders' mental models get changed and decisions taken to close the gap between the current strategic situation and the intended strategic situation. As de Geus (1988) explains, the only learning that truly counts is by those who have the power to act and impact the organization's resource allocation system. Such changes are then fed into the company's internal and external strategic plan where the *management tools* come into action.

Synthesizing the Elements Into a Holistic View

SEAM adopts the metaphor of a reed that bends but does not break in response to change (i.e., wind, rain) due to its extensive root system that provides the plant with a strong foundation to support such flexibility and adaptiveness (Savall & Zardet, 2005). In SEAM, strong internal *cohesion* is considered to represent the necessary foundation or root system on which to construct change. Such *cohesion* arises from the intermeshing of four elements within a cyclical process that facilitates self-managed, timely and effective responses to changes occurring in both the *internal and external environments* in a way that can be expected to transform the organization over time. The process underlying the analogy is illustrated in Figure 4.3 (with the root system omitted for reasons of clarity).

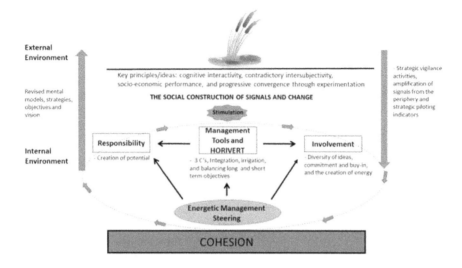

Figure 4.3.   The SEAM model for building change into the DNA of the organization.

The first element reflects the extensive set of *management tools* and processes (e.g., **HORIVERT**) that underlie the heart of the self-managed approach to change and the building of *cohesion*. These serve to stimulate the need for and response to changes occurring in *the internal and external environments*, create and manage the tension existing between the short and long runs, facilitate horizontal and vertical **cooperation**, and periodically irrigate the organization from dysfunctions arising from the natural occurrence of entropy. These outcomes occur as a result of spiraling around the three axes of change (A, B, C) on a twice yearly basis, as previously discussed. However, the **effectiveness** of these tools in promoting *cohesion* would be compromised if they did not operate within the principal of achieving sustainable **socio-economic performance** in place of the widespread shareholder profit maximization objective.

The second element is the recognition of the potential of all employees to contribute to the creation of organizational potential by being held responsible and involved with decisions associated with promoting both the short and long terms as well as the general health (*cohesion*) of the company. The *HORIVERT diagnosis* process and *management tools* reflect this fundamental belief.

The third element contributing to internal *cohesion* involves the adoption of the key **qualimetric** principles of **cognitive interactivity** and **contradictory intersubjectivity**. These principles were developed in recognition that organizational *actors* will have diverse perceptions of a complex reality and that commitment and buy-in will only occur if change is socially constructed through a *heuristic* process based on action (experimentation) and **evaluation** leading to a shared and more "objective" view for collective work (i.e., progressive convergence).

Finally, active and energetic (senior) management steering of the entire process is necessary. Such steering reflects being involved with the decision making process but not actively directing it with solutions (which must be socially constructed), believing in the validity of the elements of the system and, in particular, the potential of all employees to contribute, being prepared to act on the outputs of the system in revising mental models of the world and strategies, and always seeking to close the gap between realized strategy and strategic ambition, which further energizes and fuels the change process.

The key insight is that the SEAM model of change can only be understood through a synthesis of its component parts, consistent with a postmodern view reflecting the complexity and dynamical nature of organizations. In this sense, the final column in Table 4.1 is incomplete and fails to reveal the true operation of SEAM.

SOCIO-ECONOMIC MANAGEMENT CONTROL AND ECONOMIC PERFORMANCE

The SEAM **trihedron model** (see Figure 4.1) includes an iterative change process divided into four participative phases: **diagnosis**, **project**, **implementation** and **assessment**, combined with **policy decision-making process** and **management tools**. Its *implementation*, through an upward **spiral** of change, produces a significant increase of economic results in the organizations where SEAM is implemented, which is important in the current financial **resources** scarcity context.

SEAM management control leads to a renewal of the economic calculation for helping decision-making process through a critical analysis of the traditional accounting information systems, management accounting and control. It proposes methods and tools to change information and decision-making systems. This evolution is based on the concept of **HISOFIS** *(humanly integrated and stimulating operational and functional information system)* (Savall & Zardet, 1987). It consists in the company ability to stimulate effective behaviors of the employees for achieving objectives. Setting up HISOFIS generates better actions **synchronization** in the company, at the roots of both *effectiveness* and *efficiency*. Indeed, **sustainable effectiveness and efficiency** are **inseparable criteria** for producing socio-economic performance. This couple contributes to the sustainable **competitiveness** in a **socially responsible capitalism** (SRC) economic policy (see Chapter 3).

Hidden Costs and Performance

Unlike traditional methods in management control, solely used to measure performance produced by other methodologies, SEAM is able to measure its proper impacts the company's performance (Cappelletti & Baker, 2010; Ennajem, 2011). First, visible through hidden costs conversion into value added the impact of SEAM is also eventually measured on the visible results of the organization it is implemented in through accounting. SEAM, through a management control methodology, can demonstrate its contribution to the hidden cost conversion into visible performance in order to stimulate the managers' commitment for its use.

Case Study: Synthesis of Main Visible Performance in a Disabled People Care Center

In 2001, due to huge deficits, a French center for disabled people with 133 employees, which was created in 1984, merged at the demand by public powers with another center, as it often happens in this industry (Barry, Cristallini, & Savall, 2006). The ministry of health compelled the studied organization to reach two strategic goals: reducing costs and setting up action plans to improve patient satisfaction. Consequently, the chief executive officer decided to put in place SEAM within the organization in a context both of downsizing in 2002 and increasing the Center's activities. The intervention-research was carried out in 45 centers of this non-profit organization with 1,200 employees.

The significant visible performances evolution measured between 2003 and 2005 within the organization through a socio-economic *diagnosis* and assessment showed a profit increase of 7.8%, corresponding to gains of 280 000 euro.

The *hourly contribution to value added on variable cost (HCVAVC)* is the key indicator used in the socio-economic approach to management to enhance the hidden costs of overtime and non-production, and measure their impact on visible performance. An increase in *HCVAVC* reflects an increase of the organization's social and economic efficiency. The *HCVAVC* is a synthetic indicator of an organization's *efficiency* that truly grounds the socio-economic approach to management in the family of the management control methods, as shown in the next case vignette.

Case Study: HCVAVC Calculation in a Regional Branch of the French Social Security

The major criterion for distinguishing the variable costs is to consider that costs that may vary within a year are of two categories: *variable costs depending on strategic choices* (CV1) and *variable costs depending on the activity level* (CV2). Those last costs change with the activity level, thus if sales increase, they proportionally increase. Variable costs depending on the strategic choices (CV1) allow highlighting expenses induced by the strategic decisions *implementation*. It enables budget adjustments if the activity level does not allow these expenses over the year, without using the expenditure level required for the regular activity of the company (see Table 4.2).

Table 4.2.   HCVAVC Calculation in a Regional Branch of the French Social Security

DENOMINATION	TOTAL
A) REVENUES REPROCESSING	
ACCOUNTING TURNOVER	2,013,477 €
+ Financial and various revenues to incorporate	41,340 €
TOTAL MODIFIED TURNOVER	1,891,734 €
B) EXPENSES REPROCESSING	
TOTAL ACCOUNTING EXPENSES	1,974,202 €
Loan loss reserve on the previous financial year (fixed)	–10,795 €
Management fees	–18,288 €
TOTAL OPERATING EXPENSES	1,811,119 €
VARIABLE COSTS DEPENDING ON STRATEGIC DECISIONS (CV1)	157,233 €
Value-added on variable costs depending on strategic decisions (B = A – CV1)	1,734,501 €
VARIABLE COSTS DEPENDING ON THE ACTIVITY LEVEL (CV2)	313,914 €
Value-added on variable costs depending on activity level (C = B – CV2)	1,420,587 €
NUMBER OF HOURS WORKED PER YEAR (H)	48,366 H
Hourly Contribution to Value-Added on Variable Costs (HCVAVC = E/H or (A – CV1 – CV2)/H)	30.82 €

The *HCVAVC* measures the average value of an hour of human activity in the company, regardless of his job and tasks, whether from support function or from operational functions. It is calculated by dividing **VAVC** by **the number of expected hours worked** a year of all the employees of the company, regardless of the sector, public or private. The value added on variable costs is always higher than the value added as considered in the traditional accounting, which does not take into account the external fixed costs. Hence, it does not allow estimating value creation amount that is needed to cover the fixed *charges* whereas *HCVAVC* (through *CVAVC*) does.

In a way, *HCVAVC* is a strategic *warning* indicator coupling strategy-management control because it captures signals such as demand decrease and price variation on the market as well as internal productivity and products quality fluctuation. Therefore, *HCVAVC* measurement stems from numerous internal and external *interactions*.

Synchronized Decentralization and TFW (Taylorism, Fayolism, Weberism) Virus

To reach its goals in terms of change dynamics, SEAM implements a management control system under the principle of **synchronized decentralization**. Thus, all the managers contribute to the management control thanks to SEAM tools, through **self-management control** role. However, the whole is synchronized by the management controller and monitored by the top managers of the company.

The management self-control gradually educates all the *actors* to the economic dimension of their business practices because each individual performs, when starting the operations, a first management control step. Once the self-control achieved, the results are communicated throughout the organization, to enable the managers to identify the specific gaps in their own operations and to act on their *root causes*. This conception of management control (Ennajem, 2011) induces a behavior change in the company, but also leads to roles sharing between the operations managers and the management controller.

Thus, the socio-economic approach to management is implemented in organizations on the burnt grounds of management control methods infected by the *TFW virus* (see Chapter 2). The followers of these schools of thought recommend the maximal division of work (Taylor) by fragmenting to an excessive degree the time dedicated to activities, therefore leading to a decrease of the *actors'* responsibilities and to a lack of work interest, thus underestimating the psycho-sociological dimension of work.

Furthermore, in this model, the functions and the company departments are separated (Fayol) and the sole *efficiency* of rational and impersonal rules prevail (Weber). Thus, services working in silos would be at the base of *efficiency*, because *actors* do not speak to each other. However, many works have shown the benefits of cross-functional **communication** between departments to improve activities understanding and visibility and for a better strategic monitoring. Finally, Weberism defends that *actors* are automatically obedient to their hierarchy because of its supremacy. Each day we spent into a company shows the opposite. *Actors* are disobedient and regularly forget the rules which do not make sense for them. It leads to business models where a function is centralized on a head or a team who ultimately works separately and independently of managers.

This function separation creates a distance between managers and management control. As a result, in a lot of organizations, many managers do not know how the management control works despite their proximity to the activities to be steered, while the management controller knows how it works but is distant from activities and does not understand them. Table 4.3 compares the sharing level of the management control role in SEAM and in classical methods of management control.

Table 4.3.   Synthesis of Convergences—Specificities Between SEAM and Classical Methods of Management Control

Themes/Results	Convergence Between the Literature and Our Results	Specificities of our Results
Decentralization/ Delegation	Tools in operational units (Lorino, 2001; De Montgolfier, 1999; Kaplan & Norton, 1995; Sponem & Chatelain-Ponroy, 2007).	Investment profitability analysis at the business unit level, in addition to management controllers and regional managers
	Shared management control (Gumb, 2008; Zolnai-Saucray, 1999; Lambert, 2010)	
	Vertical and horizontal decentralization	Synchronized decentralization and ***collaborative delegation*** concepts, in response to the overall *coordination* problem and lack of adherence of the operational employees.
	(Dupuy, 1991)	
	Strengthening the role and influence of the management controller (Bollecker, 2002; Meyssonnier & Fernandez-Poisson, 2010)	
	Overall *coordination* problem and lack of adherence of the employees (Sponem & Chatelain-Ponroy, 2007).	Collaborative delegation with animation concept
	Pedagogic relation importance (Durand, 2008)	Delegation to the whole staff
	Delegation towards operational function (Pédon & Schmidt, 2002).	
	Delegation of the analyses and control activities to the middle managers	

Lorino (2007), De Montgolfier (1999), Kaplan and Norton (1995), Sponem and Chatelain-Ponroy (2007) highlight a relative evolution of management control towards a decentralization of the control tools into the operations units. For Gumb (2008), it deals with a "shared management control" or a "share of control activities" reinforcing the *interaction* and *cooperation* between operational staff and management controller (Gumb, 2008; Lambert, 2005; Zolnai-Saucray, 1999).

For Dupuy (1990), mechanism logic created by Falkenberg and Herremans (1995) is "cross-functional and dynamic," it means a real vertical and horizontal decentralization. However, a part of analysis and control activities decentralization towards the operational staff causes two issues: the overall *coordination* and the lack of will of the operational staff for achieving these operations. For Bollecker (2002), there is a paradox: delegating activities analysis and control to middle managers requires strengthening the management controller's role and influence (Meyssonnier & Fernandez-Poisson, 2010).

Concerning the above mentioned highlighted issues in the literature (Sponem & Chatelain-Ponroy, 2007), the socio-economic approach to management control responds to the overall *coordination* issue with the concepts of **synchronized decentralization** and **collaborative delegation**. For the second issue, our scientific observation show a willingness of the operational staff to perform these management control operations, since the system both delegates management control skills and gives more responsibility to the operational staff. In the SME's literature, delegation is generally preferred to animation (Pédon & Schmidt, 2000).

Our observations of companies and organizations have shown that both types are present. Delegating is useful but, without collaboration, that is, without animation, this practice is ineffective. It leads to the definition of *collaborative delegation*, consisting of a delegation process with an animation system with the person to whom the activity is delegated. The process aims at ensuring the availability of means and the regular assessment of the delegation. However, the *collaborative delegation* is not a reflex action for organizations' *actors*; it is one of the management controller's action limits whose mission is rather to support and steer the operational staff.

Profitability of Tangible and Intangible Investments

The key success factor of the socio-economic approach to management for sustainable *development* of the organization's formal and informal performance is its emphasis on **intangible investment**, unlike the conventional management control methods often focused on the sole material investments. However, when properly controlled, *intangible investments* achieved thanks to management and operations quality have a much higher investment returns, up to 4,000% (see Chapter 2).

This model (see Figure 4.4) considers intangible actions as an investment decision. Indeed, including *hidden cost*s changes the decision-making method and results for two reasons. First, the action visible cost is completed by taking into account the *hidden cost*s related to this action. Then, it is possible to estimate the expected new performance from the *hidden cost*s recycling in value added creation, and therefore to calculate a return on investment period, as it is possible for material investments.

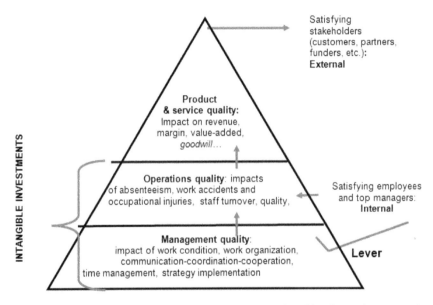

Figure 4.4.   Map of the intangible investments stimulated by the socio-economic approach to management.

The socio-economic approach to management control model proposes to assess the *intangible investment* by multiplying the number of hours spent by all categories of *actors* of the company by the *HCVAVC*.

SEAM "SATELLITE" TOOLS AND MONITORING THE PROFITABILITY OF TANGIBLE AND INTANGIBLE INVESTMENTS

The "satellite" tools of the socio-economic approach to management, such as the *economic balance*, the *operation scheduling grid (OSG)*, the *budgeted action plan (BAP)* and the *strategic activity list* are complementary to the six main tools (see Figure 4.1). The "doctrine" of **socio-economic intervention** (SEI) on the socio-economic approach to management is not to impose those tools on the organizations, but rather to encourage people within organizations to use them because they strengthen a relevant, challenging and rigorous management control **implementation**. It is even more effective in the current times of crisis and of economic turbulence.

Economic Balance

Economic balance (EB) is an essential tool for making decisions, and then for monitoring and grooming them with **effectiveness** and **efficiency**. This tool is used to quantify the economic impacts of a material and/or **intangible investment** project by listing all the actions necessary for its *implementation*, as well as the expected results. It allows identifying the variations of expenses and visible revenues, but also of **hidden cost**s-performances.

Economic balance is thus used to measure the feasibility of improvement and dysfunctions reduction actions, which may be proposed by a **focus group** after a **socio-economic diagnosis**. The *diagnosis* includes individual interviews in various departments of the company. It consists in collecting **quotes** about dysfunctions which are presented to interviewees afterwards. This step is called the **mirror-effect** because it helps all those people realize the importance of the dysfunctions.

Second, the interveners-researchers give their point of view through an **expert opinion** consisting of two parts: (1) the **key mirror-effect points** that classify by order of importance the quotes from the mirror effect into **baskets**; and (2) the **non-dit** consisting of observations of the interveners-researchers that have not been expressed in the interviews. The *economic balance* is established for assessing the feasibility of the proposals of the project group from a socio-economic point of view (Table 4.4).

The *economic balance* helps assessing the **qualitative, quantitative and financial** gains expected from an improvement action, such as the invoicing schedule *development* project aimed at improving the management and quality of production means. For this purpose, concrete actions have been identified for reducing the recognized and valued dysfunctions.

Operations Scheduling Grid

The **operations scheduling grid** of a complex action is aimed at breaking it down into operations, at indicating the persons concerned by each, and at estimating the time needed for their realization. It allows scheduling, controlling and regulating an activity in case of dysfunction, by reallocating time. The operations scheduling grid also helps in the planning, scheduling, and monitoring the activities.

Table 4.4.   Extract of an Economic Balance

Economic Balance

Basket 1: **Improving the management and the quality of means of production**

Key idea 1 : **Inadequacy of equipment and failure in the information system management**

Micro-project: **DEVELOPMENT OF INVOICING SCHEDULE**

| | | | | | Gains | |
Concrete Actions	*Elemental Dysfunction*	*Dysfunction Cost*	*Forecast Reduction Rate*	*Qualitative*	*Quantitative (h/month)*	*Financial (€ mont)*
Setting up the annual invoicing schedule	Sending invoices each month to debited clients	19 000 bills 0,492 € without value added tax (postage, supplies, service	92%			8,600
Setting up the annual invoicing schedule	Monthly invoices editing tasks for customers by the billing department	2 hours / day = 40 hours / month = 40 38 €	92%		36	1,400
		100% ■	66% ◪			
		33% ☐	0% —			

Budgeted Action Plan

The socio-economic approach to management control emerges from the observation of several critical analyses of the conventional management control. This one is usually practiced as a simple budgetary control, consisting in establishing a "budget renewal" whether by extrapolating the previous budget through a variation percentage mechanical application, which therefore does not allow a critical analysis of the past budgets; or either by a centralized budget preparation, mainly consisting in setting a desired growth or profitability rates without precisely identifying the required actions for achieving the desired results.

The **budgeted action plan** (BAP) tool consists of economically budgeting the **priority action plan** so that the leader and the persons in charge of priority actions are, upstream, familiar with the expected cost/value of these actions, and ensure downstream the reality of their forecasts. The BAP approach has two essential virtues: connecting the socio-economic approach to management to the budget-making procedure and stimulating the *actor's* respect of the budget through the ripple effect of valuing the ***cost-value*** of the planned priority actions.

Strategic Activities Nomenclature

The activities nomenclature is the basis of the socio-economic approach to management control *implementation* in the teams of an organization (see Figure Pédon). It allows each individual, at the beginning of the period, to negotiate with managers the time needed for his activities. Downstream, the tool measures the time actually spent on the various activities of the nomenclature to ensure that solvent activities finance the insolvent ones, but also to ensure that some people are not overloaded compared to others who are under-loaded. The nomenclature of activity is an effective way to individualize the management control with harmony and synchronicity. It improves the reliability of the activities production costs.

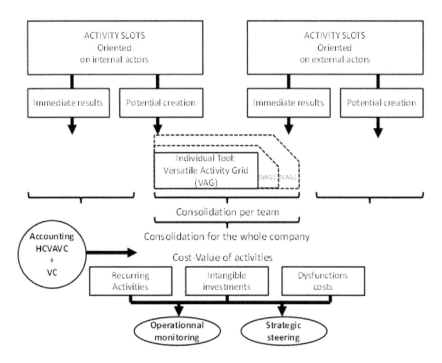

Source: Savall and Zardet (2008a).

Figure 4.5.   Activities nomenclature: A shared common tool.

In order to measure the value of activities, this approach suggests that each actor directly charges his/her working time into a nomenclature, unique for each company, which is a benchmark shared by all the internal *actors*. The activities nomenclature is a tree list of all the company activities and is used for charging time spent by destination rather than by type of task, as mentioned above.

It avoids the excessive use of fixed time allocation per work units, which is a drift as criticized by the academic literature as by practitioners. Once the individual versatile activity grids are charged, they are consolidated in the company, therefore giving the company's level of activity in terms of hours. This level of activity is enhanced by applying a coefficient called **hourly contribution to value added on variable costs** (HCVAVC) and by adding external variable costs. This valuation defines the **cost-value of the activities**.

The bottom of Figure 4.5 shows the distribution of activities of all the *actors* in three categories: recurring activities, activities resulting from *intangible investment* and activities due to dysfunctions. The division into these three activity categories allows the operational and strategic management of operations, source of **socio-economic sustainable performance** improvement.

CONCLUSION

We conclude this chapter by returning to the article by Hamel and Zanini (2014) that stimulated our thinking. They wrote that the modern organization was not designed for deep and proactive change and this has led to change being considered in exceptional rather than in normal terms. The discussion shows that SEAM builds self-managed change into the DNA of the organization by making it a natural and normal part of its **functioning** in concert with the pursuit of short term economic objectives via day to day operational activities (see Figure 4.3). While senior management has an important role to play in steering, supporting and energizing the process, as well as acting on its outputs, the responsibility and ideas for change are distributed throughout the organization based on a process of social construction following from putting ideas into action and learning from the results. The SEAM model stimulates the need for change by obtaining and amplifying information from a variety of sources, both inside and outside the organization. In this way, SEAM replaces the unfreeze-change-freeze view of change by one characterized as "permanent slush."

Moreover, the case study has sought to indicate how an innovative approach of management control such as SEAM may be used to improve the quality of people management and to contribute to the **development** of **human potential,** both being the organization's DNA in a way. The chapter has also stressed the *diagnosis* advantages to SEAM produced by measuring the value of the *human potential* using the *HCVAVC* indicator. This indicator provides a means of assessing the influence and role of people management on the *creation of value*. The premise underlying the measurement of *human potential* is that each employee in an organization makes an hourly contribution to the **creation of value added** above variable costs. The term "value added" is associated with the utility of human activity and the strategic importance of human **resources** in a company. Capital costs (e.g., financial expenses, depreciation, provisions for **risks**), constitute an inert element not activated by the **human factor**. *HCVAVC* is thus an indicator of the creation of the total **value-added** produced by all the participants in the company. This measure can be seen as a synthetic metric for both **strategic management performance** and management control performance.

The socio-economic approach to management is part of management control methods whose broad objectives are to steer and develop formal and informal performance. For this reason, the socio-economic approach to management mobilizes a change process and specific tools called "satellites" that make it a more efficient, proactive and less contemplative management control method than other methods of management control such as Kaplan and Norton's (1995) balanced scorecard.

NOTE

1. The research for this chapter has been influenced by a number of works that are not directly referred to in the text, including Boje and Rosile (2003), Gephart (2009), Savall (1974, 1975, 1977, 2012), and Savall and Zardet (1992, 2013, 2014).

REFERENCES

Ansoff, H. I. (1981). Preface. In H. Savall (Ed.), *Work and people: An economic evaluation of job enrichment*. New York, NY: Oxford University Press.

Anthony, R. N. (1988). *The management control function*. Boston, MA: Harvard Business School Press.

Anthony, R. N., & Govindarajan, V. (2007). *Management control systems* (12th ed.). New York, NY: McGraw-Hill Irwin.

Barry, S., Cristallini, V., & Savall, H. (2006). *Bilan et perspectives après deux ans de fonctionnement du management socio-économique* [Assesments and perspectives after two years SEAM fonctionning]. In H. Savall (Ed.), *L'hôpital et les réseaux de santé* [Hospital and healthcare networks] (pp. 179–188). Paris, France: Economica.

Bhide, A. (2000). *The origin and evolution of new business*. New York, NY: Oxford University Press.

Boje, D., & Rosile, G.-A. (2003). Comparison of socio-economic and other transorganizational development methods. *Journal of Change Organizational Management, 16*(1), 10–20.

Bollecker, M. (2002). Le rôle des contrôleurs de gestion dans l'apprentissage orga-nisationnel: Une analyse de la phase de suivi des réalisations [Management controller role in organizational learning: Realization analysis phase]. *Compt-abilité–Contrôle–Audit*, *2*, 109–126.

Buono, A. F., & Savall, H. (Eds.). (2007). *Socio-economic intervention in organizations: The intervener-researcher and the SEAM approach to organizational analysis.* Char-lotte, NC: Information Age Publishing.

Cappelletti, L. (2005). Designing and processing a socio-economic management control. In K. M. Weaver (Ed.), *Academy of management best paper proceedings* (pp. A1–A6). Pace, NY: Academy of Management.

Cappelletti, L., & Baker, R. C. (2010). Measuring and developing human capital through a pragmatic action research: A French case study. *Action Research*, *8*(2), 211–232.

De Geus, A. (1997). *The living company: Habits for survival in a turbulent business envi-ronment.* Boston, MA: Harvard Business School Press.

De Montgolfier, C. (1999). Quel contrôleur pour quell contrôle? [Which controller for which control] In Y. Dupuy (Ed.), *Faire de la recherche en contrôle de gestion ?* [Doing management control research] (pp. 145–160). Paris, France: Vuibert,

Duggan, W. (2007). *Strategic intuition: The creative spark in human achievement.* New York, NY: Columbia University Press.

Dupuy, Y. (1990, September). Le comptable, la comptabilité et la conception des systèmes d'information: quelques interrogations [The accountant, accoun-tancy, and information system conception: Some questions]. *Revue française de Comptabilité*, *215*, 75–81

Dupuy, Y. (1991). Les organigrammes de structure organisationnelle [Structure organizational organigram]. *Encyclopédie de management* (Vol. 2, pp. 370–381). Paris: Vuibert.

Durand, X. (2008). La relation pédagogique contrôleur de gestion–opération-nels: enjeux et déterminants [Pedagogic relationship between management controllers and operationnal teams: Stakes and determinants]. In *La compta-bilité, le contrôle et l'audit entre changement et stabilité* (CD-Rom).

Ennajem, C. (2011). *Évolution du rôle du contrôleur de gestion dans un contexte de contrôle de gestion décentralisé* [Evolution of the management controller' role in a decentralized management control context]. Sarrebruck, Deutchland: Éditions Universitaires Européennes

Falkenberg, G. L., & Herremans, I. (1995) Ethical behavior in organizations directed by the formal and informal systems?, *Journal of Business Ethics*, *14*, 133–143.

Fayol, H. (1916). *Administration générale et industrielle* [General and industrial admi-nistration]. Paris, France: Dunod.

Fayol, H. (1916–1970). *Administration industrielle et générale* [Industrial and global administration]. Paris, France: Dunod.

Foster, R., & Kaplan, S. (2001). *Creative destruction: Why companies that are built to last underperform the market—and how to successfully transform them.* New York, NY: Doubleday.

Gephart, R. P. (2009). An invitation to ethnostatistics. *Revue Sciences de gestion – Management Sciences – Ciencias de Gestión*, *70*, 85.

Gephart, R. P., Jr. (2014). Deliberating cost: Deliberative practices in qualimetrics and the socio-economic approach to management. In H. Savall, J. Conbere, A. Heorhiadi, V. Cristallini, & A. F. Buono (Eds.), *Facilitating the socio-economic approach to management* (pp. 193–207). Charlotte, NC: Information Age Publishing.

Gibson, C. (1973). Volvo increases productivity through job enrichment. *California Management Review, 15*(4), 64–66.

Gumb, B. (2008) *Les outils de gestion au service de votre stratégie* [Management tools serving your strategy]. Paris: Éditions d'Organisation.

Hamel, G., & Zanini, M. (2014). Build a change platform, not a change program. *McKinsey & Company* (October). Retrieved from http://www.mckinsey.com/insights/organization/build_a_change_platform_not_a_change_program

Kahneman, D., Lovallo, D., & Sibony, O. (2011). The big idea: Before you make that big decision. *Harvard Business Review,* (May–June), 50–60.

Kaplan, R. S., & Norton, D. P. (1995). Putting the balanced scorecard to work. *Performance Measurement, Management, and Appraisal Sourcebook, 66.*

Kotter, J. (1996). *Leading change.* Boston, MA: Harvard Business School Press.

Lafley, A. G., Martin, R., Rivkin, J., & Sigglekow, N. (2012). Bringing science to the art of strategy. *Harvard Business Review* (September–October), *90*(9), 3–12.

Lambert, C. (2005). *La fonction contrôle de gestion: Contribution à l'analyse de la place des services fonctionnels dans l'organisation* [The function management control: Contribution to the analysis of the place of the functional departments in the organization]. Doctoral dissertation, Paris IX Dauphine University.

Lambert, C. (2010). Le contrôleur de gestion et son manager [the management controller and his/her manager] In N. Berland & Y. De Rongé (Eds.), *Contrôle de gestion, perspectives stratégiques et managériales* [Management control, stategic and managerial perspectives] (pp. 97–120). Paris: Pearson.

Lindsay, R. M. (2015). *Developing robust strategy for uncertain times: Expanding our concept of management control to deal with dynamic markets* (Parts I and II). Toronto, Canada: Chartered Professional Accountants of Canada.

Lorino, P. (2001). *Méthodes et pratiques de la performance* [Methods and practices of performance]. Paris: Les Éditions d'Organisation.

Martin, R. (2009). *The opposable mind: Winning through integrative thinking.* Boston, MA: Harvard Business Press.

McGrath, R. G., & Macmillan, I. (2009). *Discovery-driven growth: A breakthrough process to reduce risk and seize opportunity.* Boston, MA: Harvard Business School.

Merchant, K., & Van der Stede, W. (2012). *Management control systems* (3rd ed.). Harlow, England: Financial Times Prentice Hall.

Meyssonnier, F., & Fernandez-Poisson, D. (2010). La réduction des coûts, enjeu majeur du contrôle de gestion [Cost-reducing, major management control view]. In N. Berland & F.-X. Simon (Eds.), *Le contrôle de gestion en mouvement-Etat de l'art et meilleures pratiques* [Moving management control—state of the art and best practices], Paris: Eyrolles.

Mintzberg, H. (1987). The strategy concept 1: Five P's for strategy. *California Management Review,* (Fall), 11–24.

Mintzberg, H. (1994). *The rise and fall of strategic planning.* New York, NY: The Free Press.

Mintzberg, H. (2008). Crafting strategy. *Harvard Business Review,* (July-August), 66–75.

Montgomery, C. (2008). Putting leadership back into strategy. *Harvard Business Review,* (January–February), 54–60.

Pédon, A., & Schmidt, G. (2002, September). L'apprentissage organisationnel en PME : Réalité et déterminants [Organizational learning in SME: Determinant and reality], *XVIèmes Journées Nationales des IAE,* 10–12.

Penrose, E. T. (1959). *The theory of the growth of the firm.* New York, NY: Wiley.

Perroux F. (1979). L'entreprise, l'équilibre rénové et les coûts cachés [The enterprise, the renovated balance and the "hidden" costs]. In H. Savall (Ed.), *Reconstruire l'entreprise, analyse socio-économique des conditions de travail* [Rebuilding the enterprise]. Paris, France: Dunod.

Perroux, F. (1979). L'entreprise, l'équilibre rénové et les coûts cachés [The enterprise, the renovated balance and the "hidden" costs]. In H. Savall (Ed.), *Reconstruire l'entreprise* [Reconstructing the enterprise] Paris, France: Dunod. (2nd ed. In H. Savall & V. Zardet. *Reconstruire l'entreprise,* Paris: Dunod. (2014))

Savall, H. (1974–1975–1977). *Enrichir le travail humain dans les entreprises et les organisations* [An economic evaluation of job enrichment]. Paris: Dunod.

Savall, H. (1979) *Reconstruire l'entreprise* [Reconstructing the enterprise] Paris, France: Dunod. (2nd ed. In H. Savall & V. Zardet. *Reconstruire l'entreprise,* Paris: Dunod (2014)).

Savall, H. (1981–2010). *Work and people: An economic evaluation of job enrichment.* 1st ed. New York: Oxford University Press ; 2nd ed. Charlotte, NC: Information Age Publishing

Savall, H. (2003). An update presentation of the socio-economic management model and international dissemination of the socio-economic model. *Journal of Organizational Change Management, 16*(1), 33–48.

Savall, H. (2012). *Origine radicale des crises économiques: Germán Bernácer, précurseur visionnaire* [Root origin of crises: Germán Bernácer, a visionary forerunner]. Charlotte, NC: Information Age Publishing.

Savall, H., & Zardet, V. (1987). *Maîtriser les coûts et les performances cachés : Le contrat d'activité périodiquement négociables* [Mastering *hidden costs* and performance: The periodically negotiable activity contract]. Paris: Economica.

Savall, H., & Zardet, V. (1992). *Le nouveau contrôle de gestion: Méthode des coûts-performances cachés* [New management control: The hidden cost-performance method]. Paris: Éditions Comptables Malesherbes-Eyrolles.

Savall, H., & Zardet, V. (1995–2005–2009). *Ingénierie stratégique du roseau, souple et enracinée* [Strategic engineering of the reed, flexible and rooted]. Paris: Economica.

Savall, H., & Zardet, V. (2008a). *Mastering hidden costs and performance.* Charlotte, NC: Information Age Publishing.

Savall, H., & Zardet, V. (2008b). Le concept de coût-valeur des activités. Contribution de la théorie socio-économique des organisations [SEAM contribution to cost-value of activities concept]. *Revue Sciences de Gestion–Management Sciences–Ciencias de Gestión, 64.*

Savall, H., & Zardet, V. (2011). *The qualimetrics approach: Observing the complex object.* Charlotte, NC: Information Age Publishing.

Savall, H., & Zardet, V. (2013a, August). *Linking individual, organizational and macro-economic performance levels: Hidden costs model*. Paper presented at the Academy of Management, Lake Buena Vista, FL.

Savall, H., & Zardet, V. (2013b). *The dynamics and challenges of tetranormalization*. Charlotte, NC: Information Age Publishing.

Savall, H., & Zardet, V. (2014). *Reconstruire l'entreprise. Fondements du management socio-économique* [Rebuilding the enterprise: The founding principle of socio-economic management]. Paris, France: Dunod.

Savall, H. Zardet, V., & Bonnet, M. (2000–2008). *Releasing the untapped potential of enterprises through socio-economic management*. Geneva: Éditions IOT-BIT.

Savall, H., Zardet, V., Bonnet, M., & Cappelletti, L. (2007, June). First Transatlantic Congress in Accounting, Auditing, Control and Costs Proceedings, AAA-IIC-ISEOR, Lyon, France.

Schoemaker, P. (2008). The future challenges of business: Rethinking management education. *California Management Review, 50*(3), 119–139.

Sponem, S., & Chatelain-Ponvoy, S. (2007). Evolution et permanence du contrôle de gestion [Evolution and permanency of management control]. *Economie et Management, 123*, 12–18.

Stubbart, C., & Knight, M. (2006). The case of disappearing firms: Empirical evidence and implications. *Journal of Organizational Behavior, 27*(1), 79–100.

Taylor, F. W. (1911). *The principles of scientific management*. New York, NY: Harpers and Brothers.

Weber, M. (1924). *The theory of social and economic organization*. New York, NY: Free Press.

Wernerfelt, B. (1984). A resource-based view of the firm. *Strategic Management Journal, 5*, 171–180.

Zolnai-Saucray, E. (1999). Vers une pédagogie du contrôle dans l'organisation [To a control pedagogy in organization] In Y. Dupuy (Ed.), *Faire de la recherche en contrôle de gestion?* [Doing management control research] (pp. 125–139). Paris, France: Vuibert.

CHAPTER 5

SOCIALLY RESPONSIBLE CAPITALISM[1]

Henri Savall and Michel Péron

The objective of this chapter is to demonstrate the coherence between the *socio-economic approach to management (SEAM)* and the economic and social environment as a whole, a territory that is seen as a vector of *social cohesion*. It also aims to emphasize the essential contribution of ISEOR's method of management, under all its aspects, within the framework of an entrepreneurial and intrapreneurial socially and sustainably responsible capitalism (SRC). This view goes beyond the restricted field of social responsibility that is limited to companies, since a company is nothing but a capitalist microcosm (Perroux, 1948) and true sustainability lies in the territory's structures. Mackey and Sisodia (2013) follow the same train of thought according to Chandler (2014) when they advocate their concept of Conscious Capitalism, that reestablishing the values-based businesses is central to reinvigorating public support for capitalism which has suffered in recent years as a result of transgressions that have caused widespread economic harm. We need to denounce a harmful drift towards a *wild, perverted* form of capitalism, one that has been led astray and expresses its opacity, at all the levels of the social, political and economic organization. This disconcerting trend touches CEOs, as well as local or national elected

The Socio-Economic Approach to Management Revisited: The Evolving Nature of SEAM in the 21st Century, pp. 103–118
Copyright © 2015 by Information Age Publishing
All rights of reproduction in any form reserved.

representatives, and even Heads of State in supporting *speculative* and/or *corrupt behaviors*, literally throwing to the nettles any ethical consideration.

In this context, **socio-economic management**, which respects humans and is committed to help them grow, promises an alternative path. No company can sustainably thrive in a hostile environment. As such, this chapter defines the *framework characteristics* that allow public and private socially responsible companies and organizations to develop and support **SEAM implementation**. We propose a framework based on a *socially, economically* and *sustainably responsible* regenerated capitalism, built on an entrepreneurship spirit, tending to behavioral exemplarity that emphasizes social responsibility. This commitment is combined with economic awareness and the ethical efforts of each citizen **actor**. Sustainably responsible capitalism emphasizes capturing the essence of individual, micro-collective, and macro-collective *human energy*.

SEAM AND THE MEANING OF CAPITALISM

Setting aside Chinese, Anglo-Saxon, and Rhine forms of capitalisms and its basic definition as "a legal statute of a human society characterized by the private property of the means of production and their implementation by workers who are not their owners" (Nouveau Larousse Universel, 1969, p. 276), capitalism is seen as a "system of production whose based on private enterprise and market freedom." This system was the engine of economic progress for centuries and it can be seen as a human energy catalyst that supports growth and **development**. This first development eliminated planned, official, and centralized economic forms, which can only lead to non-democratic, totalitarian regimes condemned by history for enslaving people and tolling the knell of free entrepreneurship. These forms of economic regime are not respectful of the dignity and fulfillment of the greatest number of people. It calls to mind the meaningful expression of François Perroux (1948, p. 106) opposing the degenerate form of hands-state capitalism, "when the entrepreneur is treated as a civil servant capitalism is sick; if a civil servant is treated as an entrepreneur, capitalism died."

When capitalism is disconnected from the social context, it brushes aside rules, becomes anarchistic and inhuman, leads to owners-hooligans' unjustifiable behaviors, and relentless stock exchange dismissals. It is called wild and untrammeled compared to the benevolent (benign) capitalism, as wished for by former British Prime Minister Tony Blair. But far worse, it becomes perverted when it answers to the sirens of the financial sphere and corrupt predators, depriving real economy entrepreneurs of their **resources** in favor of speculative bubbles that block proper running of the economy.

The result is a ceaseless process of collective creation of tangible and intangible wealth propelled by an activity engine based on the individual and collective innovations. Financial capitalism, uncontrolled and speculative, must be considered as an obstacle to intelligent growth and the establishment of a responsible and democratic development model. Indeed, this form of capitalism has been led astray, completely diverted from moral rules, refusing to grant a preeminent place to economic citizen actors who are subjected to the single objective of profit maximization. These forces deprive them from any hope to see one day a participative form of democracy established in their daily professional activity. In contrast, the type of individual responsibility put forward by SRC enhances a truly democratic model. Humanity is not reduced to the state of merchandise.

Sustainably responsible capitalism is the most pertinent dimension of the socio-economic approach to management (SEAM). These two systems are in congruence due to their underlying values and objectives. It constitutes an environment that fosters SEAM implementation, its *survival*, and its development. SEAM is the forecast of SRC on the *small perimeter* that constitutes a company or an organization, whatever its size. There is an isomorphic relationship between the two systems. The first is a miniaturized form of the second; the second is an extension of the first. SRC reflects SEAM in daily life, in proximity with all organizational members. SEAM achieves the benefits of *social performance*—in which personal needs are satisfied—and *economic performance*—the generation and repartition of rare resources, natural or produced by human action.

Sustainably responsible capitalism recognizes the benefits of the natural capacity of autonomy from individuals and teams, which permit, in concert with others, the organization to cultivate dignity in professional and personal life. SRC enhances subsidiarity—the activities are more effective and efficient when they are managed and realized as close as possible to life, action, and utilization areas.

The respect of the main fundamental values that influence human activity is more or less assured, in function with economic regime characteristics. SRC cultivates the initiative capacity and the ability to create material and intangible value, which is necessary for the well-being and the sustainable self-fulfillment of individuals. SRC limits individual dependency to public policies, far located, short-sighted, sometimes blinded, cynical and inequitable as political, administrative, syndicate and professional bureaucracies. SRC does consider the private property of the means of production means as well as the responsibility for the public policies to orchestrate the production of goods and services, to create necessary *infrastructures* and regulate their utilization. It recognizes democratically elected public powers, an eminent role in stimulating health, education, security, justice, and solidarity practices arbitrage.

Sustainably responsible capitalism energizes everybody—the individual, team, company, territorial organization (local, regional, national, and international)—through the decentralized creation of companies, associations, jobs, products (goods and services), **artistic activities**, and cultural and spiritual activities. SRC is opposed to centralized forms of planned, distant, and bureaucratic management practices that control economic and social activities, sanctioned by history such as political, military or popular dictatorships. Due to its capacity for **value creation**, linked to its **sustainable efficiency**, SRC pushes away poverty frontiers, encouraging solidarity activities and offering an advantageous alternative to speculation and corruption.

The Value Notion

In a socially responsible capitalist environment, all companies and organizations at each level (local, regional, national, or international) are expected to take care of the various categories of actors who can be put in a position to use and develop their potential in socially useful activities in order to create socio-economic value that is shared with stakeholders. By **socio-economic value**, we mean the combination of *social value*—satisfying citizen's needs—and the *economic value*—the production and repartition of rare resources. The value created, which is durable and shareable, is the "angular stone" of our socio-economic approach. This shared outcome is in direct contrast to the outrageous financial process that only considers a limited view of value—the artificial rise in stock exchange prices, which are part of an egoistic profit that does not benefit all actors. Our approach recognizes that each person, each industry, and each organization has the ability to produce economic value. It refutes that noxious archaic dichotomy, advocated by some ideologies, between the ones who produce value and those who do not—in essence, non-producers who wait passively for generous "transfers" from the value producers.

The justification of a discussion about the ins and outs of SRC in a management-oriented book is based on the concept of value shared by this type of capitalism and all the free enterprise's actors. This assimilation is well clarified by Mackey and Sisodia (2013) who argue that free enterprise, when working as it should, results in societies that maximize societal prosperity and establish conditions that promote human happiness and wellbeing—not just for the rich, but for larger society, including the poor. We share this concern aimed at contributing to the wellbeing of the society where we live and work, while going against a world of dehumanized work and the purported logic of profit maximization. The utilitarian moral proposed by Jeremy Bentham (1748–1832), whose great principles were drawn on by John Stuart Mill (1806–1873), always constitutes the theoretical base for the utilitarian goal of the greatest happiness for the greatest number. This is one of the main objectives of a socially and sustainably responsible capitalism—the essence of a more conscious form of capitalism. SCR and the democratic company are in an identical way founded on values. As pinpointed by Chandler (2014, p. 398), "values underpin our daily actions and, in the aggregate, help constitute the society in which we live."

Among these fundamental values, let us quote *freedom, human dignity*, and *democracy* as components of the principle founder of the only nation in the world born from a commercial contract (Mayflower Compact)— Life, Liberty and the Pursuit of Happiness—as featured in the United States constitution. Freedom is an important concept in our representation of SRC. In fact, capitalism is sometimes simply described as a system of economy of freedom. Perroux (1948) points out that in an interventionist and centralized state "capitalist logic is put at fault." The new-mercantilists from the 17th century did not disagree that civil law was necessary for order, but there wasn't any doubt that in their eyes an excess of laws and rules represented an attack on personal freedom and an obstacle to the proper running of the economy. In the socio-economic approach, entre- preneurship constitutes a proactive response to **regulations**.

This notion of liberty reminds us that, for Fernand Braudel (1986), there is no clear rupture between slavery, servitude, and wage-earning. This observation applies to totalitarian states as well as to present and former dictatorships. However, in our times, pope François deplores the increase of slavery and the United Nations warns states against the human trafficking upsurge all over the world. This is one of the reasons why SRC highlights the concept of *dignity*, which starts with self-respect. The SRC refuses each and every situation where human beings, transformed into dehumanized robots, lose their dignity. Our **socio-economic productivity** notion, legitimate and beneficial, refers human dignity that creates **sustainable autonomy**. The SRC has to foster the **development** of a society in which rules, institu- tions, circuits, and structures foster the respect and development of human dignity by imposing sanctions on those behaviors that degrade dignity. A staff treated with dignity is bound to show more **cooperation**. To cultivate, promote, and preserve dignity is *ethical* and **profitable**. But this latter point is part of socio-economic reasoning only by incidence. The dignity dimen- sion in SRC is based on the very foundation of **socio-economic management**, in other words shared and common work with a view to create shared value. It is in this equitable value distribution rather than the simple predation where the respect of the other dignity lies. Depriving stakeholders of the value that they have contributed to creating attacks their dignity because production and creation are manifestations of human dignity. Dignity is absent in the *speculator-parasite*, predator and unproductive. The SRC shows the value created between social performance (anthropological, physiological, sociological, economical needs satisfaction) and economic performance (rare resources exploitation and regulation).

In the objectives embedded in Hewlett Packard's mission statement in 1995, profit occupied the first rank because "Profit is the best single measure of our contribution to society and the ultimate source of our corporate strength." This affirmation was in perfect conformity with Milton Friedman's (1970) classic *New York Times Magazine* article—"The Social Responsibility of Business is to Increase its Profits." But, if we project ourselves in history, there are plenty of examples that show that humans have been seeking, in order to give meaning to their lives, deeper satisfactions than those given by sheer financial success. Mackey and Sisodia (2013), share this point of view when they wrote that the "heroic story" of free-enterprise Capitalism is one of entrepreneurs using their dreams and passions as fuel to create extraordinary value for customers, team members, suppliers, society and investors – for the whole gamut of stakeholders. For that purpose, ISEOR proposes organizational modes oriented to *persons*—individuals and teams—instead of focusing only on short-term economic objectives. The objective is not to only to seek rapid solutions but also to aim for **sustainable performance** that could be measured and experienced by all the stakeholders.

This dimension of SRC integrates the *qualimetric essence* of **performance evaluation**, connecting words to numbers, which is present in all types of organizations, for instance, hospitals as well as companies. We put forward work satisfaction, the quality of activities, and the entire responsibility of human beings along the continuum between professional and non-professional life. Our concept of **cognitive interactivity** is an essential principle of social responsibility. This principle is based on the fact that all the **actors** from all over the company should have their say in the decision-making or implementation process, in the vicinity of their local territory. One typical example is given to us by discussions about floodplains for construction without consultation from people who live here—and the resultant incoherence of the new constructible sectors, which represent as many **dysfunctions** that inevitably entail **hidden costs**. The framework that we propose recognizes the existence of frontiers, particularly legal ones, between the organization and its environment, but also insists on their *porosity* and the necessity to maintain *symbiosis* between organizations and their physical, economic, and social surrounding territory.

Synchronized Decentralization and Proximity Management

The principle of **synchronized decentralization** is a key point of the socio-economic approach to management. Within the framework of SRC, our conception of **proximity management** could be applied in territorial organizations, from the local to the national level as well within companies. The *intervention-research* carried out in these organizations lead us to demonstrate that centralization is the *root cause* of various dysfunctions and that observation could be applied to State (government) steering. Bring as close as possible the decision-making process to the perimeter, where those decisions could be applied, facilitates implementation and avoids absurd and costly consequences. For example, take the case of a highway segment built for a road that leads nowhere. We define the principle of synchronized decentralization as the "action of transferring the initiative of the decisive act to the responsibility level where its implementation will be launched, while setting up *game rules* that ensure its compatibility with actions from other zones of responsibility and with the *strategic piloting* of the entire organization" (Savall & Zardet, 1995, p. 482).

Decentralization allows developing initiatives from the most important number, undertaking forms such as human energy, creativity, engagement, and responsibility at the individual, team, and company levels. In order to be legitimate and sustainably effective, such initiatives should be compatible with one another – concerted, negotiated, orchestrated, synchronized, and stemming from the greatest number of individuals, groups, families, establishments and organizations they may concern. Socio-economic management helps to mobilize the entire *human potential*, using the synchronized decentralization of responsibilities, and the implementation of decisive acts by members of the management—the real pilots of their responsibility area. The centralized authority of decisions is balanced by more collegiality, aiming at fostering democratic reflexes relative to collective engagement.

Proximity management, at the heart of the socio-economic approach to management, is an effective response to the need of work recognition which, unsatisfied, leads organizational members to become disconnected from from objectives and frustrated. These aspects culminate with the dehumanization factor induced by wild capitalism. The socio-economic approach to management leads to an effective change management process because it facilitates staff animation and improved *communication* in all types of organization. It results in a decrease of dysfunctions, a boost in performance, and an improvement in *working conditions*. The value creation does appear in proximity. Hidden costs recycling contributes to "*micro-ecological*" well-being, in the way that it satisfies individual and collective needs—physiological, psychological, sociological, and economic —in other words *anthropological* needs. The analogy between hidden costs recycling and energy savings (human) is based on the very conviction that we could reach the same final result with lower energy spending, that we could measure both in value (cost) and in volume (time consumed).

Human Potential and Nano-GDP

No matter how important Keynes's contribution to economic thinking has been, the return to man, which he proclaimed, appears to have been rather hesitant and has not lived up to our expectations. In our attempts at economic theory, we are still a long way from incorporating man's real or potential behavior. Once new forms of job-design have been fully developed, the knowledge gained will force us to rewrite whole portions of economic theory.

Sustainably responsible capitalism readily questions the idea that by simply putting money into a company or a territorial organization one can make them more effective and dynamic. The *survival and development* of various organization types lie essentially in taking into account the underlying change strategy and *intangible investment in qualitative development of human potential*. This intangible investment is composed of costs induced by the *creation of potential* such as *integrated training* sessions, strategic and operational *project groups*, communication development, working conditions improvement, greater consideration given to the *internal and external environment*, and the development of managing skills for frontline managers. These costs should be considered as profitable investments instead of recurrent costs that reduce the operational result as they are described in accountancy norms.

Focusing efforts on intangible investment means investing in people, the key leverage point for improving and sustaining economic and *social performance*. This is the reason why we named "human potential," the primary factor of economic value production in the *socio-economic theory of organizations*, in order to separate it from the traditional concept of labor, used in various approaches of classical theory and its followers, as well neoclassic extensions, as Keynesian or Marxist critics. The *labor value theory* developed since the 19th century is incomplete and erroneous as it considers that the value of a product is composed of the amount of work and its costs. It doesn't make allowance for the fact that an *unsold* product doesn't have any value as long as no one asks for it, buys it, or pays for it.

Human potential is a factor of balance—*effectiveness and efficiency*. In order to increase efficient cooperation degree at all the company levels, it is necessary to reinforce *the intangible investment in human potential*. This investment does not consist of increasing the workforce nor activity hours but in transforming the quality of the three human potential components: individual and collective *energy, behavior, and competency*. The responsibility acquisition process that follows this investment drives to a dynamic balance in all the company sectors by facilitating the measure of individual responsibility in value creation. These are the roots of our *nano-GDP* concept.

The gross domestic product (GDP) is composed of the sum of all economic agents *value-added* for one country. It is a macroscopic and national prosperity indicator, aiming at measuring economic growth. In addition, the value-added on variable costs ratio (VAVC) measures the value created by a company and an organization. This ratio is calculated by subtracting from the turn-over the purchase value of component and supplies paid to other companies. Given that goods or services production needs to be realized as a human intervention, we could determine that the average economic value of a human activity, in a particular company, by dividing the VAVC from the sum of remunerated and realized hours – that is the *hourly contribution to the value-added on variable costs (HCVAVC)*. This economic *productivity* indicator is different from physical productivity and the production rate defined by Taylor and his disciples. This indicator takes into account not only the physical productivity from all the actors and support functions, but also of the *negotiation ability* of the company within its environment—*external stakeholders* (customers, suppliers, competitors, institutions) and *internal stakeholders* (shareholders, employees). This ability to negotiate is the primary factor of selling price level determination.

This global productivity indicator of an organization measures effectiveness and efficiency of human potential (HP) which, all things being equal, constitutes the primary value creation factor, composed of human energy, *competencies*, and behaviors (Savall, Péron, & Zardet, 2014). This factor focuses on individual responsibility, in *interaction* with team or other department's actors in the company, in order to create value and contribution to company prosperity. In contrast, this same individual could destroy value, by participating with others in various dysfunctions. As a matter of fact, the GDP depends on individual effectiveness and efficiency, combined with the collective actions at team, company, sector, local, regional and national levels. The HCVAVC could be qualified as nano-GDP because it is measuring the individual contribution of a person to his own prosperity, to his company's prosperity, and his own nation. The GDP and HCVAVC isomorphism shines the spotlight on the link between the person, the organization, and the national territory by focusing on different scales of economic responsibility (Savall, 2013a, 2013b; Savall & Zardet, 2010).

In matter of economic policy, the main issue for socio-economic theory is helping to explain *macroeconomic performance*, by focusing on each citizen's responsibility in national economic value creation. This theory plays down the macro-politic and macroeconomic (monetary and fiscal policies) factors that have dominated economic thinking since the Great Depression, which took place in 1929. It also shows their powerlessness in dealing with unemployment, economic growth, inflation, and financial crisis (Savall, 2012). Socio-economic theory and SRC restore to the citizen its rightful place in the economic concert, giving staff management in organization the key role in creating prosperity and well-being that has a democratic essence.

Taking into account human potential is a core issue in each and every sector of a company, an organization, a city, a regional state, and also a nation, whatever the size. This factor is essential in a proactive approach. Indeed, ISEOR's research focuses on misused human potential—unemployed, under-employed or over-employed—insofar as such a state of affairs leads to relationship conflicts and sources of value losses whatever the organization typology studied, and entails a plethora of *hidden costs*. In the framework of SRC, all the economic and social *actors* are considered as full members of an organization whose interests could merge. However, this convergence is not natural but established as the result of multiple negotiations between stakeholders. Our *contradictory intersubjectivity* principle consists of creating interactions between actors with different points of view, partly convergent and partly divergent or even contradictory. Our method of *successive iterations* is aimed at confronting explicitly the analysis from the different actors in order to identify convergences and specificities. These actors are not doomed to put up with their environment. They could act within the framework of a daily democratic process. This approach is in perfect conformity with our definition of human potential "*resources* that possess a person or a human group, the capacity of action, production, innovation, creation, *development* and transformation of his environment." Human potential could be defined as the *cooperation and interaction ability* of actors, companies and organizations, and also as their aptitude to create *real* economic value.

IMPLEMENTATION TOOLS OF THE SOCIO-ECONOMIC APPROACH TO MANAGEMENT

ISEOR continues to explore the development of a management method that would allow social and economic performance through the pivotal role attributed to *human potential* through the use of tools that are instrumental in *SEAM implementation*. As an example, we define our *internal and external strategic action plan (IESAP)* as a *management tool* that synchronizes all the *strategic objectives* for three, four, or five years. These objectives can be internally or externally focused within the territory in which companies operate. The strategic plan is updated each year to take into account the changes that have occurred in the environment and the objectives' degree of achievement. This bi-annual *Priority Action Plan* constitutes an effective management tool. By drawing up an inventory of the actions that they have to be accomplished, they can be translated in terms of time resources and prioritized by Priority Action Plans (PAP) to facilitate the ability to meet organizational objectives—whether concrete, virtual or even implicit in nature. They also aim to realize concrete operations, implementing adapted know-how, while insisting on the reduction of **dysfunctions** and hidden cost recycling into value-added (Savall & Zardet, 1995, p. 338).

A strategy of development implies the choice of judicious *warning indicators* aimed at a three- to five-year **strategic horizon**. Our conception of **strategic vigilance**, an active surveillance of both the **internal and external company environment**, transforms these indicators into a constructive, proactive, and dynamic aspect of **socio-economic management**.

The focus on human potential as the unique active factor in an entrepreneurial society, evolving in the framework of SRC, constitutes the key aspect of a collective engagement "culture." This is why unemployed potential represents a considerable hidden cost, because it results in psychological dissatisfaction, frustration, and lost opportunity costs. Examples abound, proving that a focus on this potential and the way it is mobilized could avoid *dysfunctions* that induce economic resources loss. In this connection when considering the growth factor, far from questioning its very existence or its basis, we have to make sure that it is compatible with a generalized improvement of **working conditions**.

The global corrupted and speculative context of wild capitalism, totalitarian regimes or military dictatorships has disastrous results for populations. This leads the electorate be disconnected with regard to elections and creates a dangerous *political absentionism*. ISEOR proposes, within its **tetranormalization** framework with its quadruple economic, social, financial, and environmental straitjacket that could slow down any creative dynamic, the concept of *managerial and entrepreneurial absentionism*. SRC is based on a prior research of factors that could impede **strategic development**, delaying or sterilizing decision-making actions, i.e., local dysfunctions in urbanism project implementation steps.

There are immediate consequences in the multitude of hidden costs, often revealed by the French Court of Auditors in their reports. As an example, a 3C (**communication-coordination-cooperation** practices) application has shown us that, in the building industry, a frequent consultation between actors from different professions enhances a more effective steering of the work, reducing conflicts between social and activity norms. The **socio-economic method** helps to measure the **profitability** of the investment in human potential. This method also demonstrates that **intangible investment** in the qualitative development of human potential is more profitable than each and every technological investment. It does take time to ensure the **integrated training** of actors and to continually renew it in innovative **project groups**, creating a **participative and structured management** for accompanying teams.

The SEAM Approach and Sustainable Responsibility

This methodology has been, thus far, introduced in 37 countries, as well as various company management levels, industries, territories, and governmental organizations. It consists of applying concepts and practices of **socio-economic theory**, founded on the only active factor that creates economic value—*human potential*—and the systematic research of *hidden costs* that could be *recycled* into value-added creation. These enhance the company's self-financing capacity and its debt level.

Forty years of interventions has allowed us to establish a rigorous typology, in a *universe* encumbered by standards and norms—in other words, *tetranormalized*. This situation requires the renewed analysis of the commercial, financial, social, and environmental models of organizations that constitute local, regional, national, or international territories. The in-depth and up-close observation of these models puts into light the distortions of the economic or social rules of the game, by confronting theories with observable reality.

The intervention and experimentation method developed by ISEOR, which has been carried out by 580 researchers on five continents in 1,310 companies and organizations, cuts across 72 industries (goods producing/industrial [35%], services [30%], and **public services** [35%]). It has also allowed us to refute the traditional two factors theory (capital and labor), by demonstrating that the real active factor in economic value creation is human potential opposed to *the inert nature of technical or financial capital*. Our **intervention-research** methodology has put light on the *gaps in and fragility of the traditional accountancy system*, also putting into question enterprise representations as they result from an anachronistic interpretation of organizational method principles stemming from Taylorism, Fayolism, and Weberism.

The kingpin in our SRC's vision is the Schumpeterian innovative and creative *entrepreneur*, opposed to the *speculator* in his or her exclusive search for profit in a led astray capitalism framework. The first one is integrated in the real economy, infusing a productive dynamic of value creation. The second one literally rejects each and every extension of entrepreneurship as well as intrapreneurship. It diverts resources to the benefits of a purely speculative virtual market, given over to sneaky predators. The SRC approach, in contrast, enhances real growth—which results in job creation. When capitalism goes astray it leads inescapably to financial bubbles, destroying resources and placing an array of economic agents and stakeholders in dangerous positions.

Economic activity often generates dysfunctions that could be observed at infra-, micro-, meso- and macro-scopic levels. These dysfunctions are destroying, at each period, effective **value-added** (historical costs) or potential value-added (opportunity costs). To these dysfunctions we can add an incessant multiplication of standards and norms that pose problems of costs and complexity. These norms are made obsolete by the technological evolution and are sometimes contradictory and considered as constraints. These constraints could have a beneficial effect on the efficient running of the company, in so far as they entailed positive behavioral and structural changes by giving a significant boost to the innovation process. Better still, anticipating future constraints could give a competitive advantage to a company. New norms could also stimulate innovative organizational practices. New constraints can serve as the yeast of creativity and responding to them can generate productive activities. Constraints are the daily routine's foe and stimulate organizational dynamic.

Such constraint, however, remains nevertheless one of the major foes of our entrepreneurial spirit. Flexibility against short-term strategies fosters this spirit. We have to be engaged for the long-term because tomorrow is more important than today. The sustainability that is the basis for our social and economic system efficacy and efficiency, which we advocate, opposes the versatility of norms that fail to meet real needs. All too often these norms are based on customer electoral considerations or pressures exerted by lobbies that aim to make money on their stock-in-trade.

This sustainability issue gets us back to the evolution of financial capitalism towards a dematerialization of time and space, in a global process. As an example, think about high frequency trading operations that focus on gaps that exist for seconds in order to influence stock transactions. These orientations don't go in the direction of a moralized market, leading instead to a perverted form of transparency. The ideal of pure and perfect information still remains a myth. The increase of this type of speculative operations, totally disconnected from the real economy, goes against SRC in the sense that it aims to contain, within reasonable limits, the destructive strengths of technology, excessive **regulation**, and oversized financial processes in order to stimulate life-quality. SRC is the closest and contributes more than any other to the concrete approach of *daily proximity democracy*, in companies as well as in territorial organizations.

Democracy in companies, and more largely at all the levels of the economic organization, is often held up to ridicule by this "unhealthy cut," which Jacques Delors mentions in his foreword *Enrichir le travail humain* (*Work and people*) (Savall, 1974). The spirit of **negotiation** is vital for a non-electoral democracy, which materializes only through daily dialogue. This spirit is supposed to prevail following the recent reform of the "labor market," with the new French pact of **competitiveness** agreed to by owners and union representatives. But this spirit seems to rarely turn up if we judge the level of tension that reigns in the course of conflicts or the brutality of planned redundancy schemes. In these latter contexts, the actors' inability to negotiate in an anticipated way compounded by a lack of courage in making anticipated decisions create an explosion of severe crises.

FINAL REFLECTION

The approach presented here is based on two postulates. Our first postulate claims that the dichotomy between life at work and life outside work is pure deception. Through SEAM and SRC we have implicitly upheld that the individual's cultural development creates new needs, which themselves imply an increase in production and work. Other scenarios, of course, have been put toward. Zero growth is one of them. Would it in this case be necessary to devote so much energy to job-design if the really important, progressive side of life were to be taking place outside work, or if the condition for the individual's development were to lie in a reduction of work? Seen from a strictly positive point of view, no present political, social, or economic regime has ever made such a choice voluntarily or consciously. We believe that there is a second factor that validates our thesis, namely the influence that working conditions have on our way of life. It is not be possible to improve the latter without improving the former.

Our second postulate assumes that the field of social and economic organization still remains untapped. The theme of specialization is a subject of universal debate. The success of the Taylor system can be explained by the convergence of a large number of evolutionary factors: ever greater scientific specialization, the subsequent educational specialization, the security provided by increasing specialized research, and increasingly hair-splitting research subjects. This evolution led to absurd situations—from the relative *incompetence* of specialists outside their own field and inability to communicate with others, to a seemingly growing inability to solve problems posed in practice. The most important recent advances have often been the result of a successful organization involved in one particular *project*, with the synthesis made by specialists who were able to communicate with one another. Perhaps this argues for a reversal of the trend forward specialization, which we advocate and which the most recent technological advances in the field of *communication* render obsolete.

The belief that *productivity* is synonymous with specialization and that the basis for an increase in productivity is to be found in mechanization and automation betrays a pessimistic view of human ability. Robots, supposed to kill employment in the not so distant future, have just shown their limits for the disposal of radioactive waste on the Fukushima site according to the deputy director of the Japanese Research Institute on intelligent systems. It has been proved that as long as it is not possible to overcome huge technical problems, there is no other solution than to organize work along lines that make for much greater human involvement.

It is our belief that the economist will find food for thought in the traditional paths that he or she clings to. Moreover, these individuals will ultimately have to accept the fact that these paths will be questioned as new contributions emerge from other areas of scientific investigation. Our study is a contribution to the epistemology of economic thought, a less and less exclusive prerogative of Marxists being currently brought into focus. Our socio-economic approach took up these issues some 40 years ago as it brought to light the necessity of widening the scope of economics to other sciences. Our research has brought to light the necessity to overcome the dichotomy between economic and social affairs, which has been institutionalized at the government level. The decentralization of semi-autonomous groups and their total quantitative and qualitative production calls into question the entire principle of economy of scale and industrial concentration benefits.

NOTE

1. The research for this chapter has been influenced by a number of works that are not directly referred to in the text, including Boje and Rosile (2003), Buono and Savall (2007), Gephart (2009), Perroux (1979), Savall (1981, 2010), Savall and Zardet (1987, 1992, 2011), and Savall, Zardet, and Bonnet (2000, 2008).

REFERENCES

Boje, D., & Rosile, G.-A. (2003). Comparison of socio-economic and other trans-organizational development methods. *Journal of Change Organizational Management, 16*(1), 10–20.

Braudel, F. (1986). *Civilisation matérielle, économie et capitalisme XVe-XVIIIe siècle* [Material civilization, economy and capitalism XVth-XVIIIth century]. Paris, France: Armand Collin.

Buono, A. F., & Savall, H. (Eds.). (2007). *Socio-economic intervention in organizations: The intervener-researcher and the SEAM approach to organizational analysis.* Charlotte, NC: Information Age Publishing.

Chandler, D. (2014). Morals, markets and values-based businesses. *Academy of Management Review, 39*(3), 396–406.

Friedman, M. (1970, September 13). The social responsibility of business is to increase its profits. *New York Times Magazine*, p. 32.

Gephart, R. P. (2009). An invitation to ethnostatistics. *Revue Sciences de gestion – Management Sciences – Ciencias de Gestión, 70*, 85.

Mackey, J., & Sisodia, R. (2013). *Conscious capitalism: Liberating the heroic spirit of business.* Boston, MA: Harvard Business School Press.

Nouveau Larousse Universel [New Universal Larousse]. (1969). *Capitalisme* [Capitalism]. *Nouveau Larousse Universel*, *1*, 276.

Perroux, F. (1948). *Capitalisme, Que sais-je? [Capitalism, I know that?]*, Paris, France: Presses Universitaires de France.

Perroux, F. (1979). L'entreprise, l'équilibre rénové et les coûts cachés [The enterprise, the renovated balance and the "hidden" costs]. Preface in H. Savall. *Reconstruire l'entreprise* [Reconstructing the enterprise] Paris, France: Dunod. 2nd ed. in H. Savall & V. Zardet. Reconstruire l'entreprise, Paris: Dunod (2014).

Savall, H. (1974–1975–1977). *Enrichir le travail humain dans les entreprises et les organisations* [An economic evaluation of job enrichment]. Paris: Dunod.

Savall, H. (1981–2010). *Work and people: An economic evaluation of job enrichment.* 1st ed. New-York: Oxford University Press ; 2nd ed. Charlotte, NC: Information Age Publishing.

Savall, H. (2010). *Individu, enterprise et nation: Comment se crée le PIB?* [Individual, enterprise and nation: How is the GDP created?]. In G. Blardone & H. Savall, Agir dans un nouveau monde: Le développement et les coûts de l'Homme [Act a new world: Development and the costs of man]. 12e journée François Perroux organized by Association François Perroux. Ecully, France: ISEOR.

Savall, H. (2012). *Origine radicale des crises économiques: Germán Bernácer, précurseur visionnaire* [Root origin of crises: Germán Bernácer, a visionary forerunner]. Charlotte, NC: Information Age Publishing.

Savall, H., Péron, M., Zardet, V. (2014, April). *Human potential at the care of socio-economic theory* (SEAM). Paper presented at the SEAM Colloquim, Minneapolis, MN.

Savall, H., & Zardet, V. (1987). *Maîtriser les coûts et les performances cachés : Le contrat d'activité périodiquement négociables* [Mastering hidden costs and performance: The periodically negotiable activity contract]. Paris: Economica.

Savall, H., & Zardet, V. (1992). *Le nouveau contrôle de gestion: Méthode des coûts-performances cachés* [New management control: The hidden cost-performance method]. Paris: Éditions Comptables Malesherbes-Eyrolles

Savall, H., & Zardet, V. (1995–2005–2009). *Ingénierie stratégique du roseau, souple et enracinée* [Strategic engineering of the reed, flexible and rooted]. Paris: Economica.

Savall, H., & Zardet, V. (2008). *Mastering hidden costs and performance.* Charlotte, NC: Information Age Publishing.

Savall, H., & Zardet, V. (2011). *The qualimetrics approach: Observing the complex object.* Charlotte, NC: Information Age Publishing.

Savall, H., & Zardet, V. (2013a). *The dynamics and challenges of tetranormalization.* Charlotte, NC: Information Age Publishing.

Savall, H., & Zardet, V. (2013b, October). *La RSE, lieu entre l'individu, l'organisation et la société: nouvel énoncé de la théorie Socio-Économique* [SCR, link between individual, organization and society: New statement of the socio-economic theory]. Paper presented at the annual ADERSE Conference, Lyon, France.

Savall, H., Zardet, V., & Bonnet, M. (2000-2008). *Releasing the untapped potential of enterprises through socio-economic management.* Geneva: Éditions IOT-BIT.

CHAPTER 6

THE IMPORTANCE OF THE QUALIMETRICS MEASUREMENT METHODOLOGY IN ASSESSING THE IMPACT OF SOCIO-ECONOMIC INTERVENTION[1]

Henri Savall, Robert Gephart, and Marc Bonnet

This chapter is aimed at showing the need for a methodology to measure the impacts of *socio-economic interventions*. Indeed, CEOs and consultants often assert that costs have been cut or that revenue and *profitability* have increased thanks to their action, proving that intervention objectives have been met. This type of anecdotal approach to evaluating interventions, however, only partially maps out the real impacts. For example, evaluations carried out by the ISEOR research center demonstrate that cutting visible costs in the short run often results in *hidden costs* increase in far higher proportion than savings on visible costs. This is particularly due to the

The Socio-Economic Approach to Management Revisited: The Evolving Nature of SEAM in the 21st Century, pp. 119–130

impacts of cost cutting on loss of skills and/or low morale. Another example is the hidden impacts of an intervention. When an intervention triggers a lot of *development* actions, it seemingly results in higher costs, because a large amount of time is devoted to *sustainable performance* as opposed to *immediate results* only. Such a development is only partly considered as an investment, while the impacts of the intervention do create potential profitability in the following years, hence underestimating the impacts of the intervention. Managers might then be prone to reduce the cost of intervention, which might be detrimental to the *project*'s overall coherence when doing away with key components, such as an accompaniment of the intervention by *external interveners*.

One can therefore form the hypothesis that the *evaluations* of intervention impacts are not at all comprehensive, which is detrimental to the quality of project implementation in companies. Indeed, usual costs and performance measurements do not fit with the need to assess sustainable performance of organizations nor their ability to change, because those measures are mostly focused on short-term visible *economic performance*. Performance metrics, when they do exist, are coarse and partial. We'll see later in this chapter that this hypothesis is shared with the ethnostatistics approach to *scientific observation* of organizations. Therefore, it is necessary to focus on intervention impact measurements, refraining from only resorting to static and partial indicators. The chapter will show how the *qualimetrics* method enables both scholars and practitioners to set up a reliable and scientific evaluation of intervention impacts.

EVALUATING THE DYNAMIC IMPACTS OF CHANGE PROCESSES

Throughout the history of science, human beings have always strived to create instruments, concepts, and tools aimed at demonstrating hypotheses. However, measuring organization life and transformation is difficult, as it requires the ability to capture complex, dynamic, and ever moving phenomena, and the conflict between quantitative and qualitative approaches to measurement is unfruitful.

Supporters of purely quantitative approaches to evaluation reject qualitative methods considered as non-scientific because of the lack of figures, which are seen as essential in the fields of management and decision making. However, figures produced in quantitative approaches to organization only have surface scientific semblance—actually, they are partial, static, and biased. Indeed, if purely quantitative data reduce complexity through a digest of data, they impoverish the relevant set of data needed to log the intervention targeted impacts. To give an example, a low rate of *absenteeism* may conceal frequent delayed arrivals that hinder organizational processes. A 10-minute delay is seemingly nothing, but the whole project team finalizing the development of a new project that customers are awaiting remains stranded. Only resorting to statistics and figures also contributes to dehumanizing management due to the focus on a partial aspect of company performance. This dynamic occurs, for example, when employees are due to prepare a project to improve the quality of service, while pay reward systems are only based on sales increase in the short run.

As for the supporters of qualitative approaches, they consider that figures are not meaningful. A customer satisfaction score may be improving, for example, but these critics would question whether it really makes sense when satisfaction criteria have not been properly defined and when the point of view of those clients who did not reply has been discarded. In addition, quantitative analyses are often criticized for skipping past the richness of qualitative data. A quantitative approach to evaluating the cancellation of a so-called costly project may downplay impacts on the involvement of company *actors*, with the *risk* of losing loyalty of highly skilled and performing employees.

Such a battle between supporters of quantitative and qualitative approaches don't contribute to overcoming the difficulties of intervention impact assessment, because they mostly result in an ill-assorted match between qualitative and quantitative evaluations, like in the case of a blind man and a cripple. An example of discrepancies is a rise of customer satisfaction rate, while potential customers have not even been considered.

The ethno-statistics approach (Gephart, 1988) sheds light on such contradictions, as it questions the reliability of data in three domains: (1) quality of data capturing; (2) data processing; and (3) the rhetoric of statistics (i.e., how the figures are used to make good of decisions that are based on implicit ideological underpinnings).

Low Quality of Data Capturing

The captured set of data that is aimed at evaluating intervention impact is typically partial and distorted. For example, a seeming increase in *productivity* may conceal employee disenchantment if they are not properly rewarded, along with a risk of low involvement or resignation within a few months. Thus, it is important to ensure an overall analysis of the multifaceted intervention impacts.

Ill-Designed Data Processing

Evaluation data on intervention impacts tend to be distorted and partial. In particular, weak signals on the evolution of a brand image may be considered as insignificant, or faded due to an overall customer satisfaction score. However, such a signal might be considered as a precursory symptom of profitability increase in the short run.

Rhetoric of the Analysis of Impacts

Often times, results that are put forward are presented and used in a biased way in order to influence decision-making processes, as each stakeholder tries to appropriate the positive impacts. For example, a management consulting company might highlight short-term results in order to renew its contract with the client, even though downsides might exist in particular with respect to the long-term impacts of the intervention.

QUALIMETRICS EVALUATION METHODOLOGY OBJECTIVES

When Henri Savall created the *socio-economic theory of organizations* in 1974, his objective was to evaluate the importance of *human potential* while rejecting the concept of human capital, which implicitly surmised the spontaneous subordination of employees to their superior as well as company ownership of the value *creation of human potential*. This objective required the development of a new ontology and epistemology of measurement, since usual performance measures were considered biased and marked by cleaving economic and social dimensions. This bias was compounded by a focus that was limited to both visible factors of value production (i.e., capital and work), discarding the pivotal role of human potential to create value.

This approach is differentiated from the attempts in the 1960s where the main objective was to analyze investments in human resources in terms of costs (Likert, 1974). The objective of *qualitative, quantitative, and financial evaluation* methods, later referred to as the qualimetrics approach (Savall & Zardet, 2004) was to turn the hidden side of organizational phenomena into visible data in order to take more thoughtful, rational, and relevant decisions. This approach consists of criticizing biased and partial measurements, which leave a large part of the underlying performance phenomena in the dark. Therefore, it was necessary to solve tricky phenomena measurement issues, such as the impact of a lack of attractiveness of a company for its employees.

The approach required more reliable data, which would be meaningful for those who analyze them to improve a situation. It was not meant to comprehensively measure all phenomena, as it is not possible for a person to capture the cost of losing one's arm or one's life, because the analysis of human life is incommensurate (Kuhn, 1962), but rather to contribute to the creation of data aimed at improving a situation. The objective of the qualimetrics approach was not only mapping out a phenomenon. It was also a phenomenon as such, because it was aimed at becoming a knowledge creation process, impacting the actors' behavior as well as their impact on the *social performance* and *economic performance* of organizations.

Definition of the Qualimetrics Methodology

The qualimetrics research method is aimed at better depicting the life and multi-faceted human behaviors in organizations and organizational dynamics, considered as a complex object, through measuring the depth and breadth of organizational phenomena. It attempts to perfect qualitative data expressed in terms of key-words through adding quantitative and financial data. The qualimetrics approach is based on the observation that a number requires an idea to convey its meaning. Conversely, an idea requires a number to make sense of it. As a result, the qualimetrics approach differs from qualitative or quantitative evaluation methods as well as those which are limited to juxtaposing qualitative and quantitative data, because qualimetrics *integrates* qualitative and quantitative data as complementary measurements of the very phenomenon.

The three types of measurements are aimed at describing the same phenomenon observed from different angles—when measurement is not feasible, words are used, but works and numbers are the components of the same measurement. During the ***intervention-research*** processes, qualimetrics measurement enhances the relevance of action and decision making thanks to improved processes of capturing and interpreting the data necessary to design innovative improvement actions.

Epistemological Pillars of the Qualimetrics Measurement

The qualimetrics approach rests on three epistemological concepts: ***cognitive interactivity***, ***contradictory intersubjectivity***, and ***generic contigency***.

Cognitive Interactivity

This principle draws on an ***interaction*** process between ***intervener-researchers*** and company actors. However clever a person might be, he or she can't produce by himself of herself a comprehensive knowledge of a complex phenomenon, because there is a need for a variety of points of view. Cognitive interactivity broadens the scope of rationality through taking into account viewpoints that are ignored by usual measurement methods (see Figure 6.1). As illustrated in Figure 6.2, it also enables a multi-dimensional analysis of data. Indeed, it is necessary to share the various actors' representations in order to better map out the complexity of a situation under survey. The qualimetrics approach assumes that each and every human being has a partial analysis of phenomena and that all of them should be involved to get a comprehensive and relevant representation of the complexity. As a result, the qualimetrics methodology enables a multi-dimensional representation (Savall,1979; Savall & Zardet, 2014).

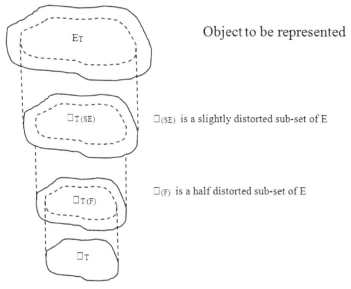

Object to be represented

$\square_{(SE)}$ is a slightly distorted sub-set of E

$\square_{(F)}$ is a half distorted sub-set of E

Source: Savall (1974, 1981).

Figure 6.1.   Compared biases of various representation models.

In the qualimetrics method, financial data are required to better take into account the **resources** needs, as they can be costly. Financial data are therefore needed in addition to qualitative and quantitative data, which interactive cognitivity makes possible through broadening the scope of data.

Contradictory Intersubjectivity

Contradictory intersubjectivity consists of capturing data provided by actors or groups of actors whose points of views are differentiating *a priori* and pointing out the intersection across elements, which can be considered as understandable by each of them. It is an alternative to objectivity, which is considered as unattainable because there is no pure truth in the field of organizational transformation. Contradictory intersubjectivity seeks to work through the unfruitful conflict between *objectivity versus subjectivity*. Successive iterations enable the creation of intangible, complex, and moving phenomena. It results in a limited and transient consensus that helps company actors enhance learning processes and better question their subjectivity. Contradictory intersubjectivity rests on a gradual knowledge creation process, thanks to the calculation of **hidden costs** and performance observed in a given situation, referred to as a *socio-technical system*. The following steps include testing innovative solutions to master

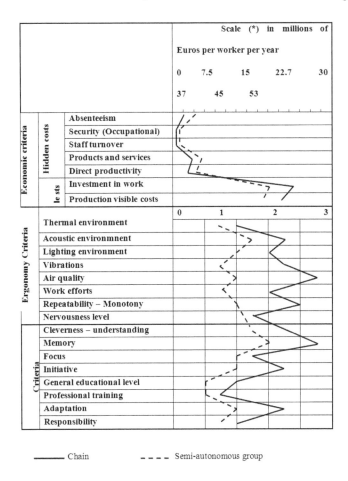

Figure 6.2.   Multi-dimensional evaluation of two organizational designs of the same production process in an industrial company.

those costs and measure the impacts of the intervention on both *social performance* and *economic performance*. The knowledge creation process is an endless phenomenon because knowledge is considered as changing in the qualimetrics approach as a way of enhancing significance. Information is dated according to the specific data capturing setting and period. The significance or interpretation of figures depends on the performance measurement period.

Generic Contingency
This perspective surmises the existence of invariants, which are generic rules (i.e., a body of knowledge featured by a minimal steadiness and uni-

versality). The qualimetrics approach simultaneously differentiates and connects *specific* and **generic knowledge**. Evaluating **intervention impacts** through the qualimetrics method facilitates the production of two complementary bodies of knowledge: (1) one that is specific to the context of the company or organization (contingency), while (2) the other is a scientific intent knowledge creation, considered as valid whatever the organization features. The **generic contingency** principle has enabled SEAM to build a generic body of knowledge that provides a framework to analyze organizations and their **socio-economic performance**, in spite of their variety.

PARTICIPATIVE DIMENSION OF QUALIMETRICS EVALUATION

There are two additional dimensions of the qualimetrics approach that further contribute to the robust nature of its data, the ability to capture: 1) the diversity of perspectives in an organization; and 2) informal insight and knowledge into what is happening in the organization.

Capturing the Diversity of Organizational Actor Cleverness

Similar to ethnostatistics, the qualimetrics approach shows that a form of intelligence is downplayed by usual performance metrics. Indeed, the qualimetrics method consists of a *shared* knowledge creation process, as opposed to other approaches where *actors* are considered as mere objects. It is thus the opposite of the *positivist* assumption where actors are not involved in order to avoid subjectivity. The qualimetrics approach can't be implemented without involving the actors because they produce information that creates value added shared by the different **stakeholders.** It results in building up and energizing collective intelligence, as a condition for team-building. Indeed, when company actors interact in a socio-economic process, they simultaneously use qualitative, quantitative, and financial data that are required to calculate hidden costs and performance. The qualimetrics methodology consists of creating those data through the interactive cognitivity process that involves all actors and groups in the organizations so as to facilitate realistic innovations and enhance **socio-economic performance**. The qualimetrics method enables one to better describe, explain, and prescribe organizational interventions based on an **information system** that is more comprehensive than usual **management tools**.

Ethnostatisics and qualimetrics are on the same page when they question the flaws of usual management performance measurements. Indicators usually implemented by **management control** do not measure **intangible investments**, nor the hidden costs stemming from decision-making processes only based on visible and partial data produced by usual measurement models.

Qualimetrics Methodology as a Negotiation Process

The qualimetrics approach helps stakeholders to better cooperate in generating data on the complexity of company performance drivers. By better mapping the complexity of organizational phenomena, the qualimetrics approach also facilitates the **negotiation** process across company actors, because it spurs the measurement of **hidden variables** that they consider as important. The qualimetrics method is *per se* a negotiation method that enhances socio-economic performance. It facilitates decision making, but it is not aimed at providing ready-made solutions in the decision process consisting of bringing together all actors to create custom-made solutions that fit a specific setting. It results in transforming the natural power of the actors to resist into a power aimed at creating value. It also prompts individual and collective intelligence.

The **qualimetrics evaluations** of **socio-economic interventions** demonstrate that such interventions enhance the coherence of objectives within companies and organizations, and that they result in improved quality of life in the short term and in more **sustainable development** in the long run. Indeed, it develops the foundation for a more humane management as well as improved individual and collective human development.

The qualimetrics methodology contributes to a **citizenship science** in the field of change management. Any private individual, as a citizen, needs measurement in his or her private life as well as time allotment, financial resources, satisfaction, delays, or distances. Individuals practice qualimetrics *mutatis mutandis* in their personal and professional life, literally owning a kind of information system and qualimetrics knowledge that takes stock of the learning drawn from experience. Whatever the position in the organization, the individual can therefore contribute to the organization, measuring and participating in the improvement of information, actions, and decision-making systems.

DEVELOPING A MORE SCIENTIFICALLY ROBUST MANAGEMENT CONSULTING PRACTICE

The qualimetrics evaluations of intervention impacts enable the creation of both a contingent knowledge, useful for the organizations, and a generic knowledge, useful for all. It differentiates from usual knowledge creation in the field of management consulting, where the objective is far too often to simply copy-paste an irrelevant solution and quick fix that have been designed in a variety of different settings. Qualimetrics methodology differs from non-scientific management consulting, where rough and partial measurement is observed, as qualimetrics enables the evaluation of intervention impacts through a structured and replicable methodology, similar to the process in all other scientific fields.

The fact that a large part of the economic performance of companies and organizations is not measured also tallies with the hidden factors of economic growth, as mentioned in Chapter 2. Each productive hour in a company corresponds to a ***nano-GDP***. Each wasted hour due to ***dysfunctions*** is a hidden micro destruction of the local, territorial dimension of national GDP, while each hour devoted to development ***projects*** in a company contributes to its future growth in terms of ***creation of potential***, as well as to local territorial or national growth.

The qualimetrics approach can be implemented at any company level, territory level or national level, based on the ***isomorphism*** principle (see Chapter 1), as it connects private individuals, organizations, and micro-, meso- and macro-levels of the social and economic fields.

Like other sciences that experience breakthroughs when measurement and analysis are improved, the qualimetrics approach contributes to creating knowledge about the dynamics of change management processes. The qualimetrics methodolology is therefore part and parcel of the history of sciences because it is aimed at creating measurement tools that enable improved ***human potential*** development and respect. Such an epistemological, methodological, and theoretical innovation calls for better information and training of academics, management consultants, and managers in order to create valid knowledge in the field of change management and organizational development.

NOTE

1. The research for this chapter has been influenced by a number of works that are not directly referred to in the text, including Boje (2001, 2004, 2008), Moisdon (1984), Nobre (2013), Perroux (1979), Savall and Zardet (1992, 1995, 2005, 2009, 2013), and Talaszka (2013).

REFERENCES

Boje, D. M. (2001). *Narrative methods for organizational and communication research*. London, England: SAGE.

Boje, D. M. (2004). Preface. In H. Savall & V. Zardet (Eds.), *Recherche en sciences de gestion: Approche qualimétrique. Observer l'objet complexe* [Research in management science: Qualimetric approach: Observing the complex object]. Paris, France: Economica.

Boje, D. M. (2008). *Storytelling organizations.* London, England: SAGE.

Boje, D., & Rosile, G.-A. (2003). Comparison of socio-economic and other trans-organizational development methods. *Journal of Change Organizational Management,* pp. 10–20

Buono, A., & Savall, H. (Eds.). (2007). *Socio-economic intervention in organizations: The intervener-researcher and the SEAM approach to organizational analysis.* Charlotte, NC: Information Ages Publishing.

Gephart, R. P. (1988). *Ethnostatistics: Qualitative foundations for quantitative research.* Newbury Park, CA: Sage.

Gephart, R. P. (1993). The textual approach: Risk and blame in disaster sense-making. *Academy of Management Journal, 36*(2), 1465–1514.

Gephart, R. P. (2009). An Invitation to Ethnostatistics. *Revue Sciences de gestion – Management Sciences – Ciencias de Gestión, 70,* 85.

Kuhn, T. S. (1962). *The structure of scientific revolutions.* Chicago, IL: University of Chicago Press.

Likert, R. (1974). *Le gouvernement participatif de l'entreprise* [Enterprise participative governance]. Paris, France: Gauthier-Villars.

Mayo, E. (1946). *The human problems of an industrial civilization,* Boston, MA: Harvard University division of research, graduate school of business administration.

Moisdon, J.-C. (1984). Recherche en gestion et intervention [Management Research and Intervention]. *Revue Française de Gestion* [French Management Review].

Nobre, T. (2013). *L'innovation managériale à l'hôpital* [Managerial innovation in hospital]. Paris, France: Dunod.

Perroux, F. (1979). L'entreprise, l'équilibre rénové et les coûts cachés [The enterprise, the renovated balance and the "hidden" costs]. Preface. In H. Savall. *Reconstruire l'entreprise* [Reconstructing the enterprise] Paris, France: Dunod. (2nd ed. in H. Savall & V. Zardet. Reconstruire l'entreprise, Paris: Dunod (2014)).

Savall, H. (1973). *G. Bernácer: L'hétérodoxie en science économique* [G. Bernácer: Heterodoxy in economics]. Paris, France: Dalloz.

Savall, H. (1974–1975–1977). *Enrichir le travail humain dans les entreprises et les organisations* [An economic evaluation of job enrichment]. Paris: Dunod.

Savall, H. (1979). *Reconstruire l'entreprise: Analyse socio-économique des conditions de travail* [Reconstructing the enterprise: Socio-economic working conditions analysis] (Preface by F. Perroux). Paris, France: Dunod.

Savall, H. (1981–2010). *Work and people: An economic evaluation of job enrichment.* (1st ed. New-York: Oxford University Press ; 2nd ed. Charlotte, NC: Information Age Publishing).

Savall, H. (2012). *Origine radicale des crises économiques: Germán Bernácer, précurseur visionnaire* [Root origin of crises: Germán Bernácer, a visionary forerunner]. Charlotte, NC: Information Age Publishing.

Savall, H., & Zardet, V. (1987). *Maîtriser les coûts et les performances cachés : Le contrat d'activité périodiquement négociables* [Mastering hidden costs and performance: The periodically negotiable activity contract]. Paris: Economica.

Savall, H., & Zardet, V. (1992). *Le nouveau contrôle de gestion: Méthode des coûts-performances cachés* [New management control: The hidden cost-performance method]. Paris: Éditions Comptables Malesherbes-Eyrolles

Savall, H. & Zardet, V. (1995-2005-2009). *Ingénierie stratégique du roseau, souple et enracinée* [Strategic engineering of the reed, flexible and rooted]. Paris: Economica.

Savall, H., & Zardet, V. (2008). *Mastering hidden costs and socio-economic performance.* Charlotte, NC: Information Age Publishing.

Savall, H., & Zardet, V. (2011). *The qualimetrics approach: Observing the complex object.* Charlotte, NC: Information Age Publishing.

Savall, H., & Zardet, V. (2013). *The dynamics and challenges of tetranormalization.* Charlotte, NC: Information Age Publishing.

Savall, H., Zardet, V., & Bonnet, M. (2000–2008). *Releasing the untapped potential of enterprises through socio-economic management.* Geneva: Éditions IOT-BIT.

Savall, H., & Zardet, V., (2014). *Reconstruire l'entreprise: Les fondements du management socio-économique* [Reconstructing the enterprise: Socio-economic analysis of working conditions]. Paris, France: Dunod.

Talaszka, H. (2013). Osons travailler ensemble [Dare to work together]. In Savall, H., Zardet, V., Bonnet, M. (Eds.), *Réindustrialisation et dynamisation multisectorielle* [Ripple effect in industrial companies, in reindustralization and multisectorial dynamic]. Paris, France: Economica.

PART III

INTRA-ORGANIZATIONAL INTERVENTION: SEAM IN DIFFERENT CONTEXTS

CHAPTER 7

ECONOMIC RECOVERY

From Company Restructuring to
Company Reconstruction[1]

Françoise Goter and Florence Noguera

In reaction to economic difficulties, companies often choose to resort to
a restructuring approach via social plans, thus hoping to restore and/or
improve their economic and financial *performance*. But if the objective of
company restructuring is to adapt to a changing environment or to restore
its *competitiveness*, the suppression or transformation of jobs that result
from it are experienced all the more painfully by the staff. Even when there
is planned redeployment towards new jobs, they still lack the necessary
effectiveness and efficiency in those new roles. For Beaujolin-Bellet (2014,
p. 5), a restructuring is a "managerial decision to modify the legal and
productive structures of the company which is likely to entail consequences
on employment and *working conditions*."

Restructurings, attributable to a sector in crisis or not, have become a
common phenomenon in the lives of companies and organizations. Yet,
while they have become increasingly frequent, they are nevertheless a very
complex phenomenon in their management, considering the elements

The Socio-Economic Approach to Management Revisited: The Evolving Nature of SEAM in the
21st Century, pp. 133–153
Copyright © 2015 by Information Age Publishing

of contingency that need to be taken into account, in particular, the economic, legal, and political environment. Indeed, restructuring constitutes one of the facets of human resource management that causes the most controversy and represents the largest potential for conflict. The literature indicates that a large number of organizations, after being restructured, are depressed and even lethargic (Appelbaum, Simpson, & Shapiro, 1987). While the objective consists of increasing efficiency and *productivity* inside the organization (Cascio, 1993; Kets De Vries & Balazs, 1997; Mishra, Spreitzer, & Mishra, 1998; Mone, 1994), numerous companies have to deal with an increase in *hidden costs* (Savall & Zardet, 1994; Mckinley, Sanchez, Schick, & Higgs, 1995). Indeed, restructuring within the framework of social plans often contributes to the deterioration of the social climate and leads to a weakening of the role of the hierarchy. Several questions arise: In what way is it possible to restore the trust of the employees after a restructuring within the framework of unaccompanied social plans? What is the role of the human resources department and the management in this reconstruction?

Our research advocates the idea that, in order to limit the perverse effects and hidden costs of restructuring, the company should set up a *socio-economic intervention* approach that relies on innovative human resources management. Based on an *intervention—research* carried out since 2010 in a company specializing in technical and ornamental textiles —this chapter attempts to capture the economic, social, and managerial difficulties of restructuring within the framework of the economic recovery of an organization. In particular, the discussion highlights the *dysfunctions* and hidden costs of badly accompanied social plans. The second part of the chapter proposes an approach to *socio-economic accompaniment* based on the implementation of a *project* reconciling economic and social imperatives (Cappelletti, Baker, & Noguera, 2011). This approach relies on the introduction of innovative managerial practices allowing us to resume the social dialogue with the *actors* of the company, delving into the conditions of well-being and sustainable performance. The third part describes the economic recovery and level of development of the *human potential* in the company after four years of socio-economic intervention, but also the limits connected to the reconstruction. The chapter concludes with our assessment of the key points linked to the reconstruction of a company.

A FAMILY COMPANY IN GREAT ECONOMIC DIFFICULTY

The socio-economic intervention was carried out in a French industrial SME (*small and medium sized enterprise*) specialized in the manufacture of ornamental and technical textiles, sold mainly to blind manufacturers

(B to B). Established in 1951, the family company's the three directors—children of the company's founder—decided to sell the company in 2005 to a large foreign group. The acquiring firm, a world leader in sun protection, had 17,000 employees and generated revenues of 2.5 billion U.S. dollars. At the time, the company consisted of a main Factory (Factory A) situated in a rural area of France where its headquarters are located, with subsidiaries in the United States, Australia, and Spain. In 2007, the Group acquired a second factory (Factory B), situated a few kilometers away from the company and belonging to one of their biggest competitors. After analyzing the possible synergies, the Group decided to eliminate all the support services in Factory B. All that was retained was the presence of the payroll accountant and some visits from an IT specialist to operate a minimum service.

At the end of 2009, the three directors who had kept their function within the company, decided to retire. One of the three brothers proposed to the new salaried manager, who had just been recruited by the Group, to stay on for 18 months to help him in the running of the company.

In less than 10 years, the arrival of Asian competition forced the directors to give up certain strategic fields of activity, such as wall coverings. The effects of the crisis on the user companies, in particular in the sectors of the hotel business and catering, also had a significant impact on sales. The *turnover* of Factory A fell by 60 percent in two years, and by 30% in Factory B.

At the time of the launch of the socio-economic intervention (April, 2010), the financial losses accumulated by the company amounted to 19 million euros. The administrative, financial, sales, and human resources directors of the time as well as the historic shareholders left the company. Factory A was ageing because of the absence of innovation and renewal of production tools (e.g., corporate offices and machines).

The Hidden Costs in Restructuring

In numerous cases, restructuring is intended to lead to financial improvement for the company. These transformations, however, become problematic when they call into question the relation between the company and its employees. Indeed, either this relation is broken, in the case of redundancies, or the working conditions are substantially modified under one or other of their dimensions (e.g., remuneration, organization, work content). In 2009, the company under study, considering its economic and financial situation, was forced to implement a workforce reduction plan. This plan mainly concerned Factory B, transitioning from 150 to 50 employees. Eventually, within one year, two plans aimed at preserving jobs were undertaken within this unit, resulting in the departure of 20 percent of the employees.

The *socio-economic diagnoses* carried out in the aftermath of the implementation of the social plan revealed that the atmosphere within the company had considerably deteriorated, largely due to a combination of the economic crisis, the acquisition of company, and difficulties within the company as reflected by verbatim statements taken from the diagnoses (see Table 7.1). This bad working atmosphere was evidenced by numerous disputes and conflicts between both merged entities (Factories A and B).

Table 7.1.   Extracts From Field-Note Quotes

- "We are still in a dynamic of layoffs and loss of skills. There is a will to close the texturation workshop of Factory B. The problem is that they have not explained why they want to do that."

- "All the people in charge of Factory B have no more decision-making power. They feel a little sidelined. They live as if in an outside factory to which we give orders."

- "The working atmosphere has strongly deteriorated. There are no exchanges and we can feel very strong tension between the people from the department."

- "People wonder where we are going and if management is making the correct strategic choices. For example, they had said that they would touch nothing in acrylic in the confection, and the people were eventually redeployed."

- "When my colleague left the company, there was no reorganization of the department."

The economic *evaluation* of the dysfunctions connected to the deterioration of the social climate and the organization of the work represented 1,539,800 euros of hidden costs (see Table 7.2). This bad feeling within the company manifested itself in the additional cost of long-term temporary staff linked to long term absences, shifts in function, defects in *work organization* and an improper division of responsibilities, or missions between employees, given the absence of an organization chart. The results also reveal important failures in the management of human resources: a mismanagement of compensatory leave connected to the reduction in working hours, holiday leave and modulation hours, a mismanagement of the *schedules*, difficulties in the *piloting* of the training plan which translates as unimplemented training initiatives. These weaknesses also come out through a lack of skills in certain professions such as weaving and coating.

The legal *diagnosis* also revealed significant liabilities. There were 53 social disputes and three cases lodged in commercial court for damages of the order of 16 million euros, which represents a very high cost for this company.

Table 7.2.   Hidden Costs of Restructuring

Diagnosed Sectors	Elementary Dysfunctions	Economic Effects
Factory A	Shifting of function in visits	1,290 €
	Additional costs of long term temporary staff	26,690 €
	Excessive breaks	2,110 €
	Unjustified changes of procedure	2,720 €
	Lack of personnel in coating.	152,730 €
	Shifting of function in sequencing – scheduling	7,180 €
Sales, Marketing and R&D	Institution of collection unimplemented	16,800 €
	Geographic distancing of the 2 sampling departments	6,040 €
	Realization of low valued added tasks by salespeople	13,380 €
	Conflict between people (sampling)	1,550 €
	Defects in the coherence of the organization of the department	12,660 €
Support Services	Unimplemented training plan	54,000 €
	Shifting of function in Purchases	4,040 €
	Absence of organization chart	8,440 €
	Difficulty in accessing staff files for one site	1,650 €
	Leave remaining, reduction in working hours, hours of modulation.	800,000 €
	Shifting of function in the IT department	55,410 €
Factory B	Shifting of function in the Quality department	24,860 €
	Mismanagement of files	14,350 €
	Lack of weaving skills	35,730 €
	Institution of partial unemployment badly managed	1,210 €
	Deactivation of weaving in the evening	8,440 €
	Lack of weavers	288,520 €
	Total Amount	1,539,800 €

Deficient Managerial Practices

The analysis of the dysfunctions through the socio-economic diagnoses allowed us to highlight the main root-causes of restructuring mismanagement in the company. The lack of leadership at every level and in all functions is one of the first root-causes, indeed, the absence of a chain of command and a lack of authority are the source of numerous dysfunctions. Second, the absence of *communication-coordination-cooperation*

(3Cs) systems in the company, as machinery for thoughtful and articulated decision making and action, provoked a serious deficiency in the contribution of managerial energy and a lack of teamwork, essential for the recovery of the company. On a related point, the important vertical subdivision between the hierarchical and horizontal (between departments) levels, caused an explosion across the departments and a lack of dialogue between the people in charge of every set of tasks (e.g., coating, warping, weaving, thermofixation). The lack of clarity in the internal-external company strategy (means-objectives) is the third cause of restructuring mismanagement. For example, from the point of view of the management of human resources, the lack of efficient managerial and weaving practices makes the allocation and realization of certain missions difficult; from the point of view of *external strategy*, the inherent difficulties with reference to the plethora of products or *research and development* also illustrate the absence of a marketing strategy. Another root-cause concerns the defect of piloting of activities and teams, one of those indicators that points to an inability to make fast and efficient decisions, because they are too complex or ineffective. Key indicators in certain domains are also missing, such as the number of customer complaints and the way in which those complaints were processed.

Failures in human resources management policy were also a root-cause of restructuring mismanagement. Indeed, in spite of a painful social plan, we noticed that the staff did not fully understand the gravity of the situation for the company. It led to unsuitable, sometimes "free-and-easy," detached behavior. For example, there was still high rate *absenteeism* and a lack of involvement turned out to be very insufficient. At the same time, the results of the diagnoses revealed a lack of consideration for the employees and the work they carried out. This engendered dissatisfaction and frustration. Furthermore, the lack of personnel in the sales, production and IT departments, as well as the unfairness of the compensation policy (between company members and between the sites) were a source of tension. Overall, when reading the results of the socio-economic diagnosis, the deterioration of the economic and *social performance* of the company allowed us to observe that the restructuring carried out through the Preservation of Jobs plan implemented in 2009 did not have the expected effects. As a result, the immediate survival and *sustainable development* of the company were at stake.

Our conclusions confirmed the results of numerous works (e.g., Appelbaum, Simpson, & Shapiro, 1987; Beaujolin & Schmidt, 2012; Cascio, 1993; Kets De Vries & Balazs, 1997; Mckinley, Sanchez, Schick, & Higgs 1995; Mishra, Spreitzer, & Mishra, 1998; Mone, 1994; Savall & Zardet, 1994) on the pernicious effects and the high *hidden costs* of restructuring within the framework of unaccompanied social plans.

DEVELOPMENT OF SOCIO-ECONOMIC MANAGERIAL PRACTICES: ORGANIZATIONAL INNOVATIONS TO FACILITATE RESTRUCTURING

As a way of improving the restructuring process, the company set up a socio-economic intervention around a *project* entitled "Ensuring the Return of the Financial Balance of the Company by Intensifying the Mobilization of The *Actors* and the In-Depth Transformation." There were seven objectives within the framework of the intervention-research, which was led by the ISEOR team:

1. Mobilize *human potential* based on innovative human resources and an improved organization of work policy.
2. Develop the *vital function of the sales* department ("We are all sellers") and the shared vision of marketing to improve the quality of service of the company.
3. Set up a management control system based on the cost-value of the activities to have a better *visibility* on performance and pilot improvements.
4. Pursue the professionalization of methods of the management of teams and their activities.
5. Increase the personalization of management and the *negotiation* capacity of organizational members.
6. Strengthen the managerial skills of all the managerial staff.
7. Structure the development of a network of internal participants.

To achieve these objectives, the *socio-economic intervention* was built according to a double approach—"The *Horivert* process." Socio-economic diagnoses were carried out with the objective of identifying *dysfunctions* from the list established by ISEOR. Individual semi-directive qualitative interviews were undertaken with the management and supervisors, and group discussions were held with employees and union representatives from every sector of the company (see Table 7.3.).

The intervention used the *qualimetric* methodology (Savall & Zardet, 1996a, 2004, 2011), combining the qualitative (Boje, Oswick, & Ford 2004; Easterby-Smith, Thorpe, & Lowe, 2002; Golden-Biddle & Locke, 1997) and quantitative (Gephart, 1988; Seale, 1999) approaches. As required by the interview method, we coded the contents of the speech (Krippendorff, 2004; Neuendorf, 2002) by choosing sentences as they were expressed by the person interviewed in their natural speech (Savall & Zardet, 1987, 2008; Savall, Zardet, Bonnet, & Péron, 2008), so-called field-note quotes, as a unit of analysis. As underlined by Allard-Poési, Drucker-Godard and Ehlinger (1999), content analysis depends on the assumption that the

Table 7.3.   Horivert Design

Diagnoses Categories	Total Number of People	Number of People Interviewed Per Population		
	244	Management and Supervisors	Basic Personnel	Unions
Horizontal diagnosis	43	43		
Vertical diagnosis production (Factory A)	103	8	92	
Vertical diagnosis production (Factory B)	47	6	41	
Vertical diagnosis Sales, marketing, and R&D	28	14	14	3
Vertical diagnosis support services	23	11	12	

Diagnoses Categories	Total Number of Interviews	Number of Interviews Per Population		
	123	Management and Supervisors	Basic Personnel	Unions
Horizontal diagnosis	43	43		
Vertical diagnosis production (Factory A)	33	8	22	
Vertical diagnosis production (Factory B)	15	6	9	
Vertical diagnosis Sales, marketing and R&D	18	14	4	3
Vertical diagnosis support services	14	11	3	

repetition of units of analysis of statements (words, expressions or similar meanings, sentences, paragraphs) reveals the centers of interest and concerns of the authors of the statements. As the dysfunctions are brought into light, an economic evaluation was undertaken to measure the economic and financial impact of the dysfunctions (Savall & Zardet, 1996b, 2011) and resultant losses in value (Cappelletti, Khouatra, & Noguera, 2011; Savall, 1974; Savall & Zardet, 1987). This destruction of existing **resources** is not featured in the accounts or the budget. It is latent in the expense accounts among the resources used that are typically recorded, that is, they are wasted or even justified. As for the destruction of potential resources, they correspond to opportunity costs that could have created added value

but did not. This involuntary or deliberate *non-creation of value* is not entered in the accounts. These two kinds of destruction of value—real and potential—constitute hidden costs in the eyes of the decision makers and stakeholders, who are nevertheless affected, unconscious victims of this destruction of resources that they are unable to share (Savall & Zardet, 2008). The amount of the hidden costs in the various sectors is high due to the state of the company, but also to the ambitious objectives of the new director (Table 7.4).

Table 7.4.   Synthesis of Hidden Costs

Diagnosed Sector	Amount of Hidden Costs Per Person and Per Year	Total Amount of Hidden Costs
Sales, Marketing et R&D Departments	44,600 €	1,300,400 €
Support Services	88,800 €	2,251,900 €
Factory A	35,900 €	4,043,700 €
Factory B	32,400 €	1,602,100 €
Total	201,700 €	9,198,100 €

Implementation of a New Organization of Work and Manufacturing

Having presented the *mirror effect* diagnosis of the interviews to the *steering committee*, groups of *horizontal and vertical projects* were set up with the objective of reducing the dysfunctions and hidden costs. These groups worked on the renovation of both factories, which allowed the progressive modernization of the methods and the *implementation of the socio-economic management* fundamental tools. The management and supervision teams were also trained in the use of *socio-economic management tools*, allowing them to clearly improve the quality of the *piloting* of the activities and the teams—from *time management, competency grid* and piloting logbook, to *priority action plans*, an *internal-external strategic action plan*, and periodically negotiable activity contracts.

During the second year of the *socio-economic intervention*, different project groups were *scheduled* on key themes: *sales and marketing*, human resources, *socio-economic organization*, and *socio-economic management control*. Due to important blockages and resistance, in particular from project managers, the project groups were terminated after a few months and working groups were later established (October, 2011) on themes such as the closure of one of the subsidiaries, reduction in stock (inventory), analysis of the *profitability* of the activity of confection, reducing costs of materials, and the introduction of new products to customers.

The objective was to succeed in the creation of a new organization of the manufacturing process.

In this industrial company, the teams were defined by phases in the manufacturing process (see Figure 7.1), which did not favor overall organizational responsibility for the quality of the product, engendering important delays in every passage of the production from one workshop to another one, with mismanagement of the work in progress. Following working session with the new industrial director (September, 2012), a target organization was defined (Figure 7.2) made up of transverse manufacturing teams going from coating to visits. Before its effective implementation (January, 2013), a *qualitative, quantitative and financial evaluation* was carried out to measure the impact of this new organization in terms of skills management and human resources management.

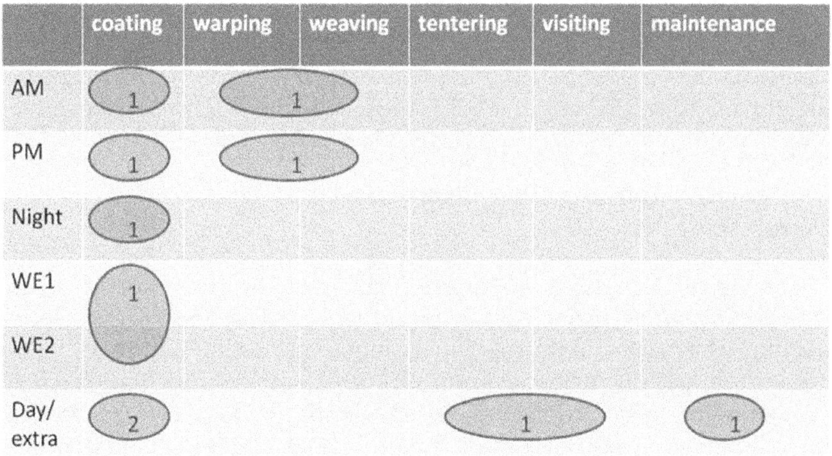

	coating	warping	weaving	tentering	visiting	maintenance
AM	1	1				
PM	1	1				
Night	1					
WE1	1					
WE2						
Day/ extra	2			1		1

Key: 1 or 2 = indicates the number of teams in the sector concerned and in the target period.

Figure 7.1. Manufacturing process before the establishment of the socio-economic.

This process of integrated manufacturing illustrates the concept of *socio-economic organization* tested by the ISEOR from 1978 onwards (Buono & Savall, 2007; Savall, 1979; Savall & Zardet, 2013; Zardet, 2007). This mode of organization facilitates *cooperation* between the various segments of a process of activity by reconstituting its unity. In contrast, the TFW virus (Taylorism, Fayolism, Weberism) (see Chapter 2) recommends a fragmentation of these processes, which provokes innumerable permanent dysfunctions and considerable chronic hidden costs (see Table 7.2).

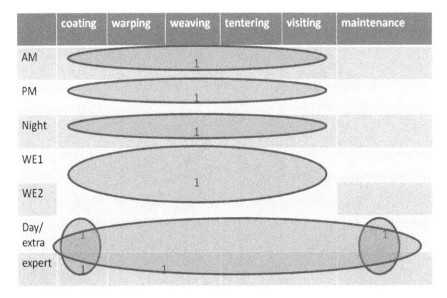

	coating	warping	weaving	tentering	visiting	maintenance
AM			1			
PM			1			
Night			1			
WE1						
WE2			1			
Day/ extra	1					1
expert	1	1				

Figure 7.2.   Integrated manufacturing process following the principles of socio-economic organization.

THE CONTRIBUTION OF SOCIO-ECONOMIC INTERVENTION TO THE RECONSTRUCTION OF A COMPANY

As the above discussion indicates, the socio-economic intervention in the company created a more effective reconstruction of its organization, reconciling economic and social *performance*. The first key point is the improvement of *cohesion* (see the theory of the strategic base in Chapter 1) around the director by ensuring the decentralization of key initiatives. To improve the quality of steering, open up the departments, and cut across the brakes connected to vertical management, a new structuring of the management team was proposed (see Figure 7.3). Within this new structure, the head the director was supported by four key managers: human resources, production, research, and development (**R&D**), and quality as well as the heads of Product, marketing and *communication*. The implementation of *coordination* committees allowed them to open the teams up vertically and horizontally, improving the *communication-coordination-cooperation* between departments. This new organization of committees favored a more dynamic organization by strengthening the capacity of the group to become a force for the proposition of new practices.

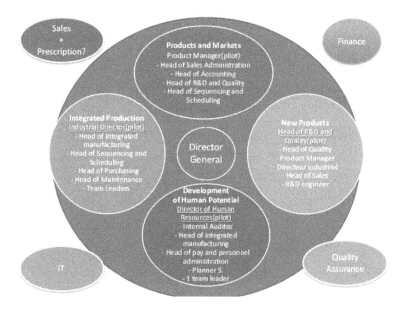

Figure 7.3.   Implementation of the coordination committees.

The second key point of the socio-economic intervention was the introduction of local management and the implementation of a transverse organization of production that set the stage for integrated manufacturing. Within this context, the idea of local management concerned all parts of the company—production, purchases, quality, and sales administration. Implementation of R&D and quality by family or product line (see Table 7.5) was also a key point of the socio-economic intervention.

Table 7.5.   Socio-Economic Organization in the R&D and Quality Departments

Product Lines	Engineers	Technicians	Quality Referents
Product 1	Engineer 1	Technician 1 + Technician 2 (part-time)	Quality Assistant 1
Product 2	Engineer 2	Technician 3	Quality Controller (part-time)
Product 3	Engineer 3	Technician 2 (part-time)	Quality Assistant 2

This new organization structure relied on higher levels of transversality between R&D and manufacturing, supporting the implementation of new methods and new work systems to improve the manufacturing process. Also, the closer relations between the quality and production departments, as well as *IT services* and Integrated Manufacturing allowed them to

integrate all the functions of the company. Overall, a multitude of improvements was observed on three performance levels of *integral quality*. These improvements are synthesized in Table 7.6. They concern improvement in the quality of products, the quality of *functioning*, and the quality of management.

Table 7.6. Synthesis of Improvement at the Three Levels of Overall Quality

Improvement in the quality of products	• Decrease in customer complaints
	• Increase in overseas sales and better achievement of the budget
	• Passage from 80% to 30% of non-corresponding products (cf. works of New Products Committee)
Improvement in the quality of functioning	• Reduction to 37 days average response time for customer complaints
	• Better productivity without having to hire or to replace some departures
	• Organization of technical support in clientele, a product manager
	• Reduction in waste and recycling of certain packaging
	• Positive response to the request for authorization to run a 3rd production line in one of the workshops
	• Development of Factory A to physically put in place inside the Factory a phase of manufacturing which was, for historic reasons, situated outside of the factory, in another building.
	• Progress in collective risk-taking relative to industrial and commercial forecasts
	• Renovation of the quality assessment (document which was very time-consuming for the quality assistant and which was little used)
	• Implementation of Quality Committees (not planned initially, but imagined by the person in charge R&D and Quality after appreciation of the quality of the other Committees)
Improvement in the quality of management	• Attainment of ISO certification 9001
	• Better negotiation of purchases (raw materials, thread)), creation of less expensive chemical formulae and implementation of a system of quality assurance with the suppliers

(Table continues on next page)

Table 7.6.   (Continued)

Improvement in the quality of management	• Abolition of more than 30 variable bonuses, simplification of payslips, settlement in the accounts of 380 K€ in 2011 of arrears of paid leave and modulation
	• For the first time, implementation of a bonus for the employees, via the use of the periodically negotiable activity contracts (PNAC), while before it concerned only the supervision.
	• Better quality of piloting thanks to the priority action plans (PAP), competency grids and piloting logbooks.
	• Implementation of local management in one of the workshops.
	• Better quality of PAP (elaboration, implementation) and PNAC + at present, rate of achievement of the PAP of 54 % compared to 30% in the previous semester
	• Improvement of the piloting of the PAP of every executive of the management committee (cf. organized by weekly and twice monthly head to heads, periodic state of progress with the assistant manager)
	• Development of the cohesion around PAP management.
	• Better distribution of the piloting of key projects (e.g., Reshaping Purchases; management of forecasts systems; the taking in hand by the director of delicate subjects [Purchases, Marketing strategy])
	• Composition of a project group on the reshaping of the organization of Purchases -Planning-Sequencing; the objective was to apply the principles of socio-economic organization in these three processes, to establish teams which integrate the skills on all of these processes and which were divided by family of production.
	• Attenuation of the hegemony of yardmen

On the economic and financial plan, the results revealed a gradual improvement in the performance of the company (see Figure 7.4). Indeed, the evolution of the net result between 2008 and 2014 shows a very clear economic recovery. The first positive signs of the recovery were visible from the second year of the socio-economic intervention. The return to financial balance appeared during the third year due to the mobilization of the *actors* and to the in-depth transformations from the intervention. As indicated by Table 7.6, the strategic actions in the intervention reflect a restructuring of the company, reconstructing the entire working process and implementing socio-economic management tools.

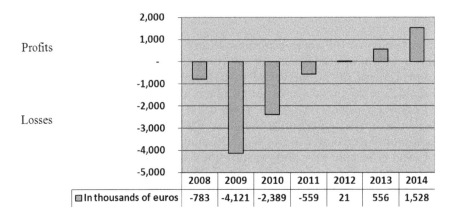

	2008	2009	2010	2011	2012	2013	2014
▫ In thousands of euros	-783	-4,121	-2,389	-559	21	556	1,528

Figure 7.4.   Evolution of net results from 2008 to 2014.

Table 7.7.   Synthesis of Strategic Action

Year	SEAM Actions	Other Actions
2008	–	–
2009	–	Staff Cuts Factory B
2010	Start of the socio-economic intervention plan: Diagnoses, implementation of assessment Introduction of *GDT*, *PAP*, *PASINTEX*, *GC* et *TDBP*, *steering committee*, Network of Internal Participants	–
2011	Implementation of PNAC and working groups	–
2012	–	Closure of a subsidiary
2013	Establishment of transversal teams linking the 5 production workshops	Staff cut and closure of Factory B
2014	Termination Method Service Naming of head of Integrated manufacturing Implementation of committees. Implementation of local management.	–

CONCLUSION

The results of the socio-economic intervention in this case illustrate the necessity of accompanying the restructuring of a company with an improvement in the quality of management and its functioning. The organizational innovations put in place in the company were sources of *value creation*. In this way, several axes can be proposed to better lead the restructuring of a company. First, the success of this socio-economic intervention relies on the simultaneous actions of setting-up of socio-economic tools and organizational transformations to reduce the *dysfunctions* and the situations of resistance to change (see Figure 7.5). The problems of cohesion and resistance to change could not have been channeled without the socio-economic tools.

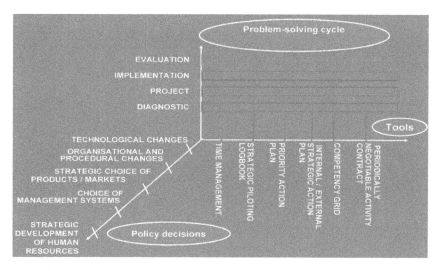

Figure 7.5.   The three forces of change (© ISEOR 1984).

Second, the use of internal-external strategic action plans divided in priority action plans within all the departments allowed them to stabilize a status quo on key themes, which limited the damage connected to the blockages of other improvements that were not implemented. Thus, the *sales*, *marketing* and communication departments defined a PAP that specified the priority actions to be set up in the semester (Figure 7.6). These action plans allowed them to clarify the *strategic objectives* of the company and set a goal for the actors of the organization.

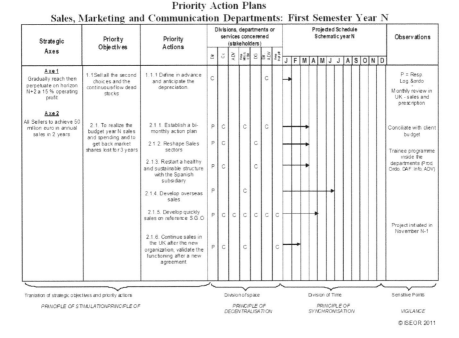

Figure 7.6. Illustrative Priority Action Plans (PAP).

The third piece of information gleaned from this case confirms the results of numerous ***intervention-researches*** led by the ISEOR. Restructuring requires the implementation of a project simultaneously reconciling economic and social objectives. In this case study, objectives were to restore authority and managerial courage at every level of leadership (managing, executives, control), to ensure the sustainable performance of the company, and to take advantage of the liberation of energy (see Chapter 1, the theory of ***human potential***) at every level to create innovative professional practices. An observation of recent restructuring efforts underscores that it is often the economic objectives that determine the structure of a company. Examples include initiatives that reduce management levels to realize savings or establish a production co-operative where employees acquire their company and take control of the organization in order to avoid closure. Social objectives are rarely included in the decisions leading to large-scale organizational transformations, such as the creation of a structure that facilitates the development of the authority of the managers.

Finally, there is an ***interaction*** between both determiners—socio-economic objectives and quality and intensity of ***piloting*** of the managers (see

Chapter 1, new statement of the *socio-economic theory*). As this case illustrates, if organizations are focused on the quality and intensity of piloting based on a desired set of socio-economic objectives, it is also important to take into account the behavior of key managers in the piloting of those objectives. Drawing on a number of socio-economic interventions, this observation helps to explain the need to reconsider between 30 and 70 percent of the executive committee members, after the failure of several tested organizational revisions.

NOTE

1. The research for this chapter has been influenced by a number of works that are not directly referred to in the text, including Boje and Rosile (2003), Buono and Savall (2007), Gephart (2009), Perroux (1979), Savall (1974, 1975, 1977, 1981, 2010, 2012), Savall and Zardet (1987, 1992, 1995, 2005, 2009, 2011, 2013), and Savall, Zardet, and Bonnet (2000, 2008).

REFERENCES

Allard-Poési, F., Drucker-Godard, C., & Ehlinger, S. (1999). Analyses de representations et de discours [Discourse and sensemaking analysis]. In R.A. Thiétard (Ed.), *Méthodes de recherche en management* [Research methods in management]. Paris, France: Dunod.

Appelbaum, S., Simpson, R., & Shapiro, B. (1987). Downsizing: The ultimate human resource strategy. *Business Quarterly, 52*(2), 52–60.

Beaujolin-Bellet, R. (2014). Les restructurations: Une sortie parle haut est-elle possible? [Restructuring: An output speaks loud is it possible?]. *Revue Économie et Management, 153*, 5–9.

Beaujolin-Bellet, R., & Schmidt, G. (2012). *Les restructurations d'entreprises* [Company restructuring]. Paris, France: Éditions La Découverte.

Boje, D., & Rosile, G.-A. (2003). Comparison of socio-economic and other transorganizational development methods. *Journal of Change Organizational Management, 16*(1), 10–20.

Boje, D. M., Oswick C., & Ford J. D. (2004). Language and organization: The doing of discourse. *Academy of Management Review, 29*, 571–577.

Buono A. F. (2003). SEAM-less post-merger integration strategies: A cause for concern. *Journal of Organizational Change Management, 16*(1), 90–98.

Buono, A. F., & Savall, H. (Eds.) (2007). *Socio-economic intervention in organizations: The intervener-researcher and the SEAM approach to organizational analysis.* Charlotte, NC: Information Age Publishing.

Cappelletti, L., Baker, R., & Noguera, F. (2011, August). *Developing human capital through action research in management control.* Paper presented at the American Accounting Association Annual Meeting, Denver, Co.

Cappelletti, L., Khouatra, D., & Noguera, F. (2011, August). *Measuring the creation of value through management consulting: The case of the hidden costs method*. Paper presented at the Academy of Management Annual Meeting, San Antonio, TX.

Cascio, W. F. (1993). Downsizing: What do we know? What have we learned? *Academy of Management Executive, 7*(1), 95–104.

Easterby-Smith, M., Thorpe R., & Lowe, A. (2002). *Management research*. London, England: Sage.

Gephart, R. (1988). *Ethnostatistics: Qualitative foundations for qualitative research*. Newbury Park, CA: Sage.

Gephart, R. P. (2009). An invitation to ethnostatistics. *Revue Sciences de gestion – Management Sciences – Ciencias de Gestión, 70*, 85.

Golden-Biddle, K., & Locke, K. (1997). *Composing qualitative research*. Thousand Oaks, CA: Sage.

Goter, F. (2005). *Etude du système de sanctions-récompenses en lien avec la performance des organisations de service public. - Cas d'Expérimentation* [Research sanctions: Reward system in connection with the performance of public service organizations—Case study]. Thèse de doctorat de sciences de gestion, Université Jean Moulin Lyon 3.

Kets De Vries, M. F. R., & Balazs, K. (1997). The downside of downsizing. *Human Relations, 50*(1), 11–50.

Krippendorff, K. (2004). *Content analysis: An introduction to its methodology*. Thousand Oaks, CA: Sage.

Lacquemanne, F. (2011). Le redressement vigoureux d'une entreprise en crise de transition [The strong recovery of a company in transition crisis. In ISEOR (Ed.), *Réussir en temps de crise: Stratégies proactives des entreprises* [Succeed in times of crisis: Proactive business strategies] (pp. 203–210). Paris, France: Economica.

Lacquemanne, F. (2012). Succession et transformation du management [*Succession Management and Transformation*]. In ISEOR (Ed.), *Les entreprise familiales: Création, succession, gouvernance et management* [Family business: Creation, succession, governance and management] (pp. 180–183). Paris, France: Economica.

Mckinley, W., Sanchez, C. M., Schick, A. G. ,& Higgs A. C. (1995). Organizational downsizing: Constraining, cloning, learning [and executive commentary]. *Academy of Management Executive, 9*, 32–44.

Mishra, K. E., Spreitzer, G., & Mishra, A. K. (1998). Preserving employee morale during downsizing. *Sloan Management Review, 39*(2), 83–95.

Mone, M. A. (1994). Relationships between self concepts, aspirations, emotional responses, and intent to leave a downsizing organization. *Human Resource Management, 33*(2), 281–298.

Neuendorf, K. A. (2002). *The content analysis guidebook*. Thousand Oaks, CA: Sage.

Perroux, F. (1979). L'entreprise, l'équilibre rénové et les coûts cachés [The enterprise, the renovated balance and the "hidden" costs]. Preface. In H. Savall. *Reconstruire l'entreprise* [Reconstructing the enterprise] Paris, France: Dunod. 2nd ed. in H. Savall & V. Zardet. Reconstruire l'entreprise, Paris: Dunod (2014)

Savall, H. (1974–1975–1977). *Enrichir le travail humain dans les entreprises et les organisations* [An economic evaluation of job enrichment]. Paris: Dunod.

Savall, H. (1979). *Reconstruire l'entreprise: Analyse socio-économique des conditions de travail* [Rebuilding the enterprise: Socio-economic analysis of working conditions]. Paris, France: Dunod.

Savall, H. (1981–2010). *Work and people: An economic evaluation of job enrichment*. 1st ed. New-York: Oxford University Press ; 2nd ed. Charlotte, NC: Information Age Publishing.

Savall, H. (2012). *Origine radicale des crises économiques: Germán Bernácer, précurseur visionnaire* [Root origin of crises: Germán Bernácer, a visionary forerunner]. Charlotte, NC: Information Age Publishing.

Savall, H., & Zardet, V. (1987). *Maîtriser les coûts et les performances cachés : Le contrat d'activité périodiquement négociables* [Mastering hidden costs and performance: The periodically negotiable activity contract]. Paris: Economica.

Savall, H., & Zardet, V. (1992). *Le nouveau contrôle de gestion: Méthode des coûts-performances cachés* [New management control: The hidden cost-performance method]. Paris: Éditions Comptables Malesherbes-Eyrolles

Savall, H., & Zardet, V. (1994). Performance économique et engagement social de l'entreprise: Jusqu'où est-ce compatible? [Economic performance and social commitment of the company: How far is this compatible?" *Stratégies Resources Humaines, 9*, 30–38.

Savall, H., & Zardet, V. (1995–2005–2009). *Ingénierie stratégique du roseau, souple et enracinée* [Strategic engineering of the reed, flexible and rooted]. Paris: Economica.

Savall, H., & Zardet, V. (1996a). *Les pratiques d'encadrement des recherches doctorales en stratégie – résultats d'enquêtes 1995 et 1996* [The supervising practices of doctoral research in strategic management: Survey analysis 1995 and 1996]. Association Internationale de Management Stratégique (AIMS) Conference, pp. 18–52.

Savall, H., & Zardet, V. (1996b). *Mesure et négociation de la performance globale de l'entreprise: Éléments pour une théorie socio-économique du contrôle de gestion* [The measurement and negocation of corporate global performance: Elements towards a socio-economic thory of management control]. IFSAM Colloquium, Montreal, Canada.

Savall, H., & Zardet V. (2004). *Recherche en Sciences de Gestion: Approche qualimétrique, Observer l'objet Complexe* [Research in management sciences: The qualimetrics approach, observing the complex object]. Paris, France: Economica.

Savall, H., & Zardet, V. (2008). *Mastering hidden costs and performance*, Charlotte, NC: Information Age Publishing.

Savall, H., & Zardet, V. (2011). *The qualimetrics approach: Observing the complex object*. Charlotte, NC: Information Age Publishing.

Savall, H., & Zardet, V. (2013). *The dynamics and challenges of tetranormalization*. Charlotte, NC: Information Age Publishing.

Savall, H., & Zardet, V. (2014). *Reconstruire l'entreprise* [Rebuilding the company]. Paris, France: Dunod.

Savall, H., Zardet V., & Goter (2012, December 5–6). Concilier modernisation de la gestion des Ressources Humaines, valeurs de service public et objectifs de performance: Analyse internationale et comparative à partir de cas de recherche-intervention [Reconcile modernization of human resources management , public service values and performance targets: International and comparative analysis from cases of intervention research], *AIRMAP Congress*, Paris, p. 8.

Savall, H., Zardet, V., & Bonnet, M. (2000–2008). *Releasing the untapped potential of enterprises through socio-economic management.* Geneva: Éditions IOT-BIT.

Savall, H., Zardet, V., Bonnet, M., & Péron, M. (2008). The Emergence of Implicit Criteria Actually Utilized by Reviewers of Qualitative Research Articles: Case of a European Journal. *Organizational Research Methods*, *11*(3), 510–540.

Seale, C. (1999). *The quality of qualitative research.* London, UK: Sage.

Zardet, V. (2007). Developing sustainable global performance in small-to medium size industrial firms: The case of Brioche Pasquier. In A. F. Buono & H. Savall (Eds.), *Socio-economic interventions in organizations: The intervener-researcher and the SEAM approach to organizational analysis* (pp. 45–70). Charlotte, NC: Information Age Publishing.

CHAPTER 8

THE TIME FACTOR IN SOCIO-ECONOMIC INTERVENTIONS

Short-Term *Versus* Long-term Performance[1]

Olivier Voyant, Alexis Roche, and Jérémy Clément Salmeron

In our contemporary context, the ability of corporations to anticipate, adapt and be adapted to their environment determines their vision and reveals their *agility*. **Piloting** the **structures**, **behaviors**, and **interactions** between both these factors (Savall & Zardet, 1987) becomes a primary issue for decider-strategists and their collaborators. The reality is that nothing is really ever "fixed" forever in organizations, ensuring that the ability to carry out change processes, rooted in practices and aimed at creating sustainable performance, is a *sine qua non* condition in order to ensure enterprise **survival** and development.

When a company decides to embark on a deep and **sustainable change process**, it is obviously important that the various **actors**—from the CEO and management to employees—who are acting on various perimeters—

The Socio-Economic Approach to Management Revisited: The Evolving Nature of SEAM in the 21st Century, pp. 155–172
Copyright © 2015 by Information Age Publishing

team, department, establishment or group—coordinate themselves around the change in order to effectively implement it. Similar to a patient asking a physician for medical advice, the CEO could have the insight to of consult with an *intervener-researcher* team.

Carrying out any organizational change process involves both internal and external pressures in a context where the alleged *rationality* and the stress created by short-term demands leads to the development of illusory **economic performance** to the detriment of **social performance**, which is subsequently atrophied. This situation impacts the temporality of the results expected by the change action pilot. In some cases, this opposition between the social and economic, ***short term and long term***, and more largely between survival and development (Savall & Zardet, 1995, 2005) entails alterations in the way the change process is carried out.

Drawing on three intervention-research case studies, the chapter attempts to bring into light the internal and external factors that bear on the change process, the role of temporary dynamics on changing action results, and the dialectic relation between the intervener and his or her partner-organization. Given the desire for short-term and long-term results – immediate and sustainable respectively—the discussion will try to clarify the role of the different time periods of an intervention process in obtaining visible and hidden results.

THE CASE CONTEXT: FROM CRISIS TO CHANGE

Since 1637, with the first economic and financial speculative bubble—"*tulip mania*"—crises have continued to multiply and diversify. Thus, after taking the effort of dating, cycle studies, and sectoral analyses, the vocabulary used to describe these bubbles have been increasingly enriched. We evoke the political, social, economic, and financial crisis but also other crises of power, institutions, morality, and the human condition. These crises are dissected in detail, suggesting that they tend to be systemic and responsible for such generic effects as the dismantling of social relations, rising unemployment, and other social ills. It is also felt that they could be resolved by simply switching the cursor from *deny* to *resistance*, and then from resistance to reconstruction. The solutions proposed follow one another and look alike. We are still seeking the one, that special person who could bring a needed response, modern times *hero*. We elaborate rhetorical sentences and crisis plans in an explicative jurisprudence cycle, modifying the changing method-product labels in an attempt to revamp them. We are simply observing the patient, particularly resilience in the face of the *disease*; in essence, we are urging States, near economic asphyxia, to react.

Crisis Context

There are numerous actors participating in this **crisis market**, but there is one basic fact—all companies and organizations are in crisis, the ones who know it and the others who ignore it, at least for the moment. The etymology of the Greek word crisis means there is something to change, but the question is what has to be changed. To start with the meaning of the very word *crisis*, it cannot be just one effect, one cycling symptom that hides deeper permanent *diseases* that company and organization *myopia* and *blindness* may conceal. An outcome is that the **root-causes** of those crises are not dealt with since they are embedded in prejudices, old reflexes, and fashion trends. As Savall (1974) pointed out, it is appropriate not to succumb to the temptation of intellectual esthetics if one focuses on managerial practice **effectiveness**. Traditionally, crisis have two consequences—the **external environment** hypertrophy, which results in an internal environment atrophy process. Pressures for immediate outcomes worship reinforcement, which does nothing but multiply and amplify the crisis phenomenon, instead of stimulating the **creation of potential**.

Starting with this reading of the crisis, with words opposition like symptom/roots cause, appearance/essence, external + immediacy/intern + potential, and after several exchanges with the leaders of the studied companies, four explanatory elements of the crisis were identified. First of all, there are failures in the development, formalization and **strategic implementation** of innovating company policies. Second, there is a lower production of **value-added** due to the absence of global workload steering. Third, a lack of **cohesion**—horizontal, vertical and transverse—is noticed. Finally, **proximity management** is atrophied.

These **four-root causes** have for vocation to give priority to the development of **endogenous performances** in a context of rarefaction of external **resources**.

Change: A Response to Crisis

CEOs place their hopes on change as an entity, not to say a deity, attempting to find solutions to the problems faced by their companies. But, we could easily observe that these discourses are not operationalized due to a lack of competency in carrying out change processes in organizations. Facing both *internal and external crises,* organizations are often lost, without the proper equipment to deal with them. Change is natural, contrary to **pro-activity** in the process of change management. However, it is this pro-activity that indicates the vitality level of the organization and influences its middle- and long-term **survival**. The **change energy** stems primarily from people who constitute the organization through their unique ability to forecast the future. In essence, this is *human potential* stimulation (Savall, 1974; Savall & Zardet, 1987; Savall, Péron, & Zardet, 2014; see also Chapter 1 in this volume) that allows the company to face its complex realities.

CEOs as employees need to *make sense* of their work and to clarify their *entrepreneurial project.* By being focused on financial objectives, they are freeing themselves from others, something that is seen as necessary for them to reach these goals. Organizational members are both the root-cause of *dysfunctions* as well as the potential that will enable an organization to face them.

Reflecting on ISEOR's database over the years, we observe that the generic goals of intervention-research always refer implicitly or explicitly to human potential stimulation. In our cases, these goals had been formulated along this line, for example: "Human potential is a strategic strength that aims to get competitive advantages"; "Developing the liberty to create new performance"; and "Working together to revive results." Change is a dynamic process linked with human vitality.

The *values* displayed in organizations consistently express human values. It is not very frequent when we observe values that are oriented to *products* or to *financial elements*. There is a gap, even a *real divergence* between people-oriented discourse and actions that are estranged from people. This malaise in the implementation phase has been observed in each and every organization we have been involved in. The *immediacy* desire masks the necessity for both people and practices to evolve. However, the efficacy is often lower, sometimes null, if individuals had not been at the origin of their creations via an appropriation process.

The Temporary Dimension of Change

The change process that we advocate is based on three dimensions: space, time, and the junction between both, the time-space. *Space* is considered as the diffusion surface of change, that is to say the different perimeters of the organization concerned by change actions. These could be vertical and be relative to hierarchical relations, starting from the head of the organization to the shop floor, or they could be horizontal and thus touch the *interfaces* between departments, working groups and establishments. A deep global change action is made on both perimeters, at the same time through a *horivert* process (Savall & Zardet, 1987, 2008), simultaneously vertical and horizontal.

Temporal rhythms management is essential in order for change to operate. *Time* is a resource that the CEO does not take lightly during *negotiation*, launching, implementation, and evaluation phases. The CEO must be aware of the efficacy rhythm of intervention. This awareness is not innate and, in some cases, the CEO has to be helped by an external agent, in this instance, the management intervener. If financial steering is usually widespread, steering (managing) *actors*' time or actions' time is a reality that requires instrumentalized time steering. Time could be properly measured in hours, days, or months in a planning cycle. This planning becomes a *coordination* tool, both individual and collective, and a realization indicator.

At the junction point between spaces (i.e. perimeters) and time lay the method-products that take the shape of *steering committees*, *diagnosis*, *training sessions*, *personalized assistance*, and *internal interveners* training. There are two types of time: calendar time and resource time. Time volume is considered as a *resource* that could be allocated to a task, an activity or a combination of activities in the same way as a financial resource. The second type of time, *calendar time*, is a feasibility indicator because time as a resource could be allocated to some actions without thinking about implementation constraints. The *agenda* is the measuring tool of this type of time. Resource and reality adequacy refers to the *performance*, both *efficacy* and *efficiency*.

When we measure time, rhythms and change actions, we come to the notion of performance. Could we obtain the same result in a shorter time frame and lightened method-products? As the number of actions influences time volume, questions can be raised concerning the efficacy of each action on the global changing process.

INTERVENTION METHODOLOGY

Our research study is based on three enterprises, two are French and one of them is Belgium. These enterprises are leaders in their national and international markets. They are *growing* and being considered as exemplary by their competitors that attempt to imitate them.

The Cases

E is a French industrial company in the metallurgical industry created 30 years ago. Its turnover (revenues) is about 18 million euros with 2.5 million euro in reserve. It has 92 employees, spread in three sites across France and Germany. T is a Belgium company specialized in high technology and working in the industrial electricity industry. This company was founded 20 years ago. It was one of the first companies to apply ISO standards. This is a family business composed of 100% private capital and transmitted to the son. It employs 335 people and 40 to 80 temporary workers on 6 sites in Belgium, France, Switzerland, and Romania. The global workforce of the company has doubled over the past 10 years. The global workforce turnover hovers around 5%, which is low for this sector. This company has approximately 52 million euro in revenues, which has also doubled in 10 years. This company realizes a 25% turnover to export and gets 7.7 million euro of own founds.

D is a French company created over 10 years by two associates in the *computing services industry* that has seen its orders increased by 10% per year. Its size has tripled over the past decade, both in turnover and workforce. D company has 55 employees and its current turnover is about 4.2 million euro with 20% annual growth.

Expressed Needs and Prescriptions

Initial expectations expressed by the three companies' CEOs were synthesized in 4 mains themes, which were at the origin of the intervention demand (see Table 8.1). We often observe a lack of formalized strategy in organizations and difficulties in implementing this strategy. These companies are calling upon us to clarify and elaborate this strategy and prepare themselves for implementation. The rising demands of customers focused on a variety and sometimes *contradictory* issues, including: execution rapidity, reduced delays, optimal quality, brand image, production capacity, personalized production, innovation, and rapid delivery. These demands are common to all the intervention-research carried out over the past few decades. This theme had been investigated in the ISEOR research-center under the name of *tetranormalization* (Savall & Zardet, 2005, 2013). Each company often put forward the importance of stimulating innovation in order to stay the leader in their market.

Table 8.1.   Comparative Analysis of the CEOs' Expressed Themes

Themes	E Company	D Company	T Company
Strategy	x	x	X
Innovation		x	X
Profitability	x	x	X
Management skills	x	x	X

The need for *profitability* is displayed, but the sensitivity and the actor's knowledge of the economy impacts of their practice are weak. This profitability question is often evoked through the necessity of developing *sales*. A good deal of strategic reasoning is typically made on turnover (revenues) instead of focusing on **value-added** margin. Institutionalized routine and work disconnection from the end product don't facilitate this awareness.

The lack of managerial skills is an important indicator of inefficacy of the societal and educational system. The system does not develop stimulating, respectful and efficient management skills. Companies point out, with discomfort, that their managers lack managerial skills. Indeed, correctives actions frequently observed on products or organizational configurations do not deal with the **root-causes** of **dysfunctions**, underscoring managerial practices inefficacy (Savall & Zardet, 1987), which hovers between authoritarianism and laxity. One fundamental concern stills remains, which is often overlooked by organizations that are not aware of its importance for their sustainability—*know-how transfer.*

In order to respond to strategic issues and their implementation, emphasizing profitability, innovation and management skills, **SEAM** provides generic method-products that are adaptable to different organizations, especially through dialogue with the actors (see Table 8.2). SEAM proposes a global approach to change that develops the organization's ability to respond to contingent needs through a methodological structure that identifies **dysfunctions**, elaborates solutions built by the actors, and enhances **learning**. This is accomplished through individual and collective theoretical and practical training, focusing on improving managerial practices categories across the board. As suggested earlier, know-how transfer and the maintenance of an on-going **improvement system** appears to us to be an essential function. However, the companies we studied were not sensitize to this problem. This challenge requires the systematic addition of the specific training of **internal interveners**, company employees who are expected to dedicate 20% of their time to the mission. This approach provides the link between **method-products** and the time necessary for the change.

Intervention Planning

The intervention planning chart (see Table 8.3) illustrates the result of the exchanges with the leaders based on their articulation of the link between method-products and implementation in order to achieve the objectives (lines), the calendar period of intervention (columns), the frequencies/rhythms, and the density of the carried out actions (intersections). For each case, a qualification of the method-products allows us to identify short and long rhythms. In the first case, the rhythm exceeds the semi-annual period and indicates a method-product that can be grounded in the company's operating modes; in the second case, the method-product implemented is produced over a shorter than six-month period—it feeds the long cycles and is not meant to be reproduced in time.

Table 8-2.   Themes and Method-Products

Themes	Method-Products
Strategy	• **Steering committee**
	• Concertation-training sessions and personalized assistance sessions on strategy and **strategic implementation**
	• **Qualitative diagnosis**
	• Project group
Innovation	• Project group
Profitability	• Financial and qualitative diagnosis
	• Project group
	• Concertation-training sessions and personalized assistance sessions on both people and activities management
Managerial skills	• Concertation-training sessions and personalized assistance sessions on: time-management, competencies management, Human and activities steering, individual and collective energy stimulation
Engineering transfers	• **Internal interveners** training in order to ensure methodology transfers and internal stimulation of **change energy**

Table 8.3.   Enterprise E Intervention Planning (Year 1)

METHOD-PRODUCT	Time nature	M1	M2	M3	M4	M5	M6	M7	M8	M9	M10	M11	M12
STEERING COMMITTEE	Long	1		2				3					4
CONCERTATION-TRAINING SESSIONS (Cluster A,B)	Long	1		2	3	4		5			6		
PERSONALIZED ASSISTANCE	Long			1		2	3					4	
INTERNAL INTERVENERS STEERING AND TECHNICAL ASSISTANCE	Long	1		2	3	4	5	6	7	8	9	10	
INTEGRAL DIAGNOSIS (HORIZONTAL PROCESS)	Short												
HORIZONTAL PROJECT GROUP (HORIZONTAL PROCESS)	Short				1	2	3						
INTEGRAL DIAGNOSIS (VERTICAL PROCESS)	Short												
INTEGRAL PROJECT GROUP (VERTICAL PROCESS)	Short							1	2	3	4		

Company E intervention planning refers to the first year of intervention. The identified method-products, overall, met the need previously expressed during the **negotiation phase** for developing a new management system. Concerning the diagnoses and the *task groups*, planning made it possible to identify the following specificities. First, the *integral* designation means that the whole company has been taken into account in the dysfunction identification phase (*diagnosis*) and solutions contrivance (***task group***). Second, the time interval between the horizontal phase (direction and management staff) and the vertical phase (middle-management and employees) focused on managerial staff training: the middle manager learns the strategy from the top manager, and then, break it down to the workers. Finally, an assumption was made on the number of taskforce meetings. The potential capacity of the direction concerning the creation of responses to the identified dysfunctions explains why the *task group* comprised three meetings, compared to four for the managerial staff.

Table 8.4.   Enterprise D Intervention Planning (Year 2)

METHOD-PRODUCT	Time nature	M1	M2	M3	M4	M5	M6	M7	M8	M9	M10	M11
STEERING COMMITTEE	Long		1		2				3			4
CONCERTATION-TRAINING SESSIONS (Cluster A)	Long		1									2
PROSPECTIVE AND STRATEGY PROJECT GROUP	Long				1	2		3				
SOCIO-ECONOMIC MANAGEMENT CONTROL PROJECT GROUP	Long		1				2			3		
TEAMWORKING SALES PROJECT GROUP	Long				1				2		3	
PERSONALIZED ASSISTANCE	Long	1			2		3		4		5	
INTERNAL INTERVENERS STEERING AND TECHNICAL ASSISTANCE	Long	1	2	3	4	5	6	7	8	9	10	11
STRATEGIC VIGILANCE DIAGNOSIS	Short											

Table 8.4 portrays Company D's intervention planning during the second year of intervention. The method-products **steering committee**, *steering and technical aid of internal interveners* facilitated the ***maintenance actions***. The other method-products consisted of going deeper to articulate management system to strategy, ***management control***, and sales.

Company T's intervention planning refers to the 19th year of intervention. The first four lines indicate long time periods related to the company operations. These method-products focused on the maintenance needs of the management system in which the CEO wanted to benefit from an external energy contribution that would to stimulate the decision-making process. The last three lines relate to the implementation methods that were employed to measure, in depth, the efficiency and ***effectiveness*** of a product line with a proactive strategic decision as a target (i.e., reinforcement or suppression of a product line in the portfolio of businesses).

Table 8.4.   Enterprise D Intervention Planning (Year 2)

METHOD-PRODUCT	Time nature	M1	M2	M3	M4	M5	M6	M7	M8	M9	M10	M11	M12
STRATEGIC SEMINARY TOP MANAGEMENT COMMITTEE	Long			1						2			
PERSONALIZED ASSITANCE TOP MANAGEMENT COMMITTEE	Long	1	2			3	4	5				6	7
STRATEGIC SEMINARY OPERATIONAL TEAM	Long				1						2		
PERSONALIZED ASSITANCE OPERATIONAL TEAM	Long				1							2	
STRATEGIC MANAGEMENT ANNUAL DAY	Long					1							
PRODUCT LINE DIAGNOSIS	Short												
PRODUCT LINE PROJECT GROUP	Short				1	2	3	4					
PRODUCT LINE IMPLEMENTATION PROJECT GROUP	Short									1	2	3	

ORGANIZATIONAL LEARNING AND INDIVIDUAL AND COLLECTIVE PLANNING STEERING

Organizational change is a modification of organizational member practices that requires an individual and collective learning training process. This process results from the interaction between external data and the mental activity necessary to create new knowledge (Piaget, 1959). It does not result from an *innate* capacity of the company but from an interaction process that, by nature, requires time.

Learning Phenomena

For *in-depth* change, it is necessary for this learning process to touch the various levels and the various people who make up the organization (Savall, 1974). A global change system seems like a "lift," going to and fro between the local and top levels to obtain sustainable results. This defragmentation of the company is not usual. Indeed, organizations are split up by integration, in mental and social processes, in the classical management theories that emphasized segmenting work. The *socio-economic method* is thus a tool of organizational defragmentation.

The need for change interiorizing requires that a *threat* is perceived by the individuals (Savall, 1974). Indeed, the words crisis, change, dysfunction, and *performance* are too often employed in an organization—but with lost meaning. They remain in perceptions by *actors* of a *discursive* and *political* level, bringing little (or no) change that will be actually observed. It is thus necessary to rebuild a common language that is used in daily action. Some socio-economic method-products are often used for this awakening, in terms of both the discursive character of change and the real threat concerning **survival** of the organization. This is why we carry out successive **mirror-effects** while doing the steps of restitution of the dysfunctions, restitution of the **expert-opinion,** and in particular the **unvoiced comments**, the basic ideas of improvement of the project. These method-products also make it possible to harmonize perceptions and the knowledge of action prospects with a view to facilitating co-operation in the implementation phase.

A company's actors do not integrate the entire change dynamic as the same pace, which is why the intervention-research is built on cycled methods that modify, little by little, individual behaviors. Organizational members are then prodded into action through successive **commitments** based on specific and generic tools: **Resolution charts, Priority Action Plan** *(PAP),* and **Periodically Negotiable Activity Contracts** *(PNAC)* (Savall & Zardet, 1987, 2008). These **management tool**s help **company actors** in formalizing their short-term (e.g., for the next meeting) and middle-term (e.g., the next six months) engagements.

To consolidate change, internal interveners are always intensively trained and supported by the intervener-researcher, in essence completing the change together. This **engineering transfer** of the change management process reinforces **organizational learning** while relying on persons who specifically control and stimulate the change process within the organization.

Planning Steering

Steering an intervention requires intervener **energy**, actors' **cooperation** and appropriate **tools** such as intervention planning. This tool reconciles resource time and calendar time, and responds to two methodological objectives: developing learning loops and training the company to carry out a sustainable change-action while assessing current activities. Observation shows that the realization cycle of a change-action lasts almost one year. Referring to the Chinese proverb—"even if it takes 9 months for a woman to conceive one child, nine women cannot conceive one child in one month"—calendar time cannot be compressed. The time required for organizational learning and for change gestation must be respected. The gap that exists between initial planning and realized planning at the end of the intervention appear in Table 8.6. After taking into account the method-products mobilized in the companies (lines), we identify in columns, per company, the number of sequences realized for each **method-product**, the time per sequence, and the global time volume that each method-product represents for each and every actor. The following columns list the sequences belatedly programmed, with a monthly measurement unit, then the sequences deferred over the following year that result in modifying the time volume devoted to change by the actors in the presence of the **external intervener**.

Table 8.6.   Gaps Between Initial and Realized Planning

METHODS	TIME NATURE	E company (Year 1) Time volume / participant	Total sequences	Sequence duration	Late sequences (month)	Next year reported sequences	Time volume / participant (corrected)	D company (Year 2) Time volume / participant	Total sequences	Sequence duration	Late sequences (month)	Next year reported sequences	Time volume / participant (corrected)	T company (Year 19) Time volume / participant	Total sequences	Sequence duration	Late sequences (month)	Next year reported sequences	Time volume / participant (corrected)
		100%					96%	100%					61%	100%					81%
MONTHLY MEAN		5,83	2,92				5,83	5,36	2,91				3,27	12,00	2,00				9,75
TOTAL MONTH		12	12		11	1	12	11	11		19	11	11	12	12		21	6	12
TIME VOLUME		70	35				67,5	59	32				36	144	24				117
		100%					94%	100%					60%	100%					84%
MONTHLY MEAN		3,25	2				3,04	5,27	2,82				3,18	9,5	1,17				8,00
TOTAL MONTH		12	12		8	1	12	11	11		19	11	11	12	12		2	3	12
TIME VOLUME		39	24				36,5	58	31				35	114	14				96
STEERING COMMITTEE	Long	10	4	2,5	0	1	7,5	10	4	2,5	6	3	2,5						
CONCERTATION+TRAINING SESSIONS	Long	15	6	2,5	1	0	15	5	2	2,5	0	1	2,5						
PERSONALIZED ASSISTANCE	Long	4	4	1	4	0	4	5	5	1	1	1	4						
INTERNAL INTERVENERS STEERING AND TECHNICAL ASSISTANCE	Long	10	10	1	3	0	10	11	11	1	2	3	8						
STRATEGY AND PROSPECTIVE PROJECT GROUP	Long							9	3	3	7	1	6						
SOCIO-ECONOMIC MANAGEMENT CONTROL PROJECT GROUP	Long							9	3	3	0	1	6						
TEAM WORKING SALES PROJECT GROUP	Long							9	3	3	3	1	6						
TOP MANAGEMENT STRATEGIC SEMINAR	Long													32	2	16	0	0	32
OPERATIONAL TEAM STRATEGIC SEMINAR	Long													16	2	8	3	0	16
PERSONALIZED ASSISTANCE TOP MANAGEMENT	Long													48	7	6,85	-1	0	48
PERSONALIZED ASSISTANCE OPERATIONAL TEAM	Long													10	2	5	0	2	0
STRATEGIC MANAGEMENT DAY	Long													8	1	8	0	1	0
		100%					100%	100%					100%	100%					70%
MONTHLY MEAN		2,58	0,92				2,58	0,09	0,09				0,09	2,50	0,83				1,75
TOTAL MONTH		12	12		3	0	12	11	11		0	0	11	12	12		19	3	12
TIME VOLUME		31	11				31	1	1				1	30	10				21
INTEGRAL DIAGNOSIS (HORIZONTAL PROCESS)	Count	1	1	1	0	0	1												
INTEGRAL PROJECT GROUP (HORIZONTAL PROCESS)	Count	9	3	3	1	0	9												
INTEGRAL DIAGNOSIS (VERTICAL PROCESS)	Count	9	3	3	0	0	9							9	3	3	2	0	9
INTEGRAL PROJECT GROUP (VERTICAL PROCESS)	Count	12	4	3	2	0	12							12	4	3	17	0	12
STRATEGIC VIGILANCE DIAGNOSIS	Count							1	1	1	0	0	1						
STRATEGIC VIGILANCE PROJECT GROUP	Count													9	3	3	0	3	0

Table 8.6 indicates that Company E, D, and T respectively cumulate 11, 19, and 21 months of programming backlog for method-products over an annual cycle. In addition, the carry forward of these methodological sequences over the following year has, as a consequence, a lesser respect of the initial calendar time, namely 96%, 61%. and 81% (Company E, D, & T respectively). In other words, the time, change energy spent indicator, envisaged by persons for an annual cycle decreased from 5.83 h to 5.63 h (Company E), 5.36 h to 3.27 h (Company D), and 12 h to 9.75 (Company T).

From an explanatory point of view, the delay observed in the company D finds its source in an ERP installation during the research-intervention period. For Company T, the variation is due to the short-time method-products used (*integral diagnosis, task group and implementation project groups*), which implies, on a product line, the line "personnel." Beyond these explanatory factors, our experiment in the steering of planning illustrates the lack of sensitivity of the actors to the frequencies/rhythms of change, and a reading of the planning lines (method-products mobilized to achieve the objectives), which are *linear* and *analytical* in contrast to a cyclic and systemic reading.

Time, Performance, and Economic Sensibility

Through our interventions, we observed changes in the way that the various actors understood the frequency/rhythm of the intervention. Indeed, at the start and in the negotiating phase, the desire of the client was for the project-driver to go more quickly than the planning suggested by the intervener. This impatience resulted in an interest in increasing meeting frequency, accelerating the rate/rhythm of the method-products, and allocating more time volumes to the entire change action. The customer was impatient and the organization wanted to act on the estimated planning in order to obtain results quickly.

In the implementation phase, the customer often, voluntarily or involuntarily, defers the dates of the sequences. All these modifications of planning affect the global process and belong to the intervention steering. At the change process level, we observe more or less important changes in the initial schedule (e.g., a customer asking for an increase in the frequency of the actions of change). Within this context, it can be negotiated with the operating team, developing a new planning that can be extended over a greater duration. The temporal sensitivity of the actors is very variable according to the organizational situations we have been working in. Nevertheless we agree that this temporal sensitivity does improve during the process stages. The time schedules also foster it. In the company's perimeter, we also observe delays in the implementation of the change actions. Taking into account the hidden time of **synchronization**, preparation and steering in order to progressively put them inside the agenda becomes a relevant indicator to measure the implication of the actors in the change process.

Some objectives cannot be carried out without a period of *fermentation* (i.e., the **development** of an improved economic sensitivity [**economic balances**]). This change is deep and can be described as an incremental and *hidden result*, acting for the intervention success in its entirety.

TIME IN THE CHANGE PROCESS

Our observations highlight the fact that individuals appropriate change perspectives by interacting and talking with one another in a constructive way. The method-products used for carrying out an intervention-research are aimed at defragmenting the organization in order to assume a better balance between **conflict-cooperation** (Savall & Zardet, 1987). There still exists an incompressible time for sense-making (Roche, 2014). There also exists a **chronobiological rhythm** for modifying practices, which is different for each individual and based on the change objective. The different speeds of individuals evolution in change process are accepted provided everyone is progressing and thus those individuals are committed to change.

Change Time and Chronobiological Rhythms

SEAM advocates **proximity management**. Our research demonstrates that the more we reduce intervention time, the more the **hidden costs** associated with this lack of **negotiation** and sense making (sources of mistakes) increase (Savall & Zardet, 1987). The excessive dematerialization of contacts seems to be toxic for change performance and **effectiveness**.

Extreme variation points in the change management process entail costs. Thus, if the rhythm is slow, the results will be delayed, the adaptation lags behind, and the actors go back to their routines. On the contrary, if the rhythm is too fast, there change is rejected and materialized by a social breakdown, which takes the forms of **absenteeism**, non-quality defects, turn-over, and social conflicts in the daily activity. These consequences are counterproductive with regard to the quest for increased performance. The results of the SEAM change process are hidden costs reduction, decision-making process stimulation, and realistic change implementation. We have to keep in mind that the **IIQDHP**[2] shows a 200 to 4,000% return on investment (Savall & Zardet, 1987).

The discussion now turns to difficulties due to the twofold nature of time—calendar time and resource time.

Calendar and Resource Time

Looking at the difficulty involved in trying to reconcile resource time, the volume of time necessary for the intervention to be carried out, and calendar time, *scheduling* seems the key factor in the successful implementation of change action. Planning is a genuine tool to diagnose the perennial diffusion of change. There still are incompressible times, relative to studied intervals and the fact that wanting to reduce these times or the frequency of the change actions does not inevitably increase the results. Planning is a living tool as well as a tool for negotiation. Initial planning is the object of a contract at the beginning of the partnership construction phase between the leader and the intervener. These exchanges constitute a testimony of the leader's willingness to accelerate the rate/rhythm of the sequences of work in the illusory hope that it will accelerate and increase the results. Updated planning (i.e., the planning which joins together the implementation [past] and the sequence to be realized [future]), takes into account possible delays, cancellations, and so forth. This planning is negotiated with the leader with a view to better understanding the gap between the CEO's *desire* and the actual *constraints* that are created in the change implementation phase.

Throughout our interventions, we have identified that taking into account the frequencies/rhythms of change by the leader and managerial staff is a success factor in the change process. The essence of a change action engages organizational members on a deeper level than actions focused solely on appearance. Therefore, the question of the instrumented steering of intervention times by the pilot of the change approach is essential. Indeed, it is necessary to reinforce the *management control* function so that it integrates the short- and long-term dimensions, in and out of its perimeter, and that it manages the *resources* (calendar time and resource time) and their allotment. The synchronization between the field, the reality of the actors, and the activity steering makes it possible for organizational members to develop their autonomy within the framework of a synchronized decentralization of decision-making processes.

The Intervener: A Realistic Catalyzer

The principle of *synchronized decentralization* is also applicable to the relationship between external interveners and *company actors*. On this point, the role of the intervener during the research-intervention concerns realistic space-time steering.

In the **expert-opinion** that is built following the diagnosis, the intervener frequently alerts the company to the fragmentation **risks** of the spaces represented by board members, the managerial staff, and the employees. Different points, validated by the actors, can shed light on the elitist forms that might exist in the company, which in turn requires, on the part of the intervener, many listening and mediating acts to implement the **Horivert** principle.

In the absence of real *temporal steering* carried out by organizational members, the intervener can resort to a number of incentives with respect to initial engagements and must show **vigilance** with respect to the many requests, in particular during the crisis period, from the actors who want to postpone scheduled actions. The explanatory factors of these deprogramming acts seem to reflect the reflex of short-term steering ability of company actors, to the benefit of apparent **immediate results**. At the same time, there can be a desire to defer work sequences under the pretense of an illusory preparation of work. We can note that the variation between the commitments entered into and those carried out does not cease to dwindle during months, thus translating training into commitment.

Finally, in terms of *realistic steering*, in the role of catalyst interveners must place their actions and words on a "soft" axis. The resulting **piloting**, comparable to soft pressure, must produce effects of positive stimulation rather than rejection. The result of our observations indicates that the intervener plays a role of thermostat. When the leader wants to intensify and accelerate work, it is necessary to alert him on the risks of exhaustion of the actors. Similarly, when leaders wants to reduce these efforts, slowing them down, the intervener must alert them on the risks of actor inertia.

CONCLUSION

ISEOR intervention-research shows that we do not necessarily obtain results more quickly while trying to reduce the rhythm of the intervention. A willingness to reduce the volume and rhythms of the **method-products** *a priori*, in the first stages of the intervention, does not result in time savings or enhanced performance earnings. On the contrary, gaps typically appear between the initial intervention planning and **implementation planning**. Acting on the method-products volume (e.g., numbers of meetings and their time valorization) does not improve the result of a change action. Indeed, some method-products are necessary even if they may appear superfluous at the beginning (e.g., **internal interveners** and inter-company trainings). Each method-product has its purpose and focus—an operating scope at the same time space (perimeter) and temporal (frequency/rhythm) —which make it possible to contribute to short-, middle- and long-term results.

The role and posture of the change agent, which is neither hard nor soft but *progressive* in working with the leader and overall organization, are essential for the success of a change process aiming at endogenous, sustainable, economic and **social performance** stimulation. The engineering transfer of the change avoids the putting under drip of the organization by the external intervener. Indeed, the opposite develop dependence to the external intervener lend to reduce the autonomy of the organization and to hinder its development.

NOTES

1. The research for this chapter has been influenced by a number of works that are not directly referred to in the text, including Boje and Rosile (2003), De Préneuf (2014), Foucart, M. (2015), Foucart, P. (2012), Gephart (2009), Perroux (1979), Savall (1981, 2010, 2012), Savall and Zardet (1987, 1992, 2011), and Savall, Zardet, and Bonnet (2000, 2008).
2. **IIQDHP** is the **intangible investment** in qualitative **development of human potential**. The intangible investment represents the time dedicated to the modification of an actor's practices. The qualitative development is composed of three components: the energy (potential), the behaviors' modification (**cooperation**), and skills development. The **human potential** is the willingness of people to act on a deep and sustainable practice modification.

REFERENCES

Boje, D., & Rosile, G.-A. (2003). Comparison of socio-economic and other trans-organizational development methods. *Journal of Change Organizational Management, 16*(1), 10–20.

Buono, A. F., & Savall, H. (Eds.) (2007). *Socio-Economic intervention in organizations: The intervener-researcher and the SEAM approach to organizational analysis.* Charlotte, NC: Information Age Publishing.

De Préneuf, G. (2014). Changer en permanence pour une adaptation sur-mesure [Permanent change to crafted adaptation]. In H. Savall & V. Zardet (Eds.), *La conduite du changement dans les entreprises et les organisations* [Change Management within Companies and Organizations]. Paris, France: Economica.

Foucart, M. (2015). Gouvernance et management socio-économique en phase de maturité [Governance and socio-economic management in maturity phase]. In H. Savall & V. Zardet (Eds.), *Gouvernance et management : quelle coopération?* [Governance and management: What cooperation?]. Paris, France: Economica.

Foucart, P. (2012). Transmission d'entreprises pratiquant le management socio-économique en Belgique [Company practicing socio-economic management transmission in Belgium]. In H. Savall & V. Zardet (Eds.), *Les entreprises familiales: Création, succession, gouvernance et management* [Family businesses. creation, succession, governance and management]. Paris, France: Economica.

Gephart, R. P. (2009). An invitation to ethnostatistics. *Revue Sciences de gestion – Management Sciences – Ciencias de Gestión, 70,* 85.

Perroux, F. (1979). L'entreprise, l'équilibre rénové et les coûts cachés [The enterprise, the renovated balance and the "hidden" costs]. Preface. In H. Savall. *Reconstruire l'entreprise* [Reconstructing the enterprise] Paris, France: Dunod.

Piaget, J. (1975). *L'équilibration des structures cognitives, problème central du développement* [Cognitive structures equilibration, development main issue]. Paris, France: Presses Universitaires de France.

Roche, A. (2014, November). *Donner du sens au travail: La question de la reconnaissance de l'utilité sociale* [Work sense making, social utility recognition]. Paper presented at the Journée de recherche IP&M [Psychoanalytical and Management Institute Research Conference].

Savall, H. (1974). *Enrichir le travail humain dans les entreprises et les organisations* [An economic evaluation of job enrichment]. Paris, France: Dunod.

Savall, H. (1981–2010). *Work and people: An economic evaluation of job enrichment.* 1st ed. New York: Oxford University Press ; 2nd ed. Charlotte, NC: Information Age Publishing

Savall, H. (2012). *Origine radicale des crises économiques: Germán Bernácer, précurseur visionnaire* [Root origin of crises: Germán Bernácer, a visionary forerunner]. Charlotte, NC: Information Age Publishing.

Savall, H., & Zardet, V. (1987). *Maîtriser les coûts et les performances cachés : Le contrat d'activité périodiquement négociables* [Mastering hidden costs and performance: The periodically negotiable activity contract]. Paris: Economica.

Savall, H., & Zardet, V. (1992). *Le nouveau contrôle de gestion: Méthode des coûts-performances cachés* [New management control: The hidden cost-performance method]. Paris: Éditions Comptables Malesherbes-Eyrolles

Savall, H. & Zardet, V. (1995–2005–2009). *Ingénierie stratégique du roseau, souple et enracinée* [Strategic engineering of the reed, flexible and rooted]. Paris, France: Economica.

Savall, H., & Zardet, V. (2008). *Mastering hidden costs and performances.* Charlotte, NC: Information Age Publishing.

Savall, H., & Zardet, V. (2011). *The qualimetrics approach: Observing the complex object.* Charlotte, NC: Information Age Publishing.

Savall, H., & Zardet, V. (2013). *The dynamics and challenges of tetranormalization.* Charlotte, NC: Information Age Publishing.

Savall, H., Péron, M., & Zardet, V. (2014). Human potential at the core of socio-economic theory (SEAM). Paper presented at the SEAM Colloquim, Minneapolis, MN (April)

Savall, H., Zardet, V., & Bonnet, M. (2000–2008). *Releasing the untapped potential of enterprises through socio-economic management.* Geneva: Éditions IOT-BIT.

CHAPTER 9

BECOMING AN ARTIST-MANAGER

The Managerial Learning of a Theater Director[1]

Isabelle Horvath and Nathalie Krief

The purpose of this chapter is to describe the socio-economic intervention process carried out within a *performing arts organization* and analyze
its contributions, particularly from the point of view of the **development** of
managerial skills. The issue we raise is that of the ability of organizational
members, especially that of the Director, to reconcile the tension between
managerial skills and artistic skills, focusing on improving the organizational and financial performance of a cultural and **artistic organization**.

The performing arts sector is difficult to define (Barbéris & Poirson,
2013) as it covers a large number of disciplines (e.g., dance, theater,
opera, music), sizes of structures (e.g., National Opera of Paris has 1,600
people, National Theater of Nice has 33, and most institutions, on average,
have less than 10), status (association, direct labor, public cultural cooperation), and labels (National Drama Center, National Theater, Opera).

*The Socio-Economic Approach to Management Revisited: The Evolving Nature of SEAM in the
21st Century*, pp. 173–192
Copyright © 2015 by Information Age Publishing

This diversity requires various funding patterns, **staff regulations**, types of relationships with public and private funders, and, as a result, different managerial approaches. Beyond this disparity, the performing arts organizations have common needs to create, buy and distribute an artistic product, and they all "depend on the creative work of artists" (Chiapello, 1997). Further, they fall within a highly institutionalized context: activity, objectives and measures that are implemented are shaped by an institutional anchoring (Aman, Mazars-Chapelon, & Villeseque-Dubus, 2014; DiMaggio & Powell, 1983; Meyer & Rowan, 1977).

Operating in a challenging economic and business environment, due to declining budgets and increased competition, the performing arts organizations seek to reduce costs, streamline the process of creating and producing shows, and increase attendance. However, they wish to preserve the creation and program planning as an area of freedom, which raises the central question of reconciliation between *managerial logic* and *artistic logic* (Benghozi, 1995; Bonnafous-Boucher, Chatelain-Ponroy, Evrard, & Mazallon, 2003; Canas, 1987; Maitlis & Lauwrence, 2003; Turbide & Laurin, 2009). They often find themselves completely unable to reach this objective and sometimes err by imitating the methods of the traditional commercial sector, which leads to "mimetic isomorphism" (DiMaggio & Powell, 1983), while they fear it. We are then talking more about filling theaters as an objective rather than about quality and artistic education through the use of static **management tools** (e.g., **evaluation**, performance monitoring tools). What emerges is a form of Taylorism (sectorization of services, sectorization of people, hermetic hierarchy) with a **risk** of decentration of the project to the benefit of technical support activities, such as **communication** functions. Artistic logic could then disappear behind the administrative logic, and the show would become a consumer product deprived of its symbolic and societal values.

Our research is based on the scientific observation of a National Drama Center (NDC) of 50 people, with a budget of 5 million euros. Although under the private status of COPS (Cooperative and Participative Society), it is funded up to 80% by the State and local government and 20% through its own receipts (ticket sales, co-productions, amateur workshops). As for all NDCs, the director is an artist, recruited for his artistic skills and appointed by the Ministry of Culture and Communication. In our case study, the Directorate is embodied by two directors. Succeeding a director who held his appointment for 27 years, in 2002 the two new directors took on the management of the theater without any experience running an institution of this size. Their plan was to integrate the functions of manager and artist, increase cross-organization **interactions**, expand the mission of employees, and increase theater attendance. At the time, the overall direction was particularly fragmented and managerial deficiency aggravated organizational segmentation.

Through the conduct of a socio-economic intervention in the theater, we examine how the process of organizational learning has helped build the managerial skills of the director-artist (the second director left the theater to oversee another during the socio-economic intervention) and thereby to better articulate the artistic project and the organizational one. In order to do this, we conducted a threefold analysis. The first and second parts, respectively, describe the process of socio-economic intervention and its results. The third attempts to show, in the problematic context of rationalization, how such a process enables an organizational transformation for fostering the artistic project, while simultaneously developing *human potential* and human and financial *internal resources*.

THE SOCIO-ECONOMIC INTERVENTION

At the time of the intervention, the NDC had a staff of 40 permanent full-time equivalent employees (administrators, technicians, *actors*, directors), and about 165 intermittent (artists, technicians, various interveners) are involved in its activities. Payroll amounted to over 1.7 million, roughly 37% of its budget.

The National Drama Center

The National Drama Center (NDC) was funded by the State and RDCA (Regional Direction of Cultural Affairs; over 40%), municipality (which also owns the buildings; 20%), department (8%), Region (6%), and another city (5%) that has a theater in which the NDC occasionally gives a performance. A framework agreement was signed for three years between these partners.

From a structural point of view, the NDC has a large theater of more than 740 seats, two rooms of 120 and 49 seats, a touring theater, and a national drama school responsible for training future professional actors. On average, approximately thirty shows (excluding tours) are offered on 150 different dates.

The activity of the NDC depends on a decentralization contract signed between the Ministry of Culture and the director, which describes the project activities defined by management and integrates its specific constraints (e.g., creation, sensitization, audience development, link with the territory). Its activities are centered mainly on the creation, distribution and co-production of plays. The program also offers activities in dance, circus, and music, and important efforts are made toward public schools (e.g., intervention in schools, booklets provided to teachers to help preparing school sessions, exchanges between students and artists). Other activities and sensitization actions were also developed, such as public lectures, open rehearsals, discussions, and training of amateur actors.

National Drama Center Problematics

Upon their arrival in 2002, the two directors inherited an institution that was heavily influenced by the personality of their predecessor, who practiced a relatively centralized and paternalistic management style. The public was faithful to the enterprise, but the theater posted a deficit of almost 200,000 euro. The new directors, with the help of the Administrator and Secretary General, led an organizational change focused on: reducing the deficit, diversifying programming and the attending public, empowering the employees, and expanding their mission. The main question concerned the ability of the organization to change in order to develop the theater's activities and, through them, the ability of its managers to train themselves for the artist-manager function. Ultimately, this dual role had to be accepted by the staff, both as artists and managers.

Stages of the Socio-Economic Intervention

The **intervention-research** lasted 27 months. It took place in accordance with ISEOR's four stages of problem solving: diagnosis, the project, **implementation**, and evaluation.

Socio-Economic Diagnosis

This section examines the different stages of the diagnosis: qualitative identification of **dysfunctions**, the quantitative stage of calculating **hidden costs**, mirror-effect restitution stage, and interpretation of results stage (**expert opinion**). As part of the *qualitative stage*, which focused on identifying *dysfunctions* in the organization, 15 interviews were conducted:

- 6 individual interviews (2 hours) with members of the management team and coaches (2 art directors, 1 property manager, 1 secretary general, 1 technical manager, 1 director of studies)
- 9 group interviews (1.5 hours with 40 permanent and intermittent employees.

Overall, 631 **fieldnote quotes** were collected on the six themes of dysfunction nomenclature: **working conditions**, **work organization**, **commu-**

nication-coordination-cooperation, *time management*, *integrated training*, and *strategic implementation*. These basic themes were then divided into 39 sub-themes and 136 generic key-ideas of dysfunctions.

The themes of "communication-coordination-cooperation" and "strategic implementation" registered the majority of the ideas expressed by organizational members (more than 300 fieldnote quotes), revealing their most sensitive concerns. These included a lack of relationship between services and management, and a lack of staff involvement in the construction and implementation of the strategic and artistic project.

For the *quantitative stage*, calculating the **hidden costs** linked to the identified dysfunctions, 13 additional interviews were conducted with 19 people. The amount of hidden costs calculated using a simplified model was 285,000 euro (see Table 9.1), approximately 6% of the budget.

Table 9.1.   Synthesis of Hidden Costs Evaluation Per Indicator and Component © ISEOR

Components / Indicators	Oversalary	Overtime	Over-consumption	Non-production	Noncreation of potential	Risk	TOTAL
Absenteeism	NE	NE	NE	NE	NE	NE	NE
Work accidents	NE	NE	NE	NE	NE	NE	NE
Personnel turnover	1,000 €	26 000 €	NE	NE	NE	NE	26,000 €
Nonquality	2,000 €	54 000 €	NE	27,000 €	NE	NE	83,000 €
Direct productivity variance	35,000 €	124 000 €	2,000 €	14,000 €	NE	NE	175,000 €
TOTAL	38,000 €	204,000 €	2,000 €	41,000 €	NE	NE	285,000 €

The basic objective was not to produce accurate numbers as much as it was to help the players generate a representation of the potential savings that could benefit the organization's **development**. The most important hidden costs concerned direct **productivity** variance and, most particularly, human **regulation** of organizational defects, definition and division of tasks.

The presentation of the qualitative and quantitative results was done according to the **mirror-effect** principle. This method allows both the **intervener-researcher** and the organizational members to compare the specific ideas of organizational members (fieldnote quotes) and the generic, permanent ideas raised by the intervener-researcher (key ideas). The mirror-effect has two functions: first, to lead organizational members to interact with each other from a common representation; and second, to interact with the researcher to build a common platform for work (Krief & Zardet, 2013). It also helps to underscore the solidarity of all the actors in the generation of the dysfunctions.

The presentation drew a map of the organization, that is to say, a set of mental representations that will evolve throughout the intervention. It enabled the interveners to highlight the representation gaps between business groups (administrative, artistic, technical) and hierarchical levels, which caused problems in the collective process of making the show, as outlined by the following quotes:

- "The administration never comes to us. (Technicians)
- "In practice the technique does not know what we do." (Administrative)

The mirror-effect was completed with an interpretative analysis of the results, through the expression of an *expert opinion*, that is, the interpretation by the intervener-researcher of the image described. This perspective is a counterfactual analysis of the "expressed" based on the ***"unvoiced" comments*** (Krief & Zardet, 2013). Several points emerged from this second degree analysis.

The contradiction between the overall design of the theatrical performances and the participation of many trades, sometimes structured as corporations, created divisions and a lack of **communication** between the departments. For example, the public relations service was not getting the programming information sufficiently in advance to inform the public; similarly, technical and administrative services were not sufficiently coordinated, which required re-planning the setting up of the scenery and interventions on stage several times.

This lack of communication and consultation also concerns the hierarchical **structure**, which caused a lack of understanding, sharing and implementation of the strategy. If managers have, artistically, their place in the organization, they struggle to find it as a *manager*. As an example, one of them noted that, "We try to have everyone is in his/her place. It is not always understood." The split between the director-artist and the director-manager causes some individualization of management, emphasized in the following fieldnote quote:

> "The Directorate pays a lot of attention to technique because if a technician says 'I'm going to stop setting up a scenery,' it's a catastrophe."

Managers rely on the Secretary General and the Administrator. As the following quotes indicate, this "many-headed" management is difficult to manage for employees:

- "It's a variable geometry management. I do not think it's good."
- "I have the feeling of that my boss is the chief secretary and not the directors."

If the diagnosis and oral presentation of the mirror-effect help to make one aware of dysfunctions, the expert opinion is a step in the awareness of the need to activate a process of improvement.

The Socio-Economic Innovation Project

After the diagnosis, five cross-disciplinary working groups were formed to address the issues identified by the actors and completed by the intervener-researcher. These working groups were set up based on baskets of dysfunctions (or areas of work), made by the intervener-researcher and reworked by the management team. The players placed themselves in an appropriation process of the socio-economic approach by demonstrating an ability to adapt process, negotiate and invent new solutions (Aubouin, Coblence, & Kletz, 2012; Benghozi, 2006), by reinterpreting the data in an ongoing dialogue with the intervener-researcher. Table 9.2 presents the axes of mobilization.

The objective of the project group was to bring proposals for improvement actions. No less than 62 proposals were made to the project team. The most significant was the Internet facility in the theater set workshops, drafting a new memo on how to borrow vehicles, defining a new organizational structure, establishing of a trading system on the objectives of each person, and redefining the mission of each person. The project group was responsible for reviewing each proposal and establishing a list of implementation priorities

Implementation and Evaluation

The implementation phase is to prepare and then perform the action. In the case of our experiment, it relied primarily on the appropriation of management tools, the principle of which was a reading grid of the organization and a way of triggering decision making. It is important to note that the implementation phase began when one of the two directors left, which gave the opportunity to the remaining director to assert further his role as manager.

The *evaluation* enabled the director and the organizational members to assess the reduction of hidden costs, highlighting improvements to the dysfunctions and stimulating new behaviors. The most important points will be emphasized in the next section.

Table 9-2 Themes of the Working Groups

GROUPS	AXES OF MOBILIZATION	PERSONS
Working group # 1	ORGANIZATION AND BUILDING	**11 persons including** 1 "artistic" 3 "tecnical" 1 "general secretariat" 2 "management" 1 cleaning lady 1 watchman 1 organizer: representing actors 1 project head
Working group # 2	PLANNING AND PACE OF WORK	**9 persons including** 1 "artistic" 2 "tecnical" 2 "general secretariat" 1 "management" 1 cleaning lady 1 organizer: general secretary, 1 project head
Working group # 3	SHOWS AND AUDIENCES	**11 persons including** 1 "artistic" 3 "tecnical" 3 "general secretariat" 1 "management" 1 cleaning lady 1 organizer: school educational director 1 project head
Working group # 4	DELEGATION AND MOTIVATION	**11 persons including** 2 "artistic" 2 "technical" 4 "general secretariat" 1 "management" 1 organizer: tecnical director 1 project head
Working group # 5	COMMUNICATION	**10 persons including** 3 "artistic" 2 "tecnical" 2 "general secretariat" 1 "management" 1 organizer: administrator 1 project head

FROM THE ARTIST DIRECTOR TO
THE ARTIST-MANAGER DIRECTOR

The following discussion focuses on the analysis of results of implementation and evaluation, with a particular examination of the emerging process of developing the director's managerial skills. In this section, we focus on the socio-economic intervention process seen as a process of *organiza-*

tional learning (Argyris & Schön, 1978). It is a modification of behaviors and mental representations through actions by company **actors** (Plane, 2000). Learning is described as organizational as soon as the acquisition of knowledge, even strictly individual, changes the behavior of the entity as a whole (Huber, 1991). It prompts introspection leading to an enhancement of existing knowledge and building skills to acquire new ones, developing a "soft **socio-economic management**, both rigorous and flexible, [which] allows the agreement between creative art and rigorous management" (Savall, 2002, pp. 8–9). The analysis attempts to identify the factors that helped transform NDC's director to rethink his position and role in the organization.

Emergence of Managerial Skills

Socio-economic intervention occurred at two levels for the director—with his relationship with the staff and his own perception as director. The diagnosis and **project phases** are "transfer tools" that are intended to improve dialogue with employees. They also underscored the problems of listening and dialogue raised by the staff:

- "What is missing is the direct exchange with the management team or rather the directors."
- "Clearly there is a communication failure with the two principals."

The very fact of accepting a diagnosis of **dysfunctions** with the participation of all employees, to be present at the restitution of the mirror-effect, and taking into account the proposals of the working groups was seen as a major mark of trust from the director vis-à-vis the workforce. An indirect dialogue had been established, which improved the direct exchange between the parties.

- The diagnosis also revealed the ambiguity of "many-headed" leadership and the role of each person:
- "Whenever we talk about art direction, there are two persons. When we talk about management, there are three persons."
- "With two directors I often ask myself the question, to whom should I speak, because they have not shared the work."

A need arose to define and affirm the scope of action of each player (directors, secretary general, administrator). The departure of one of two directors at the end of the project phase accelerated the organizational transformation, because the remaining director had to assume full responsibility.

Managerial Learning

The project *implementation* phase was based on three tools of socio-economic management: the Internal-External Strategic Plan (IESP) defined by the director for the entire structure; the *Priority Action Plan (PAP)* to breakdown the strategy at departmental level; and the *Periodically Negotiable Activity Contract (PNAC)* to match the objectives, means and actions at the individual level.

Through an application of these tools, organizational members were exposed to the breaking-down principle, shifting the focus from management to employees. They also experienced an interrogative and descriptive principle with a common lexicon for the three tools, which enabled a new common understanding of the organization in terms of common strategic axes, priority objectives, priority actions, services involved, and planning implementation.

The NDC manager has subsequently drafted a document outlining:

- *Strategic axes*: emphasizing sustainable recapture of the audience, focusing on the European dimension of the theater.
- *Objectives*: constitution of the European company, implementation of an organization (communication, technique, administration) in the service of art.
- *Actions*: recruitment of new players, defining a common message to all actors in the theater, implementation of an organizing tool for a typical season based on data from different services, and implementation of management tools adapted to the new organization.
- *Services*: focused on administrative, technical and *artistic services*.

As expressed by the director, the IESP "imposed" him to "reformulate [his] desire while integrating the various parameters of the organization" (see Horvath & Berutti, 2012, p. 103). This formalization effort began to narrow the gap between his role as manager and his artistic function. It also facilitated his ability to connect the artistic *project* and the organizational project, providing an answer to the problem of misalignment of the artistic project and the lack of clarification raised by the stakeholders in the process of diagnosis. For example:

- *"The project is not readable."*
- *"We have a project well written but there is not enough specific planning for implementation."*
- *"We do not have any common goal to move in the same direction."*

In the same vein, the secretary general implemented a number of new measures: (1) establishing a new system of meetings (thematic, inter-services and operational, limited in time); (2) redefining missions, including an enlargement of responsibility areas (especially for the communication manager or receptionist); (3) reducing the slippage of functions; and (4) developing tools for internal and external communication (e.g., internal bulletin, performance description, brochure), including in-house mail and a computer tree view to facilitate the flow of information and ***coordination*** between people.

These qualitative results have jointly brought about quantitative and financial outcomes linked to time saving (up to 25% reduction in ***hidden costs***) and an increase in the audience (11.5%).

LESSONS LEARNED

The main problem faced by performing arts companies concerns environmental constraints (commercial and financial) and, consequently, the development of the organization, which is fraught with a fear of loss of identity linked to freedom and creativity. The tension between art and management was inherited from the romantic figure of the artist of the 18th and 19th centuries. This trend is still present today, despite the fact that the 20th century reflected a "slow professionalization of managerial responsibility" (Boisbeau, 2008). Often polyphonic, it is distributed among several individuals (artistic director, executive director) and several situations (e.g., internal management and public backers). Given the diffuse nature of power, multiplicity of objectives and divergent interests, these organizations can be characterized as pluralistic (Denis, Lamothe, & Langley, 2001).

Since the beginning of the 21st century, this hybrid form focused on a single individual. While reaffirming the operational and strategic role of the administrator, and the necessary complicity with the director-artist, management becomes polymorphic (Dupuis, 2010). It requires more skills, both as internal manager but also as public relations officer with relationships with private and public partners. This does not necessarily mean "selling one's soul to the devil," but it is critical that these individuals remain respectful of the balance between economic requirements and the artistic project.

Direct observation of arts organizations and the professional literature reveals a race to questioning without proposing an access road to a new form that would be the artist-manager. From the "Talks of Valois" (2008–2009) (meeting on the future of the performing arts) and the Observatory Prospective Trades and Qualifications of Performing Arts, to specialized press files (e.g., The Stage, Performing Arts Newsletter), studies and testimonies from multitasking managers multiply. Scientists (Benghozi, 1995, 2006; Chiapello, 1998; Dupuis, 2010; Leroy, 1996) also emphasize the need for a reinterpretation of the relationship between art and management.

Several experiments show the possibility of "a new form of meeting" (Aubouin et al., 2012; Horvath & Datry, 2013) because "it is impossible to separate the work from its physical and organizational development conditions" (Benghozi, 1995, p. 85).

Intervention-research seems to be a way to guide these organizations, as we try to demonstrate in the following sections.

The Necessary Plasticity of Intervention-Research

At the beginning of this chapter we highlighted the complexity of the sector, in part because of the labels associated with it. The National Drama Center is part of these labels and its features accentuate the traits of this kind of organization. Created in 1947, as part of theater decentralization policy, NDCs fulfill a theatrical creation mission of public interest (officially recognized as a benefit to the country). Within this context, the artistic dimension immerses the organization. Hence, the resistance to change can arise—sometimes in unexpected places. This is the case of our experimentation field.

Upon his arrival in 2002, the administrator wanted to reduce the deficit, which he achieved by acting on visible costs (e.g., management of supplies, travel, building). In our first interviews, he confided his difficulty in guiding directors to work on the art project within the financial constraints. At first, he saw our intervention-research as a way of capturing and balancing the managerial logic with the artistic logic. However, he expressed some reluctance on the importance of calculating hidden costs and still more about the implementation of socio-economic *management tools*, saying: "It will no longer be a theater. Where will the share between creativity and freedom be?"

The assertion of the place and role of the director as manager somehow dislodged him from its central function in the overall organization. It will take time for him to rebuild his own identity within the *structure* (e.g., the change of name from "director" to "executive director" has certainly helped).

The *evaluation* stage, which ended our intervention-research in the theater, was invaluable, because it was the key moment for standing back from all the actions that were carried out and their development. According to the executive director, the intervention has allowed people to speak openly. Although there still appeared to be a lot of unspoken concerns, the leaders were able to take a more global approach to the organization by questioning the role and tasks of each person. The separation between the design of the artistic project and its implementation at the operational level has faded away.

The director (artist) took charge of the *socio-economic management* tools himself, not without difficulty, but with *confidence*. Several versions of the IESP were made, before being built from the artistic project while integrating organizational parameters. The director has also shown a willingness to train himself. Indeed, the transformation of the artistic project into an artistic *and* organizational project, which required a shift in his mindset with regard to his approach to his environment and his profession, was made possible by the use of IESP in its matrix dimension. The *intervener-researcher* created this dynamic by presenting a possible example of IESP and PAP (see Tables 9.3 and 9.4).

Table 9.3.   Excerpt of the IESP (© ISEOR 1986)

STRATEGIC AXES	PRIORITARY OBJECTIVE	SERVICES INVOLVED	PROVISIONNAL PLAN		
			Seasons		
			2009/2010	2010/2011	2011-2012
Give an european dimension of theater	Create an European company	Director Playwright/ Theatrical troupe leader	X		

The challenge was not necessarily to implement management tools in this precise manner, but rather to assist the director in breaking down and highlighting the stages of the project, so as to take the fullest account of the involvement of different players in the organization. The tools have played a type of matrix role by changing the representations of the organization.

Eventually, the director did not develop an IESP in a tabular form, but all the elements that would be helpful to create a new organizational form were present and responded to the deficiencies identified during the diagnosis. The reconstructed PAP from the director's presentation is presented in Table 9.5.

While the director had a relatively compartmentalized artistic representation of the project and its *implementation* from a managerial point of view, the PAP and the IESP, adapted to his needs, allowed him to develop a new way of reading the organization and a plan to implement new management practices. The plasticity of the tools and processes was a key parameter of the intervention-research and proved to be adaptable to different cultural contexts.

Table 9.4.   Excerpt of the PAP (© ISEOR 1986)

STRATEGIC AXES	PRIORITY OBJECTIVE	PRIORITY ACTION	SERVICES INVOLVED	PLANNING					
				Month 1	Month 2	Month 3	Month 4	Month 5	Month 6
Give an european dimension of theater	Create an European company	Define a theater repertory	Director						
		Organize meetings with players	Director	X	X	X	X	X	X
		Finalize the adequacy actors/repertory	Playwright/ Theatrical troupe leader						

The Anti-Virus Approach to Taylorism-Fayolism-Weberism

"The cultural sector is characterized by the special position of the artistic work in the production process. It is the ferment which feeds activity, from which it draws its rationale, its legitimacy" (Busson, 2004, p. 51). The show is the source of energy and the result of a coordinated set of actions and behaviors generated by the *actors*. The latter claim a cooperative model, whereas services and people are torn apart by dysfunctions and streamlining initiatives. This interaction leads to a *risk* of *bureaucracy*, reducing significantly relationships between people. The lack of a comprehensive approach creates a threat of standardization and homogenization of the creative process. This is what the *socio-economic theory* calls the "*TFW virus*" (for Taylorism-Fayolism-Weberism), namely the dogma of division, specialization, hierarchical organization, and impersonal rule as the operating management model of companies and organizations. This conception of the organization's activities and its management of people hold back potential players, being unaware of the changing levels of education, skills and personal aspiration as well as the new requirements of citizen-users.

Within this context, the intervention-research evaluation stage conducted in early 2010 with 37 people (5 people in the management team and 32 staff divided into 8 groups) revealed three main factors that can remedy to the risk of organization's denaturation.

The Passage from Director-Artist to Director Artist-Manager

The *artistic project* created by the Director highlights his effort to get an overall vision of the organization by defining its services or functions and the actions for its implementation. As an example, it explained that tour management responsibilities will be assumed internally by the production administrator and the program will be prepared by the secretary general in collaboration with the artistic advisor. There was a willingness on the part of the director to develop the artistic project as an organizational project.

The Hybridization of Skills

To develop inter-services **cooperation**, the secretary general established thematic inter-services meetings. For example, the issue of ticket pricing was treated by both the accountant and the public relations officer. The production administrator attended technical meetings and was then in a position to make the link between the constraints faced by the technicians and those of the administration. The creations surveillance was made by both the secretary general and the artistic advisor. This new logic further induces collaborative work and job enrichment.

Hidden Costs

The presentation of the evaluation of **hidden costs** and their reduction was a useful way to show that the savings were not only material (sometimes at the expense of creation) but they came from hidden human and social **resources** (see Table 9.6). However, just because the evaluation might show improvement results, this is not an end in itself. The appropriation of socio-economic **management tools** to enhance organizational steering promoted a dynamic of managerial learning that will become permanent over time. In particular, the director will ensure the **coordination** of all services and the generalized use of management tools, which is still partial. For example, the technical service missions are still unclear and delegation remains difficult between the technical director and the scenary construction workshops. A two-speed transformation may generate a new segmentation of the organization. This work is ongoing.

CONCLUSION

In this chapter, we have sought to show how socio-economic intervention could help an artist director of a theater in developing his managerial skills. Drawing on an intervention-research conducted between 2008 and 2010, there appear to be three ways in which the socio-economic process of change management (improvement process and management tools) is particularly suited to the performing arts sector.

The first is the questioning of the ambivalence between the nature of these organizations and their needs. Indeed, the players have, *a priori*, an attraction-repulsion with respect to management in general and management tools in particular. Anxious to maintain an identity linked to a "romantic" dimension of their activity, they expressed a distrust of anything that might hinder it. At the same time, they were seeking to create a better organization and a stronger recognition of their skills, but the context of budgetary restrictions compelled them to think about reconciling administrative and financial logic and artistic logic. However, our experiment

Table 9.5.   Reconstituted PAP by the Director (© ISEOR 1986)

STRATEGIC AXES	PRIORITY OBJECTIVE	PRIORITY ACTION	SERVICES INVOLVED	PLANNING					
				Month 1	Month 2	Month 3	Month 4	Month 5	Month 6
Sustainable recapture of the audience	Create an European company	Define a theater repertory	Director	X	X	X	X	X	X
		Define recruitment criteria	Director	X					
		Organize meetings with players	Directeur et Playwright/ Theatrical troupe		X				
		Integrate youg graduates of the school to the company	Playwright/ Theatrical troupe leader				X		
		Finalize the adequacy actors/repertory	Playwright/ Theatrical troupe leader					X	X
Improve internal and external communication	Convey a common message	Define an artistical message	Director	X					
		Develop new communication media reflecting the artistic message	Communication	X	X				
		Develop a sales leaflet for the public	Public relations and ticketing			X	X	X	
Improve external relations	Devlop relations with other NDC	Plan visits to other NDCs	Administrative officer and General Secretariat			X	X	X	X

Table 9.6.   Conversion of Dysfunctions to Performance

Dysfunction	Skills misused
Consequences	Time spent by a department head to perform tasks outside of his mission
Quantitative and financial evaluation	389h/year
	9 000 €/year
Improvement actions	Modification of workstations
	Redefining of missions
	Delegation
Investment	
Results	Investment in new development activities (program)
	Development of external relations (visits other theaters, improved corporate image, providing new information...)
	Financial gain estimated at 90% = 8 000 €

indicates that directors, without losing their artistic function, are able to build up their managerial skills, especially as part of a comprehensive approach process to the organization rather than a strictly artistic one.

The second reason is the plasticity of tools. As a template of producing actions, they are a powerful organizational learning mode that can be used to build a new mental representation of the organization (Savall & Zardet, 2001).

The third reason concerns the emergence of internal human, social and economic resources, through the recycling of hidden costs into added value. Acting exclusively on visible costs leads to a risk of misalignment of the artistic project in favor of a financial logic, and thus a weakening of the creative dynamic. In this context, *socio-economic management* seems to be a way to create a new balance between artistic logic and economic logic and thus a new organizational model for performing arts organizations. The term "artist-manager" highlights the potential reconciliation of art and management.

NOTE

1. The research for this chapter has been influenced by a number of works that are not directly referred to in the text, including Boje and Rosile (2003), Buono and Savall (2007), Gephart (2009), Perroux (1979), Savall (1974, 1975, 1977, 1981, 2010, 2012), Savall and Zardet (1987, 1992, 1995, 2005, 2009, 2013), and Savall, Zardet, and Bonnet (2000, 2008).

REFERENCES

Agid, P., & Tarondeau, J.-C. (2003). L'Opéra de Paris est-il économiquement gouvernable? [The Paris Opera is it economically governable?]. *Revue Française de Gestion, 29*(142), 147–168.

Amans, P., Mazars-Chapelon, A., & Villeseque-Dubus, F. (2014). Du "patchwork" au "canevas": Les rôles combinés des interactions et des outils de gestion autour d'un processus d'innovation dans le secteur du spectacle vivant [From the "Patchwork" to the "Canvas": The combined roles of interactions and management tools around a process of innovation in the performing arts sector]. *Innovation, 43*, 85–111.

Argyris, C., & Schön, D. (1978). *Organizational learning.* London, England: Addison-Wesley.

Aubouin, N., Coblence, E., & Kletz, F. (2012). Les outils de gestion dans les organisations culturelles: De la critique artiste au management de la création [The management tools in cultural organizations: From the critical artistic to the management of creation]. *Revue Management et Avenir, 54*, 191–214.

Barberis, I., & Poirson, M. (2013). *L'économie du spectacle vivant* [The economy of the performing arts]. Paris, France: Presses Universitaires de France.

Benghozi, P.-J. (1995). Les sentiers de la gloire: Savoir gérer pour savoir créer [The paths of glory: To know how to manage to know how to create]. In F. Charue-Duboc (Ed.), *Des savoirs en action: Contributions de la recherche en gestion* [Knowledge into action: Contributions of management research] (pp. 51–87). Paris, France: L'Harmattan.

Benghozi, P.-J. (2006). Les temps modernes: De la gestion des organisations à la gestion de projet. Le modèle du secteur culturel [Modern times: From the management of organizations to *project management*: The model of the cultural sector]. *Hermès, 44*, 71–78.

Benollet, P. (2007). Orchestrating compatibility between art and management: Socio-economic intervention in a national opera house. In A.F. Buono & H. Savall (Eds.), *Socio-economic intervention in organizations: The intervener-researcher and the SEAM approach to organizational analysis* (pp. 99–122). Charlotte, NC: Information Age Publishing.

Boisbeau, H. (2008). Évolution des contours sociologiques et juridiques de la profession (1789–1992) [Evolution of the sociological and legal contours of the profession (1789–1992)]. In P. Goetschel & J.-C. Yon (Eds.), *Directeurs de théâtre – XIXe-XXe siècles. Histoire d'une profession* [Theater Directors—19th and 20th centuries: Story of a profession] (pp. 13–29). Paris, France: Publications de la Sorbonne.

Boje, D., & Rosile, G.-A. (2003). Comparison of socio-economic and other trans-organizational development methods. *Journal of Change Organizational Management, 16*(1), 10–20.

Bonnafous-Boucher, M., Chatelain-Ponroy, S., Evrard, Y., & Mazallon, F. (2003). Quel avenir pour les théâtres lyriques? [What future for lyric theaters?]. *Revue Française de Gestion, 29*(142), 169–186.

Buono, A. F., & Savall, H. (Eds.) (2007). *Socio-economic intervention in organizations: The intervener-researcher and the SEAM approach to organizational analysis.* Charlotte, NC: Information Age Publishing.

Busson, A. (2004). Stratégie et politique d'entreprise [Strategy and business policy]. In Y. Evrard (Ed.), *Le management des entreprises artistiques et culturelles* [The management of arts and cultural enterprises] (2nd ed., pp. 15–61). Paris, France: Economica.

Canas, A. (1987). Stratégies et outils à l'usage des responsables culturels [Strategies and tools for use by cultural leaders]. *Revue Française de Gestion, 62*, 102–106.

Chiapello, E. (1997). Les organisations et le travail artistiques sont-ils contrôlables ? [Are the organizations and the artistic work controllable?]. *Réseaux, 15*(86), 77–113.

Chiapello, E. (1998). *Artistes versus managers: Le management culturel face à la critique artistique* [Artists versus managers: Cultural management faces art criticism]. Paris, France: Métailié.

Denis, J.-L., Lamothe, L., & Langley, A. (2001). The dynamics of collective leadership and strategic change in pluralistic organizations. *Academy of Management Journal, 44*(4), 809–837.

Dimaggio, P. J., & Powell, W.W. (1983). The iron-cage revisited: Institutional isomorphism and collective rationality in organizational fields. *American Sociological Review*, *48*, 147–160.

Dupuis, X. (2010). Culture et management [Culture and management]. In P. Poirrier (Ed.), *Politiques et pratiques de la culture* [Cultural policies and practices] (pp. 52–54). Paris, France: La Documentation Française.

Gephart, R. P. (2009). An INVITATION TO ETHNostatistics. *Revue Sciences de gestion – Management Sciences – Ciencias de Gestión*, *70*, 85.

Horvath, I., & Berutti, J.-C. (2012). Le management appliqué aux structures culturelles [Management applied to cultural structures]. *La Scène*, *64*, 102–103.

Horvath, I., & Datry, F. (2013). Point de vue méthodologique pour le développement des entreprises de spectacle vivant [Methodological perspective for the *development* of performing arts companies]. *Revue Recherches en Sciences de Gestion*, *94*, 111–127.

Huber, G. P. (1991). Organizational learning: The contributing processes and the literatures. *Organizational Science*, *2*, 88–115.

Krief, N., & Zardet, V. (2013). Analyse de données qualitatives et recherche-intervention [Qualitative data analysis and intervention-research]. *Revue Recherche en Sciences de Gestion*, *95*, 211–237.

Leroy, D. (1996). *Économie des arts du spectacle vivant* [Economy of performing arts]. Paris, France: L'Harmattan.

Maitlis, S., & Lauwrence, T. B. (2003). Orchestral manoeuvres in the dark: Understanding failures in organizational strategizing. *Journal of Management Studies*, *40*(1), 109–139.

Meyer, J. W., & Rowan, B. (1977). Institutional organizations: Formal structure as myth and ceremony. *American Journal of Sociology*, *83*, 340–363.

Perroux, F. (1979). L'entreprise, l'équilibre rénové et les coûts "cachés" [The enterprise, the renovated balance and the "hidden" costs]. Preface. In H. Savall. *Reconstruire l'entreprise* [Reconstructing the enterprise] Paris, France: Dunod. 2nd ed. in H. Savall & V. Zardet. Reconstruire l'entreprise, Paris: Dunod (2014)

Plane, J.-M. (2000). *Méthodes de recherche-intervention en management* [Management intervention-research methods]. Paris, France: L'Harmattan.

Savall, H. (1974–1975–1977). *Enrichir le travail humain dans les entreprises et les organisations* [An economic evaluation of job enrichment]. Paris: Dunod.

Savall, H. (1981–2010). *Work and people: An economic evaluation of job enrichment*. 1st ed. New York: Oxford University Press ; 2nd ed. Charlotte, NC: Information Age Publishing

Savall, H. (2002). *Le management des entreprises culturelles* [Management of cultural enterprises]. Actes du colloque annuel de l'ISEOR. Paris, France: Economica.

Savall, H. (2012). *Origine radicale des crises économiques: Germán Bernácer, précurseur visionnaire* [Root origin of crises: Germán Bernácer, a visionary forerunner]. Charlotte, NC: Information Age Publishing.

Savall, H., & Zardet, V. (1987). *Maîtriser les coûts et les performances cachés : Le contrat d'activité périodiquement négociables* [Mastering hidden costs and performance: The periodically negotiable activity contract]. Paris: Economica.

Savall, H., & Zardet, V. (1992). *Le nouveau contrôle de gestion: Méthode des coûts-performances cachés* [New management control: The hidden cost-performance method]. Paris: Éditions Comptables Malesherbes-Eyrolles

Savall, H., & Zardet, V. (1995–2005–2009). *Ingénierie stratégique du roseau, souple et enracinée* [Strategic engineering of the reed, flexible and rooted]. Paris: Economica.

Savall, H., & Zardet, V. (2001). L'évolution de la dépendance des acteurs à l'égard des dysfonctionnements chroniques au sein de leur organization: Résultats de processus de métamorphose [The evolution of the dependence of actors against chronic dysfunctions within their organization: Metamorphosis process results]. *Psychanalyse, Management et Dépendances au Sein des Organisations*, 179–212.

Savall, H., & Zardet, V. (2008). *Mastering hidden costs and performance*, Charlotte, NC: Information Age Publishing.

Savall, H., & Zardet, V. (2011). *The qualimetrics approach: Observing the complex object*. Charlotte, NC: Information Age Publishing.

Savall, H., & Zardet, V. (2013). *The dynamics and challenges of tetranormalization*. Charlotte, NC: Information Age Publishing.

Savall, H., Zardet, V., & Bonnet, M. (2000–2008). *Releasing the untapped potential of enterprises through socio-economic management*. Geneva: Éditions IOT-BIT.

Turbide, J., & Laurin, C. (2009). Performance measurement in the arts sector: The case of the performing arts. *International Journal of Arts Management, 11*, 56–70.

CHAPTER 10

ENTERPRISE RESOURCE PLANNING

A Tool for Understanding Hidden Costs and Performance?[1]

Nouria Harbi, Guy Saint-Léger, and Olivier Voyant

In their search for improvement, companies have heavily resorted to Enterprise Resource Planning (ERP) since the end of the 1990s. The main objective was primarily aimed at the function's partitioning in favor of a broader organization process approach. The study, deployment and implementation of this type of tool, however, generated disruptions and *in-depth* challenges in companies, both in terms of existing management methods and practices. The failures, unfortunately, were many. The chapter is focused on the factors that led to these difficulties and the underlying tensions faced by companies at a literal impasse between their *information system* and needed actions to get them out of these situations.

The discussion begins with an introduction to the general ERP context, followed by a specific case of an industrial company in trouble with its ERP system two years after its implementation. The analysis focuses on the

The Socio-Economic Approach to Management Revisited: The Evolving Nature of SEAM in the 21st Century, pp. 193–214

subsequent actions that were undertaken with the company, concluding with the lessons that emerged for ERP implementation in organizations.

THE CONTEXT OF ENTERPRISE RESOURCE PLANNING

As a way of framing our discussion of ERP, it is useful to explore several aspects of the process, focusing on how the concept has evolved over the past two decades.

Historical Properties of ERP

In the early 90s, ERP publishers were interested primarily in large groups of goods and services production. Since then *small- and medium-sized enterprises* (SMEs) have become a coveted target. These *projects* represent major investments for companies as well as a large part of uncertainty – in terms of the implementation process and its results, as the emergence of its content along the way (Besson & Rowe, 2011). Beyond the technological expertise of tool implementation, it aims above all to drive organizational transformation. This type of alteration in the company's information system requires preparation and quality support. Today it is not uncommon to find companies that are in their second or third ERP project. They are equipped with these tools and continue to use them, especially with current *technological developments* (e.g., open source, SaaS ERP, distributed networks, cloud computing). One question remains unanswered to this day —are the difficulties encountered in these projects the same as before?

The Nature of ERP

Enterprise Resource Planning is a type of modular product intended to ensure the management of all or part of the company's activities. It is composed of a single database, a single editor, a harmonized data coding across different services of the organization, *transverse and integrated processes* and *alignment* of these processes to the "Best Practices" embedded by the tool. In concept, these elements deeply meet the needs of companies that usually are equipped with redundant local heterogeneous data systems that do not interact or communicate with each other.

ERP is based on the principle of management by process, focused on creating value for the customer. So one shifts from a partitioned sequential organization to a mutual system, shared by the *actors* of the enterprise. This cross-functional approach requires and implies a willingness to cooperate and collaborate in the different phases of the migration project of information system. Indeed the intent is to achieve functional partitioning, to design a common professional reference that clarifies the definition of management concepts from one service to another and the links that drive them. This approach fundamentally changes existing management practices because it requires an understanding of global business of the company at the expense of a focus centered on the results of individual tasks. The organization management of the interdependence of trade between functions takes precedence over the individual tasks, especially as it is done in real time. The quality of the data handled by these systems is therefore a key element of their optimum operation if we want to take advantage of all the benefits of controlled informational and organizational *integration*. The question is how to support the implementation of an ERP to enable agents to cooperate and collaborate with each other. As such, it is necessary to clarify that a "lean management" type approach, focused on the optimization process mostly ignores the human dimension. Ultimately, these initiatives are not without *risk* of "backlash" from the organization.

Constraints and Changes for Final Users

The organizational transformation process is not without consequences for final users. There are a number of constraints that are imposed on the daily activities of final users that we can generally list in three major categories. First, the information system will be *modified* and must be accepted in the daily practices. Therefore it is very rare that organizational members are asked about their opinion about the tool's usefulness. Given this situation, it isn't any wonder why results point to repeated failures when the system is imposed by the decision makers. Moreover, the changes do not typically reflect the reality of everyday life for the final user.

Second, the information system will be *standardized*, that is, it will be the same for other users of other companies, while an organization will tend to believe its model is special and unique. Inevitably, it will not meet 100% of the company's needs—but it is still expected that organizational members will have to agree to change their habits because it is usually very expensive to modify existing software package (Besson, 1999). The standard version of the software involves adherence to a drive mode and a control of the organization. Can you imagine that ERP editors can design a miracle solution for all the needs of the organizations?

Third, the information system will be *built-in*, in direct **interaction** with other applications, other enterprise functions or areas. Relationships with colleagues and management will thus be changed. This interaction (exchange and data sharing) between the different business functions and hierarchical levels is problematic because it requires entities that are used to operate more or less independently to realize that their actions and their results are monitored or quotas of other functions (Beretta, 2002). Even the notion of goodwill does not suggest that the removal of borders is a guarantee for doing away with conflicting interests.

Problems Relative to ERP Deployment in SMEs

Rigor—the rigidity ERP in business planning—is often at odds with the practices of SMEs, which value their responsiveness, permanent adaptability to the market and their customers. In its formalized internal management mode, ERPs cannot handle unexpected and unstructured events. The consequences of this heaviness often manifest themselves through decisional ambiguity, where two opposing reactions are to be found—either we respect the process defined by the ERP, and lose a lot of creativity, flexibility and reactivity, or we get around the tool in ways that lose its intrinsic rigor. In other words, practitioners want to keep simple management principles rigorous and flexible, while ERP requires them to formalize and predict everything that can happen.

Visible costs to put in for the project corrupt the implementation stage —the software is considered by the manager as a ***development*** workshop packaged with less specifications. In fact, this seemingly attractive standard solution only seems less costly. The company then engages in a simplified approach of its information system. It goes to the essential and ignores its true characteristics for visible cost reasons.

In most cases, small investment devoted to the upstream phase of a project, which is to investigate the feasibility and impact of ERP, generates afterwards a large number of organizational dysfunctions. These reappear insidiously in the project during the deployment phase and post project. However, we found that companies that accept the challenges to their practice and spend time training their staff can quickly benefit from better use of the tool. ERP rarely includes a serious economic assessment of the situation in a before and after project comparison. It is the main cause of overspending, with considerable visible and ***hidden costs***. As the chapter will explore in the following sections, in-depth study of post advanced ERP phases allows for a measurement of results between what is desired by the leaders and the actual situation of the company with its information system.

THE STUDY: POST-ERP ADVANCED ASSESSMENT

The company under study is a French manufacturer (1,000 employees) that designs and manufactures electronic components for the market of major European car manufacturers. For reasons of confidentiality, anonymity of the company will be preserved.

Framework

In 2001, two years after the deployment of an ERP system (see Figure 10.1), the company's director was concerned about the lack of ownership of the software by the management. The company also had much higher inventory on stock compared to standards of the profession, which at the time was more than double the average indicated by the Federation of Industries of Equipment for Vehicles (FIEV). The expected results with the acquisition of ERP were not satisfactory and the situation was troublesome. The company's senior management wanted to understand the reasons for this situation and approached us to *diagnosis* the situation and implement the appropriate actions. Critical processes involved in the new system concerned production management, industrialization, management control, maintenance, quality, and purchasing. The number of users simultaneously connected to the software per day was about 200 organizational members.

The intervention started in January 2002. A one-year duration was initially set and later extended to two years, based on the scale of business and the actions launched on a pilot line chosen by the CEO. Questions began to emerge as to whether the delays in the deployment of the program were to be expected or unique to this particular situation. At that stage, the critical situation was rather exceptional. Decision makers even thought about abandoning the tool to select another. The priority objectives set by the top management based on the pilot line were intended to address concerns about the advanced post-project phase in critical situations by reducing the inventory levels and ensuring use of the ERP by management and employees.

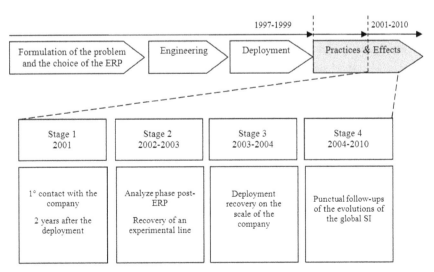

Figure 10.1.   Temporal process of the intervention.

Intervention Method

The methodology for this study case draws heavily on *socio-economic organization* theory developed by the ISEOR Research Center. Four phases make up this approach: diagnosis, the project group, implementation, and *evaluation*. These phases were aimed at transforming management practices throughout the company. This transformative intervention-research highlights the important role of *in-depth* experiments, as captured by the work of Kurt Lewin, and is it is geared toward generating assistance in organizational change. As reflected by the spirit of ISEOR's work, the researcher is involved in the field of research to help, as appropriate by offering various tools to the organization. The mission starts with the diagnosis of a pilot manufacturing line and then spread, the following year, to complete a reorganization of IT activities.

Data Acquisition

As part of this research, the leader gave us "carte blanche" to solicit input from any employee who met our needs. Thus, we were in contact with all members of the management, all staff and line managers and final users of the system (see Table 10.1).

The data came mainly from the processing of application systems and support documents used for the management of production lines and related production services. Financial and accounting data were provided by *management control* and the direction (upper management). The technical data were provided by industrialization managers, production-logistics, and the IT department.

All the data were subjected to a detailed analysis with users using the following 4-step process, each phase progressing to a deeper level of analysis.

Collection and Initial Assessment of Dysfunctions
The reasons put forward in the first level of analysis were associated with representations of the qualitative and quantitative *dysfunctions* encountered by the agents in their work as well as their enumeration, their frequency, their location in the software, and the time spent for corrections (*overtime*). As an example, the data indicated diffused and repetitive errors in transactional, basic and ERP configuration data.

Identification of Deep Causes
The second level of analysis included the previously identified causes, delving into the hidden reasons for their existence (deep causes). This analysis helped us to bring up internal practices that were incompatible

Table 10.1. Interviews and Data Collection

	Stage 1: 2001		Stage 2: 2002–2003		Stage 3: 2003–2004		Stage 4: 2004–2010
	#	Techniques for Data-Collection	#	Techniques for Data-Collection	#	Techniques for Data-Collection	Techniques for Data-Collection
Executive management	1	1st Contact with top management	5	Participation in working meetings	8	Participation in working meetings	6 (Participation in working meetings)
Managers	1	1st Contact with the managers	30	Participation in working meetings	50	Participation in working meetings	Informal dialogue (Participation in working meetings)
Project Team	1	1st Contact with the industrial direction	40	• Semi-structured interviews • Informal dialogue	80	• Semi-structured interviews • Informal dialogue	Semi-structured interviews Informal dialogue
Users			80	• Participation in working meetings • Internal documents	100	• Participation in working meetings • Internal documents	Participation in working meetings Internal documents

with the informational requirements of the software. For example, products were often introduced into production while the basic components were absent and/or the *resources* for their transformation we not available. Many such examples confirmed that basic rules of real production management (e.g., ranges, nomenclature of products, use of customer data) were not being followed. Employees were also bypassing the software in production and related services.

In-depth Analysis of the Hidden Costs and Identification of Root Causes

The third level of analysis focused on understanding the real source of dysfunctions. These are the *root causes* of the dysfunction on which substantial remedial actions should be to sustainably neutralize their impact. Using the deficiencies identified in the software, we met with organizational members in each of the company's services. In some cases, we requested the presence of the manager to ensure that suggested change in the practices of everyday life could take place over time. Within this context, an effort was made to resolve any erroneous and/or missing data from the input by authenticated users, localized in the different functions, including purchasing-procurement, design, production, and sales administration.

Validation and Results Presentation

The final stage involved valuing the dysfunction encountered in hidden costs (mainly overtime and non-production, that is, components related to human time). We relied on the indicator ***Hourly Contribution to Value-Added on Variable Costs (HCVAVC)*** (Savall, 1979; Savall & Zardet, 1987; Savall, Zardet, & Bonnet, 2008). In addition, after treatment of all data (transactional, basic and configuration), the prior three-step process served as the foundation for the identification of remedial actions to be taken in following years to eradicate the deficiencies identified throughout the organization.

The intervention research was punctuated by appointment with the director and members of the top management team to undertake remedial actions and assess the results. This process was also used to evaluate the successive transformation actions undertaken to build a new process and thus meet the objectives of the intervention.

Diagnosis of Post-ERP position on the Pilot Line

Based on the classification of six dysfunctional families in *socio-economic theory*, the main factors from our analysis of the existing pilot line are presented in Table 10.2. The first column of the table shows (by family) examples of recurring events identified during the diagnosis stage. The second column highlights the technical requirements imposed by the ERP for a quality operation.

Table 10.2.   Dysfunctions Observed in the Post-ERP Phases

Types of Dysfunction	Examples of Recurring Dysfunctional Demonstrations Raised on the Experimental Line	Reminders of Some Technical Requirements of the ERP
Communication-coordination-cooperation	Erroneous or missing data of configuration	Uniqueness of the data
	Transparency of data	Quality of the data
	Management systems	Informative integration
	Subdivision of the functions	Traceability of the transactions
	Hidden costs of SI	Interdependence of the data
		Quality of the transversality of the exchanges
Work organization	Responsibilities / SI	Organizational integration of the processes
	Questioning of the practices	Defined organizational target
	Integration of the systems	Numerous transactional seizures
	Business process	Level of granularity of the processes
	Computerization of dysfunctions	Predefined best practices
Time management	Mode of management	Update of the real time data
	Random seizures of the data	Planning of the *resources* how the long term in the short term
Strategic implementation	Technological determinism	Methodology of implementation and change management
	Strategic alignment of SI	Questioning of the existing processes
	Mode of *piloting* of the economic performance	Management by the processes
	Questioning of the direction	Expensive investments
		Partnership with providers
		Ascent the versions

(Table continues on next page)

Table 10.2.   (Continued)

Types of Dysfunction	Examples of Recurring Dysfunctional Demonstrations Raised on the Experimental Line	Reminders of Some Technical Requirements of the ERP
Integrated training	Training of the users	Control of the informative processes and corrections to be brought in case of errors
	Internal referents	
	Hierachical distance	
		Processing procedure of the anomalies ready
		Cost of entry
		Software package and management skills
Working conditions	Collective shift in functions	Adequacy of the toll compared with business
	Stress / Excess of control	
	Resistance	Adoption of the tool by the users
		Maintenance of the tool and the data
		Quality of the infrastructure hardware, software and network
		Granularity of the processes

The discussion will not detail the technical requirements of each family of dysfunctions, but as an illustration, the focus is drawn to a few lines in the 3C (*communication-coordination-cooperation*) of the *information system*. Given that there are dysfunctions (in different families), their *interactions* must be approached with the same consideration.

Integrated systems have their own intrinsic requirements, with both being structured and having structuring tools. This double feature requires a form of support discipline if the organization will be able to take advantage of controlled informational and organizational *integration*. Are the technical requirements of the tools compatible with the behavioral requirements asked of the users and management? Nothing is less certain in reality, largely because of the "natural instability" of human behavior. Dysfunctional events noted in this advanced post-ERP analysis show a number of intentional (and unintentional) shortcomings or low involvement with regard to computers. Most of the time, people are so captured by special interests, or taken in the social relations game, they eventually forget that they also work for the company's customers. They also seem to overlook the fact that their behavior very concretely translates into products, exchanged information, and service characteristics (Savall & Zardet, 2001).

These technical requirements of the ERP usually conflict with the management mode in the sense that they are completely ignored or not followed. This notion of requirement seems to us important because it requires sustainable efforts on the part of the users to respect the requirements of the integrated tools, each other, and the quality of 3C that connects us via the exchanged data. To this end, we discuss *requirements* with respect to the tool and *dysfunction* when this requirement is not respected.

The family of 3C on which we have focused this part of the research, sheds interesting light on the difficulties encountered in **organizational transformation projects**. As we have suggested earlier, the most emblematic problem for ERP projects is the increasing interdependence between the functions of the company that is accompanied by enterprise transversal management. With the integration concept, configuration elements in a situation of interdependence are now tighter than in the past.

The lack of **cooperation** with the system by the management is not here by chance. Different forms manifest this fact, especially disempowerment forms, often reflecting a lack of interest by the services manager and local management to the final user. Overall, this widespread mind-set actually prevails from one service to the other with little short-term arrangements and informal exchanges. Reflecting a theme throughout this volume, managerial practices are still heavily influenced by Taylorism as they limit hierarchical dialogue practices. Based on data from the pilot line, we identified the following **fieldnote quotes** on the existing 3C:

- "No activities synchronization meetings whatsoever, leaders say that it means lost productivity time."
- "We computerized internal dysfunctions – that's why it does not work!"
- "It seems clear that we have to make progress in this area but IS [Information Systems] is not the cup of tea of the direction, nor communication besides!"
- "The problem is that users do not enter their data correctly."

Operations Planning to Test Dysfunctions

In production management, **operations scheduling** is a critical function representative of the state of internal 3C. This function comes just before the execution of manufacturing orders by the workshops where the software for **scheduling** calculations must be utilized. When internal-external events cause fluctuations in the couple (product/resource), supervisors must conduct a re-planning of manufacturing orders in order to inform immediately the scheduling agent for changes occurring in his production programs. Only 25% of re-planning is performed on the studied manufacturing line. In roughly one-third of cases there is no re-planning, in 19% they are wrong, 25% are acceptable and 23% are highly questionable as to their reliability.

In addition, the scheduling agent explained that he spends between 40% to 60% of his time correcting incorrect or missing transactional, basic and parameter data in the software. This task must be accomplished before undertaking his or her own work—while monitoring constantly that the programs are a reflection of the reality of the workshops. In the best case scenario, the scheduling agent cannot fix more than 5% of the wrong or missing production data stemming from unscrupulous users over the working day.

The remaining 95% of these errors are absorbed by the nightly treatments of the software. This look at data quality was the main challenge we had to face in the recovery of the advanced post-ERP phase. By using the *HCVAVC* ratio specific to this company, we were able to determine the *hidden costs* associated with overtime that were generated by the scheduling operations agent during one year (see Table 10.3). The company has four schedulers facing the same difficulties with the use of the software.

Table 10.3.   Evaluation of Overtime Tabulated to Correct Data Dysfunctions

Number of Positions	*Hypothesis at the Minimum Time 40% Hidden Costs in K€*	*Hypothesis at the Maximum 60% Hidden Costs in K€*
1 agent	60 € x (192 mn/60)h x 225 j = 43, 2 K€	60 € x (288 mn/60) h x 225 j = 64, 8K€
4 agents	43,2 K€ x 4 employees = 172, 8K€	64,8 K€ x 4 employees = 259, 2 K€

Dysfunctions Propagation and Their Consequences

These powerful systems have weaknesses—and pollution from the data spread is maintained in real time by the internal mechanism of the software. Ultimately, the power of this tool backfired on the organization and turned it into a literal hidden cost machine. As such, the term "strategic misalignment" reflects quite well the overall situation of the company with respect to its information system.

Moreover, this situation is not without consequences for the *working conditions* (see working conditions [WC] in Table 10.3). The other side of the informational integration generates individual and collective stress situations. Repeated sliding of functions throughout the company tarnishes the daily life of all staff. This sliding leads to "overtime" spending in an attempt to resolve unfulfilled and/or poorly completed work. It also creates additional costs, stressing and affecting work relationships between people. *Confidence* in the IS are reduced with time when the sliding functions take place on a collective scale. Note that with ERP, landslides functions operate $360°$ in the organization in real time. Identifying sliding functions and their associated overtime provides a measure of 3C and effective transverse mode in the organization.

Summary of Actions Taken

Nine consequent actions were initiated on the pilot line during the first year of research intervention to achieve a reduction in inventory levels coupled with a satisfactory use of ERP (Table 10.4). Actions 2, 4 and 5 were the most important in terms of complexity and time. The removal of intermediate levels (Action 2) in the classified data reduced the number of entry points and facilitated a complete reorganization of physical processes. The 50% reduction in the number of transactional entry data had an immediate impact on the reliability of the data (between 0 and 10 entry errors / day instead of 120 daily errors). The number of entry points that had been established by management control was not justified in the end.

The reconfiguration of the physical and informational process (Action 4) was the most complex. Based on the principles of the optimized production technology (OPT) method, we recalculated the different smaller manufacturing and transfer batch sizes to increase flexibility of the production tool. With these new data and re-setting in the software, the running time[2] increased from 23,23h to 15,31h, leading to a theoretical saving time of 8:00 and ramping up much faster production line with a gain of 6:46. The decrease in production batches allowed the company to be more reactive in the face of changing customer demands, requiring less work in progress.

The planning reorganization of loads and capacities (Action 5) based on the principles of the constraints theory identified the machine "bottleneck" (i.e., the machine having the smallest debit of the line of manufacturing) and optimized the workflow on these machines, rather than machine "non-bottleneck "as was previously the case. The systemic combined results from the effects of all these actions coupled with Actions 1, 3, 6 and 7 (Table 10.4) allowed a fairly rapid decline in inventory stock in the order of 200 thousand euro in a few months and a "purification" of simultaneous data in the pilot production line.

Table 10.4.   Actions Leading to the Decrease of Inventory Stock and Improved Use of the Software Package

Actions on the Pilot Line	Links With the Software	Links With the Stocks
Implementation of a weekly synchronization meeting	Exploitation by actors of software data	Better planning of short term activities Internal customer-supplier relation
Cutting by about 50% of the number of transactional data entries	Number of data entry work stations Quality of transactional data	Data reliability
Suppressing erroneous or missing data by a third party	Assignment of the third party to the planning department	Oversight of data reliability by the planning agents
Total re-engineering of physical and informational processes	Standardization of the product flow	Smaller batches Minus 8 hours on the process flow Pace increase resulting in a 6 h 46 gain
Reorganization of operation management	Standardization of the pilot line bottleneck	Fine tuning the flow on the work-station bottleneck
Follow up of the operation management agent in collaboration with the design agent	Piloting the production flow	No blocking of non-bottleneck stations
Training of supervisors and users carried out by the actor of the post ERP team	Increased ERP competences	Reliability of technical and transactional data.
Questioning of existing actions	Modification of informational *structures* and management and piloting modes	Diminishing stock levels : minus €20 k within 4 months)
Proximity of uses *Communication*	Learning	Fewer transactional data entry gaps From 120 per day to 0 up to 10 per day

Evolution of Control

The support system that we have implemented for the situation recovery of this post-ERP has changed over time depending on the level of complexity and apprehended its stakes in three abstraction levels: individual, local, and business (Table 10.5). The common point of the three levels rests on the search for stability with the tool uses and activity establishment of lasting ERP activity between users. The actions described above have worked in this direction and the objectives set by the leader.

With respect to different devices, the moderating element was based on the evolution of team members, for example, volunteers working with the existing situation on a formal *competence* team that was close to the users. In levels 1 & 2, the "project group" and "implementation" phased were interwoven and often merged. Intervening directly in real time on ERP activity tends to foster this form of "agility," which is appreciated by the users and management as reflected by the comment: "I think and I act together." Contrary to the existing situation, the conditions for the ***human potential*** stimulation were gathered together to maintain the dynamics around the ***information system***. A year of work was needed to address the pilot line, followed by two years to expand the set of actions across the company.

Results and Lessons Learned

Three main phases characterize the deployment of the ERP projects: the draft, the project, and the post project (see Table 10.6). Each phase has its own factors of ***efficiency*** that cannot be considered in isolation during a project, because they are in constant ***interaction***. Looking at Table 10.6, the main recurring dysfunctional convergences of these factors sub-efficiency are shown in the first column and their characteristics observed from one company to another is captured in the second. This information is based on feedback we gathered from over 25 ERP projects from 1990–2006. These generic data provide a baseline project that we refer to as the "epistemological principle of ***generic contingency***" (Savall & Zardet, 2004). These basic invariants were completed with the projects realization.

In addition to the under-efficiency factors mentioned above, there are three other factors identified in our post-ERP intervention search.

A Learning Process Often Reduced

We often noticed a lack of "integrated" training in the learning process that is managed and designed in collaboration with users. Understanding the new procedures and new business processes is always challenging. All

Table 10- 5 Policy Implementation ArrangementsNO

Level	Stakes in the Level	Moderating Device	Major Actions Taken / Results
Individual Level: Workstation	Individual stabilization of Data Interdependency Dynamic Game, Quality (DIDGQ) and institution of an activity ERP	Informal group (restricts)	• Treatment of overtimes and slidings function • Put under control of the transactional data • Quality of the transactional data • Corrective overtime close to 0
Local Level: Experimental line of manufacturing	Local collective stabilization of DIDGQ and institution of an activity ERP	Informal group (vast)	• Questioning of the physical processes and management rules of production • Purge of source data • Reduction of the time of theoretical crossing of **8h00** • Decrease of the level of stocks: **- 200 K€** • Decrease of **80 à 90 %** of the errors on the data • Restore a closeness with the users
Company Level: 18 Lines of manufacturing	Spread stabilization of DIDGQ and institution of an activity ERP	Informal group (dedicated) *Competence* center	• Stabilize the use of the object border on the scale of the organization • Reduction of the dysfunctions • Decrease of the global overtimes • Reduction of the number of seizures by **50%.**

too often, however, the training phase that is provided to users does not take into account difficulties associated with change management. In "catalogue" formation (i.e., the standard trainings distributed by the editors and integrators), the informational *integration* requirements of ERP and their

Table 10-6 Convergences and Specificities of ERP Projects

	Convergence	*Specifics*
Inefficiency before the deployment	Relevance of the choice of this type of solution	Be lacking study of the impact on the work and the organization
	Analysis of the needs badly defined	Defect of anticipation of needs, Technical approach of the projects ERP, Computerization of the dysfunctions, Denial of the directions in front of dysfunctions
	Be lacking preparation of the company for the changes	Defect of anticipation of the **risks** in particular of the human risk
	Be lacking study of the return on investment	Time of deployment under estimated as well as the allowance of **resources**
	Absence of implication of the management team	Distance with the ground and the absence of expertise
Inefficiency during the deployment	Needs changing during the deployment	Dead end on the specificities of the company for economic reasons
	Resistances in the changes	Mode of management
	Deficit of piloting of the project	Constitution of the project team
Inefficiency after the deployment	Deficit of management	Management of skills
	Uncontrolled extension of integration concept	Strategic alignment and vision
	Instability of the ERP	Device to be implemented to raise the chaotic situations

impact on the **work organization** are rarely addressed as they are at the heart of the transformation process. It is the same concerning the concept of real-time, which modifies existing practices with an update transactional data across the organization. They give us a foundation to address several critical post-project situations.

Leaders Under Evaluate Changes and Workload in ERP Implementation

Company managements tend to prune – by overconfidence or ignorance —the content of the upstream stage of a project in favor of rapid software implementation followed by visible and concrete short-term results. The syndrome that is often presented, and is both the most characteristic and the most difficult to take into account, is the "copy and paste syndrome" (Tomas, 1999). The hypothesis of any difficulty in software implementation is often trivialized by those responsible. For some practitioners, the automation added to the review process would have an almost mechanical adjustment effect on behavior. As a result questions linger as to whether the system will be a source of value creation for the organization—or a major headache for the company.

A Management Deficit in the Broadest Sense

Of all the sub-efficiency factors leading to the failures in ERP projects, the ones concerning management should be highlighted. Without choosing user satisfaction before the relevance of uses (Fimbel, 2007), we focus on management responsibility with regard to the data quality handled by their services. In the absence of efficient and effective management, the information generated by ERP are not chosen as "filters" (e.g., DTC [Dadaists – Taboos – Litigation], AMA [News – Memory – Anticipation]; Savall, 1986) that ensure the quality of "incoming" and "outgoing" information. Managers must ensure that the document production of the ERP is consistent with the exchanges and comments made in the field. The use value of the information system is not yet perceived by management as a strategic resource that creates a value for the company (Missaoui, 2008). The study of this critical phase of post-ERP highlights a management deficit. More generally, the complexity of these projects requires a revision of the steering concept—it is no longer simply a question of operating projects or change but rather of conducting transformations. This control function requires integrating transformative methods of leading change in the current processes for the operation and management of the organization. Overall, the *development* of such organizational technologies increases the demand for professional management where the epistemological principle of *contradictory intersubjectivity* is dominant (Savall & Zardet, 2004).

To reduce these sub-efficiency factors that lead the company to an impasse with its ERP, we recommend to the leaders the following actions. First, during the first phase of the project, the implementation of a dynamic *structure* type *competence center* (as we have developed in the previous paragraph) is needed to correct the situation throughout the company. This device breaks with traditional project approaches that most often reproduce the same effects of organizations with the *TFW virus*. This competence center rests on an "agile" approach, which privileges the exchanges between designers and users to address their needs. The proximity to the users in the three phases of the project seems unavoidable, which further reflects the need for the concept of competence center.

Second, to increase efficiency, we also recommend that leaders spend more time on the upstream phase of the project, as they will avoid the problem of having to provide additional funds in latter stages to upgrade critical post-project phases. Moving to another image of the resistance to change, as it has been described by management, is part of the organizational transformation projects. It should be understood as a call for dialogue.

Finally an *economic balance* based on the study of organizational *dysfunctions* and uses of computers should anticipate weak signals leading to critical post-project situations—including a reduction in overtime spent to correct dysfunctions that can transform hidden cost into performance.

CONCLUSION

Is the ERP responsible for management failures of the organization in this advanced post-project phase? As the chapter suggests, the answer is "no." An ERP can contribute to the efficiency and to the organizational control *effectiveness* if the conditions noted in this case are implemented and controlled by key decision makers. Many major obstacles could be reduced if the latter had a deeper understanding of the human processes involved and if they were able to integrate this knowledge earlier in their project. In the recovery of this post-ERP stage, the achievement of results is related to the *regulation* actions taken to create a satisfactory equilibrium for the participants in the project. The issues associated with the definition of a realistic action plan—coming "from above"—should be based on a systematic assessment of dysfunctions focusing on their root causes. The quality of a dynamic control mode that is close to the users allows managers to transform the ERP into a mechanism that generates performance rather than creates *hidden costs*.

NOTE

1. The research for this chapter has been influenced by a number of works that are not directly referred to in the text, including Boje and Rosile (2003), Buono and Savall (2007), Gephart (2009), Perroux (1979), Savall (1974, 1975, 1977, 1981, 2010, 2012), Savall and Zardet (1992, 1995, 2005, 2008, 2009, 2011, 2013), Savall, Zardet, and Bonnet (2000, 2008), and Voyant (1997, 2001, 2010).

2. Running time refers to the transit time of a manufacturing lot in the physical process (from the starting up of the line to the achievement of its maximal pace).

REFERENCES

Beretta, S. (2002). Unleashing the integration potential of ERP systems: The role of process-based performance measurement systems. *Business Process Management Journal, 8*(3), 254–277.

Besson, P. (1999). Les ERP à l'épreuve de l'organisation [The ERP in the test of the organization]. *Systèmes d'Information et Management, 4*(4), 21–51.

Besson, P., & Rowe, F. (2011). Perspectives sur le phénomène de la transformation organisationnelle [Perspectives on the phenomenon of the organizational transformation]. *Systèmes d'Information et Management, 16*(1), 3–34.

Boje, D., & Rosile, G.-A. (2003). Comparison of socio-economic and other trans-organizational development methods. *Journal of Change Organizational Management, 16*(1), 10–20.

Buono, A. F., & Savall, H. (Eds.). (2007). *Socio-Economic intervention in organizations: The intervener-researcher and the SEAM approach to organizational analysis.* Charlotte, NC: Information Age Publishing.

Cappelletti, L. & Hoarau, C. *Finance et contrôle au quotidien.* Paris: Dunod.

Fimbel, E. (2007). *Alignement stratégique: Synchroniser les systèmes d'information avec les trajectoires et manœuvres des entreprises* [Strategic alignment: Synchronize information systems with trajectories and laborers of the companies]. Montreuil, France: Edition Pearson - Village Mondial.

Gephart, R. P. (2009). An invitation to ethnostatistics. *Revue Sciences de gestion – Management Sciences – Ciencias de Gestión, 70,* 85.

Missaoui, I. (2008). Capital immatériel et Systèmes d'Information [Immaterial capital and information systems]. *Cahier de recherche* [Working papers] *Cigref,* No. 4.

Perroux, F. (1979). L'entreprise, l'équilibre rénové et les coûts cachés [The enterprise, the renovated balance and the "hidden" costs]. Preface. In H. Savall. *Reconstruire l'entreprise* [Reconstructing the enterprise] Paris, France: Dunod. 2nd ed. in H. Savall & V. Zardet. Reconstruire l'entreprise, Paris: Dunod (2014)

Saint Léger, G. (2013). Contrôle, systèmes d'information et ERP. In L. Cappelletti & C. Hoarau, *Finance et contrôle au quotidien* [Finance and management control in the day-to-day]. Paris, France: Dunod.

Savall, H. (1974–1975–1977). *Enrichir le travail humain dans les entreprises et les organisations* [An economic evaluation of job enrichment]. Paris: Dunod.

Savall, H. (1979). *Reconstruire l'entreprise: Analyse socio-économique des conditions de travail* [Reconstructing the enterprise: Socio-economic analysis of working conditions]. Paris, France: Dunod.

Savall, H. (1981–2010). *Work and people: An economic evaluation of job enrichment.* 1st ed. New-York: Oxford University Press; 2nd ed. Charlotte, NC: Information Age Publishing

Savall H. (1986). *Le contrôle de qualité des informations émises par les acteurs des organisa-tions* [The quality control of information emitted by organizational actors]. Paper presented at the ISEOR Conference *Qualité des informations scientifiques en gestion.* Lyon, France.

Savall, H. (2012). *Origine radicale des crises économiques: Germán Bernácer, précurseur visionnaire* [Root origin of crises: Germán Bernácer, a visionary forerunner]. Charlotte, NC: Information Age Publishing.

Savall, H., & Zardet, V. (1987). *Maîtriser les coûts et les performances cachés : Le contrat d'activité périodiquement négociables* [Mastering hidden costs and performance: The periodically negotiable activity contract]. Paris, France: Economica.

Savall, H., & Zardet, V. (1992). *Le nouveau contrôle de gestion: Méthode des coûts-performances cachés* [New management control: The hidden cost-performance method]. Paris, France: Éditions Comptables Malesherbes-Eyrolles

Savall, H., & Zardet, V. (1995–2005–2009). *Ingénierie stratégique du roseau, souple et enracinée* [Strategic engineering of the reed, flexible and rooted]. Paris, France: Economica.

Savall H., & Zardet V. (2001). L'évolution de la dépendance des acteurs à l'égard des dysfonctionnements chroniques au sein de leur organisation. Résultats de processus de metamorphose [The evolution of actor dependency regarding chronic dysfunctions in organizations: Results of a process of metamorpho-sis]. In T. de Swarte (Ed.), *Psychanalyse, management et dépendances au sein des organisations* (pp. 179–212). Paris, France: L'Harmattan.

Savall, H., & Zardet V. (2004). *Recherche en Sciences de Gestion: Approche qualimétrique, Observer l'objet Complexe* [Research in management sciences: The qualimetric approach, observing the complex object]. Paris, France: Economica.

Savall, H., & Zardet, V. (2008). *Mastering hidden costs and performance*. Charlotte, NC: Information Age Publishing.

Savall, H., & Zardet, V. (2011). *The qualimetrics approach: Observing the complex object*. Charlotte, NC: Information Age Publishing.

Savall, H., & Zardet, V. (2013). *The dynamics and challenges of tetranormalization*. Charlotte, NC: Information Age Publishing.

Savall, H., Zardet, V., & Bonnet, M. (2000-2008). *Releasing the untapped potential of enterprises through socio-economic management*. Geneva: Éditions IOT-BIT.

Savall, H., Zardet, V., & Bonnet, M. (2000-2008). *Libérer les performances cachées par un management socio-*économique [Releasing the untapped potential of enterprises through socio-economic management]. Geneva, Switzerland: International Labour Office.

Tomas, J. L. (1999). *ERP and integrated software packages: The transfer of information systems.* Paris, France: Dunod.

Voyant, O. (1997). *Contribution à l'élaboration d'un système de veille stratégique intégré pour les PME-PMI* [Contribution to the elaboration of an Integrated System of Strategic Vigilance for SMEs]. Thèse de doctorat en Sciences de Gestion. Université de Lyon, France.

Voyant, O. (2001). *Les PME-PMI à l'écoute de leur environnement : élaboration d'un système de veille stratégique intégré* [SMEs' listening to their environment: Elaboration of an integrated strategic vigilance system]. Communication présentée à la 10ème Conférence Internationale de Management Stratégique, Québec, Canada.

Voyant, O. (2010). *Contribution à l'identification d'une cartographie de l'environnement externe : cas de PME familiale Belge* [Contribution to the Identification of an External Environment Map: case of a Belgian Family SME]. Communication présentée au colloque annuel de l'Association Internationale de Management Stratégique, France.

CHAPTER 11

THE CHALLENGE OF
A MEXICAN SME

Mastering Growth and Preparing the
Business Transmission[1]

Véronique Zardet and Andry Rasolofoarisoa

Sanchez Hass is a Mexican family business that has been producing and selling avocados since 1983. Despite the strong competition in this market, the company set a challenging goal of growth, evolving from a *small local company* in 2005 to a medium-sized company with more than 8 sales outlets in 2014. The *implementation of SEAM* in the company, aimed at structuring its activities and overcoming the challenges of growth, has been the key factor for setting stability and prosperity in an unstable market, and for preparing the company's transmission to the next family generation.

THE CONTEXT

The avocado is a very low value-added product, extremely perishable and with a high deterioration rate. The production organization can therefore generate significant production losses and *non-sales* in case of failure in

The Socio-Economic Approach to Management Revisited: The Evolving Nature of SEAM in the 21st Century, pp. 215–235
Copyright © 2015 by Information Age Publishing
215

the processes, such as avocado maturation, the categorization of sizes and weights, and supplying the sales outlets. The avocado production process has many constraining characteristics, which can discourage producers, but the avocado market is a highly attractive one, thus leading to a corresponding high level of competition. Sanchez Hass is located in the first avocado production area in the world, in Michoacán. Although all the farmers of this area are specialized in the same fruit, Sanchez Hass exclusively provided this local market untill 2005, before it decided to implement SEAM. In 2005, the company's sales revenues was MXN 68 million (USD 6.3 million; EUR 5.3 millions), corresponding to 8,800 tons of sales a year.

A HYPERCOMPETITIVE MARKET

Competition in the avocado market intensified with the opening of markets between the states of the Mexican Republic to worldwide distribution. In Mexico, the opening of national markets generated strong opportunities the company took advantage of to sustain its growth. This opening changed the market structure and competition from *small retail outlets* to strong price competition in *mass distribution*, particularly in supermarkets and *food services*. This price competition was characterized by a singular aggressiveness that influenced negatively the product's quality—national competitors often sold deteriorated products.

International competition took off after Mexico signed the NAFTA in 1992, opening the country's tightly closed economy to international competition. In addition, the government's small businesses support policy suddenly disappeared. Since 2014, the international competition between avocados producers has been characterized by strong price competition that also requires compliance with constraining quality standards for all exported products.

Underdeveloped Social Conditions

In 2005, the company had 90 employees, most of whom had a very low level of education due to the social and economic **development deficit** of Mexico, especially in Michoacán. This deficiency concerned the core staff and the managers—many employees were illiterate and the managers' level of education was wide ranging, from elementary school to the master's degree. Moreover, many employees only spoke one dialect, as is frequently the situation in Mexico.

In addition, the job characteristics did not encourage the company to develop education and professional training for its employees. A study

(Macías Herrera, 2007) on 10,000 Mexican companies showed that 9 working persons in 10 have never been trained in their current work, particularly for manual and simple jobs. Avocado production jobs are characterized by very simple but repetitive tasks under harsh physical conditions—working outdoors, with high temperature and dampness—generating undisputedly extremely painful conditions. The low level of education of most of the operators, including the managers, contributed to a strong disbelief in management methods because they assumed that the latter were too sophisticated for them and that they would not be skilled enough for a good appropriation.

Finally, in Mexican small- and medium-sized enterprises (SMEs), only a few people benefit from social security since it is fully paid by the employee himself. Most of the company leaders do not take this financial responsibility, considering its cost too high and the labor supply abundant. In 2005, only 15% of Sanchez Hass' employees were covered by the social security system.

Succession Challenges in a Family Business

In 2005, the founding father headed Sanchez Hass. His three sons and a son-in-law were the top managers. From then to 2014, the father, who was 70 years old, desired to transfer the company to the family's second generation, the third one already starting to take part in the company's life. However, his attempts at transmitting the business were an issue because the governance and executive responsibilities were never been clearly defined. This situation generated many *misunderstandings* and discomforts. As a result, to help sustain the business, in 2005 two main governance issues were been identified: organizing a succession plan and developing a strategy for managerial delegation, which was to be accompanied by a learning process.

Management Consulting—Perceived by Mexican SMEs Leaders as a Cost

In Mexico, agribusiness companies are not used to management consulting services, generally regarded as useless expenses and perceived as too expensive. This is the reason why many financial supports from the government and professional associations encourage Mexican CEOs to engage this type of service. As an example, Compite A.C., a *non-profit* organization, was created to provide advice to Mexican SMEs, and is mainly funded by the Mexican federal government and Ministry of Economy. In

2004, Compite A.C. organized two workshops on process **reengineering** applied to production management operations: packaging, management and process analysis. Sanchez Hass' top managers took part in these workshops, in which they were introduced to SEAM.

THE INTERVENTION PROCESS IN SANCHEZ HASS

In 2005, a first *pilot intervention* was organized by Compite A.C. and ISEOR to introduce SEAM in several SMEs, by training the companies' leaders, managers, and *internal and external consultants* to *SEAM tools* and its process of change. This pilot intervention was organized through inter-company training, referred to as *multi-SMEs Horivert* (see Figure 11.1) run by ISEOR (Savall, 2003). ISEOR trained this group in 2005–2006, in 4 sessions of 2 day-long programs during the year. The inter-company group was also trained by ISEOR through four 2-day sessions over a year. Fourteen people were involved: the leader, one to two top managers, internal consultants from each of the five companies, and five external consultants in charge of monitoring the process of change in each of the five companies between the inter-company sessions.

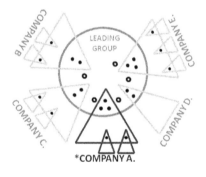

Legend:

*COMPANY A is Sanchez Hass

The inter-company group has been led by ISEOR

 HORIVERT in a Medium business

 HORIVERT in a small business (less than 15 managers)

● *Companies' leaders and top managers*

◉ *External consultants in charge of monitoring the intervention inside each company involved in the inter-company group.*

HORIVERT = HORIzontal and VERTical actions in the company

Figure 11.1.   Sanchez Hass' Involvement in the multi-SMEs Horivert Intervention—2005

The First Intervention (2005)

The first intervention, in 2005–2006, was focused on installing the SEAM basic tools and change process in the company. That year, ISEOR intervened regularly through remote technical assistance and a transfer of change management engineering to the external consultant who was in charge of monitoring the ***intra-company intervention***. Several steps in the process were carried out *within* the company: creating a change process ***steering committee***; a series of ***collaborative trainings*** on SEAM tools that involved all the managers; a ***socio-economic diagnosis*** for identifying the ***dysfunctions*** and involving all the company's ***actors***; and a ***focus group*** for exploring and resolving problems. All the departments of the company were involved in the diagnosis, focusing on the orchards, packaging, transport, and administrative services, which allowed for the ***assessment of hidden costs*** (see Figure 11.2).

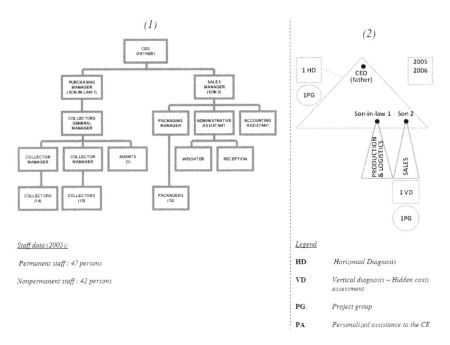

Figure 11.2.   2005 organizational chart (1) and architecture of the intra-company intervention at Sanchez Hass (2).

These initial steps were followed by the development of an ***Internal and External Strategic Action Plan (IESAP)*** and several ***Priority Action Plans (PAP),*** which preceded implementation of the ***Periodically Negotiable Activity Contract (PNAC)*** throughout the company. The technical support and actions by ISEOR at each stage of the intervention included quality control of the ***qualitative diagnoses***, hidden costs calculation, and development of the ***expert opinion, dysfunctions baskets***, and the ***economic balances*** co-constructed by the external consultant and Sanchez Hass management.

SEAM Maintenance in a Growth Context (2005–2013)

After the first intervention in Sanchez Hass, the external consultant who carried out the intra-company intervention (2005 to 2006) continued to assist the company two days per year from 2007 to 2012. The goal was to keep the management system alive and support the IESAP and PAP update by the firm's top managers. When the CEO realized the importance of maintaining the management system and sensed the organizational needs emerging from the company's *strong growth*, he decided to hire the external consultant, who became a full-time employee of Sanchez Hass in 2013 in charge of internal consulting. Moreover, the CEO solicited a new intervention in order to strengthen SEAM and to extend it to new departments after 2005, focusing on the sales outlets.

Several factors motivated his decision. Even if the company had survived the competition escalation in the avocado market, it reached a new threshold of destabilization (in 2010) due to the organic growth of the staff and sales, creating eight new sales outlets to facilitate the development of exportation. In addition, the need to clarify and define governance and executive responsibilities for the company's succession became prominent. Indeed, the problem had not been solved in 2005 since there was no formal decision about the governance and top management. In 2013, the father was still the company's "number one" and the intergenerational transmission was at standstill.

In 2013, the CEO and the top managers expressed their need for a *coherent strategy for controlling growth*, involving both material and organizational aspects. Indeed, since 2005, business growth required *material investments* to increase production capacity and to meet demand. The avocado orchards were gradually extended and new fruit orchards were created. Since 2005, eight sales outlets were also created for supplying the domestic market. It required developing local and national transport activity. In October 2013, each one of the sales outlets became profitable and together they realized 35% to 40% of Sanchez Hass' turnover (revenues). The rest of the revenue came from sales to professionals and exportation—which was also growing—to Japan, United States, and Costa Rica.

The changes during this eight year period required industrializing most of the operations—cultivation, harvesting, packaging, distribution, marketing—and structuring additional services, such as general administration. These changes also required an increase in the company's workforce. Thus, the company, which employed 90 people in 2005 (47 direct employees and 43 independent subcontractors), grew to 260 employees (including 140 direct employees) by 2013. The staff literally tripled during this time. This growth in staff created a problem—the technical and managerial skills development policy was not sufficient to prevent a shortage of experts and managers within the company. Thus, by April 2014, some of the sales outlets lacked qualified managers.

The Second Intervention (2013)

The second intervention involved a combined action of the former external consultant and the internal consultants, consisting of a series of collaborative training and *personal assistance* to *SEAM tools*, and a change process through *socio-economic diagnoses* followed by *innovation projects* in all the company departments (see Figure 11.3). This change process was mainly monitored by the internal consultants and was broken down in two waves: a first wave of diagnoses in early 2014 in the orchards and the sales outlets; and a second wave in January 2015 in the packaging, transport and administrative services departments. In order to achieve this action, four new internal consultants were trained at ISEOR during two 4-day vocational training sessions.

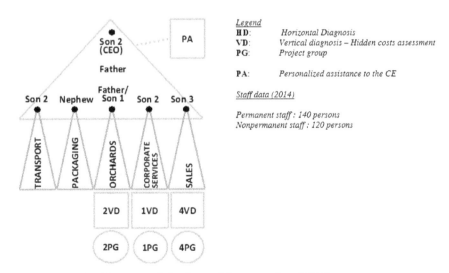

Figure 11-3 Architecture of the Second Intervention (2013)

Twice in 2014, Henri Savall and Véronique Zardet, in their role as intervener-researchers at ISEOR, completed a *SEAM in-depth training* program that involved all of the company's managers, which was also aimed at training them on assessing the effects of the change process on their economic and *social performance*. Moreover, ISEOR supervised the methodological process of the socio-economic diagnoses and ensured an engineering transfer to the *internal interveners*. Once a month, the ISEOR interveners organized personal assistance to the CEO for monitoring the change process. The internal consultants also attended two conferences in which they presented the *SEAM implementation* impacts on the company's performance, and had the opportunity to meet other companies' CEOs and managers who implemented SEAM in their own company.

Synthesis of the Dysfunctions Diagnoses

The diagnoses completed by the internal and external consultants, under the supervision of the ISEOR interveners, shed light on the major dysfunctions in the company. In 2005, *organizational structure dysfunctions* were prominent (Sánchez & Sánchez, 2007; Savall, Zardet, & Guerrero, 2005):

- The poor *synchronization* of the company's actors was amplified by a lack of tools for personal and collective planning. Top and middle managers were paralyzed by the belief that business planning was highly complex and intricate. They were convinced that they had neither the skills nor the time to plan and steer planning in company daily life. This conviction restricted the role of managers to the management of current and urgent operations, that is, dividing tasks and controlling, leaving aside their business *development* or prospective role.
- The lack of a clear definition of functions, responsibilities and processes appeared as a major issue;
- The diagnosis revealed the top and middle managers were unaware of the need to define a human resources management policy.
- Finally, the *communication-coordination-cooperation* methods were informal, focused on daily operations and the meetings did not meet the expectations of the participants.

According to the vertical diagnoses (2005), the level of hidden costs in Sanchez Hass amounted MXN 4,000,000 (EUR 312,000; USD 375,000) – 86,000 pesos per person per year[2] (USD 8,000).

The prominent dysfunctions in the diagnoses completed in 2014 were mostly related to the reorganization of the company in the context of its growth, and the preparation and implementation of the *succession plan* (Savall, Zardet, Rasolofoarisoa, & Guerrero, 2014). For a start, the focus was on *problems of growth synchronization*, which consisted of: fitting the strategy to the human and financial resources; dealing with the unfamiliarity of the top and middle managers with their staff; and poor communication, coordination, and cooperation between the head office and the sales outlets, which were recently created and scattered throughout the country.

The dysfunctions entailed by the *implementation of the* **succession strategy** included difficulties in distinguishing and dividing executive and governance responsibilities in the context of running the company, despite a well-defined succession strategy. In accordance with the strategy, the father was to gradually detach himself from executive responsibilities, share them among the top managers, and his close family would consider this succession as legitimate. However, the second son, who had followed the **pilot intervention** in 2005, was still in an ambiguous and unclear position in 2013 in terms of assuming the general direction of the company. Active in the **maintenance and development of SEAM** in the company, he thought he had taken enough responsibilities in the company management so that his father could detach from it. In addition, Sanchez Hass employees gradually recognized his leader skills and legitimacy. The next section of the chapter looks at how the **intervention-research** at the company helped to resolve the transmission issues.

Did the hidden costs evolve since 2005? As in any company, the strong growth of the company spawned a new generation of hidden costs. Thus, the vertical diagnoses in 2013 estimated that, on average in the orchards and the sales outlets, these costs were MXN 182,000 per person and per year (USD 13,900)[3] (see Figure 11.4). These **hidden costs** represented 22% of the company's turnover (revenues) and included many **opportunity costs** due to **non-sales**.

Business Unit	Turnover (pesos)	Value added on variable costs	Direct Payroll (1)	*Total Payroll	Expected hours worked	HCVAVC (2)	Hidden costs Total	Hidden costs per person per year
Whole company	$231,300,000		140	260		$156	$47,320,000	$182,000
Orchard 1	$25,026 000	$15,253,000	37	-	85,500	$178	$4,121,000	$111,00
Sales branche 1	$22,904 000	$3,036,000	6	-	20,100	$150	$1,021,000	$170, 000
Sales branche 2	$51,570 000	$8,641,000	11	-	37,800	$228	$4,732,000	$430,000
Sales branche 3	$27,769 000	$2,944,000	6	-	16,200	$180	$1,173,000	$195,000

(1) Including indirect employees (subcontractors, etc.).

(2) HCVAVC = Hourly Contribution to Value Added on Variable Costs*

Figure 11.4.   Visible and hidden economic and financial indicators in the five diagnosed business units (2014).

These **diagnoses** were presented through the **mirror-effect** to the interviewees, and generated a "shock" that stimulated several innovative actions for improving performance. The projects that followed this intervention had major impacts on the economic and social performance of the company.

SOCIO-ECONOMIC PERFORMANCE
IMPROVEMENT RESULTS

The main improvements in the company were observed through the development after the first intervention in 2005 and the evolution of the economic indicators from 2005 to 2014. The improvements following the intervention implemented in 2014 have not been assessed in depth yet.

Economic Performance

Figure 11.5 shows the evolution of the performance indicators of the company since 2004, a year before the first intervention start. An interesting result is that, for the eight year period, the company has steadily increased its *profitability* (Solid line 4) in a much stronger proportion than its turnover/revenues (Dotted lines 1 and 2). This trend suggests that the company has learned to *recycle its hidden costs* of non-sales and *overcharges* into *value-added.* The 2006 higher net profit was achieved with almost the same volume of sales than the previous year. The profit of the company has followed an upward trajectory for 8 years, despite a relative sales growth of 7% per year for 8 years. Between 2008 and 2011, the last economic crisis has had a significant impact on reducing turnover (revenues) and profitability, which, however, remained positive and followed a new and strong ascent from 2012.

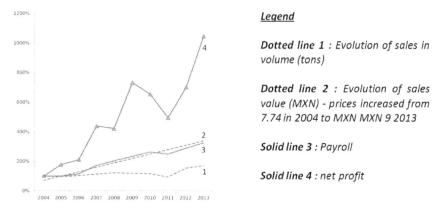

Figure 11.5.   Evolution of economic and financial indicators (2004 to 2013).

If we analyze more accurately the sales variation between 2005 and 2013, it grew in volume by 7% per year, while it grew in value by 30% per year. This growth takes into account customer losses during the crisis. The largest customer left the company in 2010, which represented a loss of a sales volume of 1,200 tons generating 1 million pesos of revenue per year, which was 12% of the total turnover (revenues) of the company. The customer argued that the company was not able to meet his requirements to offer a larger variety of fruits in its sales. This decrease was offset by additional sales from new and existing clients.

The net profit, meanwhile, was multiplied by 5 between 2004 and 2013, in 9 years, and represented between 3.1% (2005) and 6.5 % (2014) of turnover/revenues. These developments demonstrate the existence of a pool of hidden costs, which has partially been *recycled into value-added* in the period 2005–2013. Yet, the *hidden costs assessment* in 2013 showed that large pools still existed in the company, which further indicates that hidden costs are not an indicator of *economic performance* of the company per se, but rather pools of performance improvement for financing growth and future development.

Social Performance

Soon after the first intervention in 2005, the company recorded significant behavioral change in its employees—through reduced *absenteeism* and staff turnover rates, which are traditionally high in Mexico. As an example, before 2005, out of every seven people in the company in a given week, six of them would leave the following week. The improvement of the social conditions in the life of the employees and the development of the company's compliance with social laws and tax rules, consequential to the *socio-economic diagnoses*, were at the origin of the staff stabilization.

Indicators of Social Performance Improvement

At the same time, the role of *proximity management* has progressively and considerably improved. The initial authoritarian management, based on the principle of obedience to the supervisor, which actually generated a high degree of disobedience, was increasingly replaced by a management based on contracts between the managers and the employees. A higher respect for the hierarchy from the employees has been clearly perceived by the managers themselves. The *implementation of SEAM* practices promoted *synchronized decentralization* between the top and middle managers, then between middle managers and workers. The company gradually gained credibility in the eyes of its employees.

A notable improvement observed since 2006 concerned the *planning and scheduling practices* in the company, especially at the *interfaces* between production, packaging and transportation. This improvement had directly impacted the quality of service to the client and employee compliance with the work and meeting schedules.

In addition, the preparation of the business transmission itself improved. In July 2014, the father appointed his second son as new CEO after a series of interviews conducted with each family member by the *internal consultant*. He was appointed during an executive committee meeting, which consisted of the father, the sons, and the son-in-law. His new responsibilities included supervising and synchronizing all operational activities of the company. Since then, he organized bimonthly appointments with each member of the executive committee. During the same period, the third and youngest son, also trained by ISEOR to become an internal consultant, took the head of the sales outlets. The elder brother, meanwhile, was struggling to find his place in the company. Unlike his younger brothers, he was reluctant for many years to accept SEAM and to cooperate with its practices. However, after eight months of *negotiations*, he finally agreed to cooperate with his brothers.

Improvement Variables of Social and Economic Performance

The outstanding actions in the company included the combination of *intangible* and *tangible investments* in order to improve the working conditions of the employees, enhance the skills and employability development policy concerning the employees, increase wages, and extend social security to all employees. These actions also included a high quality based product-markets strategy, which was made possible by the greater stability of the staff and their commitment. The success of this quality strategy encouraged the company to expand internationally afterwards.

Tangible and Intangible Investment Policy

The primary objective of the company was not to share the dividends, but rather to achieve an investment strategy. The process of the *socio-economic innovation process* led to a major improvement plan for the physical working conditions. After the socio-economic diagnoses in the sectors of production (orchards, packaging), new equipment for transporting people and goods were purchased. The old pick-ups were replaced by trucks that were much more comfortable and safe for transporting the employees to the cultivation areas (a roughly 40 km drive). The uniforms in the crop area were also adapted to the climatic conditions, and drinking water was provided in orchards. Simultaneously, to prepare the company *development strategy*, new buildings and warehouses were built to serve the local and international markets.

Development of Corporate Social Responsibility (CSR) to Retain Employees

When the company conceived its *first internal external strategic action plan* in 2005, one of its priorities was to create local jobs and gain local notoriety. It quickly became a local reference for work, by creating a distinctive policy of qualitative development of **human potential**. The action plan focused on increasing wages, providing a better living standard for the employees and their families, and providing **socio-economic benefits** for teams and individual employees. Since 2006, Sanchez Hass has increased salaries and set up a fast and reliable wage payment process. The company has also decided to financially support social security for 92% of its employees—in 2004 80% of the employees did not have any health insurance.

A training policy designed and implemented, allowing the employees to pursue studies, supporting the skills development of the current staff rather than putting the emphasis on recruiting more educated people. In practice, many training sessions were set up—some organizational members have learned to read, and computers were purchased and used for training and learning the basics of computing. Open discussion sessions were held on life in the company and the activities that were organized, involving all the employees. Staff working hours were taken into account to organize information meetings; in return, the staff pledged to be more punctual.

An External Strategy of Differentiation Through Quality

Since 2005, one of the company's **strategic objectives** was to **increase value-added** by improving the quality and profitability of its products. This commitment led to many initiatives for achieving this goal:

- Sanchez Hass decided in 2005 to do away with its bad suppliers because they provided poor quality goods and with its bad customers because their payment practices were not acceptable.
- The company changed its procurement process to obtain product quality that was more in line with the requirements of its customers. Instead of buying products already picked in the orchards and shipping them in boxes, it set up a team of its own employees who pick avocados in the orchards of its suppliers as soon as they are ripe (about 200 local producers).
- To improve the quality of the fruits in the orchards, the company established diseases prevention and treatment practices. The scrap rate fell by 28% in 2006.
- To meet the demands of its clients, the company diversified and improved the presentation of its products, developing distribution in self-service stores.

- Finally, Sanchez Hass opted for a policy of higher prices, compared to its competitors, justified by the improvement of product quality and customer satisfaction rates. This price policy initially triggered many **internal worries**, but has paid off given the growth and development of the company's results at national and international levels (see Figure 11.5).

Market Extension

In 2006, the development strategy of the company initially focused on the local and the national market: its ambition was to become the development spearhead of the avocado producers in the region and to create a presence in different states of Mexico. Currently, four sales outlets are settled and provide about 30% of the company's turnover (revenues). Since 2013 the company aimed to become number one in the national market, particularly by diversifying the products, which is the main reason the company decided to grow blueberries and raspberries.

A second stage, from 2013, concerned the first steps of the company in the international markets, once the stability on the domestic market was achieved. Today the firm exports avocados, blueberries and raspberries to Japan, Guatemala, Costa Rica, and the United States. The company is nevertheless at the very beginning of this stage because its international revenue share is still very low. The international market has the advantage to be particularly suited to a high quality policy, and to be complementary to the national market in terms of caliber of goods.

The Evolution of Managerial Practice

After the **collaborative training** of the top and middle managers in the **SEAM tools** in 2005, which was repeated in 2014, three main tools have been used for increasing employee responsibilities and **effectiveness**, manager credibility, and the **synchronized decentralization** of operations. Those tools were the **Internal and External Strategic Action Plan (IESAP)**, **priority action plans** (PAP), and **Periodically Negotiable Activity Contract** (PNAC). The company actively uses the priority action plans to punctuate its life. Since 2005, each semester, new priority action plans were developed and monitored during the semester. These tools allowed the company both to set realistic goals and to identify concrete actions to achieve them. At the end of each semester, the company measured the implementation rate of the priority actions, and it gradually increased significantly since 2006, reaching 80% in 2013.

The company also improved **time management** practices by using simple tools for planning and scheduling. Each manager had an agenda, interdepartment regular meeting were held to ensure **synchronization** between the activities of cutting (avocados trees), production, packaging and shipping, and *resolutions charts* were regularly used to improve meeting *efficiency*, during which concrete decisions and resolutions were made. The management team was correspondingly strengthened due to the increased rate of meetings, now twice a month.

There was also more *attentive listening* to the opinions and observations of the employees, which was achieved through service meetings and the implementation of **the *periodically negotiable activity contracts*** for all managers and employees. This implementation, which started in 2006 with 27 PNACs, now concerned about 70 people. The implementation of this tool proved to be a real challenge for the managers, both when providing improvement targets, interacting with the employees, and assessing the achievement at the end of the semester to determine the amount of bonus to be awarded.

Succession Planning

Since 2006, the company set in its *internal external strategic action plan* the objective of "ensuring that the business grows and is transferred between generations," by organizing the integration of the family in the business and building an effective methodology for monitoring the business. However, between 2006 and 2013 the company hardly progressed on structuring the governance and preparation of the business transmission.

As part of the intervention launched in 2014, the second son solicited ISEOR for its methodological assistance. For several years, he had been informally managing most of the company activities without any explicit and formalized responsibility. In July 2014, he was appointed as new CEO after a series of interviews with each family member by the internal consultant. His new responsibilities consisted of supervising and synchronizing all of the operational activities of the company. He created bimonthly meetings of the executive committee, which also consisted of orchestrating the *priority action plans* campaign preparation by negotiating the *periodically negotiable activity contracts* with each of the top managers. In October 2014, the family decided to set up a *focus group* on structure and articulate governance and management, which remained strongly intertwined due to the existence of a single governing body.

The Main Remaining Challenges

This company was characterized by strong *strategic ambition*, formalized in an *internal and external strategic action plan* and priority action plans. This strategic ambition required a strong synchronization of activities and *projects* between the departments, but also time allocation for achieving the priority actions on the part of the managers. However, this ambition would only be realized through a larger delegation of responsibility from the managers to their employees. This allocation of *time resources* from the top managers to the managers is becoming increasingly common in companies and is a *strategic key of success*.

Among the remaining challenges in the company, it seems important to increase the *cohesion* between family members, to clearly structure the governance body (as owners of the company) and the role of executive managers (between heads of each of the major business units), and to define how to integrate the new generations of the family.

LESSONS LEARNED

The Sanchez Hass case raises a number if implications for the management of a family business, an agribusiness company in the primary sector, its geopolitical location, and the longevity of the SEAM practices.

Organizing the Transmission of the Family Business

The company decided to implement SEAM to develop its economic and *social performance* and to professionalize its management practices. But soon enough, the company's top management realized the simultaneous need for structuring its governance and articulating the role of executive management within the company. The reason is that the strategic and executive decisions were heavily influenced and complicated daily by the *functioning* difficulties between family members. Thus, in the context of a *SEAM intervention*, an objective of articulating the governance and the management was quite legitimate, especially considering that the emotional nature of the relationship of the main *actors* required the intervention of a third party who was part of the family. In this case, the *external consultant* and *internal consultant* played complementary roles.

A Dynamic Strategy of an Agribusiness Company in a Developing Country

The company is one of the first significant examples of SEAM implementation in an agricultural company, located in a developing country and in a region with a low socio-economic level. The 10-year *strategic trajectory* is a prime example of the deployment of a differentiation strategy favored by the implementation of SEAM to better face a highly competitive environment, without targeting growth at all costs. The basic goal was to combine profitable growth while simultaneously developing *human potential*. The company, in comparison to its competitors, cushioned the effects of the extremely severe economic crisis of 2008 due to its strong internal cohesion and the *strategic management tools* that brought flexibility to face the effects of the crisis. Best practices for *planning and scheduling* allowed the company to anticipate market reactions and keep its ability to grow, while local competitors were struggling to survive. The innovative and ambitious *development* policy of the company's human potential was initiated in 2005 and has had an impact both on the personal and professional life of the employees, their employability, stability, and the development of professional skills in the company.

A Policy of Integrated Social Responsibility

The company eventually set up a genuine policy of *integrated social responsibility* at various levels, toward: its employees, its suppliers (since it now works with 200 local producers in the State of Michoacán), and its local area because it has become the company in which local people want to work. Most of all, the company's social responsibility policy is also associated with its *economic performance*, and, thus, sustainably bearable.

Developing Proximity Management Skills

When deciding to implement SEAM in 2005, the company also chose to develop *proximity management* skills. This focus essentially concerned supervisors with a low level of initial training, who had been relatively reluctant for many years to use management tools they considered out of their reach. The top managers strongly supported those middle managers to help them move from a traditional role of agent focused on operations management to a more participatory teacher role, an organizer posture that consisted of prescribing rather than doing, helping them negotiate with their employees to set individual and collective team goals. The main levers of the transformation of roles were the use of time management tools, *competency grids*, monitoring projects through priority action plans, and *negotiation-assessment* of periodically negotiable activity contracts with the employees.

Coupling Tangible and Endogenous Intangible Investments

The technology capital investment was undoubtedly a source of ***productivity*** gains, provided it is accompanied by an investment in the people who will use the new equipment. Indeed, endogenous ***intangible investment*** has two complementary effects. The first effect is the training of the employees to adequately use the new equipment. The second effect is being more respectful of employees, facilitating their acceptance of the new methods rather than opposing these changes through more or less passive resistance. The company invested both in equipment to improve the production, transportation, and, more generally, working conditions, as well as in ***communication*** with and training of employees. This combination of initiatives helped to improve working conditions and facilitated employee understanding of the development strategy of the company, which was based on quality differentiation. Indicators of social and economic performance clearly showed that this strategy of tangible-intangible investments paid off in terms of reduced ***absenteeism***, employee turnover, wastes, and production costs and has simultaneously increased product quality and sales volumes. The combination of all these parameters explains the ***profitability*** increase, much faster than that of the turnover (revenues).

A Management System Requires Maintenance

The company set up SEAM in 2005 with the assistance of ISEOR and an external consultant. Although it quickly obtained encouraging results, Sanchez Hass required (between 2007 and 2013) the additional assistance of its external consultant to maintain the tools and management practices that were established in 2005. The external consultant brought both methodological assistance and ***external energy***, which avoided the obsolescence or the abandonment of certain innovative practices implemented in 2006. Despite this regular help, energy and methods input, the company felt (in 2013) that it was at a crucial point of its growth, with the need to more fully integrate its new employees, who had not been trained in the new managerial practices. The firm also needed to resolve its issues of governance and management.

In 2013, the company decided to hire the external consultant, who then became an internal consultant, and to solicit ISEOR for a new ***intervention*** in 2014. The new SEAM diagnoses and the ***collaborative trainings*** that were achieved in 2014 pointed to the existence of large and unexploited pools of productivity as well as the need for a larger team of internal consultants to support the newly internal senior consultant. After the training of the two first consultants in 2014, the company has already decided to train another two in 2015.

CONCLUSION

SEAM implementation in Sanchez Hass is particularly interesting with regard to its industry characteristics, its size, country, familial structure, and *strategic situation* of strong growth. Once more, this case validates the fact that strengthening *internal cohesion* is a key success factor for an ambitious *external strategy* in a highly competitive environment. In this case, the cohesion involved family members, in their dual status of owners and managers, and the top and middle managers, who have emerged as the real *key-actors* in the success of the company.

NOTES

1. The research for this chapter has been influenced by a number of works that are not directly referred to in the text, including Boje and Rosile (2003), Buono and Savall (2007), Gephart (2009), Perroux (1979), Sánchez Mateo (2014), Savall (1974, 1975, 1977, 1981, 2010, 2012), Savall and Zardet (1987, 1992, 1995, 2005, 2008, 2009, 2011, 2013), and Savall, Zardet, and Bonnet (2000, 2008).
2. These figures are expressed in Purchasing Power Parity (PPP) terms, the level of hidden costs per capita per year is 13,000 USD PPP (see Appendix 11-2).
3. Figures expressed in Purchasing Power Parity (PPP) terms (Source, OECD), the level of hidden costs per capita per year is 22,200 USD PPP.

REFERENCES

Boje, D., & Rosile, G.-A. (2003). Comparison of socio-economic and other trans-organizational development methods. *Journal of Change Organizational Management, 16*(1), 10–20.

Buono, A. F., & Savall, H. (Eds.) (2007). *Socio-economic intervention in organizations: The intervener-researcher and the SEAM approach to organizational analysis.* Charlotte, NC: Information Age Publishing.

Gephart, R. P. (2009). An invitation to ethnostatistics. *Revue Sciences de gestion – Management Sciences – Ciencias de Gestión, 70,* 85.

Macías Herrera, S. C. (2007). Enracinement de la méthode d'intervention socio-économique au sein des PME mexicaines [Strenghening SEAM intervention method in Mexican SMEs]. In H. Savall (Ed.), *L'hôpital et les réseaux de santé* (pp. 215–223). Paris, France: Economica.

Perroux, F. (1979). L'entreprise, l'équilibre rénové et les coûts cachés [The enterprise, the renovated balance and the "hidden" costs]. Preface. In H. Savall. *Reconstruire l'entreprise* [Reconstructing the enterprise] Paris, France: Dunod. 2nd ed. in H. Savall & V. Zardet. Reconstruire l'entreprise, Paris: Dunod (2014).

Sánchez Mateo, I., & Guerrero Lizardi, A. (2014). Présentation de l'entreprise Frutas Finas Hnos et de la mise en place de la démarche socio-économique [Presentation of SEAM implementation at Frutas Finas Hnos Company]. In H. Savall & V. Zardet (Ed.), *La conduite du changement dans les entreprises et les organisations* [Change Management within Companies and Organizations]. Paris, France: Economica.

Sánchez, I., & Sánchez, H. (2007). Implantation du management socio-économique et des contrats d'activités périodiquement négociables dans une PME Mexicaine. [Settling Socio-economic approach to management and Periodically Negotiable Activity Contracts in a Mexican SME]. In H. Savall (Ed.), *L'hôpital et les réseaux de santé* (pp. 227–237). Paris, France: Economica.

Savall, H. (1974–1975–1977). *Enrichir le travail humain dans les entreprises et les organisations* [An economic evaluation of job enrichment]. Paris: Dunod.

Savall, H. (1981–2010). *Work and people: An economic evaluation of job enrichment.* 1st ed. New York: Oxford University Press ; 2nd ed. Charlotte, NC: Information Age Publishing

Savall, H. (2003). International dissemination of the socioeconomic method. *Journal of Organizational Change Management, 16*(1), 107–115.

Savall, H. (2012). *Origine radicale des crises économiques: Germán Bernácer, précurseur visionnaire* [Root origin of crises: Germán Bernácer, a visionary forerunner]. Charlotte, NC: Information Age Publishing.

Savall, H., & Zardet, V. (1987). *Maîtriser les coûts et les performances cachés : Le contrat d'activité périodiquement négociable* [Mastering hidden costs and performance: The periodically negotiable activity contract]. Paris: Economica.

Savall, H., & Zardet, V. (1992). *Le nouveau contrôle de gestion: Méthode des coûts-performances cachés* [New management control: The hidden cost-performance method]. Paris: Éditions Comptables Malesherbes-Eyrolles

Savall, H., & Zardet, V. (1995–2005–2009). *Ingénierie stratégique du roseau, souple et enracinée* [Strategic engineering of the reed, flexible and rooted]. Paris: Economica.

Savall, H., & Zardet, V. (2008). *Mastering hidden costs and performance*, Charlotte, NC: Information Age Publishing.

Savall, H., & Zardet, V. (2011). *The qualimetrics approach: Observing the complex object.* Charlotte, NC: Information Age Publishing.

Savall, H., & Zardet, V. (2013). *The dynamics and challenges of tetranormalization.* Charlotte, NC: Information Age Publishing.

Savall, H., Zardet, V., & Bonnet, M. (2000–2008). *Releasing the untapped potential of enterprises through socio-economic management.* Geneva: Éditions IOT-BIT.

Savall, H., Zardet, V., & Guerrero, A. (2005). *Diagnostico socioeconomico en una empresa empacadora de frutas* [Socioeconomic diagnosis of a fruit agribusiness company]. Ecully, France: ISEOR.

Savall, H., Zardet, V., Rasolofoarisoa, A., & Guerrero, A. (2014). *Diagnosticos socioeconómicos verticales en una empresa empacadora de frutas* [Socioeconomic diagnoses of a fruit agribusiness company]. Ecully, France: ISEOR.

APPENDIX 11.1

Exchange Rate (Source: World Bank)

Year	2005	2006	2007	2008	2009	2010	2011	2012	2013
MXN	1	1	1	1	1	1	1	1	1
EUR	0,0778	0,0703	0,0623	0,0579	0,051	0,0615	0,0569	0,0581	0,0557
USD	0,0936	0,0924	0,0917	0,0735	0,0751	0,0808	0,081	0,0768	0,0766

APPENDIX 11.2

GDP Mexico expressed in parity purchasing power (Source: World Bank)

Year	2005	2013
GDP (exchange rate MXN USD)	7 824 USD	10 307 USD
GDP PPP*	11 964 USD PPP	16 463 USD PPP
Multiplicator GDP to PPP GDP	1,53	1,60

*PPP GDP or GDP per capita based on parity purchasing power (PPP): The PPP GDP is gross domestic product converted to international dollars using the parity purchasing power (PPP) rate. An international dollar has the same purchasing power over GDP of the country stating that a US dollar has in the United States.

APPENDIX 11.2

Economic and financial indicators evolution from 2004 to 2013 (appendix for Figure 11-4)

	2004	2005	2006	2007	2008	2009	2010	2011	2012	2013
Turnover (in value) pesos	70%	100%	130%	160%	190%	220%	249%	279%	309%	339%
Turnover evolution (tons)	100%	96%	104%	114%	123%	118%	117%	95%	155%	171%
Net result evolution	100%	177%	211%	437%	421%	732%	655%	494%	702%	1047%
Payroll evolution	100%	100%	115%	172%	203%	233%	262%	249%	289%	326%

PART III

INTER-ORGANIZATIONAL INTERVENTION: APPLYING SEAM ACROSS BOUNDARIES

CHAPTER 12

ADAPTATION OF HORIVERT TO ARCHITECTS[1]

Renaud Petit, Miguel Delattre, and Thibault Ruat

The architectural profession in France is a regulated vocation whose field of intervention covers the work submitted for a building permit that establishes the architectural *project*, but also involves more extended missions. Architecture is also an *artistic* occupation.

The entire architecture sector consists mainly of *small or micro-organizations*. They are framed at national level by the National Council of the Order of Architects (ANOC), which has regional relays. It is an associative organization, independent but recognized by the government, which is in charge of regulating the profession and ensuring the training activities. It is important to keep in mind that the title of architect may not be used by a person who doesn't graduate in architectural studies and who is not registered with the Order of Architects.

This chapter is based on research-interventions conducted in 22 agencies, on the request of the President of the Order of Architects Regional Council. This request was based on the need for the agencies to reinforce their internal organization, improve customer service, and increase *economic performance* and *competitiveness*, by developing the involvement and motivation of employees and architects. The research delves into a

The Socio-Economic Approach to Management Revisited: The Evolving Nature of SEAM in the 21st Century, pp. 239–263

sector that has not received much attention in the management sciences as only a few researchers have specialized in design and project management (see, for example, Midler, 1998). By contrast, the authors who have specialized in studying this profession are sociologists and economists (Callon, 1998; Gautier, 2005, 2007; Raynaud, 2004, 2009).

The chapter describes the work carried out in the *implementation* of socio-economic management in small or micro-structures in the architectural sector. After discussing the role of architecture in France, we detail the methodology deployed followed by an overview of the economic and *social performance* of the agencies in the early stage of the intervention. After emphasizing the changing socio-economic performance of the agencies with regard with the small size of these *structures*, the analysis concludes with an examination of the contribution of these research-interventions on *developments* in socio-economic management.

FROM DESIGN TO IMPLEMENTATION

This section presents the economic and social context of the architectural sector in France, focusing on its managerial, technical and environmental challenges. It also delineates the research methodology used to study these microstructures.

Economic and Social Context of the Architectural Sector in France

Currently in France, there are approximately 30,000 architects operating in 22,500 agencies: 15,000 of them operating as individuals and 7,500 employed by companies (Vial-Voiron & Cartillier, 2010). This sector is mainly composed of small or very small businesses. Indeed, there is an average of two people per office, half of them have no employees, and only 1% has more than 10 employees.[2] Only one hundred branches throughout the French territory exceed 10 people. The sector is characterized by a fragmentation of architectural design work, split between many professions: architect, urban planner, landscaper, construction economist, structural engineer, heating engineers, acoustician, and geotechnicians.

Since 1960 the gradual reduction of the size of architectural agencies increased their precariousness and led some observers to point to "underemployment" (Maurois, 1994) or even "impoverishment" (Dauge, 2004). Half of the architects have annual incomes below 25,000 euros, and the average annual income is 45,000 euros.[3] This is due to major differences between a minority of recognized architects, at the head of very large agencies, and the majority of managers and architects (the owners of the agency or employees) who oversee the daily activities in the firms.

Historically, the ideology conveyed by the School of Fine Arts accentuates the distance of the architects vis-à-vis technical issues and helps to explain why architects have accepted so easily to divest themselves of construction technical and economic issues (Raynaud, 2009). Technical skills were gradually outsourced by architectural agencies. The 1957 Protocol,[4] defining the categories of projects for which *engineering* consultants may practice project management opened a breach, confirmed by the creation in 1962 of the Ministry of Equipment. As a result, architects lost control over design and project management. Engineers have taken over the technical aspect of the construction, the main outlets for young civil engineers being in the building sector and public works and engineering firms.

The architects' situation is sensitive. Although architects play a main role, they are finding it increasingly difficult to hold. The sector and profession are recognized in the development of our living environment, but they also have the image of an elitist guild associated with a lack of pragmatism. The importance of the "artistic creation" dimension, which is central to training in the field, typically doesn't provide them with sufficient information on how to run a business and steer projects. Due to this lack of management training, an architect manager is much more of an artist than a manager. In France the architect is responsible for the act of building and skills outsourcing, assuming responsibilities related to various co-contractors services. In fact, these individuals are in the center of competitors, without being conversant enough with and trained in the working methods necessary to coordinate and manage increasingly important projects.

The Challenge of Business: Management and Technicalities

The initial training of architects is not adapted to the new requirements of professional practice in multiple aspects, particularly in business management. Project management methods, collaboration and an overall understanding of sustainable development are not taught in French schools of architecture (Terrin, 2009). Architectural studies do not prepare participants for the functions of agency or becoming a branch manager, or to be able to effectively interact with other partners such as people working in engineering design offices and surveyors. The lack of training in business and management emphasizes the uniqueness of the "artist architect" and reinforces the feeling of a low sensitivity to economic and *profitability* issues of an architectural firm—such as forgetting about billing or a lack of control of hours spent on a file. These managers are often assisted by accountants, with an expertise too remote from reality, to develop a comprehensive and integrated approach to the **survival** and development of their agency.

The agencies are also competitors and rarely work together. The sector is scarcely transverse—each participant specializes in the expertise of his or her business as well as on normative expertise and knowledge. A multiplicity of professionals currently coexists in this sector, with strong normative constraints that operate in competitive partnerships (Raynaud, 2004). Architects are all the more vulnerable due to the rise of normative requirements that them to play a coordinating role.

Faced with the economic difficulties of the profession, a focus on business and managerial skills aspects and the need to create better solutions for organizing projects with partners became important challenge for architects. According to a survey, 78% of architects consider that it will be necessary to integrate construction economists in their agencies by 2030.[5]

Technical Aspects of the Trade

The content of the traditional framework for the market of architects – called "prime contractor"—with architectural design, management and site supervision, and technical studies has greatly evolved over time. Increased **regulations** and standards further induced blur and uncertainty. Architects find themselves increasingly subject to interpretations that require greater **vigilance**. Their activities are affected by many regulations, such as the need for accessibility to public buildings, standards related to seismicity and flooding when the building site exceeds one hectare, lead and asbestos diagnoses, termite control in existing buildings, fire safety, and subdivision regulations among other demands. Building standards are becoming more numerous, and design activity is increasingly experienced by architects as a space for many important constraints (Baer, 1997; Ben-Joseph & Szold, 2005; Rowe 1993; Smith, 2002). For example, in 2012 changes in the calculation of surfaces for construction established a shift from the passage of a declarative calculation at the stage of building permits, to that of "surfaces excluding networks" in floor area.[6] This law penalizes architects since the obligation to consult an architect shifts from 170 m² to the equivalent of 185 m², ruling them out of the market for single-family home in favor of construction companies.

Tetranormalization

The daily activities of Architects are characterized by a strong normative pressure that Savall and Zardet (2005) refer to as "tétranormalisée." The **tetranormalization** approach attempts to identify the phenomena that transform and disrupt the rules of the economic and social game and establish a concept of **sustainable overall performance** to support the organizations in implementing research and a more proactive strategy. An environment "tétranormalisé" is characterized by strong density standards in four core areas: (1) accounting and financial; (2) commercial; (3) quality, safety and environment; and (4) social. These main poles of standards correspond to the major challenges, which are often contradictory, that must be applied and contribute to a more sustainable and bearable CSR for firms and organizations.

The construction sector is directly affected by the inflation of these sometimes contradictory standards, which seem to belong to "stock-in-trade theory" (Savall & Zardet, 2005) more than management practices aiming to improve construction and control the economic impacts by the *actors* involved.

Project Management Aspects

Architecture is an expression of culture—"Architectural design, the quality of buildings ... are of public interest" (Article 1, Law of 3 January 1977). As such, the architectural profession is highly regulated by public authorities. The architect's profession can be characterized as being "between work and service" and depends on the value of the architect and his or her creative ability—originality at all costs is both a myth and constraint of contemporary architecture (Habraken, 2005). The architectural activity is in tension between the representation of a creative artistic activity and the normative framework of a production process. The architect is the "conductor," the binder of the act of building. The technical and professional specialization in the construction sector has led to strong ties between architects and their stakeholders (Woudhuysen & Abley, 2004). As a result, architecture firms spend significant time managing the *interfaces* between co-contractors and the executing companies. So the authors (we) and the professionals (practitioners) encourage a reconsideration of the architects' working methods, considering that their practices are not inevitable, but only chronic *dysfunction*s of the architecture and urbanism industry (Terrin, 2009).

Environmental Issues

Since the Grenelle Environment, architects in France are committed to environmental quality and sustainable *development*. The building sector consumes 50% of natural resources and produces 30% of the nation's greenhouse gas (Dauge, 2004). Each year, it corresponds to an equivalent of 70.6 million tons of oil (70.6 Mtoe), or 43% of total final energy, which is considerable in a context of increased emissions of greenhouse gases by 14% since 1990 (ADEME, 2008).

These societal significant commitments increase the burden of standards, rules and regulatory constraints that are already facing the profession. The texts on sustainable development impose strong requirements to design activity: for example, BBC[7] (a low-energy building), high environmental quality standards (HQE), thermal regulation in 2005, 2012, and 2015, with the idea of a passive house (i.e., operating in total energy independence). The preservation of the environment is an important potential market for architects, but it also represents a threat for them if they fall behind stakeholder expectations and demands. Thus the development of managerial skills and expertise has becoming an increasingly critical determinant of the economic vitality necessary to make the architectural firms the key players in this growing market.

A Method Adapted for Microstructures

Academic research in the architecture sector is typically connected to sociological or technical frameworks. The management literature, in contrast, tends to focus on a higher degree of *intervention-research* within small firms in general without focusing on a particular profession. The organization or functioning characteristic that is specific to architecture agencies, as illustrated by our intervention-research, provides a more in-depth knowledge of the architecture business. This perspective is especially useful because architectural firms do not have the habit of engaging in the process of change to enhance socio-economic performance. The *intangible investment* necessary for the *effectiveness* and *efficiency* of the structures does not appear as fundamental for the managers-architects. This lack of attention is also noticeable in vocational training. As an example, a study of 368 agencies[8] shows that less than 2 % of their training plans concerned human management *resources*. Out of 185,053 hours of vocational training, only 3,949 hours were dedicated to management.

Given these tendencies, we hypothesize that beyond the lack of interest in management by the managers of the architectural firms, the *collaborative training* and the research in management are perceived as binding and more adapted to larger companies that have jobs dedicated exclusively to internal functioning efficiency and a search for gains on fixed costs. We have chosen to follow a very small enterprise (VSE)-adapted *implementation* method, called Multi-SME HORIVERT. The *Multi-SME HORIVERT* method follows the same principles as the *HORIVERT* method, but uses action plans that are cut-down in size to suit VSEs and professional practices. This type of intervention-research is more flexible and less binding, while being adapted, in its contents, to the daily work of the actors. For example, we considered the mis-appreciation of *piloting* tools and management in architectural firms due to the absence of consideration during initial architecture training. Concretely, **management tools** that are useful for architectural firm management are presented during the intervention-research in a simple, but not simplistic, way. This approach is recommended because the more the cost of entry of implementation of the tool is seen as low, the more the actors will test them in their daily work.

Methodology

The process of collaborative training of a group of architectural firms took place over approximately 10 months. The *inter-company* actions plans were a series of collaborative training programs that brought together one to several manager-architects who were the main collaborators in an architectural firm. The sessions focused on the construction and appropriation of managerial concepts and tools with an emphasis on the exchange of experiences between agencies. The *intra-company* actions plans delved into the process of change within each agency, based on an analysis of multi-form data according to a qualitative-quantitative-financial spectrum (Savall & Zardet, 2011). This process included four stages: diagnosis, *project*, implementation, and *evaluation*.

In each agency, individual semi-structured interviews of diagnosis of one hour were undertaken with manager-architects and collective 90-minute interviews with employees (2–5 persons) of those firms. A collective session from one to two hours ass then organized with all the members of the architectural firm to trigger an exchange on the dysfunctions and complete the qualitative data gathering by examining their quantitative and financial effects in the form of **hidden costs** (Savall & Zardet, 1987). Approximately one month later an oral and contradictory return of the diagnosis with all the actors of the agency was held to produce a **mirror-effect**.

Each agency then organized a group project, made up of the manager-architect and employees, which met three times at approximately 2-month intervals. The objective was to stimulate the **interactions** between company actors to bring to the foreground internal functioning **improvement** actions and examine relations with the **external environment**. This phase entailed strong dynamics, in the form of exchanges and dialogues. The specifications of the project were established in the form of four of six "dysfunction baskets," which included the main categories of dysfunctions prepared by the intervener-researchers. This steering tool enabled to the participants to connect the qualitative data with the calculated **hidden costs**, to help the actors assess the economic consequences of the improvement actions.

The process ended with a contradictory evaluation co-built by the intervener-researcher and the actors and presented to every architectural firm. The evaluation included management development, noticeable improvements, and improved economic and commercial performance as well as the dysfunctions that remained and the difficulties that were encountered in the process.

Concomitantly individual interviews were conducted between the inter-vener-researcher and the manager-architects called "*personal assistance*." Within this context, tools were proposed to support the implementation and process of socio-economic piloting the architectural firms.

One other peculiarity of the Multi-SME HORIVERT method is the con-stitution of inter-company groups whose purpose is to promote exchanges between the actors from different VSEs. Indeed, these agencies are often isolated—and competing with each other—with little natural ability to discuss their practices. That is why, to stimulate interactivity, it was impor-tant to create inter-company groups of the agencies that were not closely situated in a geographic or business territory so that the actors wouldn't feel threatened in the conduct of their own business activities.

Over a period of approximately two and a half years, four groups of architectural firms were set up. The duration of the collaborative training by group was spread out over 10 months with 22 agencies of architectural firms with sizes ranging from 1 to 19 people. In total, 110 people partici-pated in the intervention-research: 34 managers and 76 employees.

SOCIAL AND ECONOMIC PERFORMANCE IN ARCHITECTURE AGENCIES

This section of the chapter presents the socio-economic diagnosis in 22 architecture agencies during the research-intervention. The treatment of data allowed, initially, identifying the specific characteristics of the agen-cies, drawing on qualitative, quantitative and financial data. The discussion then turns to the observed changes that were transcribed in agencies' oper-ations, focusing on the conception of the manager-architect job.

Characteristics of the Agencies

The analysis of the architecture agencies in the study focused on three key dimensions of their performance: qualitative data from interviews and observations (*social performance*), and quantitative and financial data from their operation (economic performance).

Qualitative Data

First, we analyzed the qualitative data of the socio-economics diagnosis, according to the intervention-research time-table. After the analysis of the *actors*' field note quotes of the actors, these data revealed four types of dysfunctions in these architectural firms. The first one is a "low sensitiza-tion to economic performance." Architecture firms have a lot of difficulties anticipating economic problems, particularly on the part of the manager-architects. It results in a lack of control in billing customers and suppliers: unissued invoices after services provided, payment recovery oversights, and many unpaid bills recovered following the banks' interpellation. The lack of appropriate tools and decision-making indicators prevented the actions from understanding the *profitability* of their projects and affairs. Very often, the manager-architects or head project leaders managed a given project without being able to determine the profit margin of that project.

The second *dysfunction* is referred to as "autarkic closeness." Paradoxi-cally, the limited number of actors in an architecture firm and their working closeness do not ensure internal *communication* efficiency. We noticed that the greater proximity and lower sensitization to the structuring of the transmission of information and attention to communications *game rules* (e.g., meetings, individual interviews, written messages) was low. The com-munications game rules were insufficient, which did not allow the actors to define arrangements or ensure the necessary exchanges to arbitrate and pilot the activity. The deficit of *communication-coordination-cooperation* was also characterized by a lack of orchestration from the manager-architect and between employees. Finally, the strategic information was sometimes diluted or lost among all kinds of transmissions. This same tendency applied to procedures of transfer of knowledge and know-how.

The third theme corresponds to a sort of "collective patchwork of indi-vidualized proceedings." The company's members, according to their technical skills, worked in their own corner, with their own methods of work—physical and IT filing, procedures and processes. For example, the time individual dedicated to search for documents, paper, and emails were very different. The organizations had a propensity not to take care of themselves, to make regular and collective *clean-ups*. It became especially problematic when an actor, a quasi-only holder of numerous technical skills, was absent or left the firm. Teamwork was very important in spite of the small size of these architecture firms.

The last theme was the "commercial no-man's-land." The architectural firms did not have any other seller clearly identified than the manager-architect himself. Sales processes were not shared and there was a lack of skills appropriate for their activity. As a result, the firms were regularly confronted with activity slack from the lack of projects, which could even-tually allow the architects, and it seems to be the only way, to find time for sales *development*. Commercial relationships, in general, with customers, suppliers, and partners were insufficient and too often limited to only a resolution of problems during a project or construction. The consequences of this lack of pro-activity can, in some cases, be dramatic for the survival-development of the organization. There was not much regular attention to third parties, so that it was difficult to define exchanges as real effective business relationship.

Table 12.1 contains field note quotes that illustrate these four dysfunctions.

Table 12.1.   Examples of Dysfunctions Evoked by the Actors During the Diagnosis

Low economic sensitization:

- "We redo projects several times in a row, for example, for the construction of social housing. The corresponding time is still not charged." (Agency 1.2)

- "The agency has too many outstanding payments but the payment times are too long and we never negotiate them. With the public sector, it is the disaster for our finance." (Agency 2.4)

- "Because of problems arriving mainly at the start of the construction site, we are unable to charge services even if they are planned." (Agency 3.5)

- "The agency has a problem of positioning with regard to our customers because 90 % of the customers become friends. It is very difficult to charge friends." (Agency 4.3)

Autarkic closeness:

- "Sometimes there is important information that the manager-architects slipped at the coffee machine, for example, for a building permit filing date, between "what did you do this weekend?" Or "how are you?" Important information is lost." (2.3 Agency)

- "The assistant has valuable skills for the agency, but she puts things in place while the manager-architects are not aware. She must inform them because they have their say." (Agency 3.6)

- "We are piloting visually, there is no regular and structuring meeting to frame the work." (Agency 4.2)

Collective patchwork of individualized proceedings:

- "The model documents of the agency are not regularly updated and when they are nobody knows it." (Agency 1.4)

- "There are files that I do not know where to put on the network of the agency, in particular those that come from the outside, as the design office reports. As a result, they are to be found everywhere and I do not know who has to deal with them and who needs them." (Agency 4.4)

- "We do not have any common method of work, each person makes the small work in his or her corner and does not take time to share and work on the team. It is necessary to develop the same method of classification, identical basic files for each." (Agency 4.5)

(Table continues on next page)

Table 12.1.   (Continued)

Commercial no-man's-land:

- "There are lots of things to do on canvassing steps to be taken, however, we do not complete the work to be done." (Agency 1.1)

- "There is a concern for the office arrangement, when we receive people it is not ideal. There can be a gap with regard to the little bit of professional image of the agency we wish to give." (Agency 2.5)

- "Customers get used to our over-quality, which then becomes normal to them and is no longer a capital gain. In fact, it is somehow a loss for the agency because of the time past. It is necessary to find other selling points." (Agency 3.2)

Quantitative and Financial Data

Each identified dysfunction causes a regulatory cost for the architecture agency. The lack of quantitative and financial *piloting* indicators, however, makes the assessment of this cost almost impossible for the managers. They pilot visually, without tools, ignoring the allocation of internal *resources* and their effective use. Managers' indicators are all too often limited to the balance sheet and income statement made by the accountant a posteriori. Moreover, the economic consequences of these dysfunctions do not explicitly appear in the financial or cost accounting of the organization, although it results in a destruction of real *value-added* (pointless overcharges) or potential (opportunity cost). Hidden costs evaluation is the monetary translation of regular dysfunctional activities (Savall, 1974). For example, in Agency 1.4., people estimated that it typically took 30 minutes each day to look for documents, for two persons, which was caused by the absence of storage space. The calculation of this hidden cost was 2 persons x 0.5 h x 227 days x 54€ = €12,300, which means a hidden cost of €4,300 per person per year in this agency. In this calculation, the *Hourly Contribution to Value-added on Variable Costs* (*HCVAVC*)[9] is 54 euro.

Table 12.2 summarizes the hidden costs identified in the 22 agencies and classified by the four themes of dysfunction (see Table 12.1). The total amount of hidden costs calculated in the 22 diagnoses represents more than €2 million (i.e., an average of approximately €91,000 per agency), knowing that the minimum and maximum amounts were respectively 20,000 and 175,400 euro. If we compare this figure to the total of 110 members of the agencies during the evaluation of hidden costs, the amount of hidden costs is around 18,250 eruo per person and per year (2,007,600 € / 110 persons = 18,251 €).

This analysis indicates that hidden costs are not smaller in VSEs, in this instance, architecture agencies, compared to other organizations with larger workforces. Approximately 800,000 euro in *hidden costs* correspond

Table 12.2.   Summary of Hidden Costs in the Four Main Themes of Dysfunction

Group	Agency	Low economic sensitivity	Self-sufficient proximity	Collective patch-work	To sell without seller and internaliz ed costs	Total	Total per group
1	1.1	110 000 €	N.E	39 100 €	N.E	149 100 €	696 000 €
	1.2	7 500 €	6 500 €	15 900 €	23 800 €	53 700 €	
	1.3	35 000 €	11 600 €	34 100 €	8 800 €	89 500 €	
	1.4	112 000 €	3 000 €	60 400 €	N.E	175 400 €	
	1.5	30 000 €	N.E	8 700 €	77 000 €	115 700 €	
	1.6	N.E	15 600 €	77 800 €	19 200 €	112 600 €	
2	2.1	69 000 €	N.E	39 100 €	67 000 €	175 100 €	707 900 €
	2.2	10 000 €	4 600 €	55 000 €	36 200 €	105 800 €	
	2.3	110 000 €	N.E	11 900 €	6 500 €	128 400 €	
	2.4	71 000 €	N.E	54 300 €	18 900 €	144 200 €	
	2.5	400 €	8 900 €	126 700 €	18 400 €	154 400 €	
3	3.1	N.E	6 000 €	30 700 €	N.E	36 700 €	399 500 €
	3.2	80 400 €	51 100 €	8 800 €	N.E	140 300 €	
	3.3	4 700 €	N.E	26 300 €	9 000 €	40 000 €	
	3.4	50 800 €	N.E	20 700 €	N.E	71 500 €	
	3.5	4 900 €	1 800 €	23 000 €	15 700 €	45 400 €	
	3.6	48 100 €	1 300 €	9 200 €	7 000 €	65 600 €	
4	4.1	6 400 €	200 €	6 500 €	6 900 €	20 000 €	204 270 €
	4.2	5 700 €	N.E	24 400 €	100 €	30 200 €	
	4.3	N.E	1 770 v	39 400 €	25 500 €	66 600 €	
	4.4	20 000 €	N.E	4 500 €	6 300 €	30 800 €	
	4.5	27 300 €	1 200 €	16 800 €	11 300 €	56 600 €	
Total		803 200 €	113 570 €	733 300 €	357 600 €	2 007 670 €	2 007 670 €

to "low economic sensitivity," 40% of the hidden costs identified. The financial result corroborates with the *diagnosis qualitative* results, which underlines the significant dysfunctions due to the poor economic sensitivity of the actors. The analysis of financial data (see Table 12.3) confirms the specificity of those organizations.

Table 12.3. Summary of Economic Data for the 22 Agencies

Group	Agency	Turnover (in €)	Variable costs (en €)	VAVC (en €)	Nb of expected hours	HCVAVC (in €)	Nb of persons	turnover/Pers Ratio (in €)	Turnover/Nb hours	Hourly rate of manager (in €)	Staff Hourly rate (in €)	Operating result (in €)	Profitability rate (en %)
1	1.1	257 424	47 798	209 626	8 342	25	5	51 485	31	9	18	15 149	6.40%
	1.2	236 156	150 000	86 156	6 311	14	4	59 039	37	26.3	12.73	15 180	5.20%
	1.3	281 000	N.E	281 000	13 166	26	7	40 143	21	32.5	25.7	144 161	40%
	1.4	285 040	40 390	244 650	4 530	54	3	95 013	6	90	24	1 370	0%
	1.5	380 091	25 980	354 111	6 718	53	4	95 023	57	6	16	13 400	3.7%
	1.6	390 800	46 800	344 000	9 988	34	4	97 700	39	15	15	N.E	N.E
2	2.1	1 761 224	502 390	258 834	28 642	44	15	117 415	61	31.30	18.50	N.E	N.E
	2.2	296 424	75 861	220 563	9 580	23	6	49 404	31	30	12	N.E	N.E
	2.3	89 321	57 037	32 284	3 348	10	3	29 774	27	0	16	N.E	N.E
	2.4	563 600	86 600	477 000	16 344	29	10	56 630	34	59	40	N.E	N.E
	2.5	910 901	232 639	678 262	24 198	33	13	70 069	38	26.16	20.25	N.E	N.E
3	3.1	144 200	25 400	118 800	5 194	22	3	48 067	28	35.70	N.E	N.E	N.E
	3.2	234 645	3 948	230 697	9 194	25	3	78 215	26	N.E	N.E	N.E	N.E
	3.3	170 000	33 800	136 200	5 217	26	3	56 667	33	15	26	N.E	N.E
	3.4	137 746	13 266	124 480	3 859	32	2	68 873	36	36.37	21.25	N.E	N.E
	3.5	164 826	7 237	157 589	5 633	28	4	41 207	29	36.37	21.28	N.E	N.E
	3.6	122 482	15 031	107 451	5 450	20	3	400 827	22	16.40	21.13	N.E	N.E
4	4.1	202 533	20 300	182 233	7 767	23	3	67 511	26	10.6	21.39	N.E	N.E
	4.2	83 594	28 835	54 759	4 200	13	2	41 797	20	12.88	N.E	N.E	N.E
	4.3	377 622	40 394	337 228	8 506	40	7	53 946	44	17.62	21.64	N.E	N.E
	4.4	55 214	7 634	47 580	2 350	20	1	55 214	23	N.E	N.E	N.E	N.E
	4.5	139 655	69 915	99 740	4 671	21	4	34 914	30	11.97	12.88	N.E	N.E
Average		331 114 €	68 239 €	262 875 €	8 782 h	28 €	5	60 415 €	34 €	62 €	N.E	N.E	N.E

The average turnover (revenues) of the agencies in the study was 331,114 euro (lowest = € 83,594, highest = 1,761,224). Based on the number of workers, it represents an average turnover of 60,400 euro per person. The variable costs represent an average of 68,200 euro or 21% of revenues. The **HCVAVC** is disparate; data by the individual agencies fluctuate between 10 and 54 euro with an average of 28 euro. This amount is close to the identified average in the 1,300 research-interventions realized by ISEOR during 35 years, around 30 euro. Once again, there is no significant correlation between the organization's size and the *evaluation* of the creation of average an hourly value per person.

The specificity of agencies lies in the difference of hourly rates between employees and the manager. Indeed, in 9 out of 22 cases, the hourly rate of the manager is smaller than or equal to the one of the employees. For a manager, it is around 25 euro per hour, with a minimum of no euro (there is one case where the manager did not take any salary or remuneration for the year) and a maximum of 90 euro. The hourly rate of non-manager employees fluctuated between 12 and 40 euro with an average of 20.40 euro. The ratio of the hourly rate of managers to the hourly rate of employees is 1.225, whereas the ratio manager's worked hours to employees' worked hours is 1.53 (52,25h / 34h). The difference between those two hourly rates is quite small, less than 23% while the difference in terms of worker-hours exceeds 50% for the managers.

Learning From Intervention-Research: The Role of the Manager-Architect

The process of socio-economic *intervention-research* within architecture agencies contributed to the development of the manager's job. It highlighted the management training needed for managers and the required changes in their practices. In most cases, the approach contributed to a switch from architect-manager to manager-architect. We can see managers with more voluntarism in daily activity piloting and team management. The strategic vision and definition of the agencies took longer to develop. Sales strategies became more offensive, especially in *negotiation* steps with stakeholders. *Autarkic proximity* is better controlled through *implementation* of structured and formalized communication-consultation-*coordination*. The information was also used in a more professional way. The development of common working methods significantly reduced dysfunctions due to the *collective patchwork*. This more organizational approach allowed the agencies to better pilot needed operations, especially when they were faced with important time constraints. It also promoted the *synchronized decentralization* of knowledge and skills among employees who were now able to more independently pilot business units.

These changes were observed through the construction and use of activities and team *management tools*. The managers repossessed economic indicators that they had outsourced to their accountant in order to re-internalize their decision-making activities. Table 12.4 presents the implementation of socio-economic tools in the 22 agencies over the first 10 months of intervention. This table shows that the implementation of socio-economic tools within the agencies remained partial. Indeed, none of the 22 agencies totally controlled the tools. In the first step of the intervention, because managers and employees initially select the tools, they typically do not consider them fully interconnected to an integrated management system.

Table 12.4. Summary of Tools Implementation in the 22 Agencies

Tools	1						2					3						4				
4 Groups / 22 Agencies	1	2	3	4	5	6	1	2	3	4	5	1	2	3	4	5	6	1	2	3	4	5
110 persons	5	4	7	3	4	5	5	6	3	10	3	3	3	3	2	4	3	3	2	7	1	4
Resolution chart	■	■	■	■	▲	▲	■	■	■	■	▲	▲	■	▲	▲	■	■	▲	■	■	■	■
Time management tool	▲	□	□	▲	□	▲	▲	■	▲	■	▲	▲	■	▲	▲	■	▲	▲	▲	▲	▲	■
Cooperative delegation range	■	■	■	■	■	■	■	□	▲	▲	▲	□	□	▲	□	■	□	▲	▲	■	▲	▲
Competency grid	■	□	□	■	■	■	■	■	▲	■	▲	■	▲	■	□	■	■	▲	▲	■	▲	■
Priority action plan	□	□	□	■	■	■	□	▲	▲	▲	■	□	▲	▲	□	■	▲	■	▲	■	■	▲
Periodically negotiable activity contract	■	□	□	□	□	□	□	□	□	□	□	□	□	□	□	□	□	□	□	□	□	□
Strategic piloting logbook	▲	□	□	□	□	▲	▲	▲	▲	□	▲	▲	□	▲	□	□	▲	▲	▲	■	■	□

Legend:

■ Implemented tool

▲ Partially implemented tool or under implementation

□ Non implemented tool

253

In looking at Table 12.4, only one agency has implemented the ***Periodically Negotiable Activity Contract***[10] (PNAC). It illustrates the lack of sensitivity of employees to share the benefits of economic performance; they share the idea that the search for economic performance is only the responsibility of the manager. The manager of Agency 1.1, for example, through the implementation of PNAC tool confirmed her desire not to be the only person who would ensure the economic survival of her agency. The performance and sales objectives of PNAC are intended to stimulate the search for creation of value-added by employees. Business profits are then shared between the architects and manager, which increases their economic sensitivity toward the agency. Moreover, in this case, each PNAC includes objective of internal life ***improvement*** piloted by the employees themselves.

The ***strategic piloting*** logbook was another management tool rarely used by the agencies and, when it was implemented the indicators contained are often only known by the manager. Decentralization through delegation arrangements must be developed more intensely. Although concerted delegation was implemented in the agencies, they were more focused on the formalization of responsibilities than the distribution of the piloting of activities.

Finally, this summary illustrates the gradual improvement of the speed of tools implementation between different groups. Indeed, on average 50% of the tools were implemented in the agencies belonging to the first intervention group, compared to 17% in the agencies of the fourth group. This result could be explained by the learning effect in the involvement of the approach from the co-construction between the intervener-researchers and their stakeholders and actors in those organizations.

INTERVENTION CONTRIBUTION TO SOCIO-ECONOMIC MANAGEMENT CHANGES

Beyond the evolution of the role of the manager-architect, this section of the chapter compares the financial development in the agencies developments following the intervention-research. The discussion illustrates these observed changes by presenting two contrasted cases, examining the evolution of the methodology as the intervention-research was being conducted.

Financial Evolution of the Agencies

The agencies' changes and initiatives produced significant results in terms of the recycling of hidden costs in value-added and visible performances (see Table 12.5). The average rate of ***conversion of hidden costs*** was 50% according to agencies, with the conversion fluctuating between 9,000 and 85,000 euro. We cannot correlate the great disparity of recycled amounts to the number of actors in the agency: the volume in the number of actors is not an explanatory variable of conversion of the amount of hidden costs in value added. It is important to notice that this rate of 50% corresponds more or less to one of a "classic" **HORIVERT** approach. However, in these cases, the speed (10 months) at which this result was achieved (50% conversion rate) is specific to this type of structure.

Table 12.5.   Summary of Hidden Costs Rate Conversion

Group	Agency	Hidden costs at the beginning of intervention	Conversion of hidden costs	Conversion rates
1	1.1	149 100 €	65 000 €	44%
	1.2	53 630 €	40 500 €	76%
	1.3	89 580 €	79 000 €	88%
	1.4	175 480 €	85 000 €	48%
	1.5	115 730 €	41 000 €	35%
	1.6	112 650 €	62 700 €	56%
2	2.1	175 100 €	N.E	N.E
	2.2	105 820 €	56 700 €	54%
	2.3	128 370 €	48 120 €	37%
	2.4	144 250 €	50 000 €	35%
	2.5	154 497 €	72 500 €	47%
3	3.1	36 690 €	19 300 €	53%
	3.2	140 226 €	15 000 €	11%
	3.3	39 990 €	9000 €	23%
	3.4	71 510 €	N.E	N.E
	3.5	45 380 €	31 000 €	68%
	3.6	65 690 €	63 000 €	96%
4	4.1	20 000 €	11 900 €	60%
	4.2	30 200 €	20 500 €	68%
	4.3	97 570 €	50 000 €	51%
	4.4	87 420 €	10 600 €	12%
	4.5	56 560 €	18 800 €	33%
Total		2 095 443 €	849 620 €	46%*

*46% average conversion for the 20 evaluated agencies.

To illustrate the explanatory variables of this conversion disparity, we want to introduce some results of two contrasted cases: Agency 1.1 and Agency 1.5.

Agency 1.1

This case presents many changes in the internal operation of the agency. Improvement actions were mainly focused on internal resources control —both financial and human—and underline the strategic intent of the manager-architect to better pilot the agency. The strategy consisted of developing performance through the use of internal levers without modify the agency's market positioning or external deployment. The manager took over the PNAC tool to decentralize, among the employees, with some of responsibilities linked to the economic performance of the agency, for example, the ratio of the sales activity on the *piloting* of the mission's *profitability*. The manager has strengthened his/her role as team and activity manager during the intervention. The recycling of **hidden costs** into value-added allowed the manager to keep his architectural design time and retrieve one half-day per week for external and extra-professional activities. After the process, the manager-architect took four weeks of vacation per year—something he had not done for five years.

Concerning the financial results, the agency now had three month of cash flow in advance and the manager, who could not take a regular wage before, took a fixed salary each month. Within two years, the agency had few unpaid debts and the time spent with customers for invoicing and incomes decreased to two days (2 x 8h) a month, which were now dedicated to sales prospection. The reassignment of hours to develop a new activity in response to a public call for tenders resulted in the signing of an exclusive contract with a prestigious client (contract estimated at €2.5 million over five years). Improvement in service quality and meeting deadlines were also acknowledged by customers. As an example, a construction site of 1.5 million euro was delivered with 15 days in advance, while the average of delivery delays in France for this type of work is one month. Finally, the turnover (revenues) in the agency increased from 257,400 to 350,000 euro, maintaining the variable costs and expected hours. The HCVAVC jumped from 25 to 34 euro, which means that the value of worked hours increased and therefore the *productivity* of each member of the agency has grown. The balance sheet at the beginning of the intervention was 15,150 euro – it now reached 28,000 euro. For the first time in history, the manager gave collective premiums to all employees and two of them, for the first time, each brought in one new business client.

Agency 1.5

The intervention created a strategic refocus by the manager. This refocus can be explained by the lack of strategic plan since the agency's creation, and therefore its local image was very technical architectural project management, but less creative, preventing the agency from competing with other agencies. The manager-architect also wished to retire in five years, having "done what she never did before: architecture, competitions, for the sake of creating ..." The diagnosis of her agency allowed her to build a strategic plan, whose first implementation was to partner with her architect employee to prepare the foundation for her succession. Her future partner took control of the "classic" activities, further developing his agency management skills. The manager began to design more projects for competition, leaving her partner to present to their customers in order to change the agency's image.

The agency's turnover (revenues) decreased, within two years from 380,000 to 231,700 euro (a decrease of 39%). This outcome was the same concerning variable costs, which decreased by 50% (26,000 to 12,700€) and expected hours by 31%. The main reason for these two decreases was that one person left the workforce without being replaced. The *HCVAVC* went down from 49 to 44 euro, which means that the value-added of worked hour decreased as the balance sheet of the agency decreased from approximately 13,400 to 200 euro. The manager noticed the impacts on the visible investment costs of the new strategy created by the lack of investment in *creation of potential* since the beginning of the agency activity.

CONTRIBUTION TO "PRODUCTS-METHODS" AND "PRODUCT-SERVICES"

Historically developed in the intra-organizational perimeter, the SEAM architecture is capable of responding to requests from enterprises and organizations that are smaller in size. This methodological evolution is based on an opening of inter-organizational diagnoses and analyses, under training-consultation with the managers whose agencies are involved in the process. The approach is "miniaturized" and adjustable according to the intervention sector structure and certain conditions. The *actor*'s activation's principle is respected: the separation of perimeters not to create any scapegoats effect, the management of rhythms, support of the hierarchy, contribution of support methodologies to vital functions, and the elaboration of a challenging professional dialogue.

The overall approach on specific intervention perimeters is to promote joint action that preserves decision-making autonomy. This approach is intended to sensitize managers of their responsibilities to evolve towards a more political dimension, not just focused on technical and professional aspects.

The management of rhythms is particularly important. It is necessary for the intervener-researcher to have direct exchanges several times a month to ensure the effective implementation of the approach. Contrary to larger structure *vigilance*, the management of rhythms must be strengthened through a lack of internal relay. These information exchanges shape up as direct services in the field (training, diagnosis, *project* group, personalized assistance) and far away through phone calls and email.

Personalized assistance is the main support mechanism to the hierarchy, that is, to the manager(s). This type of service requires a lot of experience on the part of the researcher involved to create meaning in coaching, a pedagogy adapted to the specific management of the manager(s). This is even truer as applications become more heterogeneous: how to dismiss an employee? How to know the profitability of a business? How to conduct an assessment interview? How to facilitate a meeting? The questions and challenges begin to develop exponentially.

The contribution of methodologies on vital functions is a central challenge to strengthen the significance of steering and implementation. These contributions are intended to develop mutual inter-understanding on shared tools, organizational *chronobiology* (*time management*) *communication* devices, more integrated *coordination*, and concertation.

The construction of a challenging professional dialogue takes place primarily during training-concertation on *management tools* (e.g., PAP, TDBP, PNAC), personalized assistance and project group sessions. Secondly it is during the *mirror effect* stage, a device arranged to return the results of the diagnosis, that the actors have the opportunity to discuss issues concerning internal operations. Finally, regular support to the implementation of the resolutions taken by the actors leads to *interactions* depending on the implantation of devices (e.g., 3C, sales). The intervener, beyond his or her "technical" contribution, assists managers during the development phase of their function by helping them to "step back" (comparison to other contexts by the inter-agency) and put complementarity into perspective, thinking through appropriate strategic decisions, tools, and devices (e.g., the practice of *synchronized decentralization*).

This approach provides an opportunity for the agency to clarify its strategic path through a formalization-verbalization process (to ensure that the implicit becomes strategic reality) to improve the quality of the implementation. During the diagnosis phase the anonymity of people's opinion is not essential and does not stimulate resistance to change as the participants are close to the agency. In larger organization structures anonymity is an important condition, but is relativized here. The method is not "blocked" but evolves according to the reality on the ground.

The development of socio-economic interventions in small size organizations contributes to the ongoing improvement of the method due to the permanent questioning of participants. The approach allows flexibility in response to the high natural ***directivity*** from the part of the researcher. In this kind of device, the intervener should make the methodology more flexible when dealing with people who are ill-acquainted with management. The aim is not to antagonize them, but to maintain a rigorous methodology necessary to obtain tangible results. The tension in the intervention is effective, not only because the agency manager wants it but also through a subtle dosage between the internal actors and the ***external intervener***. The inter-intra balance of the intervention is fundamental here. The inter-agency device allows the intervener-researcher to create a dynamic (management of the differences) whereas the intra-dimension, a subject of vigilance for the researcher, is the locus of actual realizations. In addition, it is possible to extend this inter-intra field by combining the stakeholders of the agency. It is true that the management of stakeholder relationships is complex because each actor has his or her own issues that may contradict those of others. For example, the researcher is often regarded as a kind of rival of the accountant of the organization, the latter being the one advising the manager to make decisions based on accounting information. Thus it is necessary to clarify the position of the intervener-researcher who, is not in competition with the action of the accountant, but simply one who tries to see to it that the manager can endorse his pilot's role without depending on others.

CONCLUSION

Although the architecture sector is a little studied sector in the management sciences, its specific characteristics offer opportunities to enhance our understanding of the performance development of small business units and appropriate ways to adapt our intervention to facilitate such ***improvement***. As this chapter has illustrated, it is possible to improve the management skills of architects based on a SEAM intervention, increasing profitability and the performance of these agencies. The intervention results are tangible, quick, visible, and shared. The actors in our study have seen the connection between their efforts and agency results, resulting in a tangible increase in the requirement level of agencies – the improvement of internal professionalism. This relationship is not always as decisive in larger company interventions.

It should be noticed that the faster the results and the more the professionalism of the consultant is called upon (experience and comprehensive knowledge of the process). The quality of the consultant's ***engineering*** transfer increases his or her credibility with the stakeholders. Interventions in small structures can strengthen the role and contribution of the intervener-researcher with those professionals who lack economic and social management savvy. Considering the economic weight of small organizations in the economy, the development of inter-organizations and inter-training courses is an important challenge with a view to looking for value-added outcomes.

NOTES

1. The research for this chapter has been influenced by a number of works that are not directly referred to in the text, including Boje and Rosile (2003), Buono and Savall (2007), Gephart (2009), Perroux (1979), Savall (1974, 1975, 1977, 1981, 2010, 2012), Savall and Zardet (1992, 1995, 2005, 2009), and Savall, Zardet, and Bonnet (2000, 2008).
2. These figures are based on the annual statistics of the National Council of the Order of Architects, 2013.
3. The income figures are drawn from the annual statistics of the National Council of the Order of Architects, 2014
4. Law No. 77-2 of 3 January 1977 architecture (Consolidated version, 24 March 2012).
5. The survey was reported in *Cahiers de la profession N° 47, March 2013*.
6. See Ordonnance, n°2011-1539, 16 Novembre 2011.
7. A low-energy building must consume less than 50 kWhep/m2/year in primary energy. This can be compared to 240 for the average consumption of existing buildings, and between 80 and 110 for new buildings built to date.
8. These statistics were reported in *Entreprises d'architecture – portrait statistique*, Survey of the Observatoire des Métiers dans les Professions Libérales, may 2013.
9. ***HCVAVC*** is a synthesized measure of economic performance that can be calculated through an indicator named *Hourly Contribution to Value-Added on Variable Costs*. It is the average value of one hour of human activity in the organization, from any job, for any person, which can be calculated by dividing the value of variable costs (VAVC) by the expected annual number of hours of all employees of the organization (Savall & Zardet, 2008).
10. The PNAC is a contract of objectives and means negotiated periodically between an employee and his or her manager; the achievement of these objectives results in financial reward.

REFERENCES

ADEME. (2008). *Regard sur le Grenelle* [Look on the Grenelle]. Retrieved from http://www.comite21.org/docs/infos21/2008/octobre-2008/regard-grenelle-sept08vd.pdf.

Baer, W. C. (1997). Toward design of regulations for the built environment. *Environment and Planning B: Planning and Design*, *24*, 37–57.

Ben-Joseph, E., & Szold, T. (Eds.). (2005). *Regulating place: Standards and the shaping of urban America*. London, England: Routledge.

Boje, D., & Rosile, G.-A. (2003). Comparison of socio-economic and other transorganizational development methods. *Journal of Change Organizational Management*, *16*(1), 10–20.

Buono, A. F., & Savall, H. (Eds.) (2007). *Socio-Economic intervention in organizations: The intervener-researcher and the SEAM approach to organizational analysis*. Charlotte, NC: Information Age Publishing.

Callon, M. (1998). Rapprochement possible entre activités de service et les pratiques architecturales [Possible linking between services activities and architectural practices]. In L'élaboration des projets architecturaux et urbains en Europe, vol 3: *Les pratiques de l'architecture: Comparaisons européennes et grands enjeux* (pp. 73–89). Retrieved from http://crdaln.documentation.developpement-durable.gouv.fr/documents/Crdaln/0083/Cdu-0083539/CETTEXD0002730.pdf

Dauge, Y. (2004). *Métiers de l'architecture et du cadre de vie* [Architecture and living model jobs]. Rapport d'information n°64, fait au nom de la commission des Affaires Culturelles.

Gautier, J. (2005). *Sociologie de l'architecture: l'architecture sociologique d'un champ professionnel en mutation* [Architecture's sociology: Architectural sociology of a mutative professional field]. Master's dissertation, Tours University, Tours, France.

Gautier, J. (2007). *Complexification du marché du travail et orientation professionnelle: Analyse des fondations d'un projet professionnel chez de futurs architectes* [Job market complexification and professional orientation: Basis analysis of professional projects within future architects], N°22. Marseille, France: CÉREQ.

Gephart, R. P. (2009). An invitation to ethnostatistics. *Revue Sciences de gestion – Management Sciences – Ciencias de Gestión*, *70*, 85.

Habraken, N. J. (2005). *Palladio's children*. London, England: Taylor & Francis.

Maurois, G. (1994). La gestion d'une agence d'architectes [Architect agency management]. Compte rendu du débat du 25 Octobre.

Midler, C. (1998). Nouvelles dynamiques de la conception dans différents secteurs industriels: Quels enseignements pour le bâtiment? [New conception dynamics in different industries: What teaching for building sector?]. L'élaboration des projets architecturaux et urbains en Europe, vol 3: *Les pratiques de l'architecture: Comparaisons européennes et grands enjeux* (pp. 195–204). Retrieved from http://crdaln.documentation.developpement-durable.gouv.fr/documents/Crdaln/0083/Cdu-0083539/CETTEXD0002730.pdf

Perroux, F. (1979). L'entreprise, l'équilibre rénové et les coûts cachés [The enterprise, the renovated balance and the "hidden" costs]. Preface. In H. Savall. *Reconstruire l'entreprise* [Reconstructing the enterprise] Paris, France: Dunod. 2nd ed. in H. Savall & V. Zardet. Reconstruire l'entreprise, Paris : Dunod (2014)

Raynaud, D. (2004). Contrainte et liberté dans le travail de conception architec-
turale [Constraint and freedom in the architectural conception work]. *Revue Française de Sociologie*, *45*(2), 339–366.

Raynaud, D. (2009) La "crise invisible" des architectes dans les trente glorieuses [The "invisible crisis" of architects during the three post-war decades]. *Histoire Urbaine*, *25*, 129–147.

Rowe, P. G. (1993). *Modernity and housing*. Cambridge, MA: MIT Press.

Ruat, T. (2012). Le management socio-économique d'une agence d'architecture: Quels leviers d'amélioration de la performance globale? [Socio-economic management of architecture agency: what levers for improvement of overall performance?]. Mémoire de master Recherche en Gestion Socio-économique. [SEAM Master Program Dissertation]. Lyon, France: IAE Lyon.

Savall, H. (1974–1975–1977). *Enrichir le travail humain dans les entreprises et les organisations* [An economic evaluation of job enrichment]. Paris: Dunod.

Savall, H. (1981-2010). *Work and people: An economic evaluation of job enrichment*. 1st ed. New York: Oxford University Press ; 2nd ed. Charlotte, NC: Information Age Publishing

Savall, H. (2003). International dissemination of the socio-economic method. *Journal of Organizational Change Management*, *16*(1), 107–115.

Savall, H. (2012). *Origine radicale des crises économiques: Germán Bernácer, précurseur visionnaire* [Root origin of crises: Germán Bernácer, a visionary forerunner]. Charlotte, NC: Information Age Publishing.

Savall, H., & Zardet, V. (1987). *Maîtriser les coûts et les performances cachés : Le contrat d'activité périodiquement négociables* [Mastering hidden costs and performance: The periodically negotiable activity contract]. Paris: Economica.

Savall, H., & Zardet, V. (1992). *Le nouveau contrôle de gestion: Méthode des coûts-performances cachés* [New management control: The hidden cost-performance method]. Paris: Éditions Comptables Malesherbes-Eyrolles

Savall, H. & Zardet, V. (1995–2005–2009). *Ingénierie stratégique du roseau, souple et enracinée* [Strategic engineering of the reed, flexible and rooted]. Paris: Economica.

Savall, H., & Zardet, V. (2005). *Tétranormalisation: défis et dynamiques* [The dynamics and challenges of tetranormalization]. Paris, France: Economica.

Savall, H., & Zardet, V. (2008). *Mastering hidden costs and performance*. Charlotte, NC: Information Age Publishing.

Savall, H., & Zardet, V. (2011). *The qualimetrics approach: Observing the complex object*. Charlotte, NC: Information Age Publishing.

Savall, H., & Zardet, V. (2013). *The dynamics and challenges of tetranormalization*. Charlotte, NC: Information Age Publishing.

Savall, H., Zardet, V., & Bonnet, M. (2000–2008). *Releasing the untapped potential of enterprises through socio-economic management*. Geneva: Éditions IOT-BIT.

Smith, N. (2002). New globalism, new urbanism: Gentrification as global urban strategy. *Antipode*, *34*, 427–450.

Terrin, J.J. (2009). *Conception collaborative pour innover en architecture, processus, méthodes, outils* [Collaborative conception to innovate in architecture, process, methodologies, tools] Paris, France: L'harmattan, coll. Questions contemporaines.

Vial Voiron, V.-J., & Cartillier, M. (2010). La mise en place d'un axe stratégique: La formation au sein du Conseil régional de l'ordre des architectes de Rhône-Alpes [Implementation of a strategic axis : training in the regional council of the Architecture Association of Rhône-Alpes]. In H. Savall, V. Zardet, & M. Bonnet (Eds.), *Management des Professions Libérales Réglementées* [Accredited professionals' management]. Paris, France: Economica.

Vial Voiron, V.-J. (2013). Quand l'Ordre accompagne la formation des architectes pour valoriser le rôle de l'architecture [When the Architecture Association supports the architects'training to value the architecture role]. In H. Savall & V. Zardet (Eds.), *La conduite du changement dans les entreprises et les organisations* (pp. 69–72). Paris, France: Economica.

Woudhuysen, J. & Abley, I. (2004). *Why is construction so backward?* Chichester, England: John Wiley & Sons.

Zardet, V., Delattre, M., & Petit, R. (2012). Responsabilités sociale et économique indissociables face à la crise: Le cas du secteur de l'architecture [Social and economic responsibilities inseparable face to the crisis: Case of architecture sector]. IXème Congrès international de l'ADERSE, *RSE, globalisation et normalisation. Nouveaux enjeux liés à la crise*. Nice, France: IAE de Nice.

CHAPTER 13

GLOBAL-LOCAL (GLOCAL) CREATION OF VALUE-ADDED[1]

Frantz Datry and Amandine Savall

The challenge of balancing the needs of short-term economic results and sustainable involvement of organizational ***actors*** is a common issue for any company. In the case of listed multinational corporation subsidiaries, this issue takes on a more significant place. The management methods in these particular subsidiaries are usually based on a two-fold dimension: one is global at the international group's level; and the other is local at the country level. Corporate brand strategy and profitability objectives are usually decided at the global level. Then, the ***sales and marketing strategy*** is adapted by the subsidiary's top management to meet local market requirements and to clear sufficient profit to keep some of it at the local scale, after serving the international group's appetite.

There are two main challenges in this particular situation. The first one is to reach the shareholders' demanding and demanded profitability level. The second is to build a long-term development strategy for the local subsidiary based on a high degree of internal ***cohesion***. The cohesion issue between the subsidiary and its corporate group is also important. Here we chose not to consider this aspect in order to focus on the subsidiary's endogenous dimension.

The Socio-Economic Approach to Management Revisited: The Evolving Nature of SEAM in the 21st Century, pp. 265–285
Copyright © 2015 by Information Age Publishing
265

Is such strategy possible? This outcome would certainly aim to mobilize all the company's *resources*, including its *human potential*, to improve both the *productivity* and quality of service and to stimulate new product development. Thus, the research challenge in the chapter is to analyze the link between the degree of internal cohesion among the subsidiary's managers, and the *balancing process* between short-, medium-, and long-term performance.

The chapter reviews the management methods a service industry company decided to implement, focusing on the: (1) threshold of investment needed to develop internal cohesion; and (2) measurement of the degree of cohesion and its impacts on company performance. This case relies on an intervention-research carried out by the ISEOR team[2] within a Belgian subsidiary of a listed American corporation. Three years of intervention-research in the same company enabled us to draw on various pieces of learning and results. These outcomes will be examined in the context of the contribution of SEAM to the management control system of this organization, aimed at assessing the strategic steering system of the company. This dimension is the core aspect of measuring the profitability of the investment on human potential. Does *this* kind of investment create more value? Is internal cohesion a powerful driver that can balance economic and social performance over short- and long-term perspectives?

CONTEXT OF THE INTERVENTION-RESEARCH: RESEARCH TENSION AND HYPOTHESIS

The company case is the national subsidiary providing temporary work and related human resource solutions for an American Multinational Corporation. This 80-country-based group is *listed* on the New York Stock Exchange. The Belgian subsidiary, in which we have carried out this intervention-research, has 330 million euro in annual revenue, with 4,000 clients. It has 500 permanent staff on its payroll, 37,000 temporary workers, and 800 contractors. The contractors have permanent contracts with the subsidiary, but they work at the clients' location, carrying out specific mid-run and long-run high valued projects.

Under the four international brand names of the group, the Belgian national branch provides temporary work recruitment and placement, training services, HR consulting and carrier management, and other outsourcing solutions such as running call centers.

Initial Context of the Intervention-Research

The Belgian subsidiary CEO is also a Belgian SME administrator that made the decision to incorporate SEAM as its strategic steering method for almost 20 years. This specific position had allowed him to observe "live" the SEAM method, concepts, and results. This aspect of the case is significant since choosing a change management *engineering* method, which is intangible, is a risk-taking decision for any CEO. This **risk** is assessed according to two criteria. First, it is necessary, over a long period, to think about the compatibility between the method's concept and the strategic choices of the company. Second, observing the impact of the method's *implementation* helps the CEO to make his or her own opinion.

We can better understand the decisive factors of SEAM, crossing the social and economic situation analysis of the company made by the CEO, and the core concepts of SEAM Theory.

In 2011, the main challenges of the first intervention-research program were based on the internal and external analysis made by the CEO, which are captured in Figure 13.1.

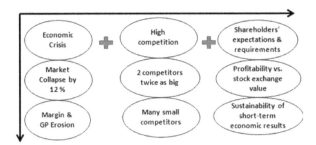

Specific Context & Environment

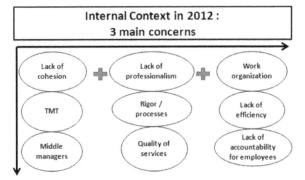

Figure 13.1. Main external and internal challenges of the company.

The ***external environment*** of the Belgian branch was mainly affected by a massive decrease in client demand. Thus, the company's sales were collapsing, especially in the Belgian manufacturing industry, which traditionally employed a significant number of temporary workers. At the internal level, the CEO highlighted three areas of concern. First, the lack of cohesion among his top management team was disappointing, as well as the cohesion between the top and the middle management. Indeed, in a highly challenging economic environment, the cohesion issue had become essential. Second, the CEO was concerned that his collaborators' practices and behaviors were not sufficiently rigorous and professional, that there were too lax in their behavior. Third, he assumed that this lack of rigor was probably tightly linked to the significant **dysfunction**s and **hidden costs** in the organization, thus impeding better productivity.

Following this analysis of the environment, there appeared to be four principles that drew CEO's attention to SEAM in an attempt to deeply change the management and strategic steering system of his company (see Figure 13.2). The first aspect was that SEAM is focused on both external and internal dimensions of the organization—the endogenous resources of the company, especially its human potential, to better resist external turbulence and convert strategic opportunities into new resources. The second important aspect for the Belgian CEO was to seek greater **effectiveness** and **efficiency** based on the internal lever for productivity, which can be measured through the amount of **hidden costs and performance**. Third, SEAM involves all the categories of actors in a structured but flexible change methodology. Finally, the CEO trusted ISEOR's experience in change process and rhythm management due his long-term relationship with the Center.

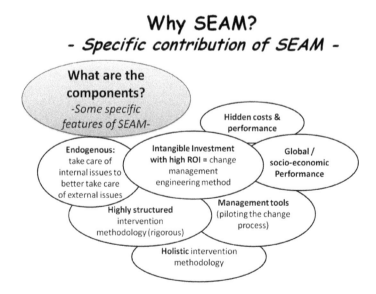

Figure 13.2.   Differentiating aspects of SEAM: Perception of the CEO.

Tension

If the American corporation would have imposed a unique management method for all the subsidiaries, this chapter would not have existed. Indeed, most CEOs of national subsidiaries consider a genuine, but essential issue—how they can obtain the financial results expected by their governance according to their local constraints and objectives. Can they simultaneously meet short-term and sustainable results using their own management method?

In this case study, the subsidiaries' CEOs have significant autonomy in terms of the methods they use to mobilize their organization in order to meet the American group's objectives. The American strategy seems demanding regarding the financial expectations, but also realistic regarding the local subsidiaries' social and economic contexts. Since 2011, the economic context has been mainly affected by a 10% annual decrease in the employment of temporary workers. This crisis resulted from the economic difficulties that European manufacturing countries, in particular, have been facing, difficulties that affected the demand for temporary workers. Thus, the challenge was to maintain gross and net profit levels in a decreasing market.

Hypothesis

Although the case raises a number of management challenges, the chapter focuses on the specific challenge of management control. Our research hypothesis is that SEAM concepts and tools can develop and reinforce the management control system of the company, simultaneously generating social and economic results—managerial **cohesion** and **efficiency-productivity**. These two variables are the levers to improve the organizational performance. Management control is a concept composed of:

- a **decentralized and synchronized strategic steering system**, taking into account the profitability measurement of **intangible investment on the qualitative development of human potential** in order to create value;
- a high level of cohesion among managers, whose new mission is to better integrate people and activity management; and
- a change management method based on permanent organizational learning, and an up-dated **work organization** according to numerous assessed and iterative experimentations.

DESCRIPTION OF THE INTERVENTION-RESEARCH: ROLLING OUT SEAM TO DEVELOP HUMAN POTENTIAL

Since the beginning of the on-going intervention-research process in January 2012, three programs were carried out. The concrete objectives of these programs were set and formalized for a 12-month period, and renegotiated every year since then. Indeed, each new program was agreed to, based on a deep assessment of the previous period's outcomes and achievements, and the adaptation of the objectives according to the company's external and *internal environment* changes.

Negotiating the First Intervention-Research Contract

The *negotiation* took a 4-step process over a 5-month period. The first meeting was an exploratory step to simultaneously identify management issues that the CEO faced and test the compatibility between SEAM concepts and the CEO's strategy. The second step was to present a first draft of the intervention-research program, based on the information that was collected during the previous interview. In this case, over a 2-month period we discussed the organization's perimeter, chronology, and the specificities of the implementation of the intervention-research. This discussion stopped during the third meeting, when the financial terms were presented to the CEO. Finally, the fourth step resulted in signing the contract and deciding the concrete aspects of the intervention-research (i.e., *scheduling* the first steps of the change process).

Five objectives were agreed upon with the company. They have been the guiding thread of the SEAM change process:

1. reducing horizontal splits among the business units ("cross-collaboration") and lack of hierarchical vertical management;
2. increasing professionalism at each organizational level towards better quality of internal and external services;
3. improving efficiency in work organization with 20% productivity savings;
4. sustaining market shares and profitability to satisfy both shareholders' and local self-financing needs; and
5. investing in human potential by training all managers and their teams in SEAM.

The Intervention-Research Process

The 2012 *intervention research* program consisted of implementing the *HORIVERT* method. "HORI" stands for a horizontal intervention involving top and middle management, while "VERT" stands for a vertical intervention in three different areas of the company. The main characteristics of the HORIVERT method are aimed at improving change effectiveness. It is a holistic and structured approach, and the process involves all categories of *actors* (top management, middle management, staff). The horizontal intervention is intended to develop better cohesion among all managers, enhancing strategic decision making and reducing problems such as business unit and profession *interface* dysfunctions. The vertical intervention is focused on different areas of the organization. This enables detecting local dysfunctions and hidden cost potential that will self-finance the improvements of the quality of management, functioning, and client service production. The HORIVERT approach is intended to strengthen team leading and the *piloting* role of managers. Then, it goes involving other staff throughout the change process in a *participative way*. This process focuses attention on a balance between necessary *directivity and participation* in the change process so to make sure that improvement actions are effectively implemented, especially through the diagnoses and project groups. The design of the first intervention-research program in 2012 is presented below (Figure 13.3).

As previously mentioned, there were various successive contracts. The first year of the intervention-research was to implement SEAM methods and tools. The following years were aimed at mixing extensive intervention in new areas of the company (Figure 13.4) and *in-depth intervention* on specific issues (Figure 13.5), while maintaining the steering intangible system. The *socio-economic intervention-research* is characterized by a progressive logic of *implementation*. Switching from the former contract to the new one resulted from regular reviews of the program. Thus, the company decision to continue its *cooperation* with ISEOR is based on these reviews according to three main criteria: (1) the degree of trust in the method of the company; (2) change action return on investment measurement; and (3) the decision to realize in-depth actions in strategic areas such as management control or *sales dynamic*

Change management steering needs investment. In order to sustainably make this investment profitable, an *engineering* process transfer was implemented at the beginning of the intervention-research. This transfer process focused on training *internal interveners*, the company's employees who dedicated 15% of their time to realize services to their colleagues in order to facilitate the change process. These services included: *management tools* training session and *personal assistance* aimed at helping middle-man

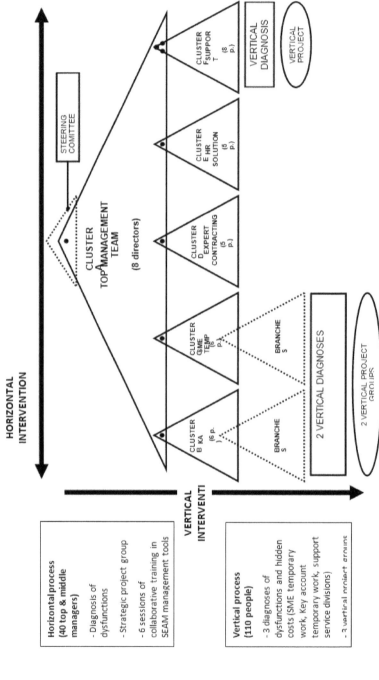

HORIZONTAL INTERVENTION

VERTICAL INTERVENTION

STEERING COMITTEE

CLUSTER A TOP MANAGEMENT TEAM (8 directors)

CLUSTER B KA (6 p.)

CLUSTER C SME TEMP (6 p.)

CLUSTER D EXPERT CONTRACTING (5 p.)

CLUSTER E HR SOLUTION (5 p.)

CLUSTER F SUPPORT (8 p.)

BRANCHES

BRANCHES

2 VERTICAL DIAGNOSES

VERTICAL DIAGNOSIS

2 VERTICAL PROJECT GROUPS

VERTICAL PROJECT

Horizontal process (40 top & middle managers)

- Diagnosis of dysfunctions
- Strategic project group
- 6 sessions of collaborative training in SEAM management tools

Vertical process (110 people)

- 3 diagnoses of dysfunctions and hidden costs (SME temporary work, key account temporary work, support service divisions)
- 3 vertical project groups

Figure 13.3 Design of the first intervention-research program (2012).

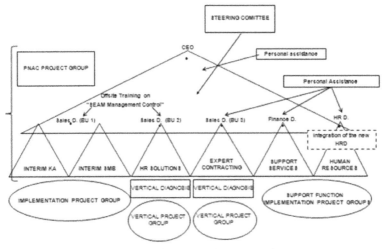

Figure 13.4. Design of the second intervention-research program (2013).

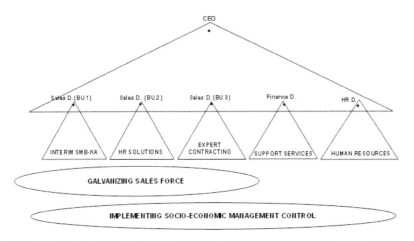

Figure 13.5. Design of the third intervention-research program (2014).

agement to implement the tools; diagnoses; and **project** groups' steering assistance. Figure 13.6 indicates the time repartition between ISEOR's intervener-researchers and internal interveners. We observed a progressive increase in loading capacities due to skills transfer that allowed them to carry a larger range of services.

2012	%	2013	%	2014	%
• 1 expert intervener researcher • 1 senior intervener researcher • 2 junior intervener researchers • 2 junior franchisees	60%	• 1 expert intervener researcher • 1 senior intervener researcher • 2 advanced intervener researchers • 2 junior franchisees	40%	• 1 expert intervener researcher • 1 senior intervener researcher • 1 advanced intervener researcher • 1 junior intervener researcher	30%
• 4 internal interveners	40%	• 8 internal interveners • *(between 10 to 20% of their time)*	60%	• 10 internal interveners • *(each one dedicated to a specific area)*	70%
10 people		**14 people**		**14 people**	

Figure 13.6.   Intervention-research team composition: ISEOR's intervener-researchers and internal interveners.

Figure 13.6 indicates that the investment nature in the changing process is progressively evolving. From 60% of the ***external intervener-researchers*** time and 40% for internal interveners during the first year, the repartition was reserved for the second year. This hybrid investment, both external interveners' consultancy fees and time economic ***evaluation*** of the internal interveners, constituted a key factor of the SEAM intervention-research process factor.

Qualimetrics Results of SEAM Diagnoses and Project Groups

SEAM diagnosis is a key step of the change process. Measuring ***hidden costs*** is one of the high points in the SEAM process. The objective is to help practitioners consider the untapped resources they could potentially have, to undertake both social and economic innovative actions without investing new resources.

Synthesis of 5 Hidden Cost Diagnoses

	OVERWAGES	OVERTIME	OVER-CONSUMPTION	NON PRODUCTION	NON CREATION OF POTENTIAL	RISKS	TOTAL
ABSENTEEISM	666 400 €	4 300 €	N.A.	121 800 €	N.A.	N.A.	792 500 €
WORK ACCIDENTS	N.A. (non assessed)	N.A.	N.A.	N.A.	N.A.	N.A.	N.A.
STAFF TURNOVER	N.A.	109 800 €	97 300 €	1 016 300 €	N.A.	N.A.	1 223 400 €
QUALITY DEFECTS	206 400 €	5 708 000 €	659 400 €	2 166 900 €	73 600 €	22 500 €	8 836 800 €
DIRECT PRODUCTIVITY GAPS	189 300 €	2 534 000 €	145 600 €	2 110 300 €	286 400 €	45 800 €	5 311 400 €
TOTAL	1 062 100 €	8 356 100 €	902 300 €	5 415 300 €	360 000 €	68 300 €	16 164 100 €

328 people, i.e.:   49 300 €   per person & per year (average)

Synthesis of 5 Hidden Cost Diagnoses

Date	Vertical Diagnosis	Amount of hidden costs	Hidden costs / person
June 2012	Key Account Temp	2'121'000 €	17'600 €
June 2012	SME Temp	3'950'000 €	91'800 €
June 2012	Support Services	3'937'000 €	55'600 €
March 2013	HR Solutions	3'126'000 €	61'300 €
March 2013	Expert Contracting	3'030'000 €	70'400 €
TOTAL		16'164'000 €	49'300 €

Figure 13.7. Synthesis of hidden cost measure (2012–2013).

In two years, the company became aware of the hidden costs volume that was evaluated at 16 million euro (see Figure 13.7). The numerous experiments that ISEOR carried out enabled the organization to recycle a portion of these hidden costs—35 to 55% of them were convertible resources from the first year of the SEAM intervention-research. This result means that the Belgian company had a value-added recycling potential between 4.8 and 8 million euro. These results also call to mind some actors, who seek improvement of their outcomes. However, we found out that after 18 months of the intervention-research process, the company's key performance indicators (e.g., sales, margins, profit) were all improving. Indeed, this trend was been validated in December 2013 when the Belgian company's accounting system recorded 8 million euro additional net profit (i.e., 50% of the assessed hidden costs during the diagnoses). Most of this achievement was due to the greater commercial dynamic—the company had a 12% increase in sales, while the competitors on the market had a 5% decrease.

Figure 13.8 presents some of the main improvement actions that were implemented throughout the project groups. The list is not exhaustive but shows the variety of actions. Some of the organizational transformations were focused on social aspects such as ***cohesion*** within the top management team and its impacts on strategic implementation; others focused on the economic dimension such as improving the ***productivity***.

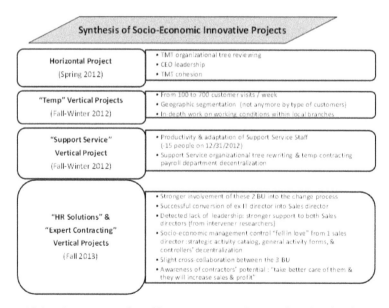

Figure 13.8.   Some examples of improvement actions undertaken by the Belgian subsidiary during the project groups.

Observing the intervention-research process and its impacts enabled two kinds of learning: learning by and for the company's actors, and by and for the intervener-researchers. These are focused on both the intervention techniques and research findings, and the company's achievements including its *economic performance*. The following sections focus on these learnings.

SPECIFIC LEARNING FOR THE COMPANY

Based on the various assessments made with the top management team, two key aspects are highlighted: (1) the change process *structure* as a key factor for change and (2) the people management impact for productivity.

Contribution of the Structured Change Process

The CEO highlighted several times that the contribution of the methodology and the intervener-researchers accompaniment was critical in getting results. Further to this point, the intervention-research process carried out by the ISEOR team has a remarkable idiosyncrasy: it never splits the conception from the action. This means that innovative ideas were always collectively elaborated on along with their implementation plan. Many innovative ideas germinate in companies without been implemented and, as a result, never create value-added for the company. These lost opportunities constitute a considerable loss of energy. Indeed, it is difficult to maintain the sustainable mobilization of actors if their ideas are never listened to by management. Indeed, managers lose the opportunity to enhance the organization and gain from the potential impacts of such changes on performance, which are not regularly measured.

The intervener-researcher's role was to help the firm's managers make concrete and actionable decisions for themselves and their collaborators. This simple managerial gesture was not as natural as it seems and required some *directivity and pedagogy* from the interveners and the managers to link the debate to the expected results of this debate. Each sequence of the intervention-research—for example, concerting-training session on management tools or project groups—set the foundation for the elaboration of a *resolution chart*.

Managing Human Potential Impacts to Productivity

While recalling the 20% productivity savings at stake when starting the intervention-research program, the link between this economic concern and *human potential* seems important to make. The concept of *socio-economic performance* typically drew the CEO's attention as a key factor for his management strategy. The assumption is that a value potential does exist and can be untapped under two basic conditions that: (1) take better care of people by renovating the managers' autonomy and their management practices, and (2) enhance the measurement of this management system on the organization's performance.

The following three strength-ideas constitute value-added development levers. First, it is useful to measure and act on the *actors*' time resource in order to help them organizing their activities. Second, it is important not to separate economic exigency from social and managerial performance. Finally, these efforts should be supported by the *implementation* of management tools in order to contractualize objectives and their underlying means in developing performance. As an example, numerous *time management* improvements were made at all organizational levels that have largely contributed to the positive increase in client visits (x 100 in less than a year). This *sales dynamic* was possible due to the low value-added tasks that the employees collectively decided to erase from their calendars and a deep reorganization of the small offices' functioning.

Activating and releasing this human potential also required significant energy from middle managers. Indeed, their key role was to explain, steer, and dose out between social and economic exigency. *Economic exigency* refers to the financial expectations from the American governance and the national top management; while *social exigency* refers to the expected rigor in the day-to-day work. The company trained its collaborators on management tools, for instance, time management and the *steering indicators logbook*. Is the middle management convinced of the efficacy of these tools and feel legitimate in requiring that each and every organizational member attends meetings with their steering logbook to assist them in integrating their activity indicators? This conception of exigency refers to working methods shared within the company. In the present case, it was clear that the middle managers realized the positive impact of rigorous internal methods on the clients' quality of service.

The contracted logical development in management practices was facilitated by the *Periodically Negotiable Activity Contract* (PNAC), which was implemented at each stage of the company since 2013. Twice a year, this tool allowed organizational members to define objectives and the means for achieving them with their managers. These objectives stand on expected improvements in terms of the development of personal competencies and help to define for the next 6-month period expected individual efforts in developing value-added for the company. These renovated management practices seem to have generated the expected outcomes. In addition, the last internal people surveys showed a much higher level of employee engagement. The turnover and ***absenteeism*** rates measurement also allowed the company to assess the management quality impacts.

LEARNING FOR THE INTERVENER-RESEARCHERS

This change process has been an important learning process for us, as intervener-researchers. The two main sources of learning were the contractors' management to activate their human potential, and the outcomes' measurement to stimulate new advancements. We recall that the contractors are employees under contract within the case studied company. They work in client's company within the frame of middle- and long-term mission.

Managing Contractors: A New Source of Shared Value-Added

During summer 2013, we carried out a diagnosis in one of the Belgian company's areas that were not initially involved in the intervention. This area was a team of contractors who were full-time employees located at an IT industry-client. This diagnosis showed new pieces of knowledge regarding the untapped ***resources*** of the company—hidden costs that were shared between the company and its client (see Figure 13.9).

First, interviewing the contractors showed us the management issue of implementing an effective management model for seconded staff in a client's company. These persons were clearly aware of their legal connection to the company, but they worked in a different place where they never actually see their employer. In their day-to-day activities, the client's employees were managing the contractors, not the company's managers. The question that emerged concerned how the company could build strong engagement with its employees/contractors when those individuals do not see that employer on a day-to-day basis. How could the firm develop simultaneous loyalty to the employer and to the client? What type of partnership would be needed to develop effective collaboration between the company, the contractors, and the client in order to develop ***decentralized, synchronized*** and effective management models? How should the effects of these management models on value creation be measured? What impact might they have on the contractors' services prices?

Second, the high level of hidden costs measured during the ***diagnosis*** validated the untapped potential in this particular area of the company: almost 150,000 euro per person/per year was evaluated in the 70-contractors area. The diagnosis describing the ***dysfunctions*** made it clear that one part of the ***hidden costs*** impacted contractor work quality and the quality of the service sold by the subsidiary. The other part of the hidden costs came from dysfunctions in the client company, which negatively impacted its margin.

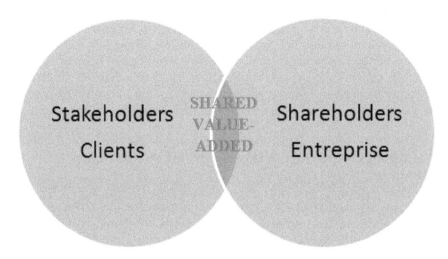

Figure 13.9.   Concept of "Shared Value-Added" between stakeholders and shareholders.

We consider that the contractors' issue illustrates the initial tension of this chapter: the quality of management and steering practice as a value creation factor. Indeed, in this case, the main challenge was to maintain coherence between management sharing and steering practices from the company and its client. It's a lever that has positive impacts on the ***creation of value-added*** and performance. First, it serves as an innovation source from the decentralized steering of collaborators. Second, it represents a way to re-discover the client partnership relation. Finally, it reflects an area of developing high valued services and margin improvements

Measuring the Outcomes of the Change Process as a Lever for Learning and Improvement

In spring 2013, we decided to assess the profitability and outcomes of the change process investment without waiting for the company's order. Within this context, it is important to examine why a company might not spontaneously undertake a deep assessment of its investment choices. As a reminder, at the beginning of this intervention-research, the CEO set a 20%-*productivity* saving objective in the first year. The explanation is about the methodology, especially since the concept of **hidden cost**s and performance is innovative and not directly captured in most management control systems. The hidden and visible cost-performance dialectic is a core concept of SEAM theory. However, integrating hidden costs and performance in budgetary and financial steering tools takes time and management control specialist training.

Figure 13.10 illustrates the financial results that were measured after one year and a half of intervention-research. The main challenge was to improve the financial information system of the company and the decision-making quality, which relates to management control. One of the main advancements in this company has been to largely decentralize the financial controllers in the *business units*. Previously reporting to the finance director, three controllers were integrated into the three brands of the company. The two objectives were to: (1) improve financial data reliability in order to monthly *report* to the American group; and (2) better stimulate the operational staff by being closer to their day-to-day activities. At the end of the intervention the three controllers had progressively integrated hidden costs, as any other financial data, in their analysis tools. On other words, **economic balances** were elaborated in order to accurately reflect the contractors' absenteeism cost calculation and its impact on the profitability of the firm's various activities.

A final methodological conclusion can also be generated from this case-study. The rigorous **evaluation** of intervention-research results constitutes an essential operation for two reasons. First, it is a question of gathering all the exploitable data for the research; second, is to produce regularly a mirror-effect to the company, in order to help it measure the changes that have taken place.

It is important to remember that this mirror-effect plays a key role in the **socio-economic diagnosis step**. Indeed, the diagnosis helps actors to be fully aware of the change challenges they face and facilitates their ability to build a practices' transformation program. This evaluation function is also necessary after the diagnosis to underpin the improvements and their effects on performance in order to avoid a change dynamic deceleration. This type of measurement of change impact, however, is not a natural process for organizational members—it has to be organized and supported in order to produce the desired effects on individual steering practices.

CONCLUSION

This intervention-research case presents significant advancement in terms of conceptual contribution and the concrete results recorded by the company. To conclude on the initial management control hypothesis,

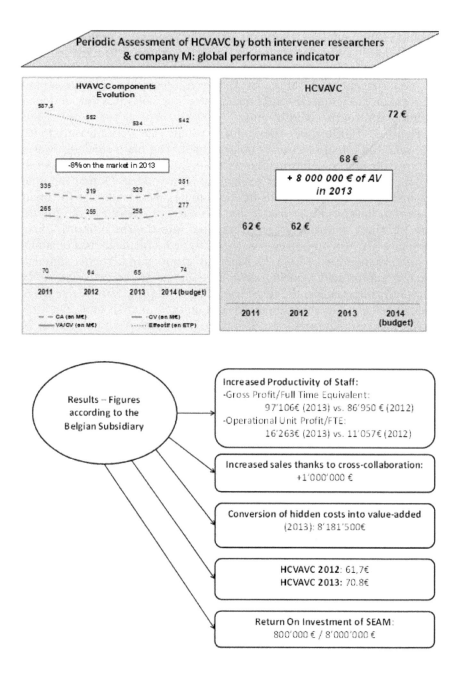

Figure 13.10.   Economic and financial outcomes of the Belgian subsidiary (after 18 months of SEAM intervention-research).

we attempted to highlight the necessary ***intangible investment in human potential development*** as a way of enhancing ***socio-economic performance***. However, experimentation puts into the light that these very positive results can quickly decrease, often due to forces beyond control of the organization. During 2014, for example, while implementing ***socio-economic management control*** principles and tools, the subsidiary's financial results did not reach a satisfactory level. Certainly, the Belgian market was highly affected by the economic crisis. Moreover, there were various low service quality dysfunctions with companies that employed two main teams of contractors, which could explain this decrease of performance.

Dysfunctions and hidden costs go through a resurgence process. Human potential does generate better productivity and creativity—but it remains fragile over time. Thus, investing in management system maintenance seems particularly indispensable to sustain organizational performance and its economic outcomes.

NOTES

1. The research for this chapter has been influenced by a number of works that are not directly referred to in the text, including Boje and Rosile (2003), Fargier (2013), Gephart (2009), Lacroix (2014), Perroux (1979), Savall (1974, 1975, 1977, 1981, 2010, 2012), and Savall and Zardet (1992, 1995, 2005, 2008, 2009, 2013).
2. The ISEOR intervention-research team was composed of Henri Savall, Frantz Datry, Amandine Savall, Ludovic Goethals, Katrien Decroos, Geoffray Picard, and Samantha Rose.

REFERENCES

Argyris, C., & Schön, D. A. (2002). *Apprentissage organisationnel: Théorie, méthode, pratique* [Organizational learning: Theory, method, practice]. Paris, France: De Boeck Université.

Argyris, C., Putnam, R., & McLain Smith, D. (1985). *Action science*. San Francisco, CA: Jossey-Bass.

Boje, D., & Rosile, G.-A. (2003). Comparison of socio-economic and other trans-organizational development methods. *Journal of Change Organizational Management, 16*(1), 10–20.

Buono, A. F. (Ed.). (2002). *Developing knowledge and value in management consulting*. Greenwich, CT: Information Age Publishing.

Buono, A. F., & Savall, H. (Eds.) (2007). *Socio-economic intervention in organizations: The intervener-researcher and the SEAM approach to organizational analysis*. Charlotte, NC: Information Age Publishing.

Buono, A. F. (2001). Consulting in an interorganizational context: Mergers, acquisitions and strategic partnerships: Knowledge and value development. *Management Consulting: Proceedings of the First International Co-sponsored Conference*, Academy of Management and ISEOR. Lyon, France: ISEOR.

Cappelletti, L. (2009). Performing an internal control function to sustain SOX 404 and improve risk management: Evidence from Europe. *Management Accounting Quaterly, 10*(4), 17–27.

Cappelletti, L. (2012). *Une nouvelle approche du capital humain* [Management control of intangible: A new approach of human capital]. Paris, France: Dunod.

Cummings, T., & Worley, C. (2008). *Organizational development and change*. Boston, MA: Cengage Learning.

Fargier, C. (2013). La connexion de la stratégie de l'entreprise à celle du territoire, le pilotage d'un investissement important ; une balance économique à la clé [The connection of the company's strategy to the territory, piloting a significant investment; economic balance key]. In H. Savall, V. Zardet, & M. Bonnet (Eds.), *Réindustrialisation et dynamisation multi-sectorielle* [Reindustrialisation and multi-sectoral dynamic]. Paris, France: Economica.

Gephart, R. P. (2009). An invitation to ethnostatistics. *Revue Sciences de gestion – Management Sciences – Ciencias de Gestión, 70,* 85.

Hayes, R. B. (2001). Using real option concepts to guide the nature and measured benefit of consulting interventions involving investment analysis. *Management Consulting: Proceedings of the First International Co-sponsored Conference,* Academy of Management and ISEOR. Lyon, France: ISEOR.

Lacroix, P. (2014). Le management socio-économique au sein d'une entreprise belge [SEAM in a Belgian company]. In H. Savall & V. Zardet (Eds.), *La conduite du changement dans les entreprises et les organisations* [Change management within companies and organizations]. Paris, France: Economica.

Lewin, K. (1948). Action research and minority problems, In G. Lewin (Ed.), *Resolving social conflicts*. New York, NY: Harper & Row.

Lewin, K. (1951). *Field theory and social science*. New York, NY: Harper & Row.

Perroux, F. (1979). L'entreprise, l'équilibre rénové et les coûts cachés [The enterprise, the renovated balance and the "hidden" costs]. Preface. In H. Savall. *Reconstruire l'entreprise* [Reconstructing the enterprise] Paris, France: Dunod. 2nd ed. in H. Savall & V. Zardet. Reconstruire l'entreprise, Paris: Dunod (2014)

Savall, H. (1974–1975–1977). *Enrichir le travail humain dans les entreprises et les organisations* [An economic evaluation of job enrichment]. Paris: Dunod.

Savall, H. (1981–2010). *Work and people: An economic evaluation of job enrichment*. 1st ed. New York: Oxford University Press ; 2nd ed. Charlotte, NC: Information Age Publishing

Savall, H. (2012). *Origine radicale des crises* économiques*: Germán Bernácer, précurseur visionnaire* [Root origin of crises: Germán Bernácer, a visionary forerunner]. Charlotte, NC: Information Age Publishing.

Savall, H., & Zardet, V. (1987). *Maîtriser les coûts et les performances cachés*: *Le contrat d'activité périodiquement négociables* [Mastering hidden costs and performance: The periodically negotiable activity contract]. Paris: Economica.

Savall, H., & Zardet, V. (1992). *Le nouveau contrôle de gestion: Méthode des coûts-performances cachés* [New management control: The hidden cost-performance method]. Paris: Éditions Comptables Malesherbes-Eyrolles

Savall, H. & Zardet, V. (1995–2005–2009). *Ingénierie stratégique du roseau, souple et enracinée* [Strategic engineering of the reed, flexible and rooted]. Paris: Economica.

Savall, H., & Zardet, V. (2008). *Mastering hidden costs and performance*, Charlotte, NC: Information Age Publishing.

Savall, H., & Zardet, V. (2011). *The qualimetrics approach: Observing the complex object.* Charlotte, NC: Information Age Publishing,.

Savall, H., & Zardet, V. (2013). *The dynamics and challenges of tetranormalization*. Charlotte, NC: Information Age Publishing.

Savall, H. Zardet, V., & Bonnet, M. (2000–2008). *Releasing the untapped potential of enterprises through socio-economic management.* Geneva: Éditions IOT-BIT.

Schein, E.H. (2001). Clinical inquiry/research. In P. Reason & H. Bradbury (Eds.), *Handbook of action research: Participative inquiry and practice.* London, England: Sage.

Schön, D. (1983). *The reflective practitioner*. New York, NY: Basic Books.

Worley, C., Hitchin, D., & Ross, W. (1995). *Integrating strategic changes: How OD builds competitive advantage.* Reading, MA: Addison Wesley.

CHAPTER 14

COOPERATION ACROSS HOSPITALS

Enhancing Quality While Reducing Costs[1]

Marc Bonnet, Patrick Tabchoury, and Pierre Francois

The quality of healthcare services is a deep concern everywhere for health-care professionals (Arndt & Bigelow, 1995). Currently, there is a trend of the ***development*** and increasing sophistication of technologies that increase healthcare costs, whereas public budgets are limited or at least have not been increasing in proportion to these rising costs. Furthermore, the aging of the population in developed countries, where ***healthcare system*** is top-of-the-range, also entails a growing demand of expensive healthcare. Moreover, standards of quality and security care, especially with accreditation agencies, add many administrative tasks in hospital administration that it now represents 10% of work time. The combination of these different factors leads to a situation where reconciling care quality and cost control objectives is harder and harder (Argyris & Schon, 1996; Dekler, 2007).

In Lebanon, these constraints are even stronger because this country has experienced internal wars for four decades. The insurance system is very

The Socio-Economic Approach to Management Revisited: The Evolving Nature of SEAM in the 21st Century, pp. 287–303
Copyright © 2015 by Information Age Publishing

inadequate and disorganized: there is a multitude of private and public insurance companies, which each have different pricing rules that complicates billing and administration. Many patients have difficulties paying their health care costs, a problem further demonstrated by a discontinuity of care. For patients under public insurance, hospital charges are refunded, on average, one year after treatment. Furthermore, the lack of *regulation* in the hospital sector by the state and trade unions leads to distorted competition. For example, some hospitals are sponsored by foreign countries or wealthy businessmen who are not looking for immediate profitability. This situation results in overcapacity and a kind of dumping. It deteriorates the financial situation of traditional hospitals, which do not benefit from these advantages. We can add that in Lebanon, pharmaceutical suppliers enjoy a monopoly and there are bribery practices, which further complicates the implementation of durable competitive strategies in this sector.

THE CONTEXT

The organization of the hospital sector is very complex (Shortell & Kaluzni, 2006; Wolf, Hanson, & Moir, 2011). Today, there are 166 hospitals in Lebanon, which employ 25,000 employees and 10,000 doctors for 800,000 internal patients per year. The majority of hospitals is concentrated in Beyrouth or in its suburbs, and most of them are private (OMS, 2012). Ten of the hospitals are university dependent and another 10 have high level accreditation. However, most hospitals have difficulties satisfying accreditation standards (Bolton, 2004). The three hospitals that have benefited from a *socio-economic intervention* are located in different sites closed to Beyrouth. These hospitals belong to a Catholic religious congregation, while the Lebanese population is Muslim in its majority.

Table 14.1.   Experimentation Site

Hospitals	H1	H2	H3	Total
Amount of beds	180	66	150	396
Turnover Million $	16	6	7	29
Employees	325	192	226	743

The cumulative capacity of the three hospitals at the beginning of the intervention was about 400 beds for 755 employees and 344 doctors (see Table 14.1). In 2013, the hospitals had 85,000 patients for 19,000 hospitalization stays, 66,000 consultations, and 8,800 surgical operations. The consolidated turnover (revenues) was 29 million dollars, which corresponds to about 100 million dollars in Western countries.

THE INTERVENTION

At the beginning of the intervention, the three hospitals had the same internal challenges: inadequacy of *resources* to the needs and care requirements, high *turnover* of nurses and key doctors, failures of information system, inter-professional tensions, and an intricate relationship between governance and management. In 2000, when noticing these problems, the director of the hospitals contacted a Canadian consulting company to help to fix the *dysfunction*s. This first intervention was a failure. The three hospitals were looking for a methodology that would facilitate the introduction of a change process that could prevent the leakage of skills and know-how, foster progress in medical and biomedical technology, and create a healthy and attractive work environment while ensuring patient security. The objective was also to progress in healthcare quality and to apply, as best as possible, national regulations and international accreditation standards while mastering costs. The leadership wanted to improve the human resource management in promoting teamwork, improving work conditions and skills, and making *sustainable development* actions.

Socio-Economic Management Implementation

In 2010, the management of the hospitals expressed their need for support in the change process and was drawn to ISEOR as the CEO had completed his thesis at the Center's research center laboratory. Some people who the director trusted went to ISEOR for training in *socio-economic methodology* and to assess its compatibility with congregation values. These "scouts" convinced the leadership that ISEOR's framework would be useful for the hospitals and an intervention contract was signed in 2010.

To start this approach, a *piloting structure* was created, composed of the superior general of the congregation, her councilors, the general treasurer, the CEO, and the three hospital directors. This piloting structure goal was to make decisions and pilot the socio-economic implementation.

The intervention had six *clusters* of trainees in accordance with the *HORIVERT method*. Cluster A was composed of the directors and religious superiors of the 3 hospitals. There was also a cluster of direction per hospital and another one with people in charge of healthcare. Considering the small size of the third hospital, the *diagnosis* and *project* included all organizational levels, from top and middle management to staff (see

Figure 14.1). The specific challenge of the socio-economic intervention was to implement the same approach in three very different hospitals and to obtain their synergy without having to merge them. The underlying goal was to enable the hospitals to succeed in a competitive market. Moreover, the distance of intervention and the use of Arabian language in the congregation required specific and rigorous organization of the intervention team. Finally, the project to implement *socio-economic cost control* was an absolute challenge because it was a new approach that had never been experimented in Lebanon and was very different from standard management methods observed in that country.

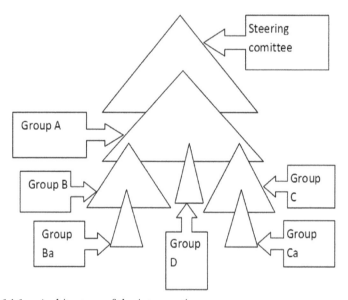

Figure 14.1. Architecture of the intervention.

During the first year of the intervention, the *horizontal diagnosis* and *vertical diagnoses* were completed by the project group. At the same time, training and personalized assistance were organized to accompany the executive staff in the application of SEAM tools. The second and third years focused on rooting the method. An *overall internal and external strategy* (IESAP) was created and applied while SEAM tools continued to be applied throughout the hospitals. In the fourth year, the direction wished to continue the intervention with a focus on socio-economic cost control tools. Figure 14.2 captures the successive steps of the SEAM implementation processes.

As in most of SEAM interventions, a team of ***internal-interveners*** were created to cooperate with the ISEOR team to institutionalize the method by taking into consideration the specific context of each hospital. These internal-interveners had carried out diagnosis and projects while keeping watch over the informed ***implementation of SEAM*** tools.

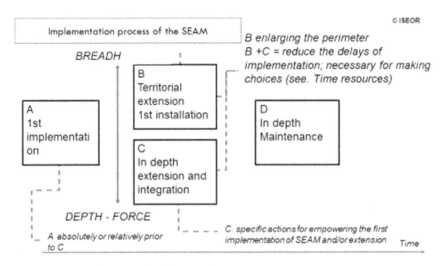

Figure 14.2.   The SEAM implementation process.

The Horizontal and Vertical Diagnosis

Three subsections were designated to embark on the ***horizontal diagnosis***. The first category concerned governance members and was composed of 10 people. The second category was a blend of 7 collaborators of the management team, and the third category included the executive staff and nurses and was composed of 66 people among them were 3 health directors and 31 supervisors (see Table 14.2).

Table 14.2.   Population Interviewed for the Horizontal Diagnosis

Population	Number of People Interviewed
Governance	10
Management Team	6
Executive staff (including nurses)	66
Total	82

After training at ISEOER, the *internal-interveners* were able to undertake a dysfunctions diagnosis. Drawing on the *fieldnote quotes* gathered in the hospitals they classified the data by keys ideas—strong ideas—subthemes —themes. The *horizontal socio-economic diagnosis* revealed serious causes of *dysfunction*s. Among the dysfunctions identified were the lack of synergy between hospitals, the lack of dialogue in strategy, and the isolation of each of the hospitals. A lack of *cooperation* between governance and strategy was also noted, as well as a lack of teamwork methods and the weaknesses of the role of executive staff. The *unsaid things* were presented in making the point about causes of dysfunctions, such as the lack of complementary organization of the hospitals, the deficiency of relationship *regulations* between governance and management, and the lack of a shared language between the managers to create *development* actions.

The *vertical diagnoses* carried out in the three hospitals had as major objectives to accompany the approach and learning of rigorous methods with regard to creating *budgeted priority action plans*. It consisted of diffusing shared management competence between the three hospitals for the *socio-economic project management*, like the use of *economic balances*. This step was necessary even though the management and executive staff had understood the principles of SEAM, and the trainings had enabled them to share common tools. These understandings had to be supported and reinforced so that the doctors and personnel in each hospital could understand by themselves that *hidden costs* recycling into *value-added* was not a utopia but a reality.

Diagnoses and socio-economic projects can transform usual representations like the common mistake of reducing visible costs to improve profitability. In fact, *vertical diagnosis* showed that the hidden costs were considerable. For example, most *hidden costs* in the operating theatre in Hospital A amounted to about $420,000 per year and were the result of a lack of *healthcare quality*, especially the lack of respect for standards, the delay of admissions, nurses leaving, a breakdown of machines, and shortage of medical instruments. Table 14.3 shows hidden costs in 10 vertical diagnoses, bringing to light the potential room to maneuver, so far hidden, to improve the performance of the hospitals.

As an example, in the *vertical diagnosis* of the maternity service in Hospital B calculating hidden costs brought to light $18,000 hidden costs per person per year. The most costly dysfunctions were personnel turnover and lack of quality. The diagnosis pointed to the vicious circle of the policy consisting of reducing visible costs. The closure of the neonatal nursery service meant a loss of income and a decrease in activity. After that, financial resources were reduced and it impacted the quality of service in the maternity ward, which had a negative impact on the corporate image of the hospitals.

Baskets and Projects Focus Groups

Projects baskets consist of bringing together the diagnosis key ideas per theme. At the end of the *horizontal diagnosis*, six baskets were created and working groups began to work on each one (see Figure 14.3).

Table 14.3. Recap Board of Hidden Costs from the Vertical Diagnoses

		Hiden costs total (in USD)	Hidden costs per person per year (in USD)	Number of employees in the diagnosed departements	Year of realization of the diagnosis
	TOTAL	$5,409,700	$ 16 800	322	
Hospital A	Surgery department	$ 484,300	$ 12,100	40	2011
	Biomedical department	$ 710,900	$ 101,500	7	2012
	Intensive care department	$ 389,100	$ 14,400	27	2012
	Emergencies department	$ 975,500	$ 69,600	14	2013
Hospital B	Maternity department	$ 361,100	$ 18,000	20	2011
	Administration department	$ 212,800	$ 9,600	22	2012
	Emergencies department	$ 794,600	$ 39,700	20	2012
	Surgery department	$ 126,200	$ 5,700	22	2013
Hospital C	Cross-functional diagnosis	$ 841,300	$ 5,600	150	2011

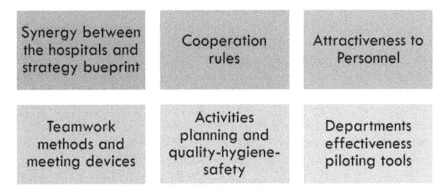

Figure 14.3. Baskets of the Horizontal Projects.

For the *vertical projects* we can use the example of the maternity service in Hospital C. The diagnosis brought to light high hidden costs in relation to nurse's turnover and a lack of equipment. In the diagnosis interviews, the strongest feelings of the direction and personnel were that there was no hope to revive the activity because the cost to recruit new nurses seemed too high. They thought the low level of activity in the maternity service, which resulted in the closure of the neo-nativity service, did not justify new equipment investment. In contrast to these negative perceptions, the work groups found ingenious and inexpensive solutions to revitalize the neo-natal service and to restore the hospital's corporate image and attractiveness. As a result, this service recovered a good level of activity, which enabled to return to profitability and avoid destabilizing the hospital balancing strategy. Moreover, strong local demographics further supported the implementation of this strategy, which was already considered a success.

Drawing on the dialogue with the gynecologist, ingenious solutions were also set up to upgrade equipment for the reasonable sum of $20,000. The hospital's purchase pool allowed such an approach, and that represented a low investment cost compared to the expected performance. This process also initiated the first inter-hospital synergies. Thanks to **actor's** mobilization and teamwork, relevant solutions were implemented. For example, a neo-natal service nurses group was formed following training periods organized in one of the hospitals. The nurses that has left were been contacted again by the healthcare manager, who proposed them to come back with job time arrangement and better work conditions. Two of the nurses agreed to return to the hospital. The economic balance (Table 14.4) was self-financed in less than a year, whereas the traditional financial approach would have meant closing the service.

Tools Implantation to Deploy Synergies

The hospital managers implemented the entire set of **socio-economic tools**, including the creation of an **Internal-External Strategic Actions Plan** (IESAP). This strategic plan (Scott, 1981) had three axes: (1) medical and biomedical aspects; (2) organizational and administrative functioning; and (3) reception, hostelry and human accompanying of patients and their family. Each one of these axes was broken down into priority objectives and priority actions. These priority actions (Savall & Zardet, 1987) had a pilot and a delivery date, and the IESAP was implemented in workgroups in the **horizontal project** and was validated by the **piloting structure**.

The **IESAP** was the result of teamwork, reflection and formalization that involved all managers by taking into consideration their points of view that were manifested in the horizontal diagnosis. It also took into consideration their proposals within the work group baskets. The IESAP allowed regrouping all hospitals projects within a structure. Everyone could thus see their contribution to the hospital's overall strategy. For example, there were specific projects aimed at medical excellence in service to patients, like operating theatre enlargement with the recruitment of specialized surgeons and IT system development. There were also other projects corresponding to hospital values, such as quality reception in patient admission.

The project content of the three hospitals was brought together in this IESAP, which also brought to light the symbiosis and synergies across the three hospitals. This tool provided the direction and the management with a larger vision, which clarified the complementarity between the hospitals from a medical point of view. For example, one hospital made an important orthopedic investment, one other in emergency wards, and the third in the architecture of the hospital. Some actions of the IESAP were accomplished

Table 14.4. Economic Balance of the Maternity Project

Costs				Performance	
	Overall amount	Years of amortization	Amount per year ($)		Amount per year($)
Recruiting 2 additional midviwes2*182 h 12 m 12$	$52,216		$52,116	Additional childbirths at $ 1,000 (236 in 2012 compared with 134 in 2011)	$102,000
Time devoted to recruitment 4 h 12$	$48	1 year	$48	More obstetrics admissions 130 in 2012 compared with 70 in 2011 ($50,600)	$30,000
Training : 15 h 12$	$180	1 year	$180		
Learning curve of existing nurses: (60 h + 991 h)*12$	$12,612	5 years	$2,522		
Training paediatrics/ neo-birht nurses 75 h 12$	$900	2years	$450		
Equipement	$20,000	5 years	$4,000		
7 beds*2000 $	$14,000	5 years	$2,710		
Negotiating recruitment with nurses (204 h$12	$2,448	2 years	$1,224		
Integrated training 12 h 12 $	$144	2 years	$72		
Training seminar 22080	$4,160	5 years	$832		
Learning curve of new nurses : 48 h*12	$576	2 years	28		
Meeting with medical doctors			PM		
Up-dating pricing policy			PM		
Improving hospitality procedures			NE		
TOTAL			$64,442	TOTAL	$130,000
				Value added in the first year	$ 65,000

by cross-teamwork of the three hospitals, as human *resources* and purchase policies. These transverse projects helped the hospitals reduce costs as in the case of sharing investments and some training activities. These synergies created value, as development of medical excellence was linked with the faculty of Medicine.

The *Priority Action Plans* (PAPs) were implemented in support of the IESAP. These plans were semestrial and featured local actions that had to be carried out (Savall & Zardet, 2008). To make them efficient, it was important to ensure their *synchronization* and coherence, which is why all services designed their PAPs through dialogue with their manager. To ensure consistency, these PAP were piloted through bimonthly sessions of the formation of a common methodology for the three hospitals. PAPs included prevention actions of dysfunction to pilot the strategy implementation, for instance an effort to improve administrative delays to avoid paying overtime hours. Actions in relation to the diminution of nosocomial infections also contributed to improved profitability. Other actions in the PAPs concerned the improvement of profitability through revenue and margin increases. For example, the increase of dialysis capacity enabled the hospitals to raise revenues. With regard to research on synergy, the priority actions represented the strategy per specific activities of each hospital, like the development of ophthalmology and maternity wards in Hospital A and the pooling of support functions across the three hospitals.

Competence grids were implemented in order to pilot team management (Savall, Zardet, & Bonnet, 2000) through skills development of every employee, enhancing flexibility and vulnerability prevention in each service. They were updated every six months by managers who negotiated improvement objectives with each employee. This competence grid helped them reduce costs, because personnel turnover costs tend to be lower when a team is multi-skilled. Moreover, training costs are also lower (Morgan, 1988; Mumford, Zaccaro, & Harding, 2000) because most training time follows the concept of "learning by doing" with direct application after training sessions. Competence grids permitted synergy between hospitals. As an example, the maternity and neo-natal services used them to design nurse formation plans. In fact, there were very few nurses with these specialties available on the labor market. As such, the competence grids were very important in developing in-house training. The competence grids also enhanced the image of the hospitals, contributing to an increase in the number of admissions due to the higher degree of professionalism. For example, the orthopedic service of Hospital A registered 4,570 operations in 2011 and 7,500 in 2013, with surplus revenue close to one million dollars.

Managers also realized that the *self-analysis time grids* allowed them to identify shifts in function that had led to costly overtime and over wages

(Savall, Zardet, & Bonnet, 2000). Control time was reduced through the professionalization and development of employee competencies. The managers were able to devote more time to development actions, which were mentioned in the PAPs (Datry & Zakkour, 2013a). As an example, they now had time to implement quality rules that were part of the accreditation process to get the highest notation in the audit.

Piloting logbooks were also implemented. These included a series of indicators like the increase of *Hourly Contribution to Value-Added on Variable Costs* (*HCVAVC*). This consolidated value-added increased by an average of 10% per year over four years since the beginning of the intervention. Common indicators of the three hospitals were set up, for instance, exit patient time after a doctor's order. This kind of indicator stimulated the search for value-added for the three hospitals, because it impacted the hospital occupancy rate. Other common indicators included there satisfaction rating of patients, the number of patients not admitted, waiting period at the emergency ward, personnel turnover costs, number and cost of medical errors, use of common resource ratings, and the economic impact of the hospitals' cooperation.

Activities classification and polyvalent activity cards per service were also established in the three hospitals in consultation with one another. For example, measurement of time spent in neo-natal service was tracked for a number of activities: post transmission, healthcare for patients, pharmacy management, pre- and post-operation preparation, patient bathes, and bedding and linen management among others. These analyses permitted the managers to think about *productivity* action amelioration, while simultaneously developing healthcare quality.

In order to transform PAP objectives into concrete actions and to implement hospital strategy, *Periodically Negotiable Activity Contracts* (PNACs) were set up. This tool aims at granting bonuses when employees reach qualitative, quantitative and financial objectives, which are assessable through precise indicators. To better master PNAC applications, especially for indicator definition and *evaluation*, this tool was implemented in three stages. The first one concerned the direction team and managers, the second one concerned the entire staff, and the third concerned the doctors. These PNACs included individual, semi-collective and collective objectives, which were negotiated between each hierarchical superior and his subordinates (Datry & Zakkour, 2013b). Creating *value-added* and recycling hidden costs were objectives included in this tool. In appearance, the PNACs constituted a cost increase because the highest bonus corresponded to a salary increase of 10% if objectives were completed. In fact, these wage increases were largely self-financed by the value-added improvement that they entailed. For example, one of the objectives of the doctors was to increase admission and reduce radiology subcontracting. The PNACs not only contributed to improve profitability in the short term, but also potential *creation of value-added* in the middle and long term. Project achievements in every service within the allotted time permit accelerated strategy implementation, especially the synergy between hospitals.

SPECIFIC LEARNINGS

This section reflects on the intervention experience and the specific contributions of the intervention to the hospitals' operations and performance.

Progress Observed After Socio-Economic Projects Implementation

Considerable progress was observed after *implementation of* the horizontal and *vertical project*. In Hospital C, for example, there was readily observable qualitative improvement. As the maternity service was saved, the neo-natal service was opened and new specialized doctors were recruited in order to improve the drawing power of the hospital. The creation of ethical and development commission was a good example of inter-services cooperation that brought together all categories of the job so as to foster *cohesion*. Moreover, new equipment was bought to modernize the hospital (e.g., radiology, scanner), the nurse *turnover* was reduced, and a training policy to improve competence and flexibility of nurses and auxiliary had been established. The functionality and quality of the buildings were improved with new parking, and renovation of the cafeteria, rooms and operating theatres. From a quantitative point of view, the hospital was now able to realize 7 operations and 100 supplementary admissions per day compared to the period before the ISEOR intervention.

From a financial stand point, the renegotiation with suppliers for equipment and medical products enabled the hospital to reduce purchase cost by 10%. The new organization was able to save $9,000 of overtime hours per year and $47,000 in serum utilization. The consolidated *HCVACV* improved to $13.8 to $20 in the four years of intervention, and revenues increased from $25 million to $34 million in the same period. The margin on variable costs improved from $15.5 million to $21.5 million. These improvements allowed the hospital to increase employee wages, especially for nurses, which accentuated the drawing power of the hospital and avoided personnel turnover.

Cooperative Learning

At the beginning of the intervention, the three hospitals had very different practices. There was no communication, except with regard to financial and cost control consolidation. Competition developed between staff, especially in Hospital A, which was more efficient than the others. The staff of the 2 other hospitals felt disadvantaged. For the first time, the *socio-economic intervention* brought the directors to work together to create a team direction. This example was carried out by the direction, encouraging project *clusters* to work in teams and a cluster of *healthcare managers* was created. They shared their practical expertise and harmonized their functioning. Medical directors, biomedical and administrative managers did the same thing. Through dialogue and regular synchronization, this cooperation accelerated the process of synergy creation. Moreover, the collaboration of the hospitals was reinforced by the *work of the internal interveners* because the managers who carried out the diagnosis and projects came from the other hospitals. During the project phase, they shared with other colleagues good practices so that they could implement this proper functioning in their own hospitals. It was a sort of internal benchmarking.

After three years, the staff in each hospital felt that they belonged to the same team and there did not appear to be any more resistance (that was observed) when they had to cooperate. For example, they were very willing to help one another with personnel assistance or sharing material and equipment. It seemed pertinent to merge some functions between the hospitals, such as the laundry room, but not to merge others, like invoicing. A lot of the procedures adopted common accords, like the ones concerning reception. Every hospital manager also practiced different jobs: the cardiology department personnel fulfilled different functions as compared with the dialysis department; financial managers and biomedical doctors had a different technical language, but in management, thanks to the SEAM, all managers shared the same language.

Priority Actions Plans (PAP) and *IESAP* implementation by every manager facilitated the ability of every service to use a common language to coordinate development actions (Datry & Zakkour, 2013a). For example, actions for improving occupation rates were different according to the service in question, but everyone understood that each service was required to release beds quickly and accelerate billing.

Performance indicators were harmonized, which favored the hospitals' cooperation (Bradford & Burke, 2005). For example, *HCVACV* had been used for *economic balances*, which were used for making decisions about development projects. All managers, including the nurses, had learned SEAM language with *hidden costs*, economic balance, *dysfunction* prevention, and *strategic piloting*. They learned the same methodology that they could use to resolve problems, such as the *mirror effect* on invoked causes, *root causes* analysis, and *communication-coordination-cooperation* tools. These common competencies encouraged more cooperation than normally found with traditional communication tools (Richard, 1969).

The appropriation of SEAM tools contributed to highlight the **human potential** within the hospitals and the need to develop managerial competencies, which allowed synergy implementation that induced performance improvement. SEAM intervention also increased management quality and intensity through human **resources** mobilization, which recycled hidden costs and improved the **socio-economic performance** of the hospitals.

GENERIC LEARNINGS

Beyond working with client organizations to improve their performance, one of the underlying objectives of SEAM is to contribute to our general body of knowledge, contributing to cross-case learning and our understanding of **generic contingency**.

Synchronized Decentralization as Key to a Successful Merger

Synergy implementation in the functioning of the three hospitals had improved the specific performance of each hospital. The objective of this pool was to set up a kind of merger that would respect the projects and strong points of each hospital. As Buono (1991, 2003) presented in his research work, for any interorganizational combination to succeed it needs to "build together synergy" and not to simply juxtapose independent firms on top of one another or to let one entity dominate the others. This case study illustrates that complementarity is possible through cooperation. It is manifested by the specialization of each hospital per activity and the set up in common of some functions. This cooperation facilitated the ability of the 3 **middle-sized hospitals** to become only one larger hospital, with huge potential to become the largest in Lebanon. The successful key of that cooperation can be characterized by the concept of **synchronized decentralization** (Savall & Zardet, 2008), which was made possible through the application of SEAM tools (e.g., **IESAP**, PAP, PNAC).

Creating Sustainable Value in a Limited Financial Resources Context

The application of SEAM in this case study illustrated that it is possible to improve hospital finances while increasing healthcare quality. These two objectives are not only compatible, but they are in synergy because the staff in each hospital has the ability to work together on teams to build **socio-economic projects** once they realized the importance of hidden costs and endogenous resources. In the case study of the hospitals examined in this chapter, the analysis underscored how priority actions plans and *economic balances* contributed to pilot potential creation (Savall & Zardet, 2005), encouraging innovation and development actions. This insight is especially important in situations where resources are limited, as the hospitals in this case study were incurring huge debts before the intervention. Through the SEAM intervention, the three hospitals were able to pay off their debts while investing in innovation projects. The hospitals also obtained the maximal notation in the accreditation test and their status changed from simple local hospitals to specialized excellence hospitals with university potential.

At the beginning of the intervention, we observed that the dysfunctions affected the hospital units' performance as *absenteeism*, personnel turnover, lack of quality, and bad management strategy were readily apparent. These dysfunctions had a considerable impact on the operations of the hospitals, which can be measured as hidden costs. These hidden costs can then be recycled into value-added, improving organization performance. To succeed in this venture, it was also important to improve management *competences* through ongoing training and support.

CONCLUSION

This SEAM case study conducted in the three hospitals illustrates that even in a turbulent environment and hard financial situation, a brutal approach through merger or restructuring was not the only possible solution. The hospitals were able to implement a sustainable method of management, through which they were able to reconcile social and *economic performance* (Huber, 1989; Savall & Zardet, 2005). The resulting organizational *metamorphosis* was rendered possible through SEAM, which as this case study indicates, can be successful even in very difficult contexts. The focused application of SEAM methodology enabled the hospitals to set up the cooperation and synergy strategies that contributed to their improved sustainable performance.

NOTE

1. The research for this chapter has been influenced by a number of works that are not directly referred to in the text, including Boje and Rosile (2003), Buono and Savall (2007), Gephart (2009), Perroux (1979), Savall (1974, 1975, 1977, 2012), Savall and Zardet (1992, 1995, 2005, 2009, 2011, 2013), and Tabchoury (2014).

REFERENCES

Argyris, C., & Schon, D. (1996). *Organizational learning II: Theory, method, and practice*. Reading, MA: Addison-Wesley Publishing.

Arndt, M., & Bigelow, B. (1995). The implementation of total quality management in hospitals: How good is the fit? *Health Care Management Review*, *20*(4), 7–14.

Boje, D., & Rosile, G.-A. (2003). Comparison of socio-economic and other trans-organizational development methods. *Journal of Change Organizational Management*, *16*(1), 10–20.

Bolton S. C. (2004). A simple matter of control? NHS hospital nurses and new management. *Journal of Management Studies*, *41*(2), 317–333.

Bradford, D., & Burke, W. (2005). *Reinventing organization development*, San Francisco, CA: Pfeiffer.

Buono, A. F. (1991). Managing strategic alliances: Organizational and human resource considerations. *Business in the Contemporary World*, *3*(4), 92–101.

Buono, A. F. (2003). SEAM-less post-merger integration strategies: A cause for concern. *Journal of Organizational Change Management*, *16*(1), 90–98.

Buono, A. F., & Savall, H. (Eds.). (2007). *Socio-economic intervention in organizations: The intervener-researcher and the SEAM approach to organizational analysis*. Charlotte, NC: Information Age Publishing.

Datry, F., & Zakkour, D. (2013a). *Audit des PAP dans les hôpitaux* [PAPs audit in hospitals] (under the direction of H. Savall & V. Zardet). Ecully, France: Rapport ISEOR.

Datry, F., & Zakkour, D. (2013b). Audit des CAPN dans les hôpitaux [PNACs audit in hospitals] (under the direction of H. Savall & V. Zardet). Ecully, France: Rapport ISEOR.

Dekler, M. (2007). Healing emotional trauma in organizations: An O.D. framework and case study. *Organizational Development Journal*, *25*, 49–56.

Gephart, R. P. (2009). An invitation to ethnostatistics. *Revue Sciences de gestion – Management Sciences – Ciencias de Gestión*, *70*, 85.

Huber. G. P. (1989). *Organizational learning: An examination of the contributing process and a review of the literature*. Pittsburgh, PA: Carnegie Mellon University.

Morgan G. (1988). *Riding the waves of change: Developing managerial competencies for a turbulent world*. San Francisco, CA: Jossey-Bass.

Mumford, M., Zaccaro, S., & Harding F. (2000). Leadership skills for a changing world: Solving complex social problems. *Leadership Quarterly*, *11*(1), 11–35

Perroux, F. (1979). L'entreprise, l'équilibre rénové et les coûts cachés [The enterprise, the renovated balance and the "hidden" costs]. Preface. In H. Savall. *Reconstruire l'entreprise* [Reconstructing the enterprise] Paris, France: Dunod. 2nd ed. in H. Savall & V. Zardet. Reconstruire l'entreprise, Paris: Dunod (2014).

Recueil National des statistiques. (2012). Recueil National des statistiques sanitaires au Liban [Health statistic national report in Lebanon]. USJ, OMS, MPH.

Richard, B. (1969). *Organization development: Strategies and models*. Reading, MA: Addison-Wesley.

Sanchez R., Martens, R., & Heene A. (2008). *Competence perspectives on learning and dynamic capabilities*. San Francisco, CA: JAI Press.

Savall, H. (1974–1975–1977). *Enrichir le travail humain dans les entreprises et les organisations* [An economic evaluation of job enrichment]. Paris: Dunod.

Savall, H. (1981–2010). *Work and people: An economic evaluation of job enrichment.* 1st ed. New-York: Oxford University Press ; 2nd ed. Charlotte, NC: Information Age Publishing

Savall, H. (2012). *Origine radicale des crises* économiques*: Germán Bernácer, précurseur visionnaire* [Root origin of crises: Germán Bernácer, a visionary forerunner]. Charlotte, NC: Information Age Publishing.

Savall, H., & Zardet, V. (1987). *Maîtriser les coûts et les performances cachés* : *Le contrat d'activité périodiquement négociables* [Mastering hidden costs and performance: The periodically negotiable activity contract]. Paris: Economica.

Savall, H., & Zardet, V. (1992). *Le nouveau contrôle de gestion: Méthode des coûts-performances cachés* [New management control: The hidden cost-performance method]. Paris: Éditions Comptables Malesherbes-Eyrolles

Savall, H., & Zardet, V. (1995–2005–2009). *Ingénierie stratégique du roseau, souple et enracinée* [Strategic engineering of the reed, flexible and rooted]. Paris: Economica.

Savall, H., & Zardet, V. (2008). *Mastering hidden costs and performance*, Charlotte, NC: Information Age Publishing.

Savall, H., & Zardet, V. (2011). *The qualimetrics approach: Observing the complex object*. Charlotte, NC: Information Age Publishing.

Savall, H., & Zardet, V. (2013). *The dynamics and challenges of tetranormalization*. Charlotte, NC: Information Age Publishing.

Savall, H. Zardet, V., & Bonnet, M. (2000–2008). *Releasing the untapped potential of enterprises through socio-economic management.* Geneva, Switzerland: International Labour Organization.

Scott, W. R. (1981). *Organizations: Rational, natural and open systems.* Englewood Cliffs, NY: Prentice Hall.

Shortell S., & Kaluzni A. (2006). *Healthcare management: Organization design and behavior* (5th ed.). Clifton Park, NY: Delmar Cengage Learning

Tabchoury, P. (2014). Création de valeur ajoutée financière dans un hôpital par la mise en place de la qualité du management socio-économique [Creation of Financial Added-Value in Hospitals through the implementation of SEAM]. In H. Savall & V. Zardet (Eds.*), La conduite du changement dans les entreprises et les organisations* [Change Management within Companies and Organizations]. Paris, France: Economica.

Wolf J., Hanson, H., & Moir, M. (2011). *Organization development in health care*. Charlotte, NC: Information Age Publishing.

CHAPTER 15

COOPERATION FOR NEW SERVICES FOR DISABLED PEOPLE[1]

Frantz Datry, Guillaume Fernandez, and Maïté Rateau

This chapter presents the results of an intervention-research by ISEOR in an institution hosting and supporting people with disabilities. As these organizations continue to face a decrease in public funding, they are looking for new solutions to ensure that they are able to deliver the required activities to support families and develop disabled people. This change of organizational pattern of coverage of disability is both a societal issue and one that opens up a *field for experimenting change* in a sector that is still deemed slightly permeable to management innovation.

The strength of *strategic motivity* is a characteristic of the case study. The management of the association understood that they must exercise *strategic pro-activity* to avoid new regulatory and financial constraints (OCDE, 2003). Within this context, the bases of an innovative strategy were built as follows: 1) developing one's own resources, 2) redefining the allocation of benefits to disabled people, and 3) developing the skills and mobility of supporting employees. The main features of this strategy concerns the method used to define the practical modes of the new organization to accompany the change.

The Socio-Economic Approach to Management Revisited: The Evolving Nature of SEAM in the 21st Century, pp. 305–322
Copyright © 2015 by Information Age Publishing

The chapter reports the achievements made by the institution during two years of *intervention-research*. We describe both the dynamic of the change process, the changes that were made, and the difficulties observed. Through this *experimental case*, we also focus on successful endogenous conditions of such a change: particularly, measuring the intangible level of *Intangible Investment in Qualitative Development of Human Potential* (*IIQDHP*) and its social and economic impacts.

In a first descriptive part, the chapter presents the organization studied, the context of the intervention, and the main research variables. The discussion then turns to a synthesis of the results of the *socio-economic diagnoses* carried out with the whole management team and one third of the employees. Finally, in the last part, different lessons that were learned from the analysis of the results of several project groups are discussed: contributions of these *project groups* to develop concrete solutions to *implement the strategy*, involvement of different *actor* categories in this participatory process, assessments of *behavior* changes, and changes of organizational *structures*.

CONTEXT

This intervention-research focuses on the main strategic choices made by the direction of the institution. This point is important because it emphasizes the necessary integration of strategy in change management. The chief executive officer of the organization described the context of his organization in a cut and dried "black and white" way, introducing the change management as inevitable:

We cannot say that the sector is changing and we don't want to change. We cannot refuse to change if we are to better respond to the needs of disabled people.

From Institutional Support to Personal Support of Disabled People

Support for disabled people is different across countries. However, the European Union, through its political organs, are increasingly encouraging its member states to work toward more personalized support, as close as possible to their social and family environment. This orientation is the case in France, which for more than 50 years has been historically in an institutionally-oriented position, where, following the identification of a population with particular symptoms of disabilities, the state provided funding and delegated care to an operator. Based on the public subsidies granted, centers were built to accommodate users according to their identified disability—which created 43 establishments and services for the organization that is the basis of our case study. Conversely, in the Nordic countries, there is virtually no longer any institutional care, except in case of high dependency. As a consequence, users do not go to institutional service anymore—the service comes to them.

Legislative frameworks by themselves, are not sufficient to anchor this significant change of practices in the organizations. Indeed, in spite of a law (January 2002), complemented by a February 2005 text that defines the principle of "equality of rights and opportunities, participation and citizenship," the institutional approach seems to persist in France, even though the 2005 law is oriented to individual and participative support. The user is considered to be an actor and co-producer of decisions that have an impact on quality of life, and is to be considered as a person in his or her own right.

A Key Player

A non-profit association was created in 1961 to respond to the needs of parents of mentally disabled children who required specific support. Contrary to what the associative legal status might suggest, this entity is an important operator because the association accommodated 2,200 handicapped persons in the 43 establishments of the department, supported by more than 1,000 employees. Its annual budget was close to 70 million euro, which largely came from public levies. As a result of these significant public subsidies, the state essentially legislated the changing environment. Despite the gradual disengagement of the main funder, in this case the State, stopping the almost systematic increase of the global budget every year (in range of 15% to 20%), this key player was in good financial health. It is important to note that this budget was allocated within the framework of "multiannual Contract of Objectives and Means" (CPOM, P for "pluriannual," i.e., multiannual), which enabled relative management independence during the five year period. This contractual relationship defined the orientation and objectives of the mission of public service delegation, while leaving the organizations free to implement their services. This real partnership aimed to build support for disabled people in the department.

Innovate Under Constraints

"Entrepreneurial capacity of the medico-social sector is subjected to the requirements of calls for *projects*. *Development* and innovation are under the control and at the suggestion of the State and department councils." This quote is how the director of the organization summed up the constraints facing him regarding the organization's ability to create innovative services, despite the fact that the competitive field required an increasingly adapted response to the needs of disabled users. Actually, these new needs, with the upsurge of addiction, autism or aging people with disabilities, questioned their core business. These constraints were compounded by budget decreases by public authorities according to their intervention.

Despite these brakes on implementation of the disabled support mission, the organization tried to suggest innovative objectives that consisted of enabling any supported person to be a citizen, gain more independence, and freely exercise his or her choice. The underlying goal was to do all the organization could to create a situation that allowed actual participation and to simplify the patient's life in a local social network.

As the evinced by actors' statements, change in the funding method of projects since 2009–2010 showed that innovation and development in the social sector were under control of public policies, and, as a consequence, of public order giving institutions. Since then, the State worked with calls for projects and chose a limited number of proposals responding to demand, instead of leaving the organizations free to propose their own projects.

THE SOCIO-ECONOMIC INTERVENTION PROCESS

Before an intervention, ISEOR attaches specific importance to defining the core objectives. Intervention requires establishing the clearest specifications of change management to which the organization and the *intervener-researchers* are committed (Savall & Zardet, 1987, 2010).

The Intervention Objectives

In this case, the objective was to change management practices to develop the adaptability of the association's *strategic project* to face the institutional, social and economic change. An efficient structuring of *collaborative delegations*, between *general management* and center managers, was implemented to stimulate team management. After implementing this decentralization of responsibilities, the authors led a reflection on the strategic choices facing the organization in terms of services provided and resources committed to increase the association's own resources. The goal of this new organization was to reinforce *managerial cohesion* around a shared strategic project that respected the associative identity. At the same time, we prepared the association to integrate new skills and share know-how and experiences between the centers in anticipation of future support for disabled people outside the institutions. Finally, one of the main issues was to raise awareness about economic constraints due to the new financial public policies of the Regional Health Authorities and reform in the general health system.

Structures of Socio-Economic Engineering

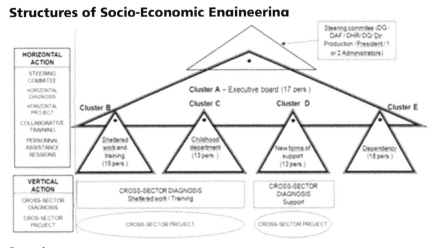

Legend:

DG: Chief Executive
DAF: Administrative and Financial Director
DRH: Human Resources Director
DQ: Quality Director

Figure 15.1.   The socio-economic intervention architecture.

Due to the size of the organization, we divided it into five *clusters*. Cluster A was composed of the 17 members of the Executive committee. Clusters B, C, D and E were the departments studied. In the present case, each cluster was composed of 12 to 18 persons who were responsible for implementation of two projects, named "Sheltered work" and "Support." The "support" activity brought together the centers that took care of disabled people who could not work or be trained for a new job. Even if the "Training" and "Sheltered work" activities concerned different centers, they were deliberately associated to improve *synchronization* between the two activities. Indeed, most children and young adults (18 or 20 years old) who were trained would be able to work in sheltered work centers. These *structures* offered a range of professional activities with health, social and educational support to promote the personal and social fulfillment of the disabled people.

There were 115 people (out of a population of 307) in the "Sheltered work" and "training" activities, representative of all sectors, who were interviewed (37% of this population). Forty percent of the "Support" population (87 people out of 217 employees) was interviewed.

Training Managers in SEAM Methods and Tools

A well-orchestrated change management process is based on a spatial and temporal logic. Following the discussion of the spatial approach, this part is devoted to the temporal process, which is illustrated in Table 15.1. Before starting, this planning was checked with the chief executive officer to be sure of the realistic with regard to activity and strategic constraints. The rhythm of intervention and sequence of actions were based on experiences of the ISEOR Research Center.

Table 15.1.   Socio-Economic Intervention Schedule

MONTH / ACTIONS	Nov 2012	Dec 2012	Jan 2013	Feb 2013	March 2013	April 2013	May 2013	June 2013	July 2013	Sept 2013
STEERING COMMITEE	1		2			3		4		5
HORIZONTAL DIAGNOSIS	▓									
HORIZONTAL PROJECT			1	2	3	4				
COLLABORATIVE TRAINING - CLUSTER A (1 cluster x 2,5h x 7 sessions)	Session #1		Sess. #2	Sess. #3	Sess. #4	Sess. #5	Sess. #6		Sess. #77	
COLLABORATIVE TRAINING - CLUSTERS B, C, D, E (4 clusters x 2,5h x 7 sessions)	Session #1		Sess. #2	Sess. #3	Sess. #4	Sess. #5	Sess. #6		Sess. #7	
PERSONAL ASSISTANCE CLUSTER A (17 persons x 1h x 5 sessions)		1	2			3		4		5
PERSONAL ASSISTANCE CLUSTER B, C, D, E IN PAIRS (17 pairs x 1h x 5 sessions)		1	2			3		4		5
2 CROSS-SECTOR DIAGNOSIS « ESATCO/CIFPRO et HHC-SUPPORT »				▓	▓	▓				
2 CROSS-SECTOR PROJECTS							1	2	3	4
TRAINING OF A 10 INTERNAL INTERVENERS TEAM	X	X	X	X	X	X	X	X	X	

(Table with Legend continues on next page)

Table 15.1.   (Continued)

Legend:
Session 1: Socio-economic analysis and time management
Session 2: Competencies
Session 3: Mirror-effect of horizontal diagnosis
Session 4: Internal and External Strategic Action Plan and Priority Action Plan
Session 5: Mirror-effect of cross-sector diagnosis
Session 6: Piloting book
Session 7: Periodically Negotiable Activity Contract

Horizontal Diagnosis

The first stage of a *dysfunctional diagnosis* is referred as "horizontal" because it focuses on the top of the organization chart. In this case, 16 executive officers and 36 managers expressed anonymously their *dysfunctions* throughout one-hour semi-guided interviews. Each employee under cover of anonymity talked about problems regarding the six dysfunctional themes: *working conditions*, *work organization*, *communication-coopera-tion-coordination (3C)*, *time management*, *integrated training*, and *strategic implementation*. Quotes were collected and classified according to the nomenclature composed by the themes, sub-themes (sometimes sub-sub-themes) and key ideas, finishing with the *actor*'s quotes. These interview results were presented in terms of the *mirror effect* (Savall & Zardet, 2011), in which the organization's dysfunctional picture are captured – with all the verbatim comments classified without the intervener's opinion. This mirror effect serves as a shock treatment to encourage people to change. Following the mirror effect process, the intervener-researcher gave his added-value, which we refer to as *expert opinion* (Savall & Zardet, 1995, 2005), which is a summing up of the *mirror effect* as well as opinions that were not explicitly expressed in the diagnosis even though they were important for change management. In addition to this discriminated contribution, we condensed information into *main ideas* regrouped in *baskets,* which became the *project groups* themes that employees would work on. Table 15.2 illustrates the *baskets* and *main ideas* of the horizontal action in this case study.

In any intervention, top management can change or refuse the pro-posed diagnosed-based work. In this case, the top management and the executive officers decided to create their own "horizontal" improvement project. As this horizontal action, a vertical one starts with a vertical diag-nosis. Generally, a vertical action concerns a single sector, service, unit or department, but it includes every level of the organization contrary to the *horizontal diagnosis*. For these reasons, the two diagnoses carried out in this organization were "cross-sectoral" because they involved different establishments and departments rather than a single unit.

Table 15.2. Baskets and Main Ideas from the Horizontal Diagnosis

	Basket	Main Ideas/Problems
1	Develop management role of managers to improve the piloting efficiency of activities	Weakness of management role and team management
		Lack of structure and piloting of activities
		Skills development less activated
2	Encourage the inclusive share of strategy to improve its implementation	Issues in concerted strategic implementation
		Insufficient quality of professional dialogue
		Risk of isolation of some staff categories
3	Develop a work organization and time management practices to work effectively and serenely	Disrespect of line manager and decisions
		Lack of time management concerted
		Complexity of work organization

Cross-Sector Diagnosis

Both diagnoses should satisfy two main goals: to multiply the socio-economic intervention and deal with the synchronization between the different centers that are supposed to work together on a common activity.

Sheltered Work and Training Sector

This sector is specific because of the multitude of centers distant from each other and from the association's head office. This double *decentralization* —vertical and transverse—was characterized by a lack of synchronization. The main objective was to create communication-coordination-cooperation actions to implement vertical and transverse synchronization to apply the concept of *synchronized decentralization* (Savall & Zardet, 1987, 2010).

Among the 115 people interviewed for the qualitative part, 28 were executive officers and managers in one hour individual interviews, and 87 employees without hierarchical responsibility were interviewed in 23 group sessions. In addition, we saw the executive officer and manager population a second time, to quantify dysfunctions that were expressed before by both populations – interviews that are referred to as *hidden costs* interviews. Each manager among the 28 was interviewed for one hour, two times. The first interview captures how much the manager knows about his team's reality; the second allows us to complete the first interview with missing information collected since that initial discussion and financially assess, as much as possible, the *regulations of the dysfunctions*.

New Forms of Support Sector

This diagnosis objective was to identify the difficulties faced by departments that participated in a support *project* to place disabled persons in their life place. This innovation requires that services come to the persons rather than the opposite, therefore a suitable organization structure was necessary.

As regards the "sheltered work" and "training" diagnosis, 87 people shared their views on dysfunctions, 21 managers were interviewed individually (for one hour) and 17 group interviews with employees with hierarchical responsibility were held as part of qualitative data gathering.

LEARNING APPLIED TO CHANGE PROCESSES

There were three diagnoses that emphasized key elements to help the customer.

Socio-Economic Productivity at the Heart of Change

One of the first lessons is that organization change during stagnation of public funding should be based on endogenous resources to be found. The chapter has already illustrated the existence of hidden costs (Savall, 1974); this section outlines how these hidden costs can be recycled into *creation of value-added*. These hidden costs, of course, are not automatically recycled; it requires improving *socio-economic productivity*. It means creating economic and sustainable added-value compatible with *social performance*, linking quality of work life and quality of service provided to users. This issue was even more important in this case when it was realized that hidden costs amounted to 4,549,000 euro for cross-sector diagnosis "sheltered work" and "training," and an additional 5,509,500 euro for the "new forms of support" sector. This organization had an enormous potential in terms of *internal resources*, but it had to deal with diffuse resources, centers scattered across a large area, and a slack management system.

Return on Investment of Change Processes

Evaluating socio-economic productivity requires an estimate of ***intangible investment*** that the change process represents. For an organization, this cost is composed of the fees of consultancy services that we charge and time spent by employees for the ***improvement process***. Table 15.3 shows the calculation elements of the intangible investment costs.

Table 15.3.   Cost of Intangible Investment (in thousands of euro)

Initial year	Workforce (end of 2012)	Completion period of intangible investment	Duration of amortization of intangible investment	Exogenous cost in K€	Endogenous cost in K€		Total intangible investment in K€	Intangible investment per person in €	Average annual amortization in K€	Average annual amortization in K€ per person	Ratios (annual basis)	
					Time spent (in hour)	Evaluation of time to HCVAVC (34€) IN K€					Intangible investment/ initial hidden costs	Intangible investment/HAVC
2012	524 pers.	2 years	3 years	292 K€	4600h	156.4 K€	**448.4 K€**	856 €	149.5 K€	285 €/ pers.	4.95%	1.09%

We can see that the cost of intangible investment (Cappelletti, 2012) that incurred in the change process amounted to about 448,400 euro. The point is to know if the ratio between the hidden costs before and after the intervention allows a sufficient ***conversion of these hidden costs into value-added*** to finance the initial investment.

Table 15.4 provides the analysis of three hypotheses for recycling hidden costs, based on the ISEOR database. According to our calculations, the most conservative assumption of conversion of hidden costs would release € 3.52 million, while the higher hypothesis estimates this figure at more than 10 million Euros. From these figures, Table 15.5 shows the profitability offered by this type of ***Intangible Investment in Qualitative Development of Human Potential*** (IIQDHP) (Savall & Zardet, 2008).

The overall rate of return on investment ranges from 2,358 % to 3,705 %. By actively participating in the change management program facilitated by the ***socio-economic intervention***, the actors of the organization were therefore able to obtain a return on investment in less than a month.

Table 15.4. Initial Hidden Costs and Creation of Value-Added by Recycling Hidden Costs (annual basis)

Initial hidden costs (annual basis)		VAVC¹ initial in K€ (source: accounting)	VAVC initial per person in €	Conversion of hidden costs in creation of value-added (annual basis)					
				Low Hypothesis 35%		Median Hypothesis 45%		High Hypothesis 55%	
Total enterprise en K€²	Per person and per year €³			☉ VAVC annual average in K€	☉ VAVC annual per person in K€	☉ VAVC annual average in K€	☉ VAVC annual per person in K€	☉ VAVC annual average in K€	☉ VAVC annual per person in K€
10,059	19,197	41,150	78,531	3,520	6.72	4,526	7.77	5,532	10.56

Legend:

¹ VAVC = Value-added on variable costs = turnover – variable costs (except wage bill considered as fixed charge)

² 4,549 000 € (diagnostis « sheltered work/training ») + 5 509 500 € (diagnostics "new forms of support")

³ Accumulated workforce of 524 persons for the both cross-sector diagnosis

Table 15.5. Profitability of Intangible Investment for Development of Overalll and Sustainable Performance (in thousands euro)

Low Hypothesis			Median Hypothesis			High Hypothesis		
Overall rate of return in %	Speed of return on investment II (annual basis)		Overall rate of return in %	Speed of return on investment II (annual basis)		Overall rate of return in %	Speed of return on investment II (annual basis)	
R = (Δ VAVC / pers / year) / (II/pers / year)	Net economic benefit (☉ VACV – II amortized)	Repayment period de l'II ((II amortized /☉ VAVC)*12)	R = (Δ VAVC / pers / year) / (II / pers / year)	Net economic benefit (☉ VACV – II amortized)	Repayment period de l'II ((II amortized /☉ VAVC)*12)	R = (Δ VAVC / pers / year) / (II / pers / year)	Net economic benefit (☉ VACV – II amortized)	Repayment period de l'II ((II amortized /☉ VAVC)*12)
2 358%	3,371€	0.5 month	2 726%	4377 €	0.40 month	3,705%	5,383€	0.32 month

A Return Speed on Investment: The Long-Term View

Beyond the cost of initial investment and its profitability, the client became aware of the magnitude of change required for all categories of staff of the association. Actually, the latter faced an insufficient number of managers, which created a mismatch between **strategic ambition** and the resources required to operate this change. The third lesson focuses on the speed of the return on investment of intangible investment to implement the right conditions for change. It is important for directors to remember that this transformation process takes a long time and will last three years at a minimum. Consequently, it appears that organizations as a whole and the association in this case in particular must be wary of underestimating the level of intangible investment related to the time required to deal with "legitimate" resistance.

THEORIZING INPUTS FROM THE LAND-BASED EPISTEMOLOGICAL PRINCIPLE OF GENERIC CONTINGENCY

The big challenge of the organization in this strategic shift is to place the user, in this case disabled people, at the heart of the work activities and organization. The underlying objective was not to function as a specialized organization in a functional way, where each center benefits from skills and specialized equipment to welcome person according to their disability and age. In the current model in France, the issue was to create the most complete coverage of the territory with the full range of specialized institutions.

Contribution of Socio-Economic Organization Principles

To face this problem, the **socio-economic organization** (Savall, 1979) offers four principles to satisfy both external and internal (e.g., employees) customers. Through their **human potential** they are the only active factors of value-added creation. The first principle develops the idea that the products and services of the organization must be taken as a whole by **actors**. The second aims at job fulfillment through empowerment and autonomy at all hierarchical levels of the organization. The third principle argues that all actors should see themselves as sellers, with a view to meeting the needs of external and/or **internal customers**. Finally, within their team, everyone should demonstrate appropriate versatility as needed.

Within in the context of the present case, these principles of socio-economic organization contributed to the success of synchronized decentralization of activities so as to provide personalized assistance support for disabled people in specialized centers through a process steered across the territory. However, it required a greater mobility of managers and disabled persons in the territory. It required a new logic in which supervisors go to meet the disabled population and not the other way around.

The challenge was to switch from a model where the support concept combined types of disability and age with specialized centers to a more decentralized model where *clusters* of centers focus on skills, resources, and availability within a territorial platform that coordinates supply (see Figure 15.2).

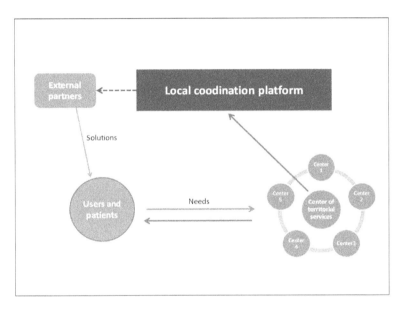

Figure 15.2.   Decentralized model of the territorial platform.

To take up this challenge, three main axes helped to build new activities, trades and the new appropriate *work organization*, reflecting the need to:

- share and pool resources, organizing synergies between different types of institutions and activities;
- revise in-depth the work organization, particularly the management *structure* of the supporting staff to increase the supervision rate (it is now it is one to twenty); and
- support and stimulate upskilling of the managers.

The Sensitive Issue of Piloting Resources

Piloting resources is more important than ever, especially the impact of intangible investments (Savall & Zardet, 2009). The economic piloting is a major challenge and *risk* for this type of institution that has lived in a logic of annuity for decades, a topic that is very sensitive, even considered taboo. Indeed, it suggests that we call into question the "good management" of the institution, at a moment when the top management of these institutions negotiate their funding from public authorities with reference to having a reputation of "healthy and sound" management.

Forthcoming Limits and Issues

One of the first limits is the impact of these changes on institutional piloting and governance. Indeed, this new model also changes family benchmarks, including the main criterion – the safety and well-being of their children. However, it must be remembered that family representatives are elected and also serve as members of the board of directors of the association. A second limitation could be the continuous instability of the actor's strategy and therefore a relative variability of the strategy.

The third limitation concerns the need to go beyond administrative constraints and conventional organizational patterns. The difficulty is that funding is built into a "locked grid." For example, an establishment gets funding for an executive job, an assistant director, and a department head, with resources calibrated on the basis of the number of disabled persons who are brought into the organization. The challenge is to develop and structure a new work organization with recognized managers that is also closer to their teams and disabled people.

CONCLUSION

Drawing on three years of observations of ongoing changes in this organization, we have drawn a number of tentative conclusions, which could be considered as work hypotheses to be investigated further.

Strategic Innovation in the Field of Medico-Social Organizations

In this example of *intervention-research*, the innovative nature of the strategy has been noted several times. The latter has many dimensions articulated in an overall project: quality and renewal of benefits for disabled people, defining a new organization of services for people according to a territorial approach, and, finally, developing activities to increase the organization's own resources and cash flow (Savall, Zardet, & Bonnet, 2011). This project shows the efforts of the association to adapt its organizational model, working methods and human management to fit evolutions in the social sector. Everyone knows that public financial resources, still relatively abundant these past few years, are no longer sufficient to continue the qualitative and quantitative *development* of the care given to the disabled without a significant transformation of management.

Learning for Organization

The method of ***socio-economic diagnosis*** (Buono & Savall, 2007), based on listening to all actor categories, has opened a space for dialogue between all the departments: adapted work centers, professional training for young people, facilities and care for multi-handicapped people, and so forth. This experience was a new one for this institution because identifying ***dysfunctions*** in the six fields of organization allowed its employees to link ***working conditions*** with the meaning and the quality of what they produced for users. ***Diagnoses*** realized the need to create a new platform of knowledge from which people can build innovative organizational solutions.

The two cross-sector projects (one on sheltered work and the other on the territorialization of services) enabled the association to decompartmentalize several institutional activities. These ***project groups*** formed the crucible of constructive and ***collaborative work*** between representatives from all trades and all departments. This working method in change management was an innovation in and of itself for the actors. These individuals were in charge of developing practical proposals linked to the new strategy developed by the association's management.

Finally, we can notice a significant step in a sector whose growth has been based on social transfers without any objective of developing one's own resources. The creation of a trademark and business line structuring provide new perspectives to rebalance the social budget and the institutional's funds. This is an in-depth change in management in the medico-social field. The border with other fields of economic activities opens up to benefits to all, including disabled persons. The latter, working in what we call protected institutions, can develop their skills and have the opportunity to better demonstrate their complete social usefulness.

Lessons from the Intervener-Researchers' Point of View

Measurement of results is a key condition for the success of any such change process (Savall, Zardet, Bonnet, & Péron, 2009). Actors need to evaluate the transformations they carry out and their impacts on organizational activities and their own working conditions. It is still a matter of conjecture in the case studied. If the ***hidden costs*** that were evaluated show significant ***productivity*** sources to self-finance improvements, the economic variable of change would be realized; this is not yet fully integrated into the tools and processes of decision making in the association under study (Savall & Zardet, 1995, 2005). The *evaluation* of the actuality and feasibility of the change actions is still only partial and largely focused on qualitative components.

The role of hierarchical level, including as the main agent of change, still seems to be undervalued by the association. The territorial platform *project* developed cross-links between departments throughout the whole area. This development could reflect significant progress if the management within the establishments and departments are in position to support these changes. Indeed, the development of cross-sector *interaction* requires considerable effort to *synchronize* activities and people in space and time. To date, the *qualitative investment in human potential* realized by the organization appears insufficient and not fully assessed concerning its impacts.

Finally, as a vigilance point, the success of this type of change project requires intensive *piloting* from the board of directors to synchronize all the change variables. In this case, reporting on the proper use of funds to the public guardianship and on the good treatment of the disabled children to their families are logically the two major criteria of good management. The endogenous dimension of change is a main learning to be drawn from the many experiments conducted by ISEOR (Savall & Zardet, 2014). The mobility of people, enhancement of their skills, and changes in work organization are levers for simultaneously improving service quality and *efficiency*. The sustainability of such change must go beyond so-called investment in human and organizational development.

NOTES

1. The research for this chapter has been influenced by a number of works that are not directly referred to in the text, including Boje and Rosile (2003), Gephart (2009), Hamayon (2015), Perroux (1979), Savall (1981, 2010, 2012), and Savall and Zardet (1992, 2008, 2013).

REFERENCES

Boje, D., & Rosile, G.-A. (2003). Comparison of socio-economic and other trans-organizational development methods. *Journal of Change Organizational Management, 16*(1), 10–20.
Buono, A. F., & Savall, H. (Eds.) (2007). *Socio-Economic intervention in organizations: The intervener-researcher and the SEAM approach to organizational analysis.* Charlotte, NC: Information Age Publishing.

Cappelleti, L. (2012). *Le contrôle de gestion de l'immatériel - Une nouvelle approche du capital humain.* [Management control of intangible: A new approach of human capital]. Paris, France: Dunod.

Gephart, R. P. (2009). An Invitation to Ethnostatistics. *Revue Sciences de gestion – Management Sciences – Ciencias de Gestión,* no. 70, p. 85.

Hamayon, D. (2015). Incidences de la crise sur les bonnes pratiques de gouvernance et les performances socio-économiques [Impact of the crisis on good governance practices and socio-economic performance]. In H. Savall & V. Zardet (Eds.), *Gouvernance et management :Quelle coopération?* [Governance and management: what cooperation?]. Paris, France : Economica.

OECD. (2003). *The non-profit sector of an economy in crisis.* Paris, France: OCDE.

Perroux, F. (1979). L'entreprise, l'équilibre rénové et les coûts cachés [The enterprise, the renovated balance and the "hidden" costs]. Preface. In H. Savall. *Reconstruire l'entreprise* [Reconstructing the enterprise] Paris, France: Dunod. 2nd ed. in H. Savall & V. Zardet. Reconstruire l'entreprise, Paris: Dunod (2014).

Savall, H. (1974–1975–1977). *Enrichir le travail humain dans les entreprises et les organisations* [An economic evaluation of job enrichment]. Paris, France: Dunod.

Savall, H. (1979). Reconstuire l'entreprise. Analyse socio-économique [Rebuild the company. Socio-economic analysis]. Paris, France: Dunod.

Savall, H. (1981–2010). *Work and people: An economic evaluation of job enrichment.* 1st ed. New-York: Oxford University Press ; 2nd ed. Charlotte, NC: Information Age Publishing

Savall, H. (2012). *Origine radicale des crises économiques: Germán Bernácer, précurseur visionnaire* [Root origin of crises: Germán Bernácer, a visionary forerunner]. Charlotte, NC: Information Age Publishing.

Savall, H., & Zardet, V. (1987). *Maîtriser les coûts et les performances cachés : Le contrat d'activité périodiquement négociables* [Mastering hidden costs and performance: The periodically negotiable activity contract]. Paris: Economica.

Savall, H., & Zardet, V. (1992). *Le nouveau contrôle de gestion: Méthode des coûts-performances cachés* [New management control: The hidden cost-performance method]. Paris: Éditions Comptables Malesherbes-Eyrolles

Savall, H. & Zardet, V. (1995–2005–2009). *Ingénierie stratégique du roseau, souple et enracinée* [Strategic engineering of the reed, flexible and rooted]. Paris: Economica.

Savall, H., & Zardet, V. (2008) Le concept de coût-valeur des activités. Contribution de la théorie socio-économique des organisations [The concept of cost-value activities. Contribution of socio-economic organization theory]. *Revue Sciences de Gestion-Management, 64,* 30–46.

Savall, H., & Zardet, V. (2008). *Mastering hidden costs and performance.* Charlotte, NC: Information Age Publishing.

Savall, H., & Zardet, V. (2009). Mesure et pilotage de la responsabilité sociale et sociétale de l'entreprise - Résultats de recherches longitudinales [Measurement and control of the corporate and social responsibility of business: Results of longitudinal research]. Louono, Spain: Revista Digital des Instituto Internacional De Costos.

Savall, H., & Zardet, V. (2010). *Maîtriser les coûts et les performances cachés: Le contrat d'activité périodiquement négociables* [Mastering hidden costs and socio-economic performance: The periodically negotiable activity contract]. Paris, France: Economica.

Savall, H., & Zardet, V. (2011). *The qualimetrics approach: Observing the complex object*. Charlotte, NC: Information Age Publishing.

Savall, H., & Zardet, V. (2013). *The dynamics and challenges of tetranormalization*. Charlotte, NC: Information Age Publishing.

Savall, H., & Zardet, V. (2014). *Reconstruire l'entreprise: les fondements du management socio-économique* [Rebuilt the organization: Socio-economic management basis]. Paris: Dunod.

Savall, H., Zardet, V., & Bonnet, M. (2000–2008). *Releasing the untapped potential of enterprises through socio-economic management*. Geneva: Éditions IOT-BIT.

Savall, H., Zardet, V., Bonnet, M., & Péron, M. (2009). *Conditions governing the performance of employment and environmental standards socio-economic considerations and proposals based on case histories from the chemicals and food manufacturing industries*. Paper presented at the 2009 International Conference and Doctoral Consortium (ISEOR & Academy of Management). Lyon, France.

Savall, H., Zardet, V., & Bonnet, M. (2011). RSE et Développement durable, fondements de la théorie socio-économique des organisations [CSR and sustainable development, socio-economic theory basis]. In N. Barthe & R. Jean-Jacques (Eds.), *RSE entre globalisation et développement durable* [CSR between globalization and sustainable development] (pp. 239–268). Bruxelles, Belgium: De Boeck.

CHAPTER 16

STEERING STRATEGIC CHANGE WITHIN A NETWORK OF COMPETITIVE AGRICULTURAL COOPERATIVES[1]

Daniel Bonnet

This chapter describes the implementation of a socio-economic diagnosis in the context of a radical crisis in a consortium of agricultural cooperatives. It explores and explains the problem of getting stuck in a competitive impasse in terms of one of the fundamental assumptions of **socio-economic organization theory** – the compatibility of social and economic variables. It shows that the rivalry in social relations between **actors** can impact the quality and **efficiency** of economic and business strategies, getting bogged down when the actors do not improve the compatibility of their social relationships.

These cooperatives bring together producers of fruits and vegetables, for whom they provide the packaging and marketing. These cooperatives cooperate with one another in the context of the Common Agricultural Policy mechanisms, but they remain in fierce **market competition**. They

The Socio-Economic Approach to Management Revisited: The Evolving Nature of SEAM in the 21st Century, pp. 323–338
Copyright © 2015 by Information Age Publishing

have faced rising competition from Spanish producers since 2009. As a result, producers suffer significant financial losses.

The radical crisis particularly affects the peach and nectarine market, but it has been already rampant for many years on the full range of products. The French peach and nectarine market are of very high quality, and the selling price to consumers is reasonable, but given the 2008 economic crisis French retailers and department stores prefer getting their supplies from Spain, whose producers benefit from a competitive cost advantage. The competitiveness gap between Spanish and French products amounts to € 0.30 / Kg. French supermarkets do not return the difference to consumers and, to maintain the competitiveness of retail prices, exert significant pressure on prices paid to French producers. The supermarkets also benefit from liberal legislation that does not fight against unfair competition. Spanish product quality is considered rather average by French consumers, and consumption in the market is declining by about 5% a year. The financial losses are very important for producers; they account for between € 0.20 / kg and € 0.40 / kg for a cost of € 0.80 / kg or € 1.20 / kg on early productions. Since 2009, the situation has become catastrophic.

Cooperative leaders have come together to study this challenge and implement a response, focusing on whether there was a need for cooperatives to regroup themselves. ISEOR was entrusted with the mission to carry out an opportunity and feasibility study for such a regrouping. It was proposed to begin the process with a *socio-economic diagnosis* supported by *clinical intervention research*. The chapter describes the *intervention methods*, the results, and the lessons learned from the *project*.

THE LOCAL INTERVENTION CONTEXT

It does not stand to reason that agricultural cooperatives should cooperate with each other to promote the production of their members. Originally, agricultural cooperatives were created to bring together producers who wanted to market their products together based on common values. This grouping, however, was made according to the terms of the local social rivalry that was initially conscribed in the production basin territory. The development of production, a correlative consumer development and commercial competition between production areas, contributed to superimpose an additional level of competition between production areas and the market. To cope with competition between production areas when the market became mature, local cooperatives were grouped, but the groups were not well accepted by farmers.

The cooperatives remained in local competition with one another, so that the development of the strategy stalled over time in the complex entanglement of commercial competition, even though the cooperatives have been able to develop relationships of professional cooperation with one another. A union of cooperatives was created in the early 1960s, but it is often referred to as the cause of all the farmers' woes.

The field of intervention is a consortium of eleven agricultural fruit and vegetable cooperatives in the south of France. It includes about 850 producers and controls a little more than half the sales of the fruit and vegetable production in the basin. For a long time, the leaders of these unions have been questioning the desirability and feasibility of consolidation. Surmising what this group could be is embedded in the myriad challenges inherent in a true fusion of these cooperatives. They do not succeed by themselves, for reasons of human relations, they say.

The investigation confirms that these cooperatives have become stuck in a competitive impasse. Given the low level of activity in the packing plants, the intervention also examines the terms of a merger as part of a cooperative redevelopment project, with the redefinition of an economic model based on merging cooperatives and a transformation of the value proposition articulated by the implementation of a real *marketing strategy*. It was determined that the transformation of the economic model could be achieved quickly, immediately restoring 50% of the convertible competitiveness deficit (i.e., about € 0.17 / kg). The *hidden cost performance* was assessed at € 0.43 / kg.

The merger was also seen as helping to improve the rate of economic concentration of the players in this market where the rate has been traditionally low. The implementation of the marketing strategy as a way of transforming the value proposition was to be carried out over a period of five to six years. The expertise of the producers was rated as very good and allowed the implementation of technological breakthroughs in production in order to offer consumers organic and extremely tasteful products.

Under this plan, the French offer corresponds to consumer expectations and would be attractive for both quality and price in the domestic market, facing competition from the Spanish producers. Leaders and all producers agreed on the diagnostic results and the proposed prescriptions – the diagnosis confirmed what they already knew and would like to do together. They realized that they would not be able to succeed by themselves.

The study of the application for assistance lays the foundation for the preliminary body of hypotheses, around the issue of a conflict of ambivalence in inter-organizational mental structures. The specifications of the intervention developed *strategic analysis* within the *socio-economic framework*, showing that there was indeed ample strategic and financial leverage. The intervention proposal was to evaluate performance and *hidden costs*, and to clarify the issue of ambivalence in the behavior of actors. This intervention proposal was chosen among four competing proposals, due to its socio-economic positioning to which producers were sensitive. The presentation led one of the members of the selection committee to note that "You have told us what we have never been able to tell ourselves."

Strategic analysis defines the issues strategy, but can leave leaders skeptical because it does not fully explain anything. In this case, a given is that the merger remains to be completed when it has been under discussion for fifteen years, raising the question of the future of the union of cooperatives. This merger has proved impossible for local human relations issues and the rivalry between the cooperatives because they want to retain control over strategic decisions. Indeed, village cooperatives mergers have historically been traumatic for producers because they were made on the basis of trying to create a balance of power in relation to one another. Finally, the economic model must ensure that producers retain direct control of strategic decisions as well as their business decisions. It was recognized that there should be only one sales office. The debate continues on the merger conditioning units, but producers also agreed on a joint production, economic and technological project at the local territory level.

THE INTERVENTION

The realization of a socio-economic diagnosis consists of two phases – the *socio-economic analysis* and the innovation project development – according to the methodological protocol of the *socio-economic intervention* (ISE) developed by ISEOR (Buono & Savall, 2007; Savall & Zardet, 1987). In this case, this protocol was encapsulated in a protocol of clinical intervention research. This is defined as a methodological approach to extract knowledge of scientific intent linked with the latent content of human behavior that is hidden by observable behaviors. This approach reflects the reality of the operations and changes in the *mental structures* of the organization in a sufficiently convincing way to guide the intervention research. Subjects have to describe and explain their own situations with the help of the researcher, which will be descriptive and explanatory hypothesis contents. The researcher refers to a theoretical knowledge corpus based on an abductive approachin order to validate these hypothesis. The researcher works out prescriptive hypothesis to advance in the research. We experimented and validated this posture to carry out investigations in the deep *mental structures* of the organization, extracting knowledge from the psychoanalytic epistemology, while respecting a posture consistent with the epistemology of ISEOR (see Table 16.1), namely that the researcher does not lead and does not assume himself the observations, but works them out in co-production with the *actors*.

Table 16.1.   Fundamentals of Intervention-Research Methodology and the ISEOR Epistemology

THE INTERVENTION-RESEARCH METHODOLOGY

A Change Process Inscribed in Organizational Development & Change Stream

Intervention research is a concept close to action-research. It implies a strong presence of the researcher within the organization for a systematic observation of the management situation under study. The researcher is clearly engaged in his or her research strategy and co-constructs knowledge with the observed actors

Principle of Generic Contingency

Epistemological framework admitting the presence of specific features in the functioning of organizations, but posing the existence of regularities and invariants that are generic rules with a core of knowledge with some stability and a certain universality. This principle establishes the framework of the theory of generic epistemological constructivism (Savall & Zardet, 1995, p. 495; 2004, p. 387).

Principle of Cognitive Interactivity

Iterative process between the researcher and the actors involved in the business of knowledge production by successive iterations curled in an ongoing effort to increase the value of significance of information within the scientific work. Knowledge is completely generated by one or the other or by the players, it is accomplished in the connecting interval Intangible actors (Savall & Zardet, 1995, p. 499; 2004, p. 221).

Contradictory Subjectivity

This method explicitly deals with different actors with their respective views and analyses, to identify similarities and differences. On these characteristics, a debate, a discussion, a tentative interpretation contribute to the creation of generic knowledge, which leads to a greater understanding of the phenomena studied. Statements (written, oral) are treated according to the method described in Figure 16.1.

It was not possible for the definition and implementation of the cooperative project to be considered without this investigation relating to the extraction of unspoken and taboo subjects that the *socio-economic diagnosis* must achieve. The first dispute was reached early in the negotiation stage of the mission on the level of association of primary cooperatives, some of which are members of the union of cooperatives; the general direction of the union wanted to represent them. It did not escape us that the position of cooperatives aimed to lead to the dismemberment of the union and that the independent cooperatives had no other intention than to make off with member cooperatives thereto, to compensate for the low level of activity of their sub-structures. Disagreement over the plan made obsolete achieving my mission. This deception was validated when the board of directions of one of the cooperative's members of the union with overthrown. Along with all the difficulties we encountered, we felt that our proposal response was robust. Scientific observation of the ambivalent behavior of the actor has been the focus of our research. We conduct our research within the theoretical framework of *generic constructivism* from which we stored the work of the leaders. The principles work in loop creating **generic knowledge** (Figure 16.1). Statements are treated according to the sorting out protocol developed by ISEOR (Figure 16.2).

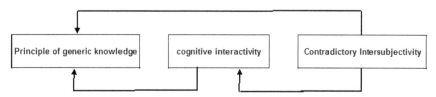

Figure 16.1. Quality of knowledge look processing of the generic knowledge.

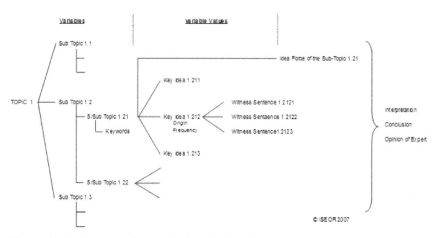

Figure 16.2. Process of examination of the talks.

CONTRIBUTION TO ORGANIZATION MANAGEMENT THEORY

This section discusses the results of the intervention research in terms of three major hypotheses that were posed at the start of the mission, around which the steering of clinical research was coordinated. These assumptions were validated over the course of the latter during the 2009–2013 periods. These assumptions were made on the basis of th**e** *generic contingency* *principle*. They provide generic knowledge, that is to say knowledge characterizing certain regularity in the organization's operation and its management from which the prescriptions and the cooperative *project* were developed. The focus of the discussion is on the nature of the rivalry between the cooperatives and the impact of the negative thoughts about the terms of the local competition.

The Inter-organizational Environment: Interstitial Space Game

The first major hypothesis held that the operation and management of the organization was in conflict with underlying systems of meaning that coexisted and were historically opposed with each organization. It spreads in the inter-organizational field that serves as an outlet, which helps maintain *cohesion* within the cooperatives. The clinical examination in this space was conducted by analyzing the content of the latent meanings, reflecting the symptom of intersubjective conflict between the actors. The intervention research analyzed the latent meaning, which operated under the obvious (observable) meaning. The qualitative interviews showed that, in particular, the arguments of the stakeholders vis-à-vis competing cooperatives and planned unconditional expectations in the register of human virtue were impossible to achieve. It was important to realize that these expectations were projecting their own values, but at the same time pointing to a tendency to refer to themselves as better than the competition.

The intervention research showed that the conflict of ambivalence lied in the relationship between the ego ideal and the ideal self. This conflict led to avoidance strategies. It helps explain that the rivalry was the means to reject outside oneself, in the inter-organizational space, which prevented *internal cooperation* within the cooperatives. Since such collaboration is only possible if the alliance between the leader and the group is strong, the leader therefore has an interest in maintaining the conflict between the consortium member organizations to maintain cohesion within the cooperative. Cooperation is justified only if the fixation of the narcissistic defenses of every actor combine transformative energy facing the organization and transformative of energy toward oneself.

In this context, the union of cooperatives and the market, particularly the department stores, have easily become scapegoats. Weak suppliers are prey for buyers of large stores, but the inter-organizational space in the cooperative consortium is where the scene of the conflict of ambivalence shows up. It is a space of diversion and derivation, especially as the economic results were not good and pointing to a scapegoat would prevent the collapse of the organization, including its governance. This could be avoided, however, in a cooperative, in which the board was overthrown. Organizational *functioning* and management were stamped by *dysfunctional strategic regulations* that transform effects into causes and lead to a competitive deadlock.

Very early in the start of the intervention, we proposed reading a text clinical at quickly identifying the behavior splits – the lament of the cooperative that did not exist or the cooperative dream veiled by the argument of Œdipus and Electra. About human inconsistencies, we recall the Latin etymology that means *sympathized with suffering,* and how it can be transformed into a consistent opposition through a motion. Cooperation agreements in this context are never anything but consistent opposition. Cooperation in the context of the consortium shall, in addition to its regular duties, civilize rivalry. Our intervention research therefore mobilizes knowledge of psychoanalytic anthropology in the outskirts of the *socio-economic theory of organizations*.

The proposal was to move the competitive rivalry in the relevant market space. The merger would have allowed the consortium to be a true leader on the national market, with 15% market share, and generate funding, equivalent to 3% of sales, to deploy marketing and communications for the better valuation of products under trademarks. This policy so far consisted only in inter-professional financial support of products withdrawn or downgraded to maintain a balance between supply and demand. We obviously proposed a repositioning of this policy in the demand sector. This achievement was to lead the transformation of the competition regime by encouraging other concentrations, as we have shown in other industries in the 1990s, including the salad, melon and potato market.

Impact of the Influence of Negative Thoughts

Let us consider the following two major hypotheses. If the operation and management of the organization come within the conflict of systems of underlying meaning that determine the latent meanings, it means that the generic knowledge must go beyond the field of figurative aspects of knowledge, that is, their *structures* and dynamics. We also need to explore the field of operative, cognitive and psychological aspects, which includes everything that works whose subject is unaware or unconscious.

If major hypothesis 1 is an constant in actor's behavior, so that the operation and management of the organization is determined in the underlying ambivalence conflict, it helps to structure alliances since everybody operates according to the same process. It is therefore a genuine regularity. It is in the meaning system that we must drive the transformation of human relations, especially in the field of intersubjectivity (see Table 16.1).

What does not belong to the alliance is rejected out of its perimeter, a subject of the rivalry. The alliance is built on the convergence of satisfactions including, of course, interest. The group then works in the grip of its symbolic structures. The group definition chosen here is that of Kaës (1999, p. 12) according to whom the group is defined by the shape and structure of an organization intersubjective links. It should, however, be understood why the exchange between *actors* get stuck in negative thoughts, whose impact on one another blocks the creativity of trade. Under this process, the actors keep the negativity, even though they know it is in their interest to achieve this merger.

Our research has explored the operation of cognitive schemas, based on the work of Piaget, to illuminate the reasons why actors operate in a model of dysfunctional thoughts. This exploration has identified a wealth of information on various subjects, particularly on the subject of trust. As a guide, it was apparent from the analysis of latent content that the actors felt they could not trust one another, to the point where a compromise on the merger would be an act of surrender, and that competitors did not wish them any good. It may be added that the merger was possible under the guarantee of unconditional conditions. Overall cognitive patterns constituted obstacles to the realization of the accommodation process, explaining that the adaptation was not achieved. This latent content allowed us to explore the influence of the negative.

Regarding the influence of the negative, Plato, in *The Sophist,* foresaw long before Descartes that thought asserts itself in attempting to negate itself. It identifies the *absolute negation* reported to nothingness, and that means a *negation* on opposition with something that is not wrong, but that is different. It is also a vehicle for creativity the work in **cognitive interactivity** and **inter-contradictory** (see Table 16.1) has illustrated, given the dysfunctional methodological option selected for the **socio-economic analysis**.

In the light of the negative, repressed content can return to consciousness and be the object of an intellectual acceptance – but denial or negation is never lifted. It seemed to us that narcissism provided a psychic anchor for accommodations, and that overall cognitive patterns were overdetermined by the actor's narcissist anchoring. However, we had to consider the issue of "evil" that represents for Plato's the denial of "good," but not the other way around, and correspondingly treat the body of hypotheses in the course of observing the functioning of cognitive schemas. Green (2011) showed that we should not study mental processes by isolating them from each other. This perspective has helped to build a body of **generic knowledge** showing that steering and development of transformation strategies can be understood starting from the central hypothesis of the transformation of invariants.

Table 16.2 serves to illustrate the work carried out with the leaders (presidents, directors, and CEOs) during our intervention. A management paper was just proposed to reading but did not lead to any chattering between group members who were skeptical. But as the president of the union of cooperatives set the time "to go further, go to the nearest," he intimated his peers. We were never asked explicitly to work on the theme of "evil," because we were working on material extracted from the qualitative interviews, that is to say, their say. However, the president of one of the independent cooperatives and president of the national union of fruit growers said a few months later that it was to "purge interpersonal relationships that know no evil and who is unable to commit it." This statement, considered as the key idea, came in the course of the intervention about the work done on the following hypothesis—local rivalry, at the first level of market structures, is determined in the social relations between local actors.

A few months later, at the general meeting of producers of the cooperative he heads, the president was debunked and the CEO was fired. Although economic results of the campaign were still not good, the actors (except for one of the cooperatives) had reached a political agreement on the merger of the cooperatives, on the basis of proposals that our study provided. This agreement was not accepted by a minority faction of the board, whose view weighed at the end of the discussions that were not serene. The statements of two of them are summarized in Table 16-3, indicating that the meaning is present in the speech whose signified contains both affirmation and negation. There the speech unites them the same as what is united in reality (Fouillée, 2005, p. 267), about the harmony between thought and language in Plato[2]). This speech is true, but it is also wrong because it holds that perception is dependent on reality and truth, on opinions and beliefs. The sales manager of the cooperative also changed his position and has since become the new general manager of the cooperative. Yet he was in favor of the merger (see Table 16.3).

Latent Content Analysis: The Influence of Group Narcissism

After these few months, we can validate two explanatory hypotheses. On the one hand, the local rivalry finds its explanation in the narcissism of small differences; on the other hand, the failure to adapt to changes in the terms of *market competition*, the second level of scale structures in the field of economic competition, finds its explanation in the fact that the local rivalry contributed to seal a denial pact between the local actors.

According to this notion of the *narcissism of small differences*, the closer the differences between individuals or groups are, the more they show them intolerant and implement mechanisms of identity defense. Narcissistic defenses help them update every time a behavior or mental process

Table 16.2.   Selection of Witnesses Sentences on the Theme of Negation (Subtheme Beliefs)

Idea Force: Local competitive rivalry maintain the cyst toxic of inter-organizational relationships?

Key Idea: Would the dispute over the prices charged to producers to do with groupal narcissism?

- The problem is that no one is put in front of his shortcomings and his poor performance compared to its neighbors.
- The machine is heavy to implement. The lack of trust is hightly. We always feel that one is better than one's neighbor.
- We compare prices between producers, and we hear that it is not the best. When you look at the numbers, there is a big difference and we are told by the cooperator

Key Idea: What rivalry is a sign of?

- Despite all the efforts that can be done, there is a relationship problem. I think we share the wrong question if one considers that the other is an enemy.
- The cooperative (F8) has always had a somewhat colonialist policy.

Key idea: Should not working here?

- The boards of directors of cooperatives did not want to delegate the sale to the union of cooperatives because they thought that cooperatives would sell better. The idea was to sell the best and send them the worst. And then we compare the price, but it does not make sense

What is the interest of going to war?

- • Men who are currently in place, I can not sit at their table because they stabbed me knives in the back.

One does not say what one actually thinks?

- We never spoke to the Board of Directors of problems, but we talk among about them producers.

Why we prevent avoids, bypasses it...?

- To combine in a single entity would be counter-productive. Mathematically, it works, but emotionally it would bother me. A global model could be designed, but preserving the specificities.
- When we talk, happen to be converge, but when you have to, there always are specifications that stand out.

---

creates an active event of resistance. This not only consists of resisting what is denied to competition in the market, such as disloyalty of economic competition at the second level of scale structures in the field of economic competition, but also resisting what is prohibited in the field of local competition. What has been denied for a long time will be refused because it is not incorporated as a reference, that is to say, a potential field in symbolic structures.

Table 16.3.   Excerpt From Interveiws with a Director and President

Director Cooperative F8

Cooperative F8 was a founding member of the Cooperative Union until 1995. Both directors were heavily involved at this time in the decision to leave the Union of Cooperatives, a few years later to form a joint venture trade with another cooperative that was independent.

If I were to have a priori, I would say it would be negative with respect to your mission. This is the 3rd or 4th time I participate in this kind of thing. I do not understand how one can even ask that kind of question. I do not see how you can not go for a collection of commercial means ... it's paradoxical to have to even ask the question of this regrouping. I think going through this kind of study will slow. It should have been things down already this year. There is already a fact that has been done. The parties *(the union of cooperatives)* are not the right ours. This is not a project that must grapple with the president and the *director general of the union*. These are the presidents of cooperatives should discuss. Cooperative F8 is not big enough and is not capable of defending its commitments. The study you are going to do, I do not care. We are in a cooperative that has this approach, and I have no a priori. At one point, it is better lto have a little a home, and it is perhaps not suitable.

President Cooperative F10

We are not leading the volumes; therefore must be recognized for something, quality and reliability for instance. It depends too much on a single client. There is no access to certain markets, because it is too small and customers are too large for us. With OP5 (name of the cooperative project), we must works on the qualitative side to advance manufacturing. When trying to sell peaches, nectarines of someone else, there are often problems. Nobody is in the top station. I feel like a liar poker. ZZ *(about the head of an association of producer organizations in this sector, including the president of the cooperative F8 is the president)*, she sharks around.

To emphasize its importance, symbolic **structures** are responsible for the development of intellectual abilities (Piaget, 2006) and cultural orientation (Levi-Strauss, 1983). Overall, we must see that this negative pattern, rooted in the grip of negative narcissism and narcissistic defenses, is holding market positions also in resistance. This is a defensive model, a model of resistance. We have seen developing over the years a causal diagram anchored in the negative, made from toxic causal attributions in relationships, which led to the competitive impasse. The medium is in this respect transitive. Transitivity is defined here as property relations in a human environment, a property that allows accommodations to happen.

This does not necessarily mean that appropriate adjustments are realized. The accommodations here have created resistance, explaining progress on some fronts, such as the development of product quality and technical and technological modernization, but not in other areas involving content associated with negative thoughts refuse. On the market that is the field of economic competition, we are rather seeing accommodation in economic resistance, as actors know one another less or little. Resistance then opposes narcissistic investments of actors in both competitive fields. But it corresponds to two independent operating processes, one turned to the local social rivalry, the other to the economic rivalry. The outcome is resistance that is all the higher as the level of intensity and transitive density, activated by the economic crisis, which is a good thing in a context of positive *interaction*, can be creative. But in the cooperative consortium, narcissistic investment crystallized divisions under the guise of the arguments of the local competitive differentiation that no longer took place on the criteria of the narcissism of small differences in the *mental structures* of the organization.

The conversion proposal in space by means of the merger is likely to uphold the most relevant criteria in defining the right strategy, if the players want to. This transformation in space would be likely to break the impact of denial of the negative pact in the field of local social rivalry, also sealed between the actors over the years. The pact of denial (Kaës, 1989), meanwhile, is a defense mechanism that actively contributes to maintaining the intersubjective link between related subjects subliminally and subsequently by one agreement on the negative. It manifests itself in the field of local competition.

The concept of the denial pact is an unconscious intersubjective pact on the negative. It includes those defenses through denial, rejection, negation, and disavowal. These help mechanisms to maintain the *internal cohesion* of the group or community. It is an offensive alliance in the constitution of a collective that accepts one's individual psychic formations given up in this mechanism. It is a psychic infrastructure of solidarity (Kaës, 2009, pp. 113–123) with two polarities. As Kaës (2009) states:

> One is founded on positive mutual investments, on common identifications, a community of ideals and beliefs, a narcissistic contract. The other jointly accept terms to achieve some desires on the illusion generating potential space reviews. Negatively around various defensive operations in any link, required of each subject, in order to maintain the social link with risking destruction: thesis are defensive operations of repression to the denial of cleavage rejection. (pp. 113–123)

CONCLUSION

The chapter presented the general rules for the implementation of a *socio-economic diagnosis* within a consortium of agricultural cooperatives. The validation of assumptions provides *generic knowledge* about organization management. The results of the *socio-economic diagnosis* illuminate the knowledge of how the organization operates in the register of *mental structures*. The challenge of change is to create and develop strategic collaboration between cooperatives that are members of the consortium; but it relates more generally to the development of **cooperation** between stakeholders in any corporate network, depending on the nature of their alliances, both in the organizational field and in the inter-organizational field. This research is also important in terms of developing new forms of organization, as a corollary of the transformation of work.

The socio-economic diagnosis adds value relative to current methods of analysis and strategic diagnosis. It requires, in fact, a definition of the problem in the combination of economic variables and social variables for the operation and management of the organization. Current approaches to strategic analysis define the strategic problematic, but only treat management and change management as an afterthought. Clinical research associated with of **socio-economic intervention research** permits one to conduct more **in-depth investigations**. Reflecting on this case, overall the investigation has led to work on the right problem and proposed a definition of the strategic plan and its implementation based on the mobilization of **human potential**—from knowledge developed by the **actors**.

This intervention research, however, was conducted in a context of radical crisis. Although one can express regret for the actors, this context is an opportunity that provides access to a level of knowledge that would not be provided as part of the normal **functioning** of the organization. It shows that the socio-economic diagnosis can be carried out in these difficult circumstances, provided one meets the **chrono-biology** of the functioning of the organization, depending on the problem to be addressed, necessary work that the actors have to do to know themselves, and appreciate better to implement the **project**. Among the recommendations which were implemented, let us point to the renewal of the generation of leaders within the board of directors of cooperatives, giving way to young producers who were recognized by their seniors. These individuals may very well be more willing to work together in the otherness, ultimately leading to the merger of cooperatives in the fruit industry within the union of cooperatives.

NOTE

1. The research for this chapter has been influenced by a number of works that are not directly referred to in the text, including Boje and Rosile (2003), Bonnet (2007), Gephart (2009), Perroux (1979), Savall (1974, 1975, 1977), and Savall and Zardet (1987, 1992, 2011, 2013).
2. The concept of *main-idea* appears in Fouillée (1888) about the formation of ideas in Plato. He is the author of the psychology of key ideas in 1893. See http://gallica.bnf.fr/ark:/12148/bpt6k771638.

REFERENCES

Barthes, R. (1957). *Mythologies* [Mythologies]. Paris, France: Éditions Du Seuil.

Boje, D., & Rosile, G.-A. (2003). Comparison of socio-economic and other trans-organizational development methods. *Journal of Change Organizational Management, 16*(1), 10–20.

Bonnet, D. (2007). *Le pilotage de la transformation en environnement de coopération inter-organisationnelle, essence socio-économique de la transformation et des stratégies de transformation* [Transformation steering of inter-organizational cooperation, socio-economic essence of transformation and strategies]. Thèse de doctorat en Sciences de Gestion. University of Lyon.

Bonnet, D. (2012). Management du risque stratégique. La transformation de l'invariance dans le mode de signification: Le schème groupal de signification [Management of strategic risk. The transformation of the invariance in the manner of service: The groupal pattern of meaning]. *Revue Gestion, 29*(4), 35–47.

Buono, A. F., & Savall, H. (Eds.). (2007). *Socio-economic intervention in organizations: The intervener-researcher and the SEAM approach to organizational analysis.* Charlotte, NC: Information Age Publishing.

Fouillée, A. (1888–2005). *La philosophie de Platon* [Plato's philosophy]. Paris, France: Elibron classics.

Freud, S. (1934). La Négation [Negation]. Translated from the German by H. Hoesli. *Revue Française de Psychanalyse, 2,* 174–177.

Gephart, R. P. (2009). An invitation to ethnostatistics. *Revue Sciences de gestion – Management Sciences – Ciencias de Gestión, 70,* 85.

Green A. (1983–2007). *Narcissisme de vie, narcissisme de mort* [Narcissism of life, death narcissism]. City: Les Éditions de Minuit.

Green A. (1993-2011). *Le travail du négatif* [The work of the negative]. Paris, France: Les Éditions de Minuit.

Kaës, R. (1999). *Les théories psychanalytiques de groupe* [Psychoanalytic theories group]. Paris, France: PUF.

Kaës, R. (2009). *Les alliances inconscientes* [The unconscious alliances]. Paris, France: Dunod.

Larue-Tondeur, J. (2009). Ambivalence et énantosémie [Ambivalence and enantiosemy]. Thèse *de Doctorat en Sciences du Langage [PhD in Linguistics]* under the direction of de M. Arrivé. Paris, France: Université de Paris X.

Levi-Strauss, C. (1983) *Le regard éloigné* [The distant look]. Paris, France: Plon.

Perroux, F. (1979). L'entreprise, l'équilibre rénové et les coûts cachés [The enterprise, the renovated balance and the "hidden" costs]. Preface. In H. Savall, *Reconstruire l'entreprise* [Reconstructing the enterprise]. Paris, France: Dunod.

Piaget, J. (2006). *Les relations entre l'intelligence et l'affectivité dans le développement de l'enfant* [The relationship between intelligence and affectivity in child development]. Cours inédit [Unpublished course]. Paris, France: Fondation Jean Piaget.

Piaget, J., Henriques, G., & Ascher, E. (1990). *Morphismes et catégories: Comparer et transformer* [Morphisms and categories: Compare and transform]. Paris, France: Delachaux et Niestlé.

Platon, X. (2006). *Le sophiste* [The sophist]. Traduction [translation] de N.L. Cordero. CityParis, France: GF Flammarion.

Savall, H. (1974–1975–1977). *Enrichir le travail humain dans les entreprises et les organisations* [An economic evaluation of job enrichment]. Paris, France: Dunod.

Savall, H. (1978). Compatibilité de l'efficience économique et du développement du potentiel humain [Compatibility of economic efficiency and development of human potential]. *VII° Colloque International au Collège de France*, organized by François Perroux & Jean Piaget. *Revue d'Economie Appliquée*. Archives de l'ISMEA. Tome XXXI (3-4), 561–593.

Savall, H. (1981–2010). *Work and people: An economic evaluation of job enrichment.* 1st ed. New York: Oxford University Press; 2nd ed. Charlotte, NC: Information Age Publishing

Savall, H. (2012). *Origine radicale des crises économiques: Germán Bernácer, précurseur visionnaire* [Root origin of crises: Germán Bernácer, a visionary forerunner]. Charlotte, NC: Information Age Publishing.

Savall H., & Zardet V., (2005). *Tétranormalisation: Défis et dynamiques* [Tetranormalization: Challenges and dynamics]. Paris, France: Economica.

Savall, H., & Zardet, V. (1987). *Maîtriser les coûts et les performances cachés : Le contrat d'activité périodiquement négociables* [Mastering hidden costs and performance: The periodically negotiable activity contract]. Paris: Economica.

Savall, H., & Zardet, V. (1992). *Le nouveau contrôle de gestion: Méthode des coûts-performances cachés* [New management control: The hidden cost-performance method]. Paris: Éditions Comptables Malesherbes-Eyrolles

Savall, H., & Zardet, V. (1995–2005–2009). *Ingénierie stratégique du roseau, souple et enracinée* [Strategic engineering of the reed, flexible and rooted]. Paris, France: Economica.

Savall, H., & Zardet, V. (2004). *Recherche en Sciences de Gestion : Approche Qualimétrique – Observer l'objet complexe* [Research in Management Sciences: Approach qualimetric—Observe the complex object]. Paris, France: Economica.

Savall, H., & Zardet, V. (2008). *Mastering hidden costs and performance.* Charlotte, NC: Information Age Publishing.

Savall, H., & Zardet, V. (2011). *The qualimetrics approach: Observing the complex object.* Charlotte, NC: Information Age Publishing.

Savall, H., & Zardet, V. (2013). *The dynamics and challenges of tetranormalization.* Charlotte, NC: Information Age Publishing.

Savall, H., Zardet, V., & Bonnet, M. (2000–2008). *Releasing the untapped potential of enterprises through socio-economic management.* Geneva: Éditions IOT-BIT.

Savall, H., Zardet, V., & Bonnet, M. (2000). *Libérer les performances cachées des entreprises par un management socio-économique* [Unlocking the hidden performance of companies with a socio-economic management]. City: Bureau International du Travail.

Simondon, G. (2005). *L'individuation à la lumière des notions de forme et d'information* [Individuation in light of notions of form and information]. Paris: Million. Collection Krisis.

CHAPTER 17

TRANSORGANIZATIONAL INTERVENTION AND MESO-SOCIO-ECONOMIC APPROACH TO TERRITORIAL MANAGEMENT

The Case of a Network of Environmental NGOs[1]

Xavier Pierre, Emmanuel Beck, and Céline Broggio

Governments have the mandate to implement public policies with a view to bringing the allocation of resources under control while obtaining the best possible results in an effective and efficient way. There is a general expectation that the implementation of such policies by the *public service* should be carried out against qualitative criteria with the minimum amount of financial and *human resources* possible. Institutions entrust the implementation of their programs to subsidiary organizations, such as non-governmental organizations (NGOs). In France, there are 1 million NGOs financed at

The Socio-Economic Approach to Management Revisited: The Evolving Nature of SEAM in the 21st Century, pp. 339–357

339

a level of 50–60% through public subsidies with an overall budget of 59 billion euros [73 billion USD], representing 3.5% of the GDP. Given the public nature of the funding of such NGOs, there is a strategic need for regional governments to become more invested in the management of networks of NGOs involved in the implementation of public policies.

This field of study focuses on energy efficiency policies (i.e., diversification of energy production sources, decreasing energy consumption) in the French region of Rhône-Alpes. To provide some context, the metropolis of the Rhône-Alpes region is Lyon, the second largest city in France. Other sizable cities include Grenoble (known for the Olympic Winter Games in 1968) and Saint-Etienne. The Rhône-Alpes region covers parts of the Alps, the center of France, and Provence. This area is about the size of Switzerland and has Denmark's population. The Rhône-Alpes regional government and the French national energy agency, referred to as "*institutional actors*" or "institutions" in the chapter, subsidize 70% of the operating budget of 13 NGOs working in the field of energy efficiency. SEAM practitioners use the term "*actors*" to talk about all employees in an organization. In sociology, the term actors is used to describe all members of an organization. The purpose of this deliberately non-hierarchical term for owners, leaders and employees is to reinforce the idea that all actors have a significant impact on the organizational *effectiveness* (Conbere & Heorhiadi, 2011). In the chapter, the term actors refers as well to the organizations involved in the implementation of the territorial strategy.

A *Socio-Economic Approach to Management (SEAM) intervention* is a method whereby an intervener-researcher engages action within an organization, focusing on all its *structures* and human behaviors by intervening in the six domains of *dysfunctions*. The organization is dealt with as a whole, in order to facilitate the emergence of sustainable, effective, and innovative solutions (Buono & Savall, 2007). In this case, a SEAM intervention took place from 2006 to 2010, implemented at the request of the regional government to identify "how to improve performance within the network of subsidized NGOs." The intervention was undertaken through the implementation of a management of change method to work on *inter-organizational cooperation* (socio-economic interventions dealing with the relationships between the actors involved in regional strategies) as well as on *intra-organizational* management (csocio-economic interventions in two NGOs; see Figure 17.1). In order to complete this research, additional interviews were conducted in 2014 as part of an evaluation of the transformation that took place during the medium- to long-term following the SEAM intervention.

The research presented in this chapter demonstrates the necessity of developing the strategic piloting of a network, which strengthens *cooperation* between its members in order to develop both the *effectiveness* and *efficiency* of a strategy implemented in a territory. Within this context, the idea of **strategic piloting** includes the implementation and application of the strategy elaborated by the decision makers, as well as the evaluation of differentials between obtained results and projected objectives through a **heuristic** process (Buono & Savall, 2007).

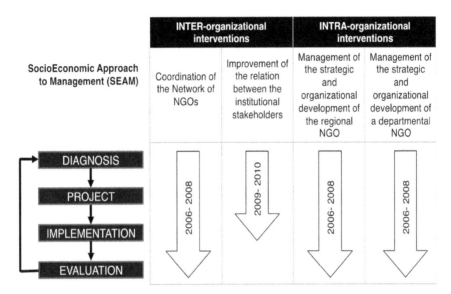

Figure 17.1.   The fields of the SEAM intervention.

The term *territory* refers to an area of land, a region, where **socio-economic activities** take place. The concept of *territorial management* is attached to the idea that there is a need to manage the actors involved in **projects** taking place in a territory, such as the implementation of **public policies**. The territory thus becomes a "meta-organization." The terms "territory" and "territorial" are preferred to "region" or "regional" because they apply to every administrative area (e.g., local, regional, national, international).

The case study referenced throughout the chapter illustrates *the value of assigning the strategic piloting role to the institutional actors*. At the present time, their role is often perceived as limited to that of regulator and public funds provider in the classical Keynesian sense. The research demonstrates that SEAM interventions are relevant for transforming their role, to become strategic pilots in the implementation of territorial strategies.

The chapter demonstrates the necessity of strengthening the **strategic force** of network members to enable them to develop a real capacity to become positive players in the implementation of the territorial strategies.

Within this context, strategic force refers to the capacity of an organization to transform intangible and material resources into activities that enable the enterprise to improve its strategic situation, namely its capacity for survival-development and its power to negotiate with **internal and external actors** (Buono & Savall, 2007).

The **socio-economic transorganizational interventions** described in the chapter, which involve **transformation efforts** both within and between the organizations involved in the project, are intended to improve the strategic piloting of the network as well as the **functioning** of its members. This text also proposes the concept of a **meso-socio-economic approach** reflecting the transfer of the SEAM to the field of territorial approach.

THE RESEARCH FIELD:
THE CHALLENGE OF MANAGING A NETWORK

In a context of economic and debt crisis of states and municipalities, there is an awareness of the urgent need to manage effectively and efficiently the allocation of **public resources** and to obtain better results out of the resources invested.

Effectiveness and Efficiency of Public Policies

Through the analysis of the regional energy efficiency policy in the present study, we found:

- increased pressure on the allocated budgets for the regional policy that resulted in a 3-15% reduction per year, which has in turn affected the subsidies granted to the NGOs;
- current goals of the regional policy remained ambitious; and
- two-thirds of the funds invested by the regional government for energy efficiency were intended to fund the network of NGOs.

The Actors' Strategies and the Territorial Approach

The implementation of a strategy in a territory is based on a number of principal actors among the organizations in the network, usually from the institutional actors that have the **resources**, skills and institutional legitimacy to assume the role of strategic pilot of the implementation of strategy, organizing the participation and **coordination** of a larger number of public, private, and non-governmental actors in a given territory (Pierre, 2011, 2014).

In the case study, the set of actors (see Figure 15.2) includes:

- *Two leading institutions*: the regional government and the national energy agency, under the supervision of three different ministries.
- *A network of non-governmental organizations* (NGOs): one regional, nine departmental, and three local. The NGOs are at different territorial levels: local, departmental and regional. The administrative divisions in France are currently based on 22 regions, which are divided into 101 departments and 36,687 municipalities organized into 2818 inter-municipalities. In the French administrative system, inter-municipalities are groupings of municipalities that share **competences** and pool resources. Local and departmental NGOs are organized in a formal network, which excludes the only regional NGO in the field of energetic efficiency in the Rhône-Alpes region.
- The *institutional actors* also want to be able to rely on departmental energy networks of municipalities in charge of managing energy **infrastructures**, as well as other governmental bodies decentralized to the regions and private operators in the energy sector.
- The goal of the energy efficiency policy is to transform consumption and production patterns of the *"target users,"* which in this case are municipalities and inter-municipalities, businesses and individuals. The large number of target users and the fact that the problems of energy efficiency may appear far from their own immediate interests require an intelligent organization of the intermediary actors involved in the **strategic implementation**.

The actors presented in Figure 17.2 was elaborated by the intervener-researcher involved in the case study (Pierre, 2011). The actors involved in the **intervention-research** were not able to create on their own a clear and structured organization chart of the organizations involved in the implementation of the regional public policy in question. This can be explained by the fact each organization wants to protect its autonomy, and for the strategic pilot(s) it is perceived as risky to take the lead because the reactions of others is unknown. They also questioned whether they are capable of taking on the strategic piloting role.

Figure 17.2 illustrates the transorganizational aspect of the intervention and the **meso-socio-economic approach**. The figure portrays a group of actors as part of a strategy unfolding over the territory in question. Here, the socio-economic intervention takes place at the junction between the microeconomic (management of firms and organizations) and macroeconomic (monetary and fiscal policies, regulations on a large scale) levels. In that sense, the intervention takes place at the meso-economic level (see Figure 17.3).

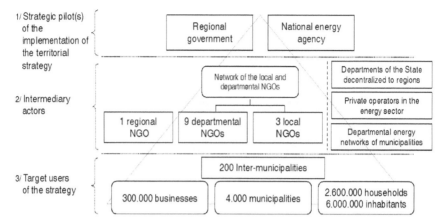

Figure 17.2.   Organization chart of the actors in the regional energy efficiency strategy.

Thus, the ***meso-socio-economic approach*** is the application of ***socio-economic analysis*** at the meso-level, in other words the SEAM intervention applied to a group of organizations linked by a strategic project in a given territory. Meso-socio-economic performance can thus be interpreted as ***social performance*** (e.g., individual and collective satisfaction through ***work conditions, work organization, communication-coordination-cooperation, time management, integrated training***, strategic implementation) as well as economic performance (e.g., efficient and effective use of resources to obtain ***immediate and sustainable economic results***, creation of new potential). The performance is generated by the group of ***actors*** involved in the implementation of a strategic plan in a defined territory.

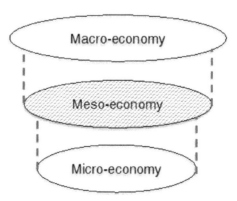

Figure 17.3.   Micro-, meso- and macro-economic levels.

The Organization of Actors is Crucial to Territorial Management

Improving the performance and *competitiveness* of a territory relies on the ability to mobilize and involve actors in a given strategy and to coordinate and get them "ready for battle" so as to implement a program of actions (more or less defined and shared) and to assess their contribution to the achievement of strategic objectives (beyond the usual self-centered and self-justifying attitude centered on obtaining subsidies) (Pierre, 2013). Work conducted on territorial innovation models (TIM) (Lagendijk, 2006; Moulaert & Sekia, 2003; Simmie, 2005) point out that appointing an effective moderator for the *interactions* between partners remains the key to success (Crevoisier, 2010).

In the case study, at the beginning of the *SEAM intervention*, the *cooperation* between the actors was described by actors as largely unsatisfying for a number of reasons. First, the cooperation within the network of NGOs was weak. Some organizations were embroiled in situations of conflict or non-communication with each other. Second, the *institutional actors* (regional government, national energy agency) felt that the collaborating NGOs did not effectively apply the public policies they were mandated to implement, and that, in some cases, they took advantage of the disagreement between themselves in order to pursue their own interests. Third, the main sources of funding for NGOs were subsidies granted by the two reference institutions. The target users did not pay for the services they received, a situation which had adverse effects on the quality of services and their relevance to the needs and constraints of the primary beneficiaries —the target users. Finally, the institutional actors collaborated mainly with the NGOs they funded and had difficulty working with other organizations, such as departmental energy networks of municipalities, governmental bodies decentralized to regions, and private operators in the energy sector. According to their own description of the situation, the institutions imagined that they were the "masters" of the NGOs that they largely subsidized. They did not know how to work in partnership with the organizations they did not fund.

The "Territory": An Organization Not Quite Like Others

The management of a territory means managing organizations with no hierarchical links between them, thus legally autonomous, acting at different levels, with different driving philosophies, and with complex relationships characterised at the same time by conflict, cooperation and negotiated interdependence (Broggio, 2012; Pierre, 2011; Zardet &

Noguera, 2006, 2014; Zardet & Pierre, 2007). Each actor in a given territory tends to pursue self-interested goals of its own, but, according to Perroux's (1969) theory of economic relationships, pure conflict is detrimental to creation of wealth, thus the pursuit of performance implies both conflict and cooperation between actors. SEAM supports this line of thinking, which differs from both classical and Marxist conceptions of economy.

There were complex relationships between the actors in the case study. The regional government and the national energy agency had a limited influence on the actors of the territorial strategy. They had a dominant position over the NGOs only because they largely financed them and they made the most of their dependency. The institutional actors did not know how to develop partnerships with other organizations, in particular when it came to the private operators. It revealed a divergence of working philosophies as well as negative preconceptions between both public and private sectors. Strong rivalries existed among the NGOs, which compete to improve their image, to hold a monopoly on certain services in a given territory, as well as to obtain subsidies from the institutional actors. Tensions also existed between the two reference institutions that had difficulty working together. Finally, the organizations did not know how to communicate with the actors working at a different level (local, departmental, regional, national, international) and articulate their services.

Managing Cooperation Within Networks

Where auto-organization takes place, "conflicts" tend not to be managed and cooperation among members of the network is weak and unsustainable (Pierre, 2011). When the *strategic piloting* of an organization improves, conflicts are managed and cooperation is more efficient. Our research underlines the need for better management of the network. The SEAM method enables the identification of *dysfunctions* and *hidden costs*, which are detrimental to the efficient running of organizations. Hidden costs are *destruction of value-added*, which is partly or completely left out of a company's accounting information system, consisting of both surplus expenditures and opportunity costs that affect the relevance of decision-making processes (Buono & Savall, 2007). Our research extends this work, underling the capacity to identify hidden costs in the context of territories (Pierre, 2011, 2014; see Table 17.1).

Hidden costs (Savall, 1975, 1981; Savall & Zardet, 2008) weaken the *efficiency* of the use of public funds and require extensive consultations and collaboration between actors to convert them into added value through *improvement actions* (Zardet & Noguera, 2014). Table 17.1shows us that the amount of the hidden costs in the case study were significant. The

Table 17.1.   Sample of Hidden Costs Observed

Identified dysfunction	Estimated hidden costs	Detail of calculation
Duplication of work: different institutional stakeholders deal with duplicate requests for subsidies from the same organization, and do not realize resulting from a lack of communication and absence of a streamlined process.	The hidden cost has been estimated at **140.000€** [177.000 USD], equal to the equivalent of 3200 hours that could be partially reallocated to restructure the agenda of the territorial engineers to manage the implementation of the territorial strategy and manage the network of NGOs.	*600 files per year processed in duplication by the regional government and national energy agency * 4 hours on average to process 1 file * 1 person doing the work uselessly * [HCVAVC] estimated at 59€ [75 USD].*
The lack of involvement of strategic stakeholders in the implementation of policies, results in a lost opportunity for engaging new resources.	The hidden cost has been estimated at **4.800.000€** [6.000.000 USD], equal approximately to the cumulated payroll of the 13 NGOs of the network, representing theoretically the possibility to double the workforce	*The estimated equivalent of 300 people that could be mobilized as intermediary partners (from departments of the State decentralized to regions, private operators in the energy sector, departmental energy networks of local authorities) and could spend 20% of their time to achieve the regional strategic goals * 200 days worked per year * 7 hours per day * HCVAVC estimated at 59€ [75 USD].*
Re-allocation of remaining funds in budgets due to the lack of strategic piloting of the projects and partners subsidies by the regional government	The hidden cost has been estimated at **2.250.000€** [2.800.000 USD], equal approximately to third of the cumulated budget of the 13 NGOs, and to more than 10% of the budget of the regional council invested in the energy efficiency policy.	*In 2008, 350.000 € [440.000 USD] have been reallocated from the operating budget used to finance NGOs and research, and 1.900.000 € [2.400.000 USD] from the investment budget.*
The lack of diversification of the funding sources represents a lost of financial resources to implement the territorial strategy	The hidden cost has been estimated at **2.100.000€** [2.600.000 USD], equal approximately to third of the cumulated budget of the 13 NGO of the network.	*The lack of development of funding alternatives of the NGOs, notably by the development of the promotion of their services to the target users of the regional strategy, in particular the municipalities and the inter-municipalities has been estimated at 30% of the cumulated budget of the 13 NGOs.*
The problems in the running of the NGOs, as identified in the NGOs that have benefited from the intra-organizational SEAM intervention, generate a loss of "strategic force" permitting the NGOs to be proactive and positive stakeholders in the network and in the implementation of the territorial strategy	The cumulated hidden costs identified in the regional NGO and in the departmental NGO have been estimated at **600.000€** [700.000 USD], equal approximately to the operating budget of the departmental NGO, or equal approximately to 10000 hours of work valued with the HCVAVC.	*Sum of the hidden costs identified in the regional NGO (350.000€ or 440.000 USD) and in the departmental NGO studied (250.000€ or 310.000 USD).*

HCVACV: Hourly Contribution to Value Added on Variable Costs (Savall, Zardet, 2008)

"recycling" of these hidden costs (see Figure 17.4) is a way to combine the management of the allocation of *resources* with the improvement of the quality of the *public action* (Pierre, 2011, 2013, 2014). Moreover, reducing working hours devoted to poor value added activities allows for the reallocation of resources to the functions of strategic piloting and partnerships management that represent very high added value.

1. Dysfunctions identified → Hidden costs identified
2. Material and immaterial investment in improvement actions Reduction of dysfunctions →Reduction of hidden costs →Self-financing of the initial investment

Figure 17.4.   The process of recycling hidden costs.

Strategic piloting is required for success in the effective recycling of the hidden costs. Effective skills, tools, and methods of management must be acquired (Pierre, 2011). Zardet and Noguera (2014) have demonstrated the value of transferring **SEAM *management tools*** within the transorganizational field of the territories. Where strategic co-piloting takes place (i.e., when implementation is shared between multiple strategic pilots), it is required that those involved communicate and coordinate among themselves to assume the strategic piloting role efficiently (Pierre, 2012).

In the case study, we observed the need for management to use strategic piloting in the network on a number of levels. NGOs expressed the need for an intervention by both institutional actors in order to stimulate cooperation in the network. The leading institutions lacked the skills to manage intermediary partners. The representatives of the regional government lacked the tools and methods necessary to intervene in the relationship between actors, to lead, coordinate and provide them with methodology in order to increase the efficiency of the contribution of each of the actors in the achievement of the territorial goals. It was also necessary to reinforce the relationships between institutional actors in order to ensure a more effective strategic co-piloting in the implementation of the territorial strategy.

ENHANCING THE STRATEGIC PILOTING OF NETWORKS

The behaviors of actors tend to be "deeply rooted" in their initial state, and their capacity to bring individually positive transformation is limited without ***external intervention***. This problem is due to the inertia generated by habits, fears, distrust of other co-operators, lack of vision of the potential gain of transformation, and so forth. In order to avoid resistance to change, a collective consultation is required, involving the "historical" actors as well as those that would be relevant for integrating the implementation of the territorial strategy. Seeking support from an external expert is recommended.

Managing the Transformation of Networks

SEAM intervention responds to these needs. The method structures collective thinking in order to (1) build a sufficient collective representation of the dysfunctions to be addressed and (2) identify a range of solutions for improvement at different levels (intra-organizational, inter-organizational). The SEAM method provides feedback, referred to as the *mirror-effect* and *expert opinion* including the reports of unvoiced comments, in order to overcome negative preconceptions and uncover taboo subjects among actors. *Non-dit* (unvoiced comments) is the second constituent of the expert opinion that finalizes the *socio-economic diagnosis*. In this instance, the intervener reports the major dysfunctions he or she perceived – but were not mentioned by actors during the diagnosis interviews (Buono & Savall, 2007). The feedback encourages increased collaboration and reduction of resistance to the change. The SEAM intervention leads the actors to express and develop possible avenues for *cooperation* in order to improve their collective performance in the context of the territorial strategy.

Another tool—the *Priority Action Plan* (PAP)—elaborated after the *project phase*, stimulates the implementation of agreed actions. This tool involves the distribution of responsibilities among piloting *actors* for each improvement action with planning timelines for each of them. In essence, PAPs are a coordinated inventory of actions to be accomplished within a period of six months to attain priority strategic objectives, once priorities have been defined and tested for feasibility (Buono & Savall, 2007).

The *SEAM intervention* also permits to consensually position the strategic pilot(s) of the implementation of the territorial strategy (see Figure 17.2). This is essential where the organizations are autonomous from a legal perspective. Moreover, the socio-economic intervention identifies organizational needs, especially in terms of acquisition of skills and *management tools* in order to be more effective and efficient in their roles. It responds to the need to deal with the deficiency of management in public organizations, a problem that has been pointed out by many authors who have elaborated the new public management theory (Gruening, 2001; Hood, 1991, 1995; Pollitt & Bouckaert, 2000).

In the case study, we observed that the SEAM intervention permitted the main actors to gather around the table to encourage strategic reflection, identify dysfunctions and strategic objectives, and develop improvement actions. These actors were also able to discuss the strategic piloting role of the regional government with the national energy agency to manage the network of NGOs. Realizing a meaningful intervention for the improvement of inter-institutional relationships, it further allowed for strengthened capacity to co-pilot the implementation of the territorial strategy. As the main actors identified areas for greater cooperation within the network of NGOs, they also began to question the negative preconceptions, harmful misbeliefs, and damaging historical relationships that had existed. By identifying ways to improve the strategic piloting of the actors of the territorial strategy, the actors formalized the identified improvement actions through the writing of a *Priority Action Plan* (PAP). Finally, the SEAM intervention helped to improve the internal *functioning* of the regional NGO and the departmental NGO to the point where both have benefited "within" their organization.

This analysis demonstrates the transorganizational effects of the intervention. We can also observe that the first effects of the SEAM intervention concerned the management of conflicts, helping to solve harmful *misunderstandings* and misconceptions by the actors. In addition, the socio-economic intervention helps foster positive cooperation between actors, and the re-allocation and the re-definition of roles in a concerted way, including the role of strategic piloting.

Long-Term Results

The effects obtained in the long term, without any action of interveners-researchers over a four-year period after the initial intervention, were significant. The authors have analyzed the improvements that remained and resulted in a profound transformation in the actors' relationships in terms of the functioning of the organizations, their philosophies, and their management processes.

Actors in the case study expressed the following comments on their experience of the SEAM intervention:

- A significant improvement of relations between the regional government and the national energy agency took place.
- Greater collaboration resulted from certain departmental NGOs with the regional NGO in the context of European projects.
- Strengthening of the governing body of the formal network of the local and departmental NGOs and the development of cooperation within this network.
- A desire by the regional government to increase the capacity of its representatives to manage the intermediary actors.
- A significant improvement in the preparation of contracts linking the *institutional actors* with the NGOs.
- The departmental NGO where a socio-economic intervention took place succeeded in its strategy for diversifying its funding sources,

by achieving its goal to limit donors to those funding under 20% of its overall budget.

Overall, the authors noted that actors overcame negative preconceptions against some private actors in the energy sector and against the strategy of the promotion of services by NGOs to target-users.

Need for Continued Improvement

It is relevant for continued improvement to identify the elements that have not considerably changed despite the SEAM intervention that represent potential possibilities for improvement. In the case study, the interviewees indicated a number of areas for improvement. One concern reflected the cooperation between the regional NGO and the rest of the network, which the actors felt needed to be developed further. There was a persisting need to enhance the strategic piloting of the implementation of the territorial strategy by institutional actors. This required greater involvement of elected representatives of the regional government in the implementation strategy and efforts to integrate management tools.

The use of tools, such as SEAM *competency grids*, to accompany the implementation of projects on territories would allow increased skills transfers and the facilitation of the distribution of responsibilities among intermediary actors, in particular between NGOs at different territorial levels. The competency grid is a synoptic tool displaying the *competences* currently available in a team and their concrete deployment (Buono & Savall, 2007). In the context of territories, the authors have named the tool "*meso-competency-grid*" (see Table 17.2). Another tool was the *Priority Action Plan* (PAP), a coordinated inventory of actions to be accomplished within a period of six months to attain priority strategic objectives, once priorities have been defined and tested for feasibility (Buono & Savall, 2007). There was also a desire to carry on with the development of contractual *negotiation tools*, using the *Periodically Negotiable Activity Contract* (PNAC). The PNAC is a *management tool* that formally states the priority objectives and the means made available for attaining them, involving every employee in the enterprise (including workers and office employees), based on a biannual personal dialogue with the employee's direct hierarchical superior (see Buono & Savall, 2007).

The actors also thought that it was important to "multiply" the number of operations that provided methodology to municipalities to manage their territorial projects, which could lead to better skills transfer and experience sharing among the NGO network. The reinforcement of the quality of the internal functioning of the NGOs needed to be developed by improving

Stakeholders	REALIZED OPERATIONS							
	Manage the implementation of the regional strategy	Deal with the requests for subsidies	Offer thematic expertise	Carry out feasibility studies	Provide methodology to the municipalities	Implement material installation	Capitalize and distribute strategic information	Evaluate the results of the implementations of the solution
Regional council	◖	■	■					◣
National Energy Agency	◖	■	■					◣
Regional NGO			■	◣	■		◣	◣
Departmental NGO			■	■	◖		◣	◣
Local NGO			■	■	◖		◣	◣
Energy networks of local authorities				■		■		◣
Vulnerability of the operation	VS	w	VS	vw	VS	w	S	S
Observation	To be developed		Risk of dispersion		Carry out a skills transfer		Need to allocate the focus point role	Conduct collective training

■	Total mastery of the operation	**VS** : Very Strong
◣	Need assistance at time	**S** : Strong
☐	Theorical knowledge without practice	**w** : weak
—	Neither theorical knowledge or practice	**vw** : Very weak
◯	To realize	

Source: Adapted from the ©ISEOR 1978 competency grid and applied to the case of territorial project; see Pierre (2013).

Table 17.2.   Simulation of a meso-skills-grid.

the *efficiency* and *effectiveness* of the use of their resources. There was also a strong interest in pursuing a continued collective reflection on ways to increase the efficiency of the regional policy, taking into account the decrease in the budgets of the institutional actors that affected the funds allocated to the NGOs. In that sense, it would be relevant to extend the strategy of diversifying funding sources of the departmental NGO, in which the SEAM intervention took place, to the entirety of the NGOs in the network.

The *meso-competency-grid* permits a synoptic vision of the skills required to implement the *strategic project*, the actors involved in the project, the distribution of roles, and the level of skills of each actor. This *meso-skills-grid* is a decision-making tool that identifies which skills need to be improved on a priority basis. It also allows for the identification of the possible skills transfers that could take place between actors in order to enhance versatility and flexibility.

The analysis and the control of **hidden costs**, as well as the **multi-Horivert** approach, which were tested by the ISEOR team in other sectors of activity and in other territories, seem to be relevant for responding to the current needs for improvement identified by the study. Based on the Horivert model created by the ISEOR team to implement socio-economic interventions within organizations, the multi-Horivert model has been developed to reduce the cost of **intervention-research projects** and create positive effects of competition between the multiple participating businesses, whose top-managers collectively received some services from the intervener-researchers.

The multi-Horivert model makes it possible to bring together in the SEAM process five or six **small organizations** from the same region as well as members of the institutional actors (e.g., Chamber of Commerce, Chamber of Notaries, regional government) that take part in the **collaborative-training** sessions dealing with **SEAM tools** and methods. The case study in this chapter presents some characteristics of the multi-Horivert process (e.g., realization of inter-organizational project's sessions), but the initial architecture did not strictly integrate this **socio-economic engineering** because only two NGOs benefitted from the SEAM intervention within their organization, and this without gathering together for training sessions. However the intra- and inter-organizational method (Pierre, 2007), which was proposed in the studied case, allowed the consolidation of an action plan to address the **dysfunctions** identified in the inter-organizational relationships and the **strategic piloting** of the implementation of the territorial strategy. Nevertheless, it is pertinent to reinforce our methodology with socio-economic interventions focused on the internal functioning of the actors, with certain elements of **diagnosis**, training and project sessions gathering the entire NGO network and institutional actors around the same table. This process would increase the **strategic force** of each member and, in turn, their capacity to integrate the territorial projects and achieve its strategic goals.

At the present time, the gap between set objectives and obtained results remains significant, demonstrating that it is necessary to pursue the deployment of the **strategic implementation** based on the multiple intermediary actors. The following questions were raised when the intermediate **evaluation** was presented in 2014, outlining the need for managerial innovation on territories:

- *Manager of the Regional Government:* "How [can we] get organized in order to deploy on the territory an intelligent network of actors?"
- *CEO from a departmental NGO:* "What kind of governing body [should we] adopt to work efficiently together based on the needs expressed in the field?"

CONCLUSION

This study underlines the value of enhancing the strategic piloting of a network to obtain better collective results than simply the sum of the individual performance of each actor. The individual performance of each NGO, as referenced in this paper, is diminished where conflict between members exists. The results of the research show the need to equip the strategic pilot(s) of the network (in the case study the regional government and the national energy agency) with new skills and management tools. It is also important to reinforce the *structure* of the relationships between the strategic pilots in the specific situation of strategic co-piloting of the network. The research illustrates the value of helping institutional actors to complete their role of regulator and public funds provider, with a role of strategic piloting of the actors involved in the implementation of the territorial strategy for which they are responsible (Pierre, 2011). The goal is to enhance the involvement of the actors and the quality of their contribution in order to achieve the territorial goals.

The evolution of the role of the institutional actors requires organizational change and *development*. The study demonstrates the value of the SEAM method in managing transformation in a structured way, facilitating a constructive dialogue between the actors of the territorial strategy. The chapter observes the manner in which a SEAM intervention helps to overcome an initial situation characterized by negative preconceptions between actors. The initial situation was also characterized by taboos and seemingly crystalized historical elements. The results of the research demonstrate the value of carrying out a *transorganizational socio-economic intervention* simultaneously at the *inter-organizational level* on the relationship between members of a network and at the *intra-organizational level*, enhancing the *internal cohesion* and the strategic force of each member in order to be proactive and act as positive players in the network and implementation of the territorial strategy.

The research demonstrates the potential to apply the SEAM method in the context of territorial strategies. Thus the method facilitates the identification of dysfunctions, hidden costs, and concrete *improvement actions* (i.e., auto-financed by the reduction of hidden costs they generate) by the intervener-researcher and actors. Territorial strategies or *projects* correspond to a level of action in between macro-economy (that have limits in terms of leverage on performance of territories) and micro-economy (that does not take enough in consideration the external cooperative environment of organizations). Therefore the meso-socio-economic approach offers interesting tools to manage the transformation requested by actors to address challenges faced by territories, in particular in terms of the management of the allocation of *public resources*.

NOTE

1. The research for this chapter has been influenced by a number of works that are not directly referred to in the text, including Boje and Rosile (2003), Gephart (2009), Perroux (1979), Savall (2012), Savall and Zardet (1987, 1992, 1995, 2005, 2009, 2011, 2013), and Savall, Zardet, and Bonnet (2000, 2008).

REFERENCES

Boje, D., & Rosile, G.-A. (2003). Comparison of socio-economic and other trans-organizational development methods. *Journal of Change Organizational Management, 16*(1), 10–20.

Broggio, C. (2012). La région, cadre privilégié du management territorial [French Regions, the ideal level of government for territorial management]. In J. Bonnett (Ed.), *Aménagement et développement territorial* [Installation and territorial development] (pp. 29–52). Paris, France: Ellipses.

Buono, A. F., & Savall, H. (Eds.) (2007). *Socio-Economic intervention in organizations: The intervener-researcher and the SEAM approach to organizational analysis.* Charlotte, NC: Information Age Publishing.

Cappelletti, L. (2007). Intervening in small professional enterprises: Enhancing management quality in French notary publics. In A.F. Buono & H. Savall (Eds). *Socio-economic intervention in organizations: The intervener-researcher and the SEAM approach to organizational analysis* (pp. 331–353). Charlotte, NC: Information Age Publishing.

Conbere, J., & Heorhiardi, A. (2011). Socio-economic approach to management: A successful systemic approach to organizational change. *OD Practitioner, 43*(1), 6–10.

Crevoisier, O. (2010). La pertinence de l'approche territoriale [The relevance of applying a territorial approach]. Revue d'Économie Régionale & Urbaine, 5(December), 969–985.

Gephart, R. P. (2009). An invitation to ethnostatistics. *Revue Sciences de gestion – Management Sciences – Ciencias de Gestión, 70,* 85.

Gruening, G. (2001). Origin and theoretical basis of new public management. *International Public Management Journal, 4,* 1–25.

Hood, C. (1991). A public management for all seasons. *Public Administration, 69*(1), 3–19.

Hood, C. (1995). The "new public management" in the 1980s: Variations on a theme. *Accounting, Organizations and Society, 20*(2–3), 93–109.

Lagendijk, A. (2006). Learning from conceptual flow in regional studies: Framing present debates, unbracketing past debates. *Regional Studies, 40*(4), 385–399.

Moulaert, F. & Sekia, F. (2003). Territorial Innovation Models. *Regional Studies, 37*(3), 289–302.

Perroux, F. (1969). *L'économie du XXe siècle* [The economy of the 20th century]. Grenoble, France: Presse Universitaire de Grenoble.

Perroux, F. (1979). L'entreprise, l'équilibre rénové et les coûts cachés [The enterprise, the renovated balance and the "hidden" costs]. Preface. In H. Savall. *Reconstruire l'entreprise* [Reconstructing the enterprise] Paris, France: Dunod. 2nd ed. in H. Savall & V. Zardet. Reconstruire l'entreprise, Paris : Dunod (2014)

Pierre, X. (2007). Méthode de diagnostic intra et interorganisationnel dans le cadre de démarches territoriales [Intra and Inter-organizational Diagnosis Method in the Context of Territorial Projects]. Colloquium sponsored by ISEOR and the Research Methods Division, Academy of Management. Lyon, France (June).

Pierre, X. (2011). *Pilotage institutionnel des coopérations interorganisationnelles – La mise en œuvre de stratégies territoriales* [Institutional Piloting of Inter-organizational Cooperation – the Implementation of Territorial Strategies]. Sarrebruck: Éditions Universitaires Européennes.

Pierre, X. (2012). *Coopérations interinstitutionnelles : Enjeux, difficultés, impacts économiques, actions possibles* [Inter-institutional cooperation: Stakes, difficulties, economic impacts, and possible actions for improvement]. Colloquium sponsored by ISEOR and the Organization Development and Change Division, Academy of Management. Lyon, France (June).

Pierre, X. (2013). *Compétitivité des territoires : les coopérations entre les acteurs du territoire source d'avantages concurrentiels?* [Competitiveness of Territories: Cooperation between Local Actors as a Source of Competitive Advantage?]. Journée François Perroux, Lyon, France (September).

Pierre, X. (2013). *Résoudre l'équation – maitrise des dépenses tout en améliorant l'action publique – par l'analyse à la loupe de la mise en œuvre des politiques sur les territoires* [Solve the equation—control public spending while improving public action—by observing the implementation of policies on territories with a magnifying glass]. 3rd Congrès Transatlantique de Comptabilité, Contrôle, Audit, Contrôle de Gestion et Gestion des coûts, in partnership with ISEOR, American Accounting Association, and l'Institut International des Coûts (IIC). Lyon (June).

Pierre, X. (2014). *Efficacité et efficience de l'action territoriale* [Efficiency and effectiveness of territorial action]. 3rd Colloque de l'AIRMAP [Management public], Aix-en-Provence, France (May).

Pollitt, C., & Bouckaert, G. (2000). *Public management reform : A comparative analysis.* Oxford, UK: University Press.

Savall, H. (1974–1975–1977). *Enrichir le travail humain dans les entreprises et les organisations* [An economic evaluation of job enrichment]. Paris: Dunod.

Savall, H. (1981–2010). *Work and people: An economic evaluation of job enrichment.* 1st ed. New York: Oxford University Press ; 2nd ed. Charlotte, NC: Information Age Publishing

Savall, H. (2007). ISEOR's socio-economic method: A case of scientific consultancy. In A. F. Buono & H. Savall (Eds.), *Socio-economic intervention in organizations: The intervener-researcher and the SEAM approach to organizational analysis* (pp. 1–31). Charlotte, NC: Information Age Publishing.

Savall, H. (2012). *Origine radicale des crises économiques: Germán Bernácer, précurseur visionnaire* [Root origin of crises: Germán Bernácer, a visionary forerunner]. Charlotte, NC: Information Age Publishing.

Savall, H., & Zardet, V. (1987). *Maîtriser les coûts et les performances cachés : Le contrat d'activité périodiquement négociables* [Mastering hidden costs and performance: The periodically negotiable activity contract]. Paris: Economica.

Savall, H., & Zardet, V. (1992). *Le nouveau contrôle de gestion: Méthode des coûts-performances cachés* [New management control: The hidden cost-performance method]. Paris: Éditions Comptables Malesherbes-Eyrolles

Savall, H., & Zardet, V. (1995–2005–2009). *Ingénierie stratégique du roseau, souple et enracinée* [Strategic engineering of the reed, flexible and rooted]. Paris: Economica.

Savall, H., & Zardet, V. (2008). *Mastering hidden costs and performance*. Charlotte, NC: Information Age Publishing.

Savall, H., & Zardet, V. (2011). *The qualimetrics approach: Observing the complex object*. Charlotte, NC: Information Age Publishing.

Savall, H. & Zardet, V. (2013). *The dynamics and challenges of tetranormalization*. Charlotte, NC: Information Age Publishing.

Savall, H., Zardet, V., & Bonnet, M. (2000–2008). *Releasing the untapped potential of enterprises through socio-economic management*. Geneva: Éditions IOT-BIT.

Simmie, J. (2005). Critical surveys edited by Stephen Roper innovation and space: A critical review of the literature. *Regional Studies, 39*(6), 789–804.

Zardet, V. & Noguera, F. (2006). Cas de recherche-intervention de trois territoires-pilotes d'une Région [The case of a research-intervention on three pilot-territories in a French region]. In ISEOR (Ed.), *Le Management du développement des territoires* (pp. 131–149). Paris, France: Economica.

Zardet, V., & Noguera, F. (2014). Quelle contribution du management au développement de la dynamique territoriale ? Expérimentation d'outils de contractualisation sur trois territoires [What is the contribution of management to the development of territories? The testing of contractual tools on three territories]. *Gestion et Management Public, 2*(2), 5–31.

Zardet, V., & Pierre, X. (2007). *Distance spatiale et cognitive entre acteurs impliqués dans le management d'un territoire* [Spatial and cognitive distances between actors involved in the management of a French region]. Paper presented at Atelier de l'AIMS : Stratégies, Espaces et Territoires, Loin, proche : la dimension spatiale dans le management des organisations. Orléans, France (November).

CHAPTER 18

PUBLIC SERVICE MODERNIZATION AND SOCIO-ECONOMIC PERFORMANCE[1]

Véronique Zardet and Samantha Rose

The modernization of public services is a major issue for public authorities and delegated public service organizations. The latter are faced with challenges that necessitate *in-depth organizational change*. This chapter presents the case of a French delegate *public service* entity, designated by the letter U, in which we have conducted since 1995 a *socio-economic intervention-research*.

THE CHALLENGES OF PUBLIC SERVICE ORGANIZATIONS

In all the countries of the Organization for Economic Cooperation and Development (OECD), the modernization of public service is an important challenge following the 2002 launch of a proposed relaxation of the public sector by the public Governance Committee of OECD. The requirements,

The Socio-Economic Approach to Management Revisited: The Evolving Nature of SEAM in the 21st Century, pp. 359–376
Copyright © 2015 by Information Age Publishing
359

in terms of quality and *productivity*, increases because citizens demand a faster and higher level of quality of services rendered.

Modernization of Public Services in Developed Countries

Financial constraints that weigh on delegated public service organizations have become more stringent. Users increasingly require more transparency in the allocation of their taxes, and the government puts pressure on the public sector organizations to increase their performance. Finally, business requirements rise and new services appear. This results in increased automation and computerization of the tertiary public sector. However, public-private partnerships are particularly slow to develop, especially in France. It took, for example, three years to convince French parliamentarians to accept that a departmental public sector entity, in which we intervened, provides payroll service to refreshment employers, which was until now exclusively provided by accountants.

Scarcity of Public Financial Resources

Like businesses, public services are called upon to change rapidly, with declining *resources*. They are experiencing "financing gaps because of excessive debt and political and social reactions that reject new taxes and social contributions" (Savall & Zardet, 2011, p. 2). However, "despite budgetary constraints, public services can be *competitive*, improving the quality of management, the degree of staff involvement and their skills *development*" (Savall & Zardet, 2011, p. 3). Thus, while it is true that increasing the *efficiency* and *effectiveness* of public service organizations (PSOs) has become a true necessity because the procedures and working methods are outdated, these organizations have considerable productivity reserves but "that can only be mobilized by stronger involvement (behavior and skills) of personal at all levels of the Administration" (p. 2).

Proliferation in Government and Public Service Organization Mergers

Organizational strategies once reserved for the private sector now extend to the public one. Mergers of PSOs have been increasing in an attempt to obtain *economies of scale*. One of the challenges is to increase synergies while under financial constraint, increasing the services rendered to contributors. Nonetheless, due to resistance to change in PSOs, existence of statutory protections for certain behaviors, and/or difficulties encountered by management in the performance of its duties, merger processes in government and PSOs (e.g., Social Security organisms, chambers of commerce and industry, public agencies employment) are difficult and slow.

The organization in which we intervened is composed of a national network with national public policy missions, consisting of various private organizations, with 14,000 employees, who fall under a collective agreement. It depends on a national agency, itself attached and financed by the French State. The national agency is in charge of cash management, with flows of 450 billion euros per year. In 2013, the entire network collected about 235 billion euros. At the national level, this represents 7.8 million employer contributor accounts.

U collects social security contributions (sickness, maternity, old age, unemployment) of French employers and employees, and manages those resources in real time. Its activities include the identification of taxpayers, collection of contributions, distribution to the beneficiaries (e.g., health insurance, employment center, old age insurance), statements control, and litigation management. It plays the role of statements and payments facilitator for the contributors. In 2013, U had 390 employees and managed 208,000 contributor accounts.

U sought to develop its services on a continuous basis. Thus, it managed to improve information access for users through the creation of a website providing new opportunities, such as documentation and information available online and updated frequently. Dematerialization also facilitated and secured returns and payments. In addition, U developed services of regulatory conformity control, diagnosis before a decision, and service offers with *external partners* (e.g., securing contracts and employee savings agreements, guarantee of a uniform application of the legislation). Of course, all of these services, in particular those based on the consultant's advice, do not have the same success and are not known to the public. Indeed, the French PSOs, particularly those responsible for collecting taxes and contributions, suffered from a somewhat degraded image among users, especially in terms of the quality of services rendered.

An important issue in any merger or acquisition is to establish adequate and structured support for all the *actors* affected by the reorganization. Otherwise, and at all levels of an organization, the *risk* of lower productivity and an increase in quality defects is high, as shown by Buono and Savall (2007).

THE SOCIO-ECONOMIC INTERVENTION:
A LONGITUDINAL LEARNING PROCESS

Prior to 1990, U was old, expensive, and rated poorly with regard to counterpart organizations, with a Taylorist and bureaucratic organizational operating approach without any account of expected results. From 1990 to 1995, *participative management* practices had appeared, but with a lack of *coordination* and synchronization of actions. Nevertheless, this marked the beginning of the modernization of the U management.

The Installation Phase: 1995 to 1998

Since 1995, in search of a management method "likely to make lasting change its internal *functioning*" (Director of U, 2009) and to retain the benefits of participatory management while developing U synchronization, U requested ISEOR's assistance. Thus, U began practicing *socio-economic management* and cooperating with ISEOR since 1995, after the discovery by the agency head of the *synchronized decentralization* concept, in a thesis directed by Henri Savall at ISEOR. U's challenge was to steer local energies, multiply the poles of initiatives, and articulate and ensure consistency between those poles. The practice of operating performance contracts, such as *priority action plans*, which formalize an inventory of concerted actions to carry out in a semester to achieve *strategic objectives*, appeared to U's leader as an opportunity to develop synchronized decentralization. Its goal was to move from the 95th to the first place in the national ranking of organisms. The underlying aim was to put the concept of development in the center of the organization's management.

From 1995 to 1998, ISEOR undertook a *horizontal diagnosis* followed by a *project group*, two *vertical diagnoses* in the logistics and management departments of contributor accounts, followed by *vertical projects* and socio-economic management training for top and middle management. The methodology and tools were transferred to nearly 100 people, by ISEOR interveners and *internal-interveners* trained in socio-economic management *engineering*. At the same time, in an effort to solidify the *implementation* of this approach, two senior executives obtained master's degrees in socio-economic management at the University where ISEOR interveners-researchers teach.

Low Maintenance: 2000–2011

For 12 years, from 2000 to 2012, new executives recruited in U followed the inter-company training courses offered by ISEOR, namely "Making Change," "Self-Finance Company," and "The Number 1" followed by U's CEO. These courses provided the opportunity for U executives to meet with other companies, exchanging information on changes already implemented, comparing the challenges, looking for solutions to overcome them. These inter-companies training sessions contributed greatly to consolidate the implementation of socio-economic management in an organization, combining the contributions of approaches within and between companies.

Although the first results were obtained in the short term, the most important appeared in the early 2000s. Operating costs were reduced based on a *recycling of dysfunctions*. U management costs decreased between 2002 and 2008 from 0.63% to 0.26% of the amount received in contributions, potentially equivalent to 15% of progressive downsizing by voluntary departure rather than by redundancy. But instead of reducing them, U negotiated with the National Agency to reallocate these potential performance deposits created by the reduction in operating costs to the deployment of new services to contributors, such as the management of "universal service employment checks," recovering 40 billion euro (discussed later in the chapter). It is in this way that U has supported, without any additional personnel, the management of national major accounts, which until then was centralized in the Paris office.

Preparing Regionalization Without Outside Intervention

The decision to regionalize the network of organizations, that is to say, to adopt a territorial organization mode focused on regions, came from the French government and was led by the National Agency. The number of organizations decreased from 88 departmental entities to 22 regional entities. This was a major focus of the 2012–2013 objectives and management convention, which is a contracting tool, concluded between the French government and the National Agency. The national objective set for regionalization was to improve services rendered to users (e.g., telephone response), fight against fraud, and development of services. As for U, the merger project of eight departmental entities (including U) in a regional entity began in September 2011 and was completed on January 1, 2014 by the actual start of the new regional entity. This reform was based on the assumption that, thanks to their size increase, the entities would pool all resources and standardize processes between different agencies, which were expected to enhance the coherence of decisions with regard to contributors and improve overall performance. The eight entities included from 50 to 350 agents; the new regional entity boasted 1,500 agents.

This change had multiple impacts on functioning and management. Thus, in this context of *rapid growth*, the CEO of the new entity saw, literally overnight, his number of collaborators multiplied by five. Indeed, the incumbent CEO of U since 1995 was selected as future director of the regional entity. His goal was to maintain, at the regional entity level, the principle of synchronized decentralization despite constraining national organizational instructions. Indeed, the National Agency determined

13 processes and, for each of them, a national commission was set up by region, and had a functional role. The principle of synchronized decentralization of U resulted in the implementation of *priority action plans* put forward by departmental sites, articulated at the regional level, and co-piloted by regional and departmental levels.

The national goal of regionalization was to drive directly all transverse processes from the national headquarters in drafting the action plans. Directors of the business units drove these functions at the national headquarters and 22 regional head offices. Their role was to decline national action plans, which was a strong change for people used to be independent in their units. The history of public management, as well as *large groups* in general, shows that managing from the central level malfunctions, causing dysfunctions at the *interfaces* between operational and functional units. The peculiarity of the regional U was its quality partnership with the different business support departments, state wise or local long. Thus, in 2008, the economic crisis led to the creation of a new *horizontal partnership* structure of business support at the regional level, including financial support, composed of various public regional agencies, a committee of local banks, and U. The Committee partnership had quality and financial aids granted to important enterprises.

The preparation of the regional merger from 2011 to 2013 was carefully carried out by a *plenary regional steering committee*, with the involvement of 100 managers. The aim was to harmonize the different working methods and procedures of the eight entities and adapt the management of human resources. The numbers of executives were reduced by approximately 20 to 25% as a result of retirements and transfers. A 10% decrease of staff in support functions was reallocated to operational functions.

Socio-Economic Management Intervention: 2013–2014

Since January 2014, the eight departmental entities were a regional entity composed of a regional team and eight departmental sites. The eight former departmental directors took a function at the headquarters or became site manager. In doing so, they all lost, except the Regional Director, their "number 1" status in the departmental U, which enjoyed legal independence. The legal status of the personnel, which until this point was very protective, is evolving, and five-year contracts for the Directors were formalized in order to put the emphasis on the objectives expected of them.

Challenges of the New Regional Entity

At this point, the regional body had the lone legal responsibility for the sites, which represented 1,500 employees, 700,000 contributor accounts, and 33 billion euros of contributions received. These sites were of great diversity, both in terms of situations and/or sizes and were geographically distant, at considerable distances from each other up to 200 kilometers. **Work organizations** and management methods were disparate, even if the will of the region was to gradually have a unified operation system.

A New HORIVERT at the Region Level

The objective was to implement socio-economic management across the regional entity, so as to find the "right" level of autonomy for the departmental directors. The advantage of socio-economic management is its *agility* (Worley, Bonnet, Zardet, & Savall, 2015), taking into account the actors' needs with regard to the company.

In addition to this challenge, the skills of the people present on the sites did not necessarily correspond to the new activities of these sites. That strong mismatch between training and employment was an important organizational and human issue, and the use of **competency grid** facilitated the process of driving and reducing this gap. Another important challenge was the complexity in the management of 30 directors, whose vast majority has lost autonomy and responsibility following the merger. This situation required intense steering, supported by the implementation of **priority action plan**, competency grids, and the realization of **socio-economic diagnoses**. As noted by one of the participants at the department level,

> With regionalization, we went from eight directors and eight accountants to only one director and only one accountant, the full-managers and accounting agents lost their prerogatives and their status. It is difficult to live [in this situation]. (Accountant, Departmental Entity, 2013)

In 2013, during the preparation of the merger, to initiate the **extension** of socio-economic management, a **horizontal diagnosis** of future regional direction agents, about 20 people, was carried out, starting with the two larger sites with 350 and 150 persons (see Figure 18.1). The objectives were to:

- organize **communication-coordination-cooperation** between both the regional and departmental levels, between business and support functions;
- organize **collaborative delegation** between those levels; and
- enhance the contribution of the regional management members and executives in the proposed strategic actions and their steering, based on a business executive testimony who implanted the **socio-economic management**.

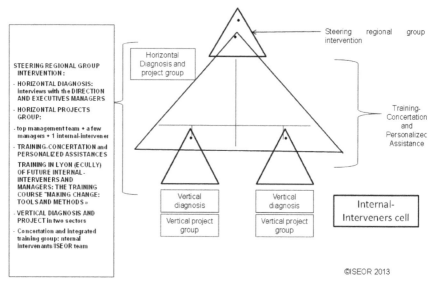

Figure 18.1.   2013 HORIVERT action.

The horizontal diagnosis and training-concertations were conducted in U. The collective axis of the intervention was to ensure that some services would not find themselves in difficulty in January 2, 2014, starting date of the regionalization.

In 2014, the possibility of deploying socio-economic management throughout the region was raised. A **HORIVERT** action, five **vertical actions** and the strengthening of an **internal-intervener** cell, was proposed (see Figure 18.2). The objective was to accompany the regional U to achieve its goals and commitments, clarify internal roles, and preserve and consolidate the achievements of socio-economic management through the support of an internal-intervener cell, which was strengthened in numbers and skills. The intervention required training 24 members of the top management team in a common set of **socio-economic management tools**, through training-concertation and deploying these tools in all eight sites among middle managers.

RESULTS OF THE SOCIO-ECONOMIC INTERVENTION

One of the objectives desired by the national agency with regard to the merger was the centralization of operational and support functions of each regional union. An obligation was made to regional unions to organize support functions centrally, while for the business functions it was a national

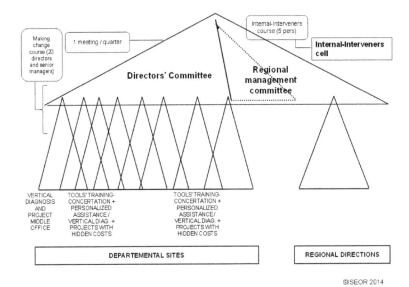

Figure 18.2. 2014 HORIVERT action.

recommendation without any obligation. However, the regional director wanted to combine this national recommendation with the principle of *synchronized decentralization*, which had been applied since 1995 in the departmental organization he led. This political will was justified by the conviction, based on his experience—that the only responsibility of each *actor* in the organization was to jointly improve *productivity* time, personnel and contributor satisfaction.

Synchronized Decentralization: Management Engineering

The governance of social security institutions has been assured for decades by contracting in two stages. First, the ministry in charge of social security signs an objectives agreement of management (OAOM) with the national agency. The latter then formalizes multiannual management contracts (MMC) with each of the regional agencies, with particular emphasis on *directly productivity time*, *efficiency*, *effectiveness* and service quality objectives.

U had implemented a management *engineering* initiative, translating multi-year objectives of the MMC in an *Internal and External Strategic Action Plan* (IESAP) consisting of formalizing, in addition to multi-year objectives, axes and strategic actions deployed over the contract period.

Then, the **IESAP**, in turn, is translated into semi-annual **priority actions plans**, successively broken down as follows: regional entity PAP, departmental entities PAP, services and departments PAP within each departmental entity, and PAP of support directions of the regional entity. Finally, concerning the executives, the **periodically negotiable activity contract (PNAC)** allows contractualizing team and individual objectives containing an additional variable remuneration. Indeed, the national collective agreement allowed a performance bonus for executives.

During so important a transition period due to regionalization, **priority action plans** installed in the entire region also allowed, without waiting for the complete validation of the MMC, the organization of steps to be taken and priority actions associated with the merger of departmental entities. The regional director also decided that each site director would be hierarchically responsible for operational employees from his site. By national decision, collaborators from support functions (e.g., Human Resources, Logistics), most of them located in the regional office and a smaller part in the sites, were hierarchically linked to a "function driver" (equivalent to a functional director) located at the regional headquarters. These 22 regional function drivers were connected to the national function driver (see Figure 18.3).

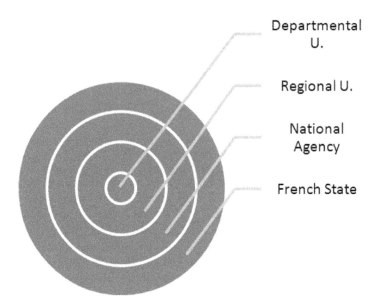

Figure 18.3.   From French State to Departmental U by National Agency and Regional U.

The Measured Increased Effectiveness and Efficiency

Since 1995, performance improvement results were recorded on a number of dimensions.

Social Performance

The installation of socio-economic management facilitated increased *internal cohesion* between the direction and management, deploying personnel training actions, especially regarding management technicians and obtaining services and management tools certification. The *development* of the professional skills of the collaborators was also accomplished through *integrated training*, mentoring, and *concerted delegation*. Part of this increase was also due to the allocation of skill points defined in national collective agreement, which was a major lever. These skills were acquired through support of the trainee in professional situations by a tutor, whether it was for taking a new position or on account of innovation. The mentoring principle was very important in the skills development of this organization – the tutor, often a colleague, supported his colleagues in their learning process. The training by mentoring was conducted at short intervals, every week, and by short sequences as the training needs were identified.

Economic and Business Performance

Organizational performance ratios all increased, thanks to productivity gains from *hidden costs recycling*, which led to improvements in short-term performance and the self-financing of medium-term developments in the organization. Business performance measures also increased. There was a general strengthening of management control practices and internal control, combined with productivity gains, which enabled the deployment of new services. Thus, the redeployment of "job titles services companies" had an impact on the relief of administrative formalities that *small businesses*, with less than 10 people, had previously to provide.

The first step in the *implementation of socio-economic management* in the departmental entity in 1995 led to an increase in productivity and quality of service. To contain downsizing, the leaders spontaneously proposed to the National Agency the need to support the national missions with constant *resources*. Thus, with the same workforce more missions were ensured. As an example, among the national missions entrusted to the department then regional agency, these new missions included the management of national major clients accounts, the management of "universal service check," the management of "title employment service business," and, more recently, the French cross-border management service of employees in Switzerland. In the 2008–2011 period, over 3 million salary slips were made by the organization in favor of more than 180,000 small businesses throughout the French territory.

Quality performance of services is certified by the French standards agency (AFNOR) for certification concerning telephone reception, which includes: being available 10:30 daily for five working days of the week, response rate to calls exceeding 90%, physical reception of contributors up to 40 hours per week, limited waiting time at the counter, the possibility of personalized appointments, and email response commitment, within 48 hours regarding simple questions and 15 days for complex subjects. The adaptation of the organization, processes, operation methods and behaviors to new challenges and constraints of public service enabled faster and more responsive management of the organization, better *vertical and horizontal synchronization*, and larger collective mobilization and involvement. The following are field note quotes illustrating these results as expressed by U-executives.

- We succeeded in building a strong internal cohesion while training our personnel and involving basic technicians in this approach. We also increased our ratios and self-financed our development, which may seem extravagant for a public company. However, this has allowed us to generate productivity gains, to hunt for *hidden costs* and develop services taking advantage of released margin of manœuvre. (General Director of U, 2013).
- We were able to absorb the shock thanks to the efforts made for a certain number of years at the U. of Lyon. Multiple and significant efforts such as phone platforms of experts, charged with studying the economic problems of businesses and the adaptation of our litigation proceedings (General Director of U, 2011).
- So we can say that there has been a huge success rate as for payment delays that were sometimes accompanied by remission of debts by the company's creditors and public creditors (General Director of U, 2011).

LESSONS LEARNED

The work done by the team of ISEOR for 40 years with more than 1,350 companies and organizations, in both public and private sectors, made it possible to conclude that public sector organizations do not incur more hidden costs than private sector companies (see Chapter 2). As Savall and Zardet (2011, p. 1) have argued, "The production reserves in the public sector are of the same order of magnitude as in the private sector, contrary to generally accused ideas." Similarly the *recycling of hidden costs into value-added* is possible in both public and private sectors organizations. In the case of U, the efficiency increase that was observed was not a source of downsizing, as long as the organization could increase its bargaining power towards its environment, a purveyor of its economic resources. Indeed, the general direction of U has negotiated, with the National Agency which assigns its budgetary resources, the acceptance of new activities to avoid downsizing while increasing its efficiency and effectiveness.

This case also highlights the importance of three important conditions for improving the *socio-economic performance*: *synchronized decentralization*, the development of the role of *proximity management*, and *negotiation* with the governance of the founding principles of socio-economic management to ensure its acceptability and sustainability.

Synchronized Decentralization: A Highly Meaningful Principle

The implementation of socio-economic management in this organization was based on the principle of synchronized decentralization. Its durability in this case confirms that this principle is applicable in both public service and private sector organizations. This concept was first applied at the departmental entity level from 1995 to 2013, then served as the basis for the organization of the new regional entity with eight operating entities, as well as support services related directly to the regional direction. The fact that U practiced socio-economic management, and more precisely synchronized decentralization for 18 years, producing the durable performance described above, helped reinforce the position of the leader of U. This individual was appointed head of the new regional entity, in a careful preparation of the reorganization that the merger represented, and developed a preventive approach to avoid *dysfunctions*.

Dysfunctions related to merger and acquisition activities can affect all types of businesses and organizations. If they are not taken seriously, these dysfunctions have serious effects, because they cause such important hidden costs that they cancel the savings expected from the pooling of services and activities sought in a merger. Thus, bringing together the regional direction of headquarters, the service, and the people in charge of premises spread over a large geographical area is an economy that is only apparent, when the remoteness of these people vis-à-vis local entities entails delays in maintenance, significant travel expenses of maintenance personnel, additional travel time, and more complicated *communication-coordination-cooperation* between the regional and local entities (Buono & Savall, 2007).

Synchronized decentralization in the regional entity concretely led to set up local sites with hierarchical responsibility towards all personnel performing the operational activities. Leaders of these local sites were then in a position to develop their own *priority actions plan**, to negotiate with the regional direction, and to accompany their own collaborators to develop their own plan. It is how local management and regional management are articulated in this new configuration.

> The first analysis we can do on the socio-economic management is that its holistic, active in the short and long term, and ideally suited to national policies implemented in the administrative networks. You can compare this phenomenon with the principle of Russian dolls, because the ***value-added*** created is broken down with the help of ***strategic gear*** at each political, national, regional and local level.... The fight against these hidden costs is constant today in our organization. (CEO of U, 2011)

Development of the Managerial Role of Local Managers

The implementation of socio-economic management is an important challenge in all enterprises and organizations. It concerns the accompaniment of managers and, in particular, local managers who run the operational field teams, to shift from a technical and operational role to a role that provides more autonomy and operational responsibilities to field staff. This then allows managers to develop their own role in the management of people and activities. This transformation of the role of ***proximity managers*** is carried out especially with the training-concertation sessions in ***socio-economic management tools*** and ***socio-economic innovation project groups*** following diagnoses of dysfunctions and hidden costs. People management includes the management of jobs and ***competences*** of employees, the ***development*** and implementation of ***integrated training plans***, the development of employee involvement, the organization of team meetings, and individual interviews of negotiation and evaluation of ***periodically negotiable activity contracts***. Management activities consist of managing information, guiding people in achieving their activities, accompanying them, training them, controlling them so that they complete these terms in *time* and in the expected manner, and using established ***management tools*** such as ***piloting logbooks***, priority action plans, and objectives from periodically negotiable activity contracts.

The deployment of socio-economic management is thus accompanied, for all executives with managerial responsibilities, with a transformation of their role. As articulated by Henri Savall during ISEOR's "Making Change Successful" training course, "Take care of your employees, they will take care of your machines, your products and your customers."

Negotiating Governance

One might think that the choice of a management method is the sole responsibility of the top management team, in a subsidiary company or *public service* organization financed by regional or national governance, enjoying t a certain operational and *strategic autonomy*. However, multiple pilot actions we conducted in organizations and companies that are dependent on a public or private group or guardianship have taught us that, when the first performance improvement results are recorded and visible, the direction has interest in informing its governance of setting up of a management method it has chosen and the positive effects it has produced. This approach has two advantages. It shows the proactive approach of the organization or company in its quest to increase *sustainable socio-economic performance*. It prevents the possible phenomena of competition with other management methods, which could be driven or imposed by the group. In this case, U negotiated with its national supervision that it could rely on the socio-economic management as a method of public service modernization, even though other performance and management methods were advocated by the governance, such as the approach by process or "lean management."

> The first analysis we can do on socio-economic management is that its overall approach, active in the short and long term, is ideally suited to national policies implemented in the administrative systems. (CEO of U, 2009).

At the same time, as part of the preparation of regionalization, which lasted three years, the U entity encountered difficulties in having its advance in modernity and efficiency recognized by departmental colleagues. Since 1998, however, it has been the leader in terms of performance indicators among the eight departmental entities. But it was the victim of a phenomenon often observed in change processes when implanted in a process known as "oil spreading" (Savall & Zardet 1987, 2010): the more an entity is successful, the more it isolates itself and becomes vulnerable. In this case, it is not a design defect of the *engineering implementation* of change, it is the regionalization decision taken at the national level that created this situation. However, we have encountered similar situations, when a company practicing socio-economic management merges with one or more companies that do not practice this approach. In these situations there is often tension and jealousy inherent in the merger process due to the significant differential performance of the company—the good student is envied!

Finally, let us note once again a difficulty specific to merger and acquisition transactions. The director responsible for leading the regionalization process grew from a peer position when he was a colleague of other departmental entities directors to position of superior hierarchical over these directors. This entails brakes and resistance to change in the action of regionalization, which requires a lot of diplomacy and education from the regional entity director.

CONCLUSION

In organization U, the value-added of management tools came from a strong involvement of all managers in the preparation of different priority action plans, and from transverse and *vertical synchronization* of the different actions included in those tools.

We are, therefore, in the presence of a strategic gearing up from the State to the service of a few dozen people constituting the operating entities at the regional level. But the development of these tools also helps organize the up and down process, inserting in the *priority action plans* different levels of dysfunctional recycling actions identified through different *socio-economic diagnoses*. The upstream process is a major originality in an activity sector dominated by centralized decision-making processes and downstream declination of national policies.

This pilot action is also emblematic of the process of reallocation of time recovered by *recycling hidden costs into value-added*. The latter does not inevitably lead to downsizing, even if sometimes it is the only issue wished for or imposed by the governance.

NOTES

1. The research for this chapter has been influenced by a number of works that are not directly referred to in the text, including Boje and Rosile (2003), Gephart (2009), Perroux (1979), Savall (1974, 1975, 1977, 1981, 2010, 2012), Savall and Zardet (1987, 1992, 1995, 2005, 2009, 2011, 2013), and Savall, Zardet, and Bonnet (2000, 2008).

REFERENCES

Boje, D., & Rosile, G.-A. (2003). Comparison of socio-economic and other trans-organizational development methods. *Journal of Change Organizational Management, 16*(1), 10–20.

Buono, A.F., & Savall, H. (Eds.) (2007). *Socio-economic intervention in organizations: The intervener-researcher and the SEAM approach to organizational analysis.* Charlotte, NC: Information Age Publishing.

Gephart, R. P. (2009). An invitation to ethnostatistics. *Revue Sciences de gestion – Management Sciences – Ciencias de Gestión*, 70, 85.

Pansard, J.-C. (2012). *Panorama et particularités des entreprises familiales, dans Les entreprises familiales: Création, succession, gouvernance et management* [Panorama and peculiarities of family businesses, in family businesses: Creation, succession, governance and management]. Paris, France: Economica.

Pansard, J.-C. (2014). *Management socio-économique et projet stratégique,* dans La conduite du changement dans les entreprises et les organisations [Socio-economic management and strategic project, in change process in businesses and organizations]. Paris, France: Economica.

Perroux, F. (1979). L'entreprise, l'équilibre rénové et les coûts cachés [The enterprise, the renovated balance and the "hidden" costs]. Preface in H. Savall. *Reconstruire l'entreprise* [Reconstructing the enterprise] Paris, France: Dunod.

Pigaglio, G. (2009). *Management socio-économique dans les organisations de service public, dans Management socio-économique, une approche innovante* [Socio-economic management in organizations in public sector, in Socio-economic management, an innovative approach]. Paris, France: Economica.

Pigaglio, G. (2011). Crise, dynamique et perspectives nouvelles, dans Réussir en temps de crise, stratégies proactives des entreprises [Crisis, dynamic and new perspectives, in success in time of crisis]. Paris, France: Economica.

Pigaglio, G. (2013). *Effet d'entraînement des entreprises industrielles, dans Réindustrialisation et dynamisation multisectorielle* [Ripple effect in industrial companies, in reindustralization and multisectorial dynamic]. Paris, France: Economica.

Savall, H. (1974–1975–1977). *Enrichir le travail humain dans les entreprises et les organisations* [An economic evaluation of job enrichment]. Paris: Dunod.

Savall, H. (1981–2010). *Work and people: An economic evaluation of job enrichment.* 1st ed. New York: Oxford University Press ; 2nd ed. Charlotte, NC: Information Age Publishing

Savall, H. (2012). *Origine radicale des crises économiques: Germán Bernácer, précurseur visionnaire* [Root origin of crises: Germán Bernácer, a visionary forerunner]. Charlotte, NC: Information Age Publishing.

Savall, H., & Zardet, V. (1987). *Maîtriser les coûts et les performances cachés : Le contrat d'activité périodiquement négociable* [Mastering hidden costs and performance: The periodically negotiable activity contract]. Paris: Economica.

Savall, H., & Zardet, V. (1992). *Le nouveau contrôle de gestion: Méthode des coûts-performances cachés* [New management control: The hidden cost-performance method]. Paris: Éditions Comptables Malesherbes-Eyrolles

Savall, H., & Zardet, V. (1995–2005–2009). *Ingénierie stratégique du roseau, souple et enracinée* [Strategic engineering of the reed, flexible and rooted]. Paris: Economica.

Savall, H., & Zardet, V. (2008). *Mastering hidden costs and performance.* Charlotte, NC: Information Age Publishing.

Savall, H., & Zardet, V. (2011). *Présentation du modèle de gestion socio-économique [Presentation of the socio-economic management model*. Working paper. *OECD Conference*. Paris, France.

Savall, H., & Zardet, V. (2011). *The qualimetrics approach: Observing the complex object*. Charlotte, NC: Information Age Publishing.

Savall, H., & Zardet, V. (2013). *The dynamics and challenges of tetranormalization*. Charlotte, NC: Information Age Publishing.

Savall, H., Zardet, V. & Bonnet, M. (2000–2008). *Releasing the untapped potential of enterprises through socio-economic management*. Geneva: Éditions IOT-BIT.

Worley, C., Zardet, V., Bonnet, M., & Savall, A. (2015). *Becoming agile: How the SEAM approach to management builds adaptability*. New York, NY: John Wiley and Sons.

GENERAL BIBLIOGRAPHY

ADEME. (2008). *Regard sur le Grenelle* [Look on the Grenelle]. Retrieved from http://www.comite21.org/docs/infos21/2008/octobre-2008/regard-grenelle-sept08vd.pdf.

Agid, P., & Tarondeau, J.-C. (2003). L'Opéra de Paris est-il économiquement gouvernable? [The Paris Opera is it economically governable?]. *Revue Française de Gestion, 29*(142), 147–168.

Allard-Poési, F., Drucker-Godard, C. & Ehlinger, S. (1999). Analyses de representations et de discours [Discourse and sensemaking analysis], In R.-A. Thiétard, R.-A, (Ed.), Méthodes de recherche en management (Research methods in management]. Paris, France: Dunod.

Amans, P., Mazars-Chapelon, A., & Villeseque-Dubus, F. (2014). Du patchwork' au 'canevas': Les rôles combinés des interactions et des outils de gestion autour d'un processus d'innovation dans le secteur du spectacle vivant [From the 'Patchwork' to the 'Canvas': The combined roles of interactions and management tools around a process of innovation in the performing arts sector]. *Innovation, 43*, 85–111.

Ansoff, H. I. (1981–2010). Preface. In H. Savall, *Work and people: An economic evaluation of job enrichment.* 1st ed. New York: Oxford University Press; 2nd ed. Charlotte, NC: Information Age Publishing

Anthony, R. N., & Govindarajan, V. (2007). *Management control systems* (12th ed.). New York, NY: McGraw-Hill Irwin.

Anthony, R. N. (1988). *The management control function.* Boston, MA: Harvard Business School Press.

Appelbaum, S., Simpson, R., & Shapiro, B. (1987). Downsizing: The ultimate human resource strategy. *Business Quarterly, 52*(2), 52–60.

Argyris, C., Putnam, R., & McLain Smith, D. (1985). *Action science.* San Francisco, CA: Jossey-Bass.

Argyris, C., & Schön, D. (1978). *Organizational learning*. London, England: Addison-Wesley Publishing.

Argyris, C., & Schon, D. (1996). *Organizational learning II: Theory, method, and practice*. Reading, MA: Addison-Wesley.

Argyris, C., & Schön, D. A. (2002). *Apprentissage organisationnel: Théorie, méthode, pratique* [Organizational learning: Theory, method, practice]. Paris, France: De Boeck Université.

Aristote. (2014a). Éthique à Nicomaque [Ethics to Nicomaque]. In P. Pellegrin (Ed.), *Aristote, œuvres complètes* [*Aristote, integral work*] (pp. 1975–2226). Paris, France: Flammarion.

Aristote. (2014b). Réfutations sophistiques [Sophistical Refutations]. In P. Pellergin (Ed.), *Aristote, œuvres complètes* [Aristote, integral work] (pp. 453–506). Paris, France: Flammarion.

Aristote. (2014c). Les Politiques [Politics]. In P. Pellegrin (Ed.), *Aristote, œuvres complètes* [Aristote, integral work] (pp. 2321–2636). Paris, France: Flammarion.

Arndt, M., & Bigelow, B. (1995). The implementation of total quality management in hospitals: How good is the fit? *Health Care Management Review*, *20*(4), 7–14.

Aubouin, N., Coblence, E., & Kletz, F. (2012). Les outils de gestion dans les organisations culturelles: De la critique artiste au management de la création [The management tools in cultural organizations: From the critical artistic to the management of creation]. *Management et Avenir*, *54*, 191–214.

Baer, W. C. (1997). Toward design of regulations for the built environment. Environment and Planning B: *Planning and Design*, *24*, 37–57.

Barberis, I., & Poirson, M. (2013). *L'économie du spectacle vivant* [*The economy of the performing arts*]. Paris, France: Presses Universitaires de France.

Barry, S. (2006). Bilan et perspectives après deux ans de fonctionnement du management socio-économique [Assessments and perspectives after two years SEAM fonctionning]. In Savall, H. (Ed.), *L'hôpital et les réseaux de santé* [*Hospital and healthcare networks*] (pp. 179–188). Paris, France: Economica.

Barth, I., & Martin, Y.-H. (2014). *Le manager et le philosophe* [*The manager and the philosopher*]. Paris, France: Le Passeur Éditeur.

Barthes, R. (1957). *Mythologies* [mythologies]. Paris, France: Éditions Du Seuil.

Beaujolin-Bellet, R. (2014). Les restructurations: Une sortie parle haut est-elle possible? [Restructuring: An output speaks loud is it possible?]. *Revue Économie et Management*, *153*, 5–9.

Beaujolin-Bellet, R., & Schmidt, G. (2012). *Les restructurations d'entreprises* [Company restructuring]. Paris, France: Éditions La Découverte.

Becker, G. S. (1964). *Human capital*. Chicago, IL: University of Chicago Press.

Becker, G., Murphy, K., & Tamura, R. (1990). Economic growth, human capital and population growth. *Journal of Political Economy*, *98*(5), S12–S137.

Beine, M., & Docquier, F. (2000). *Croissance et convergence économiques* [Economic growth and convergence]. Louvain-la-Neuve, France: De Boeck.

Benghozi, P.-J. (1995). Les sentiers de la gloire: Savoir gérer pour savoir créer [The paths of glory: To know how to manage to know how to create]. In F. Charue-Duboc (Ed.), *Des savoirs en action: Contributions de la recherche en gestion* [Knowledge into action: Contributions of management research] (pp. 51–87). Paris, France: L'Harmattan.

Benghozi, P.-J. (2006). Les temps modernes: De la gestion des organisations à la gestion de projet. Le modèle du secteur culturel [Modern times: From the management of organizations to project management: The model of the cultural sector]. *Hermès, 44*, 71–78.

Ben-Joseph, E., & Szold, T. (Eds.). (2005). *Regulating place: Standards and the shaping of urban America*. London, England: Routledge.

Benollet, P. (2007). Orchestrating compatibility between art and management: Socio-economic intervention in a national opera house. In A. F. Buono & H. Savall (Eds.), *Socio-economic intervention in organizations: The intervener-researcher and the SEAM approach to organizational analysis* (pp. 99–122). Charlotte, NC: Information Age Publishing.

Beretta, S. (2002). Unleashing the integration potential of ERP systems: The role of process-based performance measurement systems. *Business Process Management Journal, 8*(3), 254–277.

Bernácer, G. (1922). La teoría de las disponibilidades como interpretación de las crisis y del problema social [The theory of availability and interpretation of the crisis and the social problema]. *Revista Nacional de Economía, 40*, 128–158.

Bernácer, G. (1925). *El interés del capital: El problema de sus orígenes* [The interest of capital: The problem of its origin]. Alicante, Spain: Ed. Lucentum.

Bernácer, G. (1945). *La teoría funcional del dinero* [The functional theory of money]. Madrid, Spain: Consejo Superior de Investigaciones Científicas.

Bernácer, G. (1955). Una economía libre, sin crisis y sin paro [A free economy without crisis and without unemployment]. Madrid, Spain: Aguilar.

Besson, P. (1999). Les ERP à l'épreuve de l'organisation [The ERP in the test of the organization]. *Systèmes d'Information et Management, 4*(4), 21–51.

Besson, P., & Rowe, F. (2011). Perspectives sur le phénomène de la transformation organisationnelle [Perspectives on the phenomenon of the organizational transformation]. *Systèmes d'Information et Management, 16*(1), 3–34.

Bhide, A. (2000). *The origin and evolution of new business*. New York, NY: Oxford University Press.

Boisbeau, H. (2008). Évolution des contours sociologiques et juridiques de la profession (1789–1992) [Evolution of the sociological and legal contours of the profession (1789–1992)]. In P. Goetschel & J.-C. Yon (Eds.), *Directeurs de théâtre – XIXe-XXe siècles. Histoire d'une profession* [Theater Directors – 19th and 20th centuries: Story of a profession] (pp. 13–29). Paris, France: Publications de la Sorbonne.

Boje, D. M. (2001). *Narrative methods for organizational and communication research*. London, England: SAGE.

Boje, D. M. (2004). Preface. In H. Savall & V. Zardet (Eds.), *Recherche en sciences de gestion: Approche qualimétrique. Observer l'objet complexe* [Research in management science: Qualimetric approach: Observing the complex object]. Paris, France: Economica.

Boje, D. M. (2007). Globalization antenarratives. In A. Mills, J. C. Helms-Mills, & C. Forshaw (Eds.), *Organizational behavior in a global context* (pp. 505–549). Toronto, Ontario, Canada: Garamond.

Boje, D. M. (2008). *Storytelling organizations*. London, England: SAGE.

Boje, D. M. (2008). *Critical theory ethics for business and public administration*. Charlotte, NC: Information Age.

Boje, D. M. (2009). Storytelling, appreciative inquiry, and tetranormalization. Paper presented at the international conference organized in partnership with the ISEOR and Divisions of the Academy of Management, Lyon, France.

Boje, D. M., Oswick C., & Ford J. D. (2004). Language and organization: The doing of discourse. *Academy of Management Review, 29*, 571–577.

Boje, D., & Rosile, G.-A. (2003). Comparison of socio-economic and other transorganizational development methods. *Journal of Organizational Change Management, 16*(1), 10–20.

Boje, D. M., & Rosile, G. A. (2003). Theatrics of SEAM. *Journal of Organizational Change Management, 16*(1), 21–32.

Bollecker, M. (2002). Le rôle des contrôleurs de gestion dans l'apprentissage organisationnel: Une analyse de la phase de suivi des réalisations [Management controller role in organizational learning: realization analysis phase]. *Comptabilité–Contrôle–Audit, 2*, 109–126.

Boltanski, L., & Chiapello, E. (1999). *Le nouvel esprit du capitalisme* [The new spirit of capitalism]. Paris, France: Gallimard.

Boltanski, L., & Thévenot, L. (1987). *Les économies de la Grandeur: Cahier du centre d'étude pour l'emploi* [*The Economies of the Immensity: Journal of Employment Study Center*]. Paris, France: Presses Universitaires de France.

Bolton S. C. (2004). A simple matter of control? NHS hospital nurses and new management. *Journal of Management Studies, 41*(2), 317–333.

Bonnafous-Boucher, M., Chatelain-Ponroy, S., Evrard, Y., & Mazallon, F. (2003). Quel avenir pour les théâtres lyriques? [What future for lyric theaters?]. *Revue Française de Gestion, 29*(142), 169–186.

Bonnet, D. (2007). *Le pilotage de la transformation en environnement de coopération inter-organisationnelle, essence socio-économique de la transformation et des stratégies de transformation* [Transformation steering of inter-organizational cooperation, socio-economic essence of transformation and strategies]. Thèse de doctorat en Sciences de Gestion. University of Lyon.

Bonnet, D. (2012). Management du risque stratégique. La transformation de l'invariance dans le mode de signification: Le schème groupal de signification [Management of strategic risk. The transformation of the invariance in the manner of service: The groupal pattern of meaning]. *Revue Gestion, 29*(4), 35–47.

Bradford, D., & Burke, W. (2005). *Reinventing organization development*, San Francisco, CA: Pfeiffer.

Braudel, F. (1986). *Civilisation matérielle, économie et capitalisme XVe-XVIIIe siècle* [*Material civilization, economy and capitalism XVth-XVIIIth century*]. Paris, France: Armand Collin.

Broggio, C. (2012). La région, cadre privilégié du management territorial [French Regions, the ideal level of government for territorial management]. In J. Bonnet (Ed.), *Aménagement et développement territorial* [Installation and territorial development] (pp. 29–52). Paris: Ellipses.

Brunetti, A. (1997). *Politique et croissance économique : comparaison de données internationales* [Politic and economic growth: Comparison of international data]. Paris, France: OECD.

Buono, A. F. (1991). Managing strategic alliances: Organizational and human resource considerations. *Business in the Contemporary World*, *3*(4), 92–101.

Buono, A. F. (2001). Consulting in an Interorganizational Context: Mergers, Acquisitions and Strategic Partnerships: Knowledge and Value Development. Management Consulting: *Proceedings of the First International Co-sponsored Conference*, Academy of Management and ISEOR. Lyon, France: ISEOR.

Buono, A. F. (Ed.). (2002). *Developing knowledge and value in management consulting*. Greenwich, CT: Information Age Publishing.

Buono A. F. (2003). SEAM-less post-merger integration strategies: A cause for concern. *Journal of Organizational Change Management*, *16*(1), 90–98.

Buono, A., & Savall, H. (Eds.) (2007). *Socio-economic intervention in organizations: The intervener-researcher and the SEAM approach to organizational analysis*. Charlotte, NC: Information Age Publishing.

Busson, A. (2004). Stratégie et politique d'entreprise [Strategy and business policy]. In Y. Evrard (Ed.), *Le management des entreprises artistiques et culturelles* [The management of arts and cultural enterprises] (2nd ed., pp. 15–61). Paris, France: Economica.

Caghassi, J. (2009). Articulation gouvernance / management [Governance / management articulation]. In Savall, H., Zardet, V., Bonnet, M. (Eds.), *Management socio-économique, une approche innovante* [Socio-economic approach to management. An innovative approach]. Paris, France: Economica.

Callon, M. (1998). Rapprochement possible entre activités de service et les pratiques architecturales. [Possible linking between services activities and architectural practices]. In L'élaboration des projets architecturaux et urbains en Europe, vol 3: *Les pratiques de l'architecture: Comparaisons européennes et grands enjeux* (pp. 73-89). Retrieved from http://crdaln.documentation.developpement-durable.gouv.fr/documents/Crdaln/0083/Cdu-0083539/CETTEXD0002730.pdf

Cameron, R. (1967). *Banking in the early stages of industrialization*. New York, NY: Oxford University Press

Canas, A. (1987). Stratégies et outils à l'usage des responsables culturels [Strategies and tools for use by cultural leaders]. *Revue Française de Gestion*, *62*, 102–106.

Cappelletti, L. (2005). Designing and processing a socio-economic management control. In K. M. Weaver (Ed.), *Academy of Management best paper proceedings* (A1–A6). Pace, NY: Academy of Management.

Cappelletti, L. (2007). Intervening in small professional enterprises: Enhancing management quality in French notary publics. In A. F. Buono & H. Savall (Eds.), *Socio-economic intervention in organizations: The intervener-researcher and the SEAM approach to organizational analysis* (pp. 331–353). Charlotte, NC: Information Age Publishing.

Cappelletti, L. (2009). Performing an internal control function to sustain SOX 404 and improve risk management: Evidence from Europe. *Management Accounting Quaterly*, *10*(4), 17–27.

Cappelleti, L. (2012). *Le contrôle de gestion de l'immatériel - Une nouvelle approche du capital humain* [Management control of intangible: A new approach of human capital]. Paris: Management Sup: Dunod.

Cappelletti, L., & Baker, R. C. (2010). Measuring and developing human capital through a pragmatic action research: A French case study. *Action Research, 8*(2), 211–232.

Cappelletti, L., Baker, R., & Noguera, F. (2011). *Developing human capital through action research in management control.* Paper presented at the American Accounting Association Annual Meeting, Denver, Co, August.

Cappelletti, L., & Hoarau, C. (2013) *Finance et contrôle au quotidien* [Finance and control in the day-to-day]. Paris: Dunod

Cappelletti, L., Khouatra, D., & Noguera, F. (2011). Measuring the creation of value through management consulting: The case of the hidden costs method. Paper presented at the Academy of Management Annual Meeting, San Antonio, TX, August.

Carré, J.-J., Dubois, P., & Malinvaud, E. (1972). *La croissance française: Un essai d'analyse causale de l'après-guerre. [French growth: A causal analysis test of the postwar].* Paris, France: Édition du Seuil.

Cascio, W. F. (1993). Downsizing: What do we know? What have we learned? *Academy of Management Executive, 7*(1), 95–104.

Chandler, D. (2014). Morals, Markets and Values-based Businesses. *Academy of Management Review, 39*(3), 396–406.

Chiapello, E. (1997). Les organisations et le travail artistiques sont-ils contrôlables? [Are the organizations and the artistic work controllable?]. *Réseaux, 15*(86), 77–113.

Chiapello, E. (1998). *Artistes versus managers. Le management culturel face à la critique artistique* [Artists versus managers. Cultural management faces art criticism]. Paris, France: Métailié.

Conbere, J., & Heorhiadi, A. (2011). Socio-economic approach to management. *Organization Development Practitioner, 43*(1), 6–10.

Corsi, M., & Guarini, G., (2007). La fonction de productivité de Sylos Labini: Aspects théoriques et empiriques [The productivity function of Sylos Labini: Theoretical and empirical aspects]. *Revue d'économie industrielle, 118,* 1–25.

Crevoisier, O. (2010). La pertinence de l'approche territoriale [The relevance of applying a territorial approach]. *Revue d'Économie Régionale & Urbaine, 5*(December), 969–985.

Crozier, M., & Friedberg, E. (1981). *L'acteur et le système: Les contraintes de l'action collective* [The Actor and the System: Collective action constraints]. Paris, France: Seuil.

Cummings, T., & Worley, C. (2008). *Organizational development and change.* Boston, MA: Cengage Learning.

Cyert, R. M., & March, J. G (1956). Organizational factors in the theory of oligopoly. *Quarterly Journal of Economics, 70,* 44–64.

Darreau, P. (2002). *Croissance et politique économique* [Growth and economic policy]. Bruxelles, Belgique: De Boeck.

Datry, F., & Savall, A. (2014) Seeking economic resources: SEAM intervention-research. Case in a Belgian subsidiary of a NYSE listed American group. SEAM Conference in North America. Minneapolis, MN (May).

Datry, F., & Zakkour, D (2013a). Audit des PAP dans les hôpitaux [PAPs audit in hospitals] (under the direction of H. Savall & V. Zardet). Ecully, France: Rapport ISEOR.

Dauge, Y. (2004). *Métiers de l'architecture et du cadre de vie* [Architecture and living model jobs]. Rapport d'information n°64, fait au nom de la commission des Affaires Culturelles.

De Boeck, P., & E. Denison (1967). *Why growth rates differ*. New York, NY: The Brookings Institution.

De Geus, A. (1997). *The living company: Habits for survival in a turbulent business environment*. Boston, MA: Harvard Business School Press.

De Montgolfier, C. (1999). Quel contrôleur pour quel contrôle? [Which controller for which control] in Y. Dupuy, *Faire de la recherche en contrôle de gestion?* [Doing management control research?], Paris, France: Vuibert, 145–160.

De Montmollin, M. (1981). *Le Taylorisme à visage humain*. [*Human face of Taylorism*]. Paris, France: L'Harmattan.

De Préneuf, G. (2014). Changer en permanence pour une adaptation sur-mesure [Permanent Change to Crafted Adaptation]. In Savall, H. & Zardet, V. (Eds.), *La conduite du changement dans les entreprises et les organisations* [Change Management within Companies and Organizations]. Paris, France: Economica.

Dekler, M. (2007). Healing emotional trauma in organizations: An O.D. framework and case study. *Organizational Development Journal, 25*, 49–56.

Denis, J.-L., Lamothe, L., & Langley, A. (2001). The dynamics of collective leadership and strategic change in pluralistic organizations. *Academy of Management Journal, 44*(4), 809–837.

Dimaggio, P. J., & Powell, W. W. (1983). The iron-cage revisited: Institutional isomorphism and collective rationality in organizational fields. *American Sociological Review, 48*, 147–160.

Duggan, W. (2007). *Strategic Intuition: The creative spark in human achievement*. New York, NY: Columbia University Press.

Dul, J., Ceylan, C., & Jaspers, F. (2011). Knowledge worker's creativity and the role of the physical work environment, *Human Resource Management, 50*(6), 715–734.

Dupuis, X. (2010). Culture et management [Culture and management]. In P. Poirrier (Ed.), *Politiques et pratiques de la culture* [Cultural policies and practices] (pp. 52–54). Paris, France: La Documentation Française.

Dupuy, Y. (1991). Les organigrammes de structure organisationnelle [Structure organizational organigram], *Encyclopédie de management* (Vol. 2). ParisVuibert, pp. 370–381.

Dupuy, Y. (1990) Le comptable, la comptabilité et la conception des systèmes d'information : quelques interrogations [The accountant, accountancy, and information system conception: Some questions]. *Revue française de Comptabilité*, 215, septembre, pp. 75–81.

Durand, X. (2008). La relation pédagogique contrôleur de gestion–opérationnels: enjeux et déterminants [Pedagogic relationship between management controllers and operationnal teams : stakes and determinants]. In *La compta-bilité, le contrôle et l'audit entre changement et stabilité* (CD-Rom).

Easterby-Smith, M., Thorpe R., & Lowe, A. (2002). *Management research*. London, England: Sage.

Elkington, J. (1997). *Cannibals with forks: Triple bottom line of 21st century business*. Oxford, England: Capstone Publishing.

Ennajem, C. (2011). Évolution du rôle du contrôleur de gestion [Evolution of the management controller role]. Sarrebruck, Deutchland: Éditions Universi-taires Européennes.

Enriquez, E. (2002). *L'organisation en analyse* [The organization in analysis]. Paris, France: Presses Universitaires de France.

Fahr, R. (2011). Job design and job satisfaction: Empirical evidence for Germany. *Management Revue, 22*(1), 28–46.

Falkenberg, G. L., & Herremans, I. (1995) Ethical behavior in organizations di-rected by the formal and informal systems?, *Journal of Business Ethics, 14,* 133–143.

Fargier, C. (2013). La connexion de la stratégie de l'entreprise à celle du territoire, le pilotage d'un investissement important ; une balance économique à la clé [The connection of the company's strategy to the territory, piloting a signifi-cant investment; economic balance key]. In Savall, H., Zardet, V., Bonnet, M. (Eds.), *Réindustrialisation et dynamisation multi-sectorielle* [Reindustrialisation and multi-sectoral dynamic]. Paris, France: Economica.

Fayol, H. (1916). *Administration industrielle et générale* [Industrial and global admi-nistration]. Paris, France: Dunod.

Fimbel, E. (2007). *Alignement stratégique: Synchroniser les systèmes d'information avec les trajectoires et manœuvres des entreprises* [Strategic alignment: Synchronize infor-mation systems with trajectories and laborers of the companies]. Montreuil, France: Edition Pearson - Village Mondial.

Foster, R., & Kaplan, S. (2001). *Creative destruction: Why companies that are built to last underperform the market—and how to successfully transform them*. New York, NY: Doubleday.

Foucart, M. (2015). Gouvernance et management socio-économique en phase de maturité [Governance and socio-economic management in maturity phase]. In Savall, H. & Zardet, V., (Eds.), *Gouvernance et management : quelle coopé-ration?* [Governance and management: What cooperation?]. Paris, France: Economica.

Foucart, P. (2012). Transmission d'entreprises pratiquant le management so-cio-économique en Belgique [Company practicing socio-economic manage-ment transmission in Belgium]. In H. Savall & V. Zardet (Eds.), *Les entreprises familiales : création, succession, gouvernance et management* [Family businesses. creation, succession, governance and management]. Paris, France: Econo-mica.

Fouillée, A. (1888). *La philosophie de Platon* [*Plato's philosophy*]. Paris: Elibron classics.

Freud, S. (1934). La Négation [Negation].Translated from the German by H. Hoesli. *Revue Française de Psychanalyse, 2,* 174–177.

Friedman, M. (1970, September 13). The social responsibility of business is to in-crease its profits. *New York Times Magazine,* p. 32.

Gautier, J. (2005). *Sociologie de l'architecture: l'architecture sociologique d'un champ professionnel en mutation* [Architecture's sociology: Architectural sociology of a mutative professional field]. Master's dissertation, Tours University, Tours, France.

Gautier, J. (2007). *Complexification du marché du travail et orientation professionnelle: Analyse des fondations d'un projet professionnel chez de futurs architectes* [Job market complexification and professional orientation: Basis analysis of professional projects within future architects], N°22. Marseille, France: CÉREQ.

Gephart, R.P. (1988). *Ethnostatistics: Qualitative foundations for quantitative research.* Newbury Park, CA: Sage.

Gephart, R. P. (1993). The textual approach: Risk and blame in disaster sensemaking. *Academy of Management Journal, 36*(2), 1465–1514.

Gephart, R. P. (2009). An Invitation to Ethnostatistics. *Revue Sciences de gestion – Management Sciences – Ciencias de Gestión*, 785.

Gephart, R. P. (2013). Doing research with words: Qualitative methodologies and industrial/organizational psychology. In J. M. Cortina & R. S. Landis (Eds.), *Modern research methods for the study of behavior in organizations* (pp. 265–318). New York, NY: Routledge.

Gephart, R. P., Jr. (2014). Deliberating cost: Deliberative practices in qualimetrics and the socio-economic approach to management. In H. Savall, J. Conbere, A. Heorhiadi, V. Cristallini & A.F. Buono (Eds.), *Facilitating the socio-economic approach to management* (pp. 193–207). Charlotte, NC: Information Age Publishing.

Gibson, C. (1973). Volvo increases productivity through job enrichment. *California Management Review, 15*(4), 64–66.

Golden-Biddle, K., & Locke, K. (1997). *Composing qualitative research.* Thousand Oaks, CA: Sage.

Goldsmith, R. (1969). *Financial structure and development*, New Haven, CT: Yale University Press.

Goter, F. (2005). *Étude du système de sanctions-récompenses en lien avec la performance des organisations de service public. – Cas d'expérimentation* [Research sanctions: Reward system in connection with the performance of public service organizations—Case study]. Thèse de doctorat de sciences de gestion, Université Jean Moulin Lyon 3.

Green A. (2007). *Narcissisme de vie, narcissisme de mort* [Narcissism of life, death narcissism]. City: Les Éditions de Minuit.

Green A. (2011). Le travail du négatif [The work of the negative]. Paris: Les Éditions de Minuit. Gruening, G. (2001). Origin and theoretical basis of new public management. *International Public Management Journal, 4*, 1–25.

Gumb, B. (2008). *Les outils de gestion au service de votre stratégie* [Management tools serving your strategy], Paris: Éditions d'Organisation

Habraken, N. J. (2005). *Palladio's children.* London, England: Taylor & Francis.

Hallowell, R., Schlesinger, L. A., & Zornitsky, J. (1996). Internal service quality, customer and job satisfaction: Linkages and implications for management. *Human Resource Planning, 19*, 20–31.

Hamayon, D. (2015). Incidences de la crise sur les bonnes pratiques de gouvernance et les performances socio-économiques [Impact of the crisis on good governance practices and socio-economic performance]. In Savall, H. & Zardet, V. (Eds.), *Gouvernance et management : quelle coopération?* [Governance and management: what cooperation?]. Paris, France : Economica.

Hamel, G., & M. Zanini (2014). Build a change platform, not a change program. McKinsey & Company, (October). Retrieved from http://www.mckinsey.com/insights/organization/build_a_change_platform_not_a_change_program

Hansen, G. S., & Wernerfelt, B. (1989). Determinants of firm performance: The relative importance of economic and organizational factors. *Strategic Management Journal, 10*(5), 399–411.

Hayes, R. B. (2001). Using real option concepts to guide the nature and measured benefit of consulting interventions involving investment analysis. *Management Consulting: Proceedings* of the First International Co-sponsored Conference, Academy of Management and ISEOR. Lyon, France: ISEOR.

Heertje, A., Pieretti, P., & Barthélémy, P. (2003). *Principes d'économie politique.* [*Principles of economic policy*]. Louvain-la-Neuve, Belgique: De Boeck.

Hood, C. (1991). A public management for all seasons. *Public Administration, 69*(1), 3–19.

Hood, C. (1995). The "new public management" in the 1980s: Variations on a theme. *Accounting, Organizations and Society, 20*(2–3), 93–109.

Horvath, I., & Berutti, J.-C. (2012). Le management appliqué aux structures culturelles [Management applied to cultural structures]. *La Scène, 64,* 102–103.

Horvath, I., & Datry, F. (2013). Point de vue méthodologique pour le développement des entreprises de spectacle vivant [Methodological perspective for the development of performing arts companies]. *Recherches en Sciences de Gestion – Management Sciences - Ciencias de Gestión, 94,* 111–127.

Huber. G. P. (1989). *Organizational learning: An examination of the contributing process and a review of the literature.* Pittsburgh, PA: Carnegie Mellon University.

Huber, G. P. (1991). Organizational learning: The contributing processes and the literatures. *Organizational Science, 2,* 88–115.

ISEOR. (2001). Knowledge and value development in management consulting. International conference co-sponsored by Management Consulting Division of the Academy of Management (USA), ISEOR (France), HEC School of Management (France), Copenhagen Business School (Denmark) and Central Michigan University (USA). Lyon, France.

ISEOR. (2004). Crossing Frontiers in Quantitative and Qualitative Research Methods. International conference co-sponsored by Research Methods Division of the Academy of Management (USA) and ISEOR (France). Lyon, France.

ISEOR. (2005). International conference on Corporate Social Responsibility co-sponsored by ISEOR (France), ADERSE (France) and The Social Issues in Management Division of the Academy of Management (USA). Lyon, France.

ISEOR. (2006, 2008). Organizational Development and Change. International conference co-sponsored by Organization Development and Change Division of the Academy of Management (USA) and ISEOR (France). Lyon, France.

ISEOR. (2007a). *L'hôpital et les réseaux de santé* [Hospital and Health Networks]. Paris, France: Economica.

ISEOR. (2007b). Research Methods. International conference co-sponsored by Research Methods Division of the Academy of Management (USA) and ISEOR (France). Lyon, France.

ISEOR. (2008). *Modernisation des services publics : fécondité, des partenariats publics-privés* [Modernization of public services: Fertility of public-private partnerships]. Paris, France: Economica.

ISEOR. (2009). International conference and Doctoral Consortium co-sponsored by MC, ODC, ONE, RM, SIM, PTC Divisions of the Academy of Management (USA) and ISEOR (France). Lyon, France.

ISEOR. (2010). International conference co-sponsored by Management Consulting and Organizational Development and Change Divisions of the Academy of Management (USA), ISEOR (France), American Accounting Association (USA), Benedictine University (USA), New Mexico State University (USA), ADERSE (France) and FNEGE (France). Lyon, France.

ISEOR. (2011). Impacts of performance metrics on management research. International conference co-sponsored by Research Methods Division of the Academy of Management (USA) and ISEOR (France). Lyon, France.

ISEOR. (2012). Organizational Development and Change. International conference co-sponsored by Organizational Development and Change Division of the Academy of Management (USA), ISEOR (France), Benedictine University (USA), New Mexico State University (USA), ADERSE (France) and FNEGE (France). Lyon, France.

ISEOR. (2013). Crisis and Prosperity. Transatlantic Conference on Accounting, Auditing, Financial Control and Cost Control co-sponsored by Organization Development and Change Division of the Academy of Management (USA), ISEOR (France), American Accounting Association (USA), CNAM (France), Association Francophone de Comptabilité (France), Universidad Nacional Autonoma de Mexico (Mexico), ADERSE (France) and FNEGE (France). Lyon, France.

ISEOR. (2014). Current Challenges in Organizational change and interventions. International Conference co-sponsored by Management Consulting and Organizational Development and Change Divisions of the Academy of Management (USA), ISEOR (France), Benedictine University (USA), ADERSE (France) and FNEGE (France). Lyon, France.

Kaës, R. (1999). *Les théories psychanalytiques de groupe* [Psychoanalytic theories group]. Paris: PUF.

Kaës, R. (2009). *Les alliances inconscientes* [The unconscious alliances]. Paris, France: Dunod.

Kahneman, D., Lovallo, D., & Sibony, O. (2011). The big idea: Before you make that big decision. *Harvard Business Review*, (May–June), 50–60.

Kaplan, R. S., & Norton, D. P. (1992). The Balanced Scored Card: Measures that Drive Performances. *Harvard Business Review*, 70(1), 71–79.

Kaplan, R. S., & Norton, D. P. (1995). *Putting the balanced scorecard to work. Performance measurement, management, and appraisal sourcebook*. Amherst, USA: HRD Press.

Kets De Vries, M. F. R., & Balazs, K. (1997). The downside of downsizing. *Human Relations*, 50(1), 11–50.

Keynes, J. M. (1936). *The general theory of employment, interest, and money*. Cambridge, England: Cambridge University Press.

Kotter, J. (1996). *Leading change*. Boston, MA: Harvard Business School Press.

Krief, N., & Zardet, V. (2013). Analyse de données qualitatives et recherche-intervention [Qualitative data analysis and intervention-research], *Recherches en Sciences de Gestion - Management Sciences - Ciencias de Gestión*, 95, 211–237

Krippendorff, K. (2004). *Content analysis: An introduction to its methodology*. Thousand Oaks, CA: Sage.

Kuhn, T. S. (1962). *The Structure of Scientific Revolutions*. Chicago: University of Chicago Press.

Lacquemanne, F. (2011). Le redressement vigoureux d'une entreprise en crise de transition [The strong recovery of a company in transition crisis. In Savall, H. & Zardet, V. (Eds.), *Réussir en temps de crise : Stratégies proactives des entreprises [Succeed in times of crisis: Proactive business strategies]* (pp. 203–210). Paris, France: Economica.

Lacquemanne, F. (2012). Succession et transformation du management [Succession Management and Transformation]. In ISEOR (Ed.), *Les entreprise familiales : Création, succession, gouvernance et management* [Family business: Creation, succession , governance and management] (pp. 180–183). Paris, France: Economica.

Lacroix, P. (2014). Le management socio-économique au sein d'une entreprise belge [SEAM in a Belgian company]. In Savall, H. & Zardet, V. (Eds.), *La conduite du changement dans les entreprises et les organisations* [Change management within companies and organizations]. Paris, France: Economica.

Lafley, A. G., Martin, R., Rivkin, J., & Sigglekow, N. (2012, September–October). Bringing science to the art of strategy. *Harvard Business Review*, *90*(9), 3–12.

Lagendijk, A. (2006). Learning from conceptual flow in regional studies: Framing present debates, unbracketing past debates. *Regional Studies*, 40 (4), 385–399.

Lambert, C. (2005). *La fonction contrôle de gestion: Contribution à l'analyse de la place des services fonctionnels dans l'organisation* [The function management control: Contribution to the analysis of the place of the functional departments in the organization]. Doctoral dissertation, Paris IX Dauphine University.

Lambert, C. (2010). Le contrôleur de gestion et son manager [The management controller and his/her manager]. In N. Berland & Y. De Rongé (Ed.), *Contrôle de gestion, perspectives stratégiques et managériales* [Management control, stategic and managerial perspectives] (pp. 97–120). Paris: Pearson,

Larue-Tondeur, J. (2009). *Ambivalence et énantosémie* [Ambivalence and enantiosemy]. Thèse de Doctorat en Sciences du Langage [PhD in Linguistics]. Paris, France: Université de Paris X.

Lenhardt, V. (1992). *Les responsables porteurs de sens : Culture et pratique du coaching et du team-building* [Coaching for Meaning: the culture and practice of coaching and team building]. 2nd Ed. Paris, France: INSEP.

Leroy, D. (1996). *Économie des arts du spectacle vivant* [Economy of performing arts]. Paris, France: L'Harmattan.

Levi-Strauss, C. (1983). *Le regard éloigné* [The distant look]. Paris, France: Plon.

Lewin, K. (1948). Action research and minority problems, In G. Lewin (Ed.), *Resolving social conflicts*. New York, NY: Harper & Row.

Lewin, K. (1951). *Field theory and social science*. New York: Harper & Row.

Likert, R. (1974). *Le gouvernement participatif de l'entreprise* [Enterprise participative governance]. Paris, France: Gauthier-Villars.

Lindsay, R. M. (2015). Developing robust strategy for uncertain times: Expanding our concept of management control to deal with dynamic markets (Parts I and II). Toronto, Canada: Chartered Professional Accountants of Canada.

Lorino, P. (2001). *Méthodes et pratiques de la performance* [Methods and practices of performance]. Paris, France: Les Éditions d'Organisation

Lucas, R. (1988). On the mechanics of economic development. *Journal of Monetary Economics, 22,* 3–42.

Lussato, B. (1977). *Introduction critique aux théories d'organisation* [Critical introduction to organizational theories]. Paris, France: Bordas.

Macías Herrera, S. C. (2007). Enracinement de la méthode d'intervention socio-économique au sein des PME mexicaines [Strenghening SEAM intervention method in Mexican SMEs]. In ISEOR (Ed.), *L'hôpital et les réseaux de santé* [Hospital and health networks] (pp. 215–223). Paris, France: Economica.

Mackey, J., & Sisodia, R. (2013). *Conscious capitalism: Liberating the heroic spirit of business.* Boston, MA: Harvard Business School Press.

Maitlis, S., & Lauwrence, T. B. (2003). Orchestral manoeuvres in the dark: Understanding failures in organizational strategizing. *Journal of Management Studies, 40*(1), 109–139.

March, J. G., & Simon, H.A. (1958). *Organizations.* Boston, MA: Harvard Book List.

Martin, R. (2009). *The opposable mind: Winning through integrative thinking.* Boston, MA: Harvard Business Press.

Marx, K. (1848). *Critique de l'économie politique: Contribution à la critique de l'économie politique* [The critique of political economy: Contribution to the critique of political economy]. Paris, France: Éditions sociales.

Marx, K. (1862). *Le Capital* [The Capital]. Paris, France: M. Lachâtre.

Maurois, G. (1994). *La gestion d'une agence d'architectes* [Architect agency management]. Compte rendu du débat du 25 Octobre.

Mayo, E. (1946). *The human problems of an industrial civilization*, Boston, MA: Harvard University division of research, graduate school of business administration.

McKinnon, R. (1973). *Money and capital in economic development.* Washington, DC: Brookings Institution

McGrath, R. G., & Macmillan, I. 2009). *Discovery-driven growth: A breakthrough process to reduce risk and seize opportunity.* Boston, MA: Harvard Business School.

Mckinley, W., Sanchez, C. M., Schick, A. G., & Higgs A. C. (1995). Organizational Downsizing: Constraining, Cloning, Learning [and Executive Commentary]. *Academy of Management Executive, 9,* 32–44.

Mean, J. P., & Ombelets, N. (2008). Politiques publiques, contractualisation des objectifs et évaluation des performances [Public policies, contracting goals and performance evaluation]. In ISEOR (Ed.), *Modernisation des services publics, fécondité des partenariats publics-privés* [Public services modernization: Public-private partnerships fecondity]. Paris, France: Economica

Merchant, K., & Van der Stede, W. (2012). *Management control systems* (3rd Ed.). Harlow, England: Financial Times Prentice Hall.

Meyer, J. W., & Rowan, B. (1977). Institutional organizations: Formal structure as myth and ceremony. *American Journal of Sociology*, *83*, 340–363.

Meyssonnier, F., & Fernandez-Poisson, D. (2010). La réduction des coûts, enjeu majeur du contrôle de gestion [cost-reducting, major management control view]. In Berland, N. & Simon, F.-X., *Le contrôle de gestion en mouvement- État de l'art et meilleures pratiques* [Moving management control: State of the art and best practices]. Paris: Eyrolles.

Midler, C. (1998). Nouvelles dynamiques de la conception dans différents secteurs industriels: Quels enseignements pour le bâtiment? [New conception dynamics in different industries: What teaching for building sector?]. L'élaboration des projets architecturaux et urbains en Europe, vol 3: *Les pratiques de l'architecture: Comparaisons européennes et grands enjeux* (pp. 195–204). Retrieved from http://crdaln.documentation.developpement-durable.gouv.fr/documents/Crdaln/0083/Cdu-0083539/CETTEXD0002730.pdf

Mintzberg, H. (1987). The strategy concept 1: Five P's for strategy. *California Management Review*, (Fall), 11–24.

Mintzberg, H. (1994). *The rise and fall of strategic planning*. New York, NY: The Free Press.

Mintzberg, H. (2008, July–August). Crafting strategy. *Harvard Business Review*, 66–75.

Mishra, K. E., Spreitzer, G., & Mishra, A. K. (1998). Preserving employee morale during downsizing. *Sloan Management Review*, *39*(2), 83–95.

Missaoui, I. (2008). Capital immatériel et Systèmes d'Information [Immaterial capital and information systems]. Cahier de recherche [Working papers] Cigref, No. 4.

Moisdon, J.-C. (1984). Recherche en gestion et intervention [Management research and intervention]. *Revue Française de Gestion*.

Mone, M. A. (1994). Relationships between self concepts, aspirations, emotional responses, and intent to leave a downsizing organization. *Human Resource Management*, *33*(2), 281–298.

Montgomery, C. (2008, January–February). Putting leadership back into strategy. *Harvard Business Review*, 54–60.

Morgan G. (1988). *Riding the waves of change: Developing managerial competencies for a turbulent world*. San Francisco, CA: Jossey-Bass.

Moulaert, F., & Sekia, F. (2003). Territorial Innovation Models. *Regional Studies*, *37*(3), 289–302.

Mumford, M., Zaccaro, S., & Harding F. (2000). Leadership skills for a changing world: Solving complex social problems. *Leadership Quarterly*, *11*(1), 11–35

Näslund, B. (1964). Organizational slack. *Ekonomisk Tidskrift*, *1*, 26–31.

Neuendorf, K. A. (2002). *The content analysis guidebook*. Thousand Oaks, CA: Sage.

Nobre, T. (Ed.). (2013). *L'innovation managériale à l'hôpital* [Managerial innovation in hospital]. Paris, France : Dunod.

Nouveau Larousse Universel [New Universal Larousse]. (1969). Capitalisme [Capitalism]. Nouveau Larousse Universel, 1, 276.

OECD. (2003). *The non-profit sector of an economy in crisis*. Paris, France: Author.

Pansard, J.-C. (2012). Panorama et particularités des entreprises familiales. In Savall, H. & Zardet, V, *Les entreprises familiales : Création, succession, gouvernance et management* [Panorama and peculiarities of family businesses, in family businesses: creation, succession, governance and management]. Paris, France: Economica.

Pansard, J.-C. (2014). Management socio-économique et projet stratégique. In Savall, H. & Zardet, V, *La conduite du changement dans les entreprises et les organisations* [*Socio-economic management and strategic project, in change process in businesses and organizations*]. Paris, France: Economica.

Pareto, V. (1927). *Manual of Political Economy*. London, England: Macmillan.

Pascale, R. (2011). *La empresa en tiempos de la economía del conocimiento. Desafíos estrategia, costos e interdisciplinaridad* [The Enterprise in time of knowledge economy. Challenges strategy, costs and interdisciplinary]. XII Congrès International des Coûts, Punta del Este, Uruguay.

Pasquier, S. (1995). Préface [Preface]. In H. Savall, & V. Zardet, *Ingénierie stratégique du roseau, souple et enracinée* [*Strategic engineering of the reed, flexible and rooted*]. Paris, France: Economica.

Pasquier, P. (2009). Deux cas emblématiques de développement économique durable des entreprises [Two emblematic cases of sustainable economic development of enterprises]. In H. Savall, V. Zardet, & M. Bonnet (Eds.), *Management socio-économique, une approche innovante* [Socio-rconomic approach to management. An innovative approach]. Paris, France: Economica.

Pédon, A., & Schmidt, G. (2002). L'apprentissage organisationnel en PME : réalité et déterminants [Organizational learning in SME: Determinant and reality], paper, XVIèmes Journées Nationales des IAE, Paris, 10–12 septembre 2002.

Péron, M., & Bonnet, M., (2008). CSR in intervention-research: Example of an implementation of the SEAM model. *Revue Sciences de Gestion – Management Sciences – Ciencias de Gestión*, 239–257.

Péron, M., & Péron, M. (2003). Postmodernism and the socio-economic approach to organizations. *Journal of Organizational Change Management, 16*(1), 49–55.

Penrose, E. T. (1959). *The theory of the growth of the firm*. New York, NY: Wiley.

Perroux, F. (1948). *Capitalisme* [Capitalism]. Paris, France: Presses Universitaires de France.

Perroux, F. (1965). *La pensée économique de Joseph Schumpeter. Les dynamiques du capitalisme* [The economic thought of Joseph Schumpeter: Dynamics of capitalism]. Geneva, Switzerland: Droz. (Original work published 1935)

Perroux, F. (1969). *L'économie du XXe siècle* [The economy of the 20th Century]. Grenoble: Presse Universitaire de Grenoble.

Perroux, F. (1973). *Pouvoir et économie* [Power and economy]. Paris, France: Bordas.

Perroux, F. (1974). Économie de la ressource humaine [Economics of human resources]. *Mondes en développement*. ISMEA, 15–81.

Perroux (1975). *Unités actives et mathématiques nouvelles. Révision de la théorie de l'équilibre économique général* [Active unities and new mathematics. General equilibrium theory revision]. Paris, France: Dunod

Perroux, F. (1979). L'entreprise, l'équilibre rénové et les coûts cachés [The enterprise, the renovated balance and the "hidden" costs]. Preface. In Savall, H. *Reconstruire l'entreprise* [*Rebuild the enterprise*] Paris, France: Dunod. 2nd ed. Savall, H. & Zardet, V. *Reconstruire l'entreprise* [Rebuild the enterprise], Paris: Dunod (2014)

Pfeffer, J. (1994). *Competitive advantage through people: Unleashing the power of the work force*. Boston, MA: Harvard Business School Press.

Piaget, J. (1975). *L'équilibration des structures cognitives, problème central du développement* [Cognitive structures equilibration, development main issue]. Paris, France: Presses Universitaires de France.

Piaget, J. (2006). Les relations entre l'intelligence et l'affectivité dans le développement de l'enfant [The relationship between intelligence and affectivity in child development]. Cours inédit [Unpublished course]. Paris: Fondation Jean Piaget.

Piaget, J., Henriques, G., & Ascher, E. (1990). *Morphismes et catégories: Comparer et transformer* [Morphisms and categories: Compare and transform]. Paris: Delachaux et Niestlé.

Pierre, X. (2007). Méthode de diagnostic intra et interorganisationnel dans le cadre de démarches territoriales [Intra and Inter-organizational Diagnosis Method in the Context of Territorial Projects]. Colloquium sponsored by IS-EOR and the Research Methods Division, Academy of Management. Lyon, France (June).

Pierre, X. (2011). *Pilotage institutionnel des coopérations interorganisationnelles – La mise en œuvre de stratégies territoriales* [Institutional piloting of inter-organizational cooperation: The Implementation of territorial strategies]. Sarrebruck: Éditions Universitaires Européennes.

Pierre, X. (2012). Coopérations interinstitutionnelles : Enjeux, difficultés, impacts économiques, actions possibles [Inter-institutional Cooperation: Stakes, Difficulties, Economic Impacts, and Possible Actions for Improvement]. Colloquium sponsored by ISEOR and the Organization Development and Change Division, Academy of Management. Lyon, France (June).

Pierre, X. (2013). Compétitivité des territoires : les coopérations entre les acteurs du territoire source d'avantages concurrentiels? [Competitiveness of Territories: Cooperation between Local Actors as a Source of Competitive Advantage?], paper, Journée François Perroux, Lyon, France (September).

Pierre, X. (2013). Résoudre l'équation – maitrise des dépenses tout en améliorant l'action publique – par l'analyse à la loupe de la mise en œuvre des politiques sur les territoires [Solve the equation—control public spending while improving public action—by observing the implementation of policies on territories with a magnifying glass]. 3rd Congrès Transatlantique de Comptabilité, Contrôle, Audit, Contrôle de Gestion et Gestion des coûts, in partnership with ISEOR, American Accounting Association, and l'Institut International des Coûts (IIC). Lyon (June).

Pierre, X. (2014). Efficacité et efficience de l'action territoriale [Efficiency and effectiveness of territorial action], paper, 3rd Colloque de l'AIRMAP [Management public], Aix-en-Provence, France (May).

Pigaglio, G. (2009). Les mutations stratégiques d'un organisme public: Cas de l'ISE à l'URSSAF de Lyon [Strategic Mutations of a Public Company: case of socio-economic intervention-research at URSSAF Lyon]. In H. Savall, V. Zardet, & M. Bonnet (Eds.), *Management socio-économique, une approche innovante* [Socio-economic management, an innovative approach]. Paris, France: Economica

Pigaglio, G. (2009). Management socio-économique dans les organisations de service public [Socio-economic management in organizations in public sector]. In Savall, H., Zardet, V., Bonnet, M. (Eds.), *Management socio-économique, une approche innovante* [Socio-economic management, an innovative approach]. Paris, France: Economica

Pigaglio, G. (2011). Crise, dynamique et perspectives nouvelles. In Savall, H. & Zardet, V. *Réussir en temps de crise, stratégies proactives des entreprises* [Crisis, dynamic and new perspectives, in success in time of crisis]. Paris, France: Economica.

Pigaglio, G. (2013). Effet d'entraînement des entreprises industrielles. In Savall, H., Zardet, V., Bonnet, M. (Eds.). *Réindustrialisation et dynamisation multisectorielle* [*Ripple effect in industrial companies, in reindustralization and multisectorial dynamic*]. Paris, France: Economica.

Plane, J.-M. (2000). *Méthodes de recherche-intervention en management* [Management intervention-research methods]. Paris, France: L'Harmattan.

Platon, (2006). *Le sophiste* [*The sophist*]. Traduction [translation] de N. L. Cordero. Paris: GF Flammarion.

Pollitt, C. & Bouckaert, G. (2000). *Public management reform: A comparative analysis*. Oxford, England: University Press.

Rainey, H. G., Backoff, R. W., & Levine, C. H. (1976). Comparing public and private organizations. *Public Administration Review*, *36*(2), 233–244.

Rainey, H. G., & Chun, Y. H. (2005). Public and private management compared. *The Oxford Handbook of Public Management*, *72, 102.*

Rainey, H. G., Pandey, S., & Bozeman, B. (1995). Research note: Public and private managers' perceptions of red tape. *Public Administration Review*, *55*(6), 567–574.

Raynaud, D. (2004). Contrainte et liberté dans le travail de conception architecturale [Constraint and freedom in the architectural conception work]. *Revue Française de Sociologie*, *45*(2), 339–366.

Raynaud, D. (2009) La 'crise invisible' des architectes dans les trente glorieuses [The «invisible crisis» of architects during the three post-war decades], *Histoire Urbaine*, *25,* 129–147.

Recueil National des statistiques. (2012). Recueil National des statistiques sanitaires au Liban [Health statistic national report in Lebanon]. USJ, OMS, MPH.

Reder, M. W. (1947). A reconsideration of marginal productivity theory. *Journal of Political Economy*, *55,* 450–458.

Richard, B. (1969). *Organization development: Strategies and models*. Reading, MA: Addison-Wesley.

Roche, A. (2014). Donner du sens au travail: La question de la reconnaissance de l'utilité sociale [Work sense making, social utility recognition]. Paper, Journée de recherche IP&M [Psychoanalytical and Management Institute Research Conference], (November).

Romer, P. (1986). Increasing returns and long run growth. *Journal of Political Economy*, *94*(5), 1002–1037.

Rousseau, D. (2011). Reinforcing the micro/macro bridge: organizational thinking and pluralistic vehicles. *Journal of Management*, *37*(2), 429–442

Rowe, P. G. (1993). *Modernity and Housing*. Cambridge, MA: MIT Press.

Ruat, T. (2012). *Le management socio-économique d'une agence d'architecture : Quels leviers d'amélioration de la performance globale?* [Socio-economic management of architecture agency: What levers for improvement of overall performance?], Mémoire de master Recherche en Gestion Socio-économique. [SEAM Master Program Dissertation]. Lyon, France: IAE Lyon.

Saint Léger, G. (2013). Contrôle, systèmes d'information et ERP. In L. Cappelletti & C. Hoarau, *Finance et contrôle au quotidien* [*Finance and management control in the day-to-day*]. Paris, France: Dunod.

Sanchez R., Martens, R. & Heene A. (2008). *Competence perspectives on learning and dynamic capabilities*. San Francisco, CA: JAI press.

Sánchez Mateo, I., & Guerrero Lizardi, A. (2014). Présentation de l'entreprise Frutas Finas Hnos et de la mise en place de la démarche socio-économique [Presentation of SEAM implementation at Frutas Finas Hnos Company]. In Savall, H. & Zardet, V., *La conduite du changement dans les entreprises et les organisations* [Change management within companies and organizations]. Paris, France: Economica.

Sánchez, I., & Sánchez, H. (2007). Implantation du management socio-économique et des contrats d'activités périodiquement négociables dans une PME Mexicaine. [Settling Socio-economic approach to management and Periodically Negotiable Activity Contracts in a Mexican SME]. In ISEOR (Ed.), *L'hôpital et les réseaux de santé* [Hospital and Health Networks] (pp. 227–237). Paris, France: Economica.

Savall, H. (1973, 1975). *G. Bernácer: L'hétérodoxie en science économique* [G. Bernácer: Heterodoxy in economics]. Col. Les grands Économistes, Paris, France: Dalloz.

Savall, H. (1974). *Enrichir le travail humain dans les entreprises et les organisations* [An economic evaluation of job enrichment]. Paris, France: Dunod.

Savall, H. (1978). Compatibilité de l'efficience économique et du développement du potentiel humain [Compatibility of economic efficiency and human development], *Économie Appliquée, 4,* 965–998.

Savall, H. (1978). Compatibilité de l'efficience économique et du développement du potentiel humain [Compatibility of economic efficiency and development of human potential]. VII° Colloque International au Collège de France, organized by François Perroux & Jean Piaget. *Économie Appliquée.* Tome XXXI (3–4), 561–593.

Savall, H. (1979). *Reconstruire l'entreprise : Analyse socio-économique des conditions de travail* [Rebuild the enterprise: Socio-economic analysis of working conditions]. Paris, France: Dunod.

Savall, H. (1981–2010). *Work and people: An economic evaluation of job enrichment*. 1st ed. NewYork: Oxford University Press ; 2nd ed. Charlotte, NC: Information Age Publishing

Savall H. (1986). Le contrôle de qualité des informations émises par les acteurs des organisations [The quality control of information emitted by organizational actors]. Paper, ISEOR Conference Qualité des informations scientifiques en gestion [Quality of management scientific data]. Lyon, France.

Savall, H. (2002). *Le management des entreprises culturelles* [Management of cultural enterprises]. Paris, France: Economica.

Savall, H. (2003a). An update presentation of the socio-economic management model and international dissemination of the socio-economic model. *Journal of Organizational Change Management*, *16*(1), 33–48.

Savall, H. (2003b). International dissemination of the socio economic method . *Journal of Organizational Change Management*, *16*(1), 107–115.

Savall, H. (2007). ISEOR's socio-economic method: A case of scientific consultancy. In A. F. Buono & H. Savall (Eds.), *Socio-economic intervention in organizations: The intervener-researcher and the SEAM approach to organizational analysis*. Charlotte, NC: Information Age Publishing.

Savall, H. (2010). Individu, enterprise et nation: Comment se crée le PIB? [Individual, enterprise and nation: how does the GDP is created?]. In G. Blardone & H. Savall, Agir dans un nouveau monde: le développement et les coûts de l'Homme, 12e journée François Perroux organized by Association François Perroux. Écully: ISEOR Éditeur.

Savall, H. (2011). Keynote speaker, Petite lecture épistémologique sans prétention de la responsabilité sociale de l'entreprise [Little epistemological reading without arrogance of corporate social responsibility]. ADERSE Conference. In Le Flanchec, Uzan & Doucin (Eds.). 2012. *RSE et gouvernance mondiale*, [*CSR and global governance*], 3–22.

Savall, H. (2012). *Origine radicale des crises économiques: Germán Bernácer, précurseur visionnaire* [Root origin of crises: Germán Bernácer, a visionary forerunner]. Charlotte, NC: Information Age Publishing.

Savall, H., & Zardet, V. (1987a). Les coûts cachés et l'analyse socio-économique des organizations [Hidden costs and the socio-economic analysis of organizations]. In *Encyclopédie du Management*. Paris, France: Economica

Savall, H., & Zardet, V. (1987b). *Maîtriser les coûts et les performances cachés* [Mastering hidden costs and Socio-economic performance]. Paris, France: Economica. 5th ed, 2010.

Savall, H., & Zardet, V. (1992). *Le nouveau contrôle de gestion: Méthode des coûts-performances cachés* [New management control: The hidden cost-performance method]. Paris, France: Éditions Comptables Malesherbes-Eyrolles

Savall, H., & Zardet, V. (1994). Performance économique et engagement social de l'entreprise: Jusqu'où est-ce compatible? [Economic performance and social commitment of the company: How far is this compatible?]. *Stratégies Resources Humaines*, *9*, 30–38.

Savall, H., & Zardet, V. (1995). *Ingénierie stratégique du roseau, souple et enracinée* [Strategic engineering of the reed, flexible and rooted]. Paris, France: Economica. 2nd ed, 2005.

Savall, H., & Zardet, V. (1996a). La dimension cognitive de la recherche-intervention: la production de connaissances par interactivité cognitive [The cognitive dimension of intervention-research: The production of knowledge through cognivitive interactivity]. *Revue Internationale de Systémique*, *10*(1–2), 157–189.

Savall, H., & Zardet, V. (1996b). Les pratiques d'encadrement des recherches doctorales en stratégie – résultats d'enquêtes 1995 et 1996 [The supervising practices of doctoral research in strategic management: Survey analysis 1995 and 1996]. *AIMS*, 18-52.

Savall, H., & Zardet, V. (1996). *Mesure et négociation de la performance globale de l'entreprise: Éléments pour une théorie socio-économique du contrôle de gestion* [The measurement and negociation of corporate global performance: Elements towards a socio-economic theory of management control]. IFSAM colloquium, Montreal, Canada.

Savall H., & Zardet V. (2001). L'évolution de la dépendance des acteurs à l'égard des dysfonctionnements chroniques au sein de leur organisation. Résultats de processus de metamorphose [The evolution of actor dependency regarding chronic dysfunctions in organizations: Results of a process of metamorphosis]. In T. de Swarte (Ed.), *Psychanalyse, management et dépendances au sein des organisations* (pp. 179–212). Paris, France: L'Harmattan.

Savall, H., & Zardet V. (2004). *Recherche en Sciences de Gestion: Approche qualimétrique, Observer l'objet Complexe* [Research in management sciences: The qualimetric approach, observing the complex object]. Paris, France: Economica.

Savall H., & Zardet V. (2005). *Tétranormalisation : Défis et dynamiques* [Tetranormalization: Challenges and dynamics]. Paris, France: Economica.

Savall, H., & Zardet, V. (2006). *Théorie socio-économique des organisations : impacts sur quelques concepts dominants dans les théories et pratiques managériales* [Socio-economic theory : impacts on some mainstream concepts in management theories and pratices] Academy of Management (ODC Division) & ISEOR Conference, Lyon, France. April, 267–302.

Savall, H., & Zardet, V. (2008). *Mastering hidden costs and performance*. Charlotte NC: Information Age Publishing.

Savall, H., & Zardet, V. (2009a). *Mesure et pilotage de la responsabilité sociale et sociétale de l'entreprise : résultats de recherches longitudinales* [Measuring and piloting corporate social responsibility : results from longitudinal research]. Paper, International conference proceedings and doctoral consortium, partnership between the Academy Of Management (AOM) and ISEOR, Lyon, France. June, 25–53.

Savall, H., & Zardet, V. (2009b). *Responsabilidad social y societal de la empresa: indicadores para dialogar con las partes interesadas* [The corporate social responsibility : indicators to converse with stakeholders]. Paper, ACACIA Conference. July, UAM – México, 31–59.

Savall, H., & Zardet, V. (2010a). Le non-dit dans la théorie socio-économique des organisations : situations de management et pièces de théâtre [Unvoiced comment in the socio-economic theory of organizations: Management situations and theatrics]. In Rodolphe OCLER (Ed.). *Fantasmes, mythes, non-dits et quiproquo : Analyse de discours et organisation [Fantasy, myths, unvoiced and misunderstanding : Analysis of speech and organization*], Paris, France: L'Harmattan, 9–35.

Savall, H., & Zardet, V. (2010b). *Management stratégique des professions libérales réglementées* [Strategic management of the professions regulated]. Paris, France: Economica.

Savall, H., & Zardet, V. (2011) *The qualimetrics approach: Observing the complex object*. Charlotte, NC: Information Age Publishing.

Savall, H., & Zardet, V. (2011). *Réussir en temps de crise : stratégies proactives d'entreprises* [Succeed in times of crisis: Proactive business strategies]. Paris, France: Economica.

Savall, H., & Zardet, V. (2012a). *Les entreprises familiales : création, succession, gouvernance et management* [Family businesses. creation, succession, governance and management]. Paris, Franc: Economica.

Savall, H., & Zardet, V. (2012b, octobre) Nouvel énoncé de la théorie socio-économique des organisations et des territoires [New statements of the socio-economic theory of organizations and territory]. Lyon, France: Cahier de recherche ISEOR.

Savall, H., & Zardet, V. (2013). *Linking individual, organizational and macro-economic performance levels: Hidden costs model.* Paper presented at the Academy of Management, Lake Buena Vista, FL (August).

Savall, H., & Zardet, V. (2013a). *The dynamics and challenges of tetranormalization.* Charlotte, NC: Information Age Publishing

Savall, H., & Zardet, V. (2013b). La RSE, lien entre l'individu, l'organisation et la société: nouvel énoncé de la théorie Socio-Économique [SCR, link between individual, organization and society: New statement of the socio-economic theory]. Paper, ADERSE Conference, Lyon, France (October).

Savall, H., & Zardet, V. (2014). *Reconstruire l'entreprise : les fondements du management socio-économique* [Rebuild the enterprise: socio-economic management basis]. Paris, France: Dunod.

Savall, H., & Zardet, V. (2014a) La théorie du socle stratégique et l'effet de levier de la cohésion [The strategic bedrock theory and the cohesion leverage effect] 5ème colloque et séminaire doctoral international de l'ISEOR - AOM, June, 27–58.

Savall, H., & Zardet, V. (2014b). *La conduite du changement dans les entreprises et les organisations* [Change management within companies and organizations]. Paris, France : Economica.

Savall, H., &. Zardet, V. (2008) Le concept de coût-valeur des activités. Contribution de la théorie socio-économique des organisations [The concept of cost-value activities. Contribution of socio-economic organization theory]. *Revue Sciences de gestion – Management Sciences – Ciencias de Gestión*, *64*, 30–46

Savall, H., & Zardet, V. (2007). *L'importance stratégique de l'investissement incorporel: résultats qualimétriques de cas d'entreprises* [The strategic importance of intangible investment : qualimetric results of company cases]. In Colloque IIC-ISEOR-American Accounting Association, Lyon, France (June).

Savall, H., & Zardet, V. (2009a). Mesure et pilotage de la responsabilité sociale et sociétale de l'entreprise – Résultats de recherches longitudinales [Measurement and control of the corporate and social responsibility of business: Results of longitudinal research.]. *Revista Digital del Instituto Internacional de Costos* (4), 7–36

Savall, H., & Zardet, V. (2011). Présentation du modèle de gestion socio-économique [Presentation of the socio-economic management model]. Working paper. OECD Conference. Paris, France.

Savall, H., Zardet, V., & Bonnet, M. (2000, 2008). *Releasing the untapped potential of enterprises through socio-economic management.* Geneva, Switzerland: Editions BIT.

Savall, H., Péron, M., & Zardet, V. (2014). Human potential at the core of socio-economic theory (SEAM). Paper presented at the SEAM Colloquim, Minneapolis, MN (April).

Savall, H., Zardet, V., & Bonnet, M. (2000, 2008). *Libérer les performances cachées par un management socio-économique* [Releasing the untapped potential of enterprises through socio-economic management]. Geneva, Switzerland: International Labour Office.

Savall, H., Zardet, V. & Bonnet, M. (2009). *Management socio-économique : une approche innovante* [Socio-economic approach to management. An innovative approach]. Paris, France: Economica.

Savall, H., Zardet, V., & Bonnet, M. (2010). RSE et développement durable, fondements de la théorie socio-économique des organisations [CSR and sustainable development, basis of socio-economic theory]. Paper, ADERSE Conference. La Rochelle, France. In Barthe, N. & Rosé, J.-J. (Eds.). 2011. *RSE et développement durable* [CSR between globalization and sustainable development]. Bruxelles, Belgique: De Boeck, 239–268, 3–36.

Savall, H., Zardet, V., & Bonnet, M. (2013). *Réindustrialisation et dynamisation multi-sectorielle* [Reindustrialisation and multi-sectoral dynamic]. Paris, France : Economica.

Savall, H., Zardet, V., Bonnet, M., & Péron, M. (2008). The emergence of implicit criteria actually utilized by reviewers of qualitative research articles: Case of a European journal. *Organizational Research Methods, 11*(3), 510–540.

Savall, H., Zardet, V., Bonnet, M., & Péron, M. (2009). *Conditions governing the performance of employment and environmental standards socio-economic considerations and proposals based on case histories from the chemicals and food manufacturing industries.* Paper, International Conference and Doctoral Consortium, ISEOR & Academy of Management. Lyon, France.

Savall, H., Zardet V., & Goter (2012). *Concilier modernisation de la gestion des Ressources Humaines, valeurs de service public et objectifs de performance: Analyse internationale et comparative à partir de cas de recherche-intervention* [Reconcile modernization of human resources management , public service values and performance targets: International and comparative analysis from cases of intervention research], paper, AIRMAP Congress, Paris, France. December, 8–31.

Savall, H., Zardet, V., & Guerrero, A. (2005). Diagnostico socioeconómico en una empresa empacadora de frutas [Socio-economic diagnosis of a fruit agribusiness company]. Rapport, Écully, France: ISEOR.

Savall, H., Zardet, V., Rasolofoarisoa, A., & Guerrero, A. (2014). Diagnosticos socioeconómicos verticales en una empresa empacadora de frutas [Socio-economic diagnoses of a fruit agribusiness company]. Écully, France: ISEOR.

Schein, E. H. (2001). Clinical inquiry/research. In P. Reason & H. Bradbury (Eds.), *Handbook of action research: Participative inquiry and practice*. London, England: Sage.

Schoemaker, P. (2008). The future challenges of business: Rethinking management education. *California Management Review*, *50*(3), 119–139.

Schön, D. (1983). *The reflective practitioner*. New York, NY: Basic Books.

Schuler, R., & Jackson, S. (1987). Linking competitive strategies and human resource management practices. *Academy of Management Executive*, *1*(3), 207–219.

Schumpeter, J. A. (1934). *A theory of economic development*. Cambridge, MA: Harvard University Press.

Scott, W. R. (1981). *Organizations: Rational, natural and open systems*. Englewood Cliffs, NY: Prentice Hall.

Seale, C. (1999). *The quality of qualitative research*. London, UK: Sage.

Shortell S., & Kaluzni A. (2006). *Healthcare management: Organization design and behavior*, 5th edition, Clifton Park, NY: Delmar Cengage Learning.

Simmie, J. (2005). Critical surveys edited by Stephen Roper innovation and space: A critical review of the literature. *Regional Studies*, *39*(6), 789–804.

Simondon, G. (2005). *L'individuation à la lumière des notions de forme et d'information* [Individuation in light of notions of form and information]. Paris: Million. Collection Krisis.

Sleesman D. J., Conlon D. E., McNamara G., & Miles J. E. (2012). Cleaning up the Big Muddy: A meta-analytic review of the determinants of the escalation of commitment. *Academy of Management Journal*, *55*(3), 541–562.

Smith, A. (1776). *Inquiry into the nature and causes of the wealth of nations*. London, England: W. Strahan & T. Cadell.

Smith, N. (2002). New globalism, new urbanism: Gentrification as global urban strategy. *Antipode*, *34*, 427–450.

Solow, R. M. (1956). A contribution to the theory of economic growth. *The Quarterly Journal of Economics*, *70*(1), 65–94.

Sorensen, P. F., Yaeger, T. F., Savall, H., Zardet, V., Bonnet, M., & Peron, M. (2010). A review of two major global and international approaches to organizational change: SEAM and appreciative inquiry. *Organization Development Journal*, *28*(4), 31–39.

Sponem, S., & Chatelain-Ponvoy, S. (2007). Evolution et permanence du contrôle de gestion [Evolution and permanency of management control], Économie et Management, *123*, 12–18.

Stoléru, L. (1969). *L'équilibre et la croissance économique* [Balance and economic growth]. Paris, France: Dunod.

Stubbart, C., & Knight, M. (2006). The case of disappearing firms: Empirical evidence and implications. *Journal of Organizational Behavior*, *27*(1), 79–100.

Tabchoury, P. (2014). Création de valeur ajoutée financière dans un hôpital par la mise en place de la qualité du management socio-économique [Creation of Financial Added-Value in Hospitals through the implementation of SEAM]. In Savall, H. & Zardet, V. (Eds.), *La conduite du changement dans les entreprises et les organisations* [Change Management within Companies and Organizations]. Paris, France: Economica.

Talaszka, H. (2013). Osons travailler ensemble [Dare to work together]. In Savall, H., Zardet, V., Bonnet, M. (Eds.), *Réindustrialisation et dynamisation multisec-*

torielle [Reindustralization and multisectorial dynamic]. Paris, France: Economica.

Taylor, F. W. (1911). *The principles of scientific management*. New York, NY: Harpers and Brothers.

Terrin, J. J. (2009). *Conception collaborative pour innover en architecture, processus, méthodes, outils* [Collaborative conception to innovate in architecture, process, methodologies, tools]. Paris, France: L'harmattan.

Tomas, J. L. (1999). *ERP and integrated software packages: The transfer of information systems*. Paris, France: Dunod.

Turbide, J., & Laurin, C. (2009). Performance measurement in the arts sector: The case of the performing arts. *International Journal of Arts Management, 11*, 56–70.

Van de Ven, A., & Johnson, P. (2006). Knowledge for theory and practice. *Academy of Management, 31*(4), 802–821.

Vial Voiron, V.-J. (2013). Quand l'Ordre accompagne la formation des architectes pour valoriser le rôle de l'architecture [When the Architecture Association supports the architects'training to value the architecture role]. In H. Savall & V. Zardet (Eds.), *La conduite du changement dans les entreprises et les organisations* [Change management within companies and organizations] (pp. 69–72). Paris, France: Economica.

Vial Voiron, V.-J., & Cartillier, M. (2010). La mise en place d'un axe stratégique: La formation au sein du Conseil régional de l'ordre des architectes de Rhône-Alpes [Implementation of a strategic axis : training in the regional council of the Architecture Association of Rhône-Alpes]. IIn H. Savall & V. Zardet (Eds.), *Management des Professions Libérales Réglementées* [Accredited Professionals' Management]. Paris, France: Economica.

Voyant, O. (1997). *Contribution à l'élaboration d'un système de veille stratégique intégré pour les PME-PMI* [Contribution to the elaboration of an Integrated System of Strategic Vigilance for SMEs]. Thèse de doctorat en Sciences de Gestion. Université de Lyon, France.

Voyant, O. (2001). *Les PME-PMI à l'écoute de leur environnement : élaboration d'un système de veille stratégique intégré* [SMEs' Listening to their Environment: elaboration of an integrated strategic vigilance system]. Paper, 10ème Conférence Internationale de Management Stratégique, Québec, Canada.

Voyant, O. (2010). *Contribution à l'identification d'une cartographie de l'environnement externe : cas de PME familiale Belge* [Contribution to the Identification of an External Environment Map: case of a Belgian Family SME]. Paper, Association Internationale de Management Stratégique Conference, France.

Walker, J. W. (2001). Human capital: Beyond HR?. *Human Resources Planning, 24*(2), 4–5.

Walras, L. (1877). *Éléments d'économie politique pure ou théorie de la richesse sociale* [Elements of pure economic policy or social wealth theory]. Lausanne, Switzerland: Imprimerie L. Corbaz.

Weber, M. (1924–1964). *The theory of social and economic organization*. New York, NY: Free Press.

Wernerfelt, B. (1984). A resource-based view of the firm. *Strategic Management Journal, 5*, 171–180.

Wilkens, U., & Nemerich, D. (2011). Love it, change it, or leave it: Understanding highly-skilled flexible workers' job satisfaction from a psychological contract perspective, *Management Revue*, *22*(1), 65–83.

Wolf, J., Hanson, H., & Moir, M. (2011). *Organization development in healthcare*. Charlotte, NC: Information Age Publishing.

Worley, C., Hitchin, D., & Ross, W. (1995). *Integrating strategic changes: How OD builds competitive advantage*. Reading, MA: Addison Wesley.

Worley, C., Zardet, V., Bonnet, M., & Savall, A. (2015). *Becoming agile: How the SEAM approach to management builds adaptability*. New York, NY: John Wiley and Sons.

Woudhuysen, J., & Abley, I. (2004). *Why is construction so backward?* Chichester, England: John Wiley & Sons.

Zardet, V. (2007). Developing sustainable global performance in small-to medium size industrial firms: The case of Brioche Pasquier. In A. F. Buono & H. Savall (Eds.), *Socio-economic interventions in organizations: The Intervener-researcher and the SEAM approach to organizational analysis* (pp. 45–70). Charlotte, NC: Information Age Publishing.

Zardet, V., Delattre, M., & Petit, R. (2012). Responsabilités sociale et économique indissociables face à la crise: Le cas du secteur de l'architecture [Social and economic responsibilities inseparable face to the crisis: Case of architecture sector]. Paper, ADERSE Conference. Nice, France: IAE de Nice.

Zardet, V., & Harbi, (2007). SEAMES®. A Professional Knowledge Management Software Program. In A. F. Buono & H. Savall (Eds.). *Socio-economic Interventions in Organizations: The intervener-researcher and the SEAM Approach to Organizational Analysis* (pp. 33–42). Charlotte NC: Information Age Publishing.

Zardet, V., & Noguera, F. (2006). Cas de recherche-intervention de trois territoires-pilotes d'une Région [The case of a research-intervention on three pilot-territories in a French region]. In ISEOR (Ed.). *Le Management du développement des territoires* (pp. 131–149). Paris, France: Economica.

Zardet, V., & Noguera, F. (2014). Quelle contribution du management au développement de la dynamique territoriale? Expérimentation d'outils de contractualisation sur trois territoires [What is the contribution of management to the development of territories? The testing of contractual tools on three territories]. *Gestion et Management Public*, *2*(2), 5–31.

Zardet, V., & Pierre, X. (2007). Distance spatiale et cognitive entre acteurs impliqués dans le management d'un territoire [Spatial and cognitive distances between actors involved in the management of a French region]. AIMS Workshop. Orléans, France (November).

Zardet, V., & Voyant, O. (2003). Organizational transformation through the socio-economic approach in an industrial context. *Journal of Organizational Change Management*, *16*(1), 56–71.

Zolnai-Saucray, E. (1999). Vers une pédagogie du contrôle dans l'organisation [To a control pedagogy in organization]. In Y. Dupuy, *Faire de la recherche en contrôle de gestion?* [Doing management control research?] (pp. 125–139). Paris, France: Vuibert.

GLOSSARY
SEAM-Related Concepts and Terminology

This glossary contains references to the use of terms and concepts used in the various chapters in this volume, and specific keywords with a brief definition. As appropriate, the reader is also referred to A.F. Buono & H. Savall (Eds.), *Socio-economic intervention in organizations: The intervener-researcher and the SEAM approach to organizational analysis* (Charlotte, NC: Information Age Publishing, 2007).

Absenteeism: One of the five indicators of hidden costs, both the consequence of certain dysfunctions and the cause of other dysfunctions (Chapters 6, 7, 8, 11, 13, 14).

Active listening (or attentive): Active listening is founded in interaction, a heuristic approach composed of three phases: (1) pure (nonjudgmental) listening, (2) reformulation and validation, (3) followed by listening anew (Chapter 11).

Activity piloting intensity: Chapter 1

Actor: External actor designates a person pertaining to the organization's relevant external environment. Internal actor designates a person belonging to the organization's internal environment (e.g., owner, director, employee, volunteer) (Chapters 3, 4, 6, 7, 8, 9, 10, 11, 12, 13, 14, 15, 16, 17, 18).

Agenda: Chapter 8

Agility: Chapters 3, 8, 11

Alignment: Chapter 10

Anthropological: Chapter 5

Applied research: Scientific research that is focused on the effective implementation of discoveries or models to be tested [see Chapter 11 in Buono & Savall (2007)].

Artistic: activities, logic, organization, project, services (Chapter 5, 9, 12)

Assessment of achievements [See Chapter 7 in Buono & Savall (2007)].

Assessment: See evaluation (also Chapter 4)

Balanced budget: Chapter 1

Basket: A basket of dysfunctions is a gathering of dysfunctions based on a *root-cause* in order to address, in a systemic and holistic way, solutions research-process. The *focus group* designs its improvement action plan, based on 3 or 5 baskets that sum up the main dysfunctions indentified along the diagnosis phase. Each basket label is related to an improvement axis, such as "Improving cooperation level between factory and sales force". See *dysfunction basket* (Chapter 4, 14, 15)

Behavior grid: [See Chapter 8 in Buono & Savall (2007)].

Behaviors: Observable human conducts, which have an impact on their physical and social environment. Behaviors are different from a human being's attitude or personality and can be observed through actions. Behaviors play an essential role, on the one hand as source of dysfunctions, on the other hand, in the innovation dynamic to reduce them. (Chapter 5, 15)

Boomerang-effect: Reaction of the external environment to the externalization of costs (externalized costs) forcing an organization to transform them into internal costs (internalized costs) [see Chapter 15 in Buono & Savall (2007)].

Budgeted Action Plan (B.A.P.): A budgeted action plan is a Priority Action Plan (PAP) [see ***Priority Action Plan***] completed by a measurement of its economic impacts: external time and costs of implementation; and expected performances in terms of charges reduction and revenue increase. A budgeted action plan is the priority action plan and economic balance [see ***economic balance***] synthesis. (Chapter 4, 14)

Bureaucracy: Chapter 2

Change axis: see ***trihedron model*** (also Chapter 4)

Change energy: Given the environment evolution and the actors' resistance to change, the success of change processes requires a stronger expenditure of human energy than the evolutions in day-to-day activities. (Chapter 1, 8)

Charges: Chapter 2, 4, 14

Chronobiology: Study of the life rhythms of a person or organization. The chronology of socio-economic intervention respects both the natural rhythms of the organization where the intervention takes place and certain intervention-process rhythms necessary for effectiveness (Chapter 8, 12, 14).

Citizenship science: Chapter 6

Clean-up: Maintenance or renovation of the material or intangible objects that make up an organization (e.g., structures, procedures and behaviors) which suffer from inexorable deterioration over time. Clean-up is one of the three efficiency factors (see HISOFIS and synchronization) and one of the main sources of reduced dysfunction and hidden costs (Chapter 1, 12).

Clinical intervention-research: See ***intervention-research*** (Chapter 16)

Cluster: A cluster is a team composed of internal actors with their hierarchical superiors. Clusters are core elements in the collaborative-training structure, which is part of the Horivert process (Chapter 5, 14, 15, 16).

Cognitive interactivity: Interactive process (between intervener-researcher and company actors) of knowledge production through successive feedback loops, with the steadfast goal of increasing the value of significant information processed by scientific work (Chapter 1, 3, 4, 5, 6, 7, 16).

Cohesion: Level of cooperation among actors within a team or an enterprise, which is a source of sustainable performance according to SEAM (Chapter 1, 2, 4, 7, 11, 13, 14, 16).

Collaborative delegation: Entrusting an operation to a delegate, while ensuring that the delegate has the necessary means to carry it out, which include pedagogical support from the instructing party on behalf of the delegate. (Chapter 4, 15, 18)

Collaborative initiatives: Chapter 2

Collaborative learning: See *learning by doing*. [Also Chapter 1 in Buono & Savall (2007)].

Collaborative training: Theoretical and practical training of managers in a zone of responsibility in the organization, led by the hierarchical superior, adapting training content to the real work situation (Chapter 3, 11, 12, 17).

Collaborative work: Chapter 15

Commitment: Behavior that testifies high involvement in work, support to the corporate strategy, and contribution to the carrying out of its objectives. One of the commitment's signs is the achievement of objectives in time and the expected quality level. (Chapter 1, 8)

Communication: All types of information exchange among actors, formal and informal, top-down and horizontal, frequent and rare, regular and irregular, professional and nonprofessional content, of major importance or not (Chapter 3, 4, 7, 9, 10, 11, 12).

Communication-Coordination-Cooperation (3C): Referred to as 3C, this concept covers all communication, coordination and cooperation as defined in the present glossary (Chapter 1, 4, 5, 7, 9, 10, 11, 12, 14, 15, 17, 18).

Competence: Theoretical and practical knowledge held by an actor, which is implemented in the exercise of his or her professional activity (Chapter 2, 10, 14, 17, 18).

Competency grid: Synoptic tool displaying the competencies currently available in a team and their concrete deployment (Chapter 3, 4, 7, 11, 14, 17, 18).

Competitiveness: Chapter 1, 2, 4, 7, 12, 17, 18.

Confidence: Positive relationship between individuals or teams, which facilitates cohesion (Chapter 9, 10).

Conflict-cooperation: Professional relationships among people and groups are always characterized by dialectical tension between partly conflictive and cooperative relations. The socio-economic theory considers that natural conflictual impulse is inherent to human and social life. Conflict management is at the core of management activities, and may be a source of creativity. (Chapter 1, 8).

Constraints: Chapter 5, 8.

Content analysis: Chapter 1.

Contradictory intersubjectivity: Technique for creating consensus based on the subjective perceptions of different actors, in order to create more "objective" grounds for working together (Chapter 3, 4, 6, 10).

Cooperation and transversality: Chapter 1.

Cooperation deficiency: Chapter 2

Cooperation: Characterizes the exchanges between actors that permit (1) defining a common operational or functional objective to be carried out within a determined period and (2) defining the game rules of the cooperation (Chapter 1, 2, 4, 5, 7, 9, 10, 13, 14, 16, 17)

Cooperative delegation span (CDS): Schematic representation of concerted delegation relationships between two people or two entities "A" and "B", hierarchically or functional linked. It divides the activities into 4 zones : (a) full autonomy of "B" without any information to "A", (b) initiatives from "B" with retrospective information to "A", (c) preliminary consultation of "A" from "B" prior to any action from "B", (d) decision and action made by "A". (Chapter 18)

Cooperative delegation: See *collaborative delegation*. Assigning missions for operations and tasks to a collaborator or a team, combined with integrated training action by the hierarchical superior to guarantee adequate competency and leeway for individual initiative; see also collaborative delegation (Chapter 18).

Cooperative learning: Chapter 14

Coordination: Information-exchange frameworks between actors with the goal of attaining an operational objective or completing a functional activity (Chapter 4, 7, 9, 12, 17, 18)

Core group: [See Chapter 1, 6, 11 in Buono & Savall (2007)].

Cost estimate: [See Chapter 1, 10 in Buono & Savall (2007)].

Cost reduction: reduction of charges (visible costs) of the company (Chapter 2).

Cost-value of the activities: Chapter 4.

Cost-value: The cost-value of an activity is twofold: it is a cost for one of the partners, and a value for the other one. One can measure it by the dedicated amount of time to achieve this activity (in hours) multiplied by the HC-VAVC, whether it be a dysfunction regulation activity, a production activity, or an endogenous creation of potential activity. This amount includes the overall production cost (including the wages and structure costs) and the contribution of this activity to the company's profit. (Chapter 4)

Creation of economic value: Chapter 3.

Creation of human potential: Chapter 6.

Creation of potential: Action that will have positive effects on future financial years, mainly composed of intangible investments (Chapter 1, 6, 12)

Creation of value-added: Goal of internal human activity, responding to the needs of external actors (stakeholders) (Chapter 1, 4, 7, 13, 14, 15).

Crisis: Chapter 8.

Daily proximity democracy: Chapter 5.

Decentralization: Chapter 15.

Decentralized and synchronized strategic steering system: Chapter 13.

Decentralized and synchronized: Chapter 13.

Decider-payer: Individual in the intervention process with the legitimate power to commit the necessary resources and make change decisions [See Chapter 1 in Buono & Savall (2007)].

Democracy: Chapter 5.

Deontology: See *ethics* [See Chapter 1 in Buono & Savall (2007)].

Depersonalization: See *TFW* virus. Impersonal characteristic of rules, organization charts, logical charts, instructions, processes, and procedures based on the Weberian principle that stipulates: the rational organization should not take into account the specific characteristics of people, because they have to be interchangeable. It is one of the three principles of TFW virus (Chapter 2).

Destruction of value-added: Waste of economic resources due to useless expenditures or noncreation of value-added by internal actors (Chapter 17).

Development of Corporate Social Responsibility (CSR) to Retain Employees: Chapter 11.

Development: Qualitative and quantitative transformation of the enterprise, its activities, its structures, its behaviors and its results, including both economic and social performance (Chapter 2, 3, 4, 6, 7, 10, 11, 12, 14, 15, 17, 18).

Development-management: [See Chapter 15 in Buono & Savall (2007)].

Diagnosis: See *socio-economic diagnosis* (Chapter 3, 4, 7, 8, 10, 13, 14, 16, 17).

Dialectics: Chapter 1.

Dichotomy: Chapter 2.

Differentiation strategy through quality: Chapter 11.

Dignity: Chapter 5.

Direct productivity gaps: One of the five indicators of hidden costs indicating that the volume of production of goods or services is inferior to the standard volume that could be expected [See Chapter 15 in Buono & Savall (2007)].

Directivity and participation: Chapter 13.

Directivity and pedagogy: Chapter 13.

Directivity: Component of participative processes that enables their sustainable socio-economic effectiveness and efficiency, thanks to actors' projects and actions, according to the orchestra conductor's metaphor, who manages the synchronization of competent musicians. (Chapter 12)

Directly productive time: Human time devoted to the completion of tasks, operations or activities directly impacting the immediate operational activity of the organization. According to socio-economic theory, directly productive time is only efficient if coupled with indirectly productive time (Chapter 18).

Discriminating value-added: [See Chapter 7 in Buono & Savall (2007)].

Double and interactive responsibility: Chapter 1.

Dysfunction basket: see *basket*. Method grouping together dysfunctions under three to six relevant themes to facilitate the focus-group's search for solutions during the project phase (Chapter 1, 11).

Dysfunction: Consequence of interaction between an organization's structures and the behaviors of internal and external actors. They are described by actors in terms of discrepancies with reference to orthofunctions (Chapter 3, 4, 6, 7, 9, 10, 11, 12, 13, 14, 15, 17, 18).

Dysfunctional thought: Chapter 16.

Economic balance: The economic balance of a project is a tool that compares, on the one hand project implementation costs, including time spent; and on the other hand the project expected performance: hidden costs of dysfunction recycling level thanks to the new project, in terms of charges reduction and revenue increase : turnover and margin. (Chapter 4, 8, 10, 11, 13, 14)

Economic performance: Rational short and long-term utilization of the organization's resources, in keeping with socio-economic rationale, which is multidimensional and takes into account psychosociological and anthropological criteria in defining the ultimate goal of economic action (Chapter 3, 4, 6, 11, 13, 14)

Economies of scale: Chapter 2, 18.

Effectiveness: Degree to which a predefined objective is attained (Chapter 2, 3, 4, 7, 8, 10, 11, 12, 13, 17, 18).

Efficiency: Judicious utilization of resources engaged to attain a result (Chapter 3, 4, 7, 11, 13, 15, 16, 17, 18).

Effort/benefit balance for actors: Tool that synthesizes the principal change efforts as well as the principal advantages to be drawn by the various categories of actors involved in a socio-economic innovation project [See Chapter 11 in Buono & Savall (2007)].

Endogenous investment: Production of goods and services, generated by company's internal resources and supposed to create effects and socio-economic value in the coming periods. (Chapter 2).

Endogenous performances: Chapter 8.

Energy, behavior and competency: Chapter 5.

Energy: See *human energy* (Chapter 8).

Engineering transfer: A sustainable effective and efficient change process in the organizations requires a methodical engineering implying structured, though flexible, knowledge rules, while transferring know-how to the actors so they can integrate the organizational metamorphosis (Chapter 8).

Engineering: Chapter 8, 12, 13, 18.

Entrepreneurial and economic abstention: Chapter 1.

Entrepreneurship and intrapreneurship capitalism: Chapter 1.

Entropy: Chapter 1.

Ethics: Fundamental values embodied in a code of good conduct shared among actors when cohesion is adequate (Chapter 5).

Evaluation phase: Fourth stage of the socio-economic intervention on the improvement-process axis (following the diagnostic, the project and the implementation phases). The evaluation is qualitative, quantitative and financial in nature, and expresses progress in social and economic performance (Chapter 3).

Evaluation: Measure of the result obtained through a real activity with regards to an objective that was defined a priori (Chapter 2, 3, 4, 6, 7, 9, 13, 14, 15, 17).

Excess salary: Component of the cost of certain dysfunctions corresponding to wage differential due to a higher-paid employee performing a task that should have been performed by a lesser-paid employee (downward shift of functions) [See Chapter 1, 9 11, 14, 17 in Buono & Savall (2007)].

Exhaustive fieldnote quotes: See *fieldnote quotes* [see also Chapter 1 in Buono & Savall (2007)].

Exogenous investment: Chapter 2.

Expected hours worked (number of): Chapter 4.

Experimental research: Scientific research that submits ideas for factual experimentation (Chapter 15). This concept was borrowed from C. Bernard, *Introduction to the Study of Experimental Medicine*, New York: Dover, 1957).

Expert opinion: Chapter 4, 8, 9, 11, 15, 17.

Extension phase: See *(territorial) extension (phase)* [see also Chapter 1, 3, 4, 5 in Buono & Savall (2007)].

Extension: Chapter 18.

External actor: Chapter 17

External consultant: See *external intervener*; Chapter 11

External energy: Chapter 11.

External environment: All economic actors outside the organization (stakeholders) whose action directly or indirectly affects the organization (Chapter 2, 3, 4, 7, 8, 12, 13).

External intervener: Professional consultant from the external environment implementing a set of actions involving the modification of structures and behaviors of the organization (Chapter 4, 6, 8, 11, 12, 13).

External intervener-researcher: Chapter 13.

External stakeholders: Chapter 5.

External strategy: Chapters 1, 7, 11.

External validation: Capacity of a theoretical model to be applied to other contexts [see Buono & Savall (2007)].

Externalized cost: Cost generated by the organization and imposed upon its external environment; see also ***boomerang-effect*** [see Buono & Savall (2007)].

Field for scientific observation: Chapter 6.

Fieldnote quote: Short citation -or sentence- of an organizational actor collected through exhaustive fieldnotes during the socio-economic intervention. In the socio-economic diagnosis phase, a fieldnote quote expresses a dysfunction, in a natural language, perceived by the interviewed. It is then categorized in a generic key idea of dysfunction (Chapter 1, 9, 10, 14).

Focus group: A focus group is a temporary workgroup implemented in order to conceive an improvement action plan that solves dysfunctions. The proposal actions are validated in the permanent decision-making organs of the organization. The focus group is composed of managers and animated by a project leader who is responsible of the concerned perimeter. In a SME, the project leader is the CEO him/herself. The focus group alternatively gathers (a) in *restricted group*: to identify priorities, to define objectives-constraints of the project and to validate advances of the plenary group; and (b) in *a plenary session group* to cooperatively conceive and create improvement action proposals. The plenary group creates workgroups to explore themes in-depth. Their composition is totally free, exception due to the fact that each workgroup has to be led by a manager member of the plenary group. (Chapter 4, 11, 14)

Functioning: The observable operation of an organization is a mixture of orthofunctions and dysfunctions (Chapter 3, 4, 7, 11, 16, 17, 18).

Game rules: Set of the rules that determine the functioning, the cooperation, the good practices and processes thanks to which the organizational actors are able to play their roles, with sustainable effectiveness and efficiency, and to avoid dysfunctions and hidden costs. (Chapter 5, 12)

Gears: Made up of human behaviors and frameworks that make procedures and processes of activity and communication-coordination-cooperation function correctly [See Chapter 5 in Buono & Savall (2007)].

Generic constructivism: Epistemological framework advocated by the socio-economic theory of organizations, based on individual and collective knowledge creation mechanisms. Unlike the constructivism which better considers specificity and contingency in knowledge creation process, the generic constructivism does not renounce to the quest of some universality, such as in life and nature sciences, without taking the too much external or superficial, optic of traditional positivism. (Chapter 16)

Generic contingency: Epistemological principle introduced by the socio-economic theory that, while recognizing the operational specificities of organizations, postulates the existence of invariants that constitute generic rules embodying core knowledge that possesses a certain degree of stability and "universality" (Chapter 6, 10, 14, 16).

Generic dysfunction: Non-specific kind of dysfunction that one can observe in different types of organizations. ISEOR has counted 3 534 generic dysfunctions throughout the intervention-researches carried-out in 1 350 companies and organizations of 40 countries. (Chapter 1)

Generic key idea: [See Chapter 1 in Buono & Savall (2007)].

Generic knowledge: Core, decontextualized knowledge (Chapter 6, 16).

HCMVC: See *HCVAVC* (Chapter 4, 10, 12).

HCVAVC: See *hourly contribution to value-added on variable costs* (Chapter 4, 5, 10, 12, 14).

Heuristic: A process that produces knowledge by processing factual information through "intelligent groping" in which the search for solutions incorporates, step by step, the rules for discovering relevant information (Chapter 4, 6, 17).

Hidden cost recycling: Part of the hidden costs is compressible. The compression of hidden costs is named recycling or conversion of hidden costs into value-added since it includes at the same time charge decrease and revenue increase thanks to time expenditure decrease, a source of over-wage, overtime and non-production, reallocated to additional production and sales activities (the "recycling" expression refers to the metaphor of "recycling energy"). Recycling hidden costs works without staff reduction, by developing activities that create value-added. (Chapter 18)

Hidden cost: Destruction of value-added, which is partly or completely left out of a company's accounting information system, consisting of both surplus expenditures and opportunity costs that affect the relevance of decision-making processes (Chapter 3, 4, 6, 7, 9, 10, 11, 12, 13, 14, 15, 16, 17, 18).

Hidden cost-and performance (theory): Full title of the theory of hidden costs; an interaction exists between such costs and performance (i.e., reducing hidden costs is a performance and reduced performance is a cost) (Chapter 1, 3, 4, 6, 7, 8, 9, 10, 11, 12, 13, 14, 15, 16, 17, 18).

Hidden costs and performances: Chapter 2, 16.

Hidden costs conversion into value-added: Chapter 3, 4, 11, 12, 15.

Hidden costs versus profitability: Chapter 2, 3, 4, 5, 6, 7, 8, 11, 12.

Hidden infrastructure: An organization's infrastructure composed of modes of operation and management that are not visible to external actors [See Chapter 2 in Buono & Savall (2007)].

Hidden life: Chapter 3.

Hidden performance: [See Chapter 1 in Buono & Savall (2007)].

Hidden products/services: The spontaneous functioning of an organization often generates microproducts that have a value but are not sold by the enterprise [see Chapter 18 in Buono & Savall (2007)].

Hidden variables: Chapter 6.

Hidden: Chapter 2.

High level of profitability of IIQDHP: Chapter 2.

HISOFIS: Humanly Integrated and Stimulating Operational and Functional Information System: HISOFIS-type information stimulates the receiver, individual or group, and incites the receiver to engage in decisive action, which implies the expenditure of human energy. HISOFIS is one of the three efficiency factors (see synchronization and clean-up) and one of the main sources of reduced dysfunctions and hidden costs. OFIS (Operational and Functional Information System) represents the total volume of information emitted and circulated in an organization. HIOFIS (Humanly Integrated OFIS) is the subset of information assimilated by the receivers. HISOFIS (Stimulating HIOFIS) is the part of HIOFIS that stimulates human action, source of performance (Chapter 4).

HISOFISGENESIS: Generating HISOFIS effects [see Chapter 6 in Buono & Savall (2007)].

Horivert (architecture or intervention or model or method or process): Socio-economic innovation intervention in an organization composed of two simultaneous actions: (1) a HORIzontal action, a diagnostic of dysfunctions with the board of directors and the management team, as well as setting up socio-economic management tools, followed by a horizontal project; and (2) a VERTical action: in at least two departments including vertical diagnostics. Vertical action involves the line personnel as well (Chapter 2, 3, 4, 7, 8, 12, 14, 15, 18).

Horizontal action (or intervention): [See Chapter 1, 2, 3, 4, 7, 11, 12, 17 in Buono & Savall (2007)].

Horizontal and vertical intervention: Chapter 15.

Horizontal and vertical projects: Chapter 7.

Horizontal diagnosis: First phase of the intervention, in parallel with the first training sessions in socio-economic management tools, consisting in drawing up an inventory of major dysfunctions through one-on-one interviews with every senior and middle manager (Chapter 14, 15, 18).

Horizontal project: Action projects responding to the dysfunctions that were revealed during the horizontal diagnostic at the beginning of the Horivert process, setting the stage for improving policies and general procedures (Chapter 7, 14).

Horizontal socio-economic diagnosis: See *horizontal diagnosis* (Chapter 14).

Horizontal synchronization: Chapter 18.

Hourly contribution to value-added on variable costs (HCVAVC): It is the average value-added generated by one activity hour of the whole staff. The overall value-added on variable cost (VAVC) of a company is measured by deducting from its turn-over the variable expenditures depending on the level of activity, excluding the personnel expenditures. We calculate the HCVAVC by dividing the VAVC by the total annual number of hours of human activity (Chapter 4, 5, 10, 12, 14).

Human energy: See *energy*. Metaphor that expresses the individual and collective action capacity of one person. Management actions and practices enable stimulating energy by arousing actions. It is one of the three components of *human potential*, along with *competence* and *behavior*, and thus, a factor of *socio-economic performance*. Human energy is both composed of profession-based energy (capacity to achieve tasks of a defined profession) and change energy. The energy level declines over time (entropic phenomenon) which requires a periodical stimulation (Chapter 5).

Human factor: The socio-economic theory replaces the materialistic and utilitarian concept of the human "factor" with that of human "potential" (Chapter 3, 4).

Human potential: The all-important factor for creating economic value lies in the individual, who can give or withhold his or her energy based on the quality of the informal and formal bond with the organization. This is measured by the HCVAVC indicator (hourly contribution to value-added on variable costs) (Chapter 1, 2, 3, 4, 5, 6, 7, 8, 9, 10, 11, 12, 13, 14, 15, 16, 17).

IESAP: Internal/external strategic action plan (Chapter 2, 7, 11, 14, 18).

IIQDHP Intangible Investment on Qualitative Development of Human Potential: The IIQDHP is an extrafinancial measurement in time and monetary terms. The IIQDHP cost includes external costs (e.g., training, fees, travel expenses, small equipment purchases) and internal costs, i.e. the time dedicated to creation of potential by all the company's actors. The creation of potential is the time dedicated by the company's actors to training others or themselves, creating new procedures and working methods more effective, participating to focus groups, creating new products, preparing the conquest of new markets... Any internal project can be assessed in terms of investment cost (IIQDHP), as well as its profitability tied to the value-added increase (Chapter 1, 5, 15).

IIQDHP profitability: Chapter 1, 4, 5, 8, 10, 11, 13, 15.

Immaterial (or intangible) investment: See *intangible investment* [see Chapter 15 in Buono & Savall (2007)].

Immediate result: Results under the headings of visible costs and visible products that are identified and assessed by the actors; often referred to as short-term economic results, such as they appear in the company profit and loss statement (Chapter 1, 3, 6, 17).

Immediate-result indicators: See *immediate results* [see Chapter 1, 13 in Buono & Savall (2007)].

Implementation of management control: Chapter 2, 4.

Implementation of SEAM: Chapter 2, 3, 7, 9, 11, 12, 13.

Implementation phase: Chapter 15.

Implementation planning: Chapter 8.

Implementation: Chapter 4, 9, 13, 14 18.

Improvement actions (or process): Chapter 15, 17.

Improvement-process axis: See *(SEAM) three key forces of change* (Chapter 15).

In-depth intervention (or integration) phase: Chapter 10, 13.

Indicators of Social Performance Improvement: Chapter 11.

Indirectly productive time: Human time indirectly impacting the immediate operation activities of the organization. According to socio-economic theory, indirectly productive time is insufficient for certain categories of actors (e.g., line personnel) and excessive for others (e.g., integrated training, communication-coordination-cooperation, evaluation of actions) [see Chapter 2 in Buono & Savall (2007)].

Individual and collective commitment: See *commitment* (Chapter 1).

Individual and collective conflict-cooperation behaviors: See *conflict-cooperation* (Chapter 1).

Individual job satisfaction: Chapter 1.

Industrial injuries: one of the five indicators (see *work accidents*) [see also Chapter 1 in Buono & Savall (2007)].

Inert knowledge: Chapter 1, 2.

Inert nature of technical or financial capital: Chapter 5.

Informal powers: Chapter 1.

Informal Production System: Chapter 1.

Infrastructure: Framework that organizes and codetermines the quality, coherency, effectiveness and efficiency of the organization's operations, such as synchronization-stimulation frameworks (HISOFIS) and "clean-up." These frameworks are not readily visible and are often omitted when carrying out decisive actions. Dysfunctions are usually lodged in the six "infrastructure" domains: working conditions, work organization, time management, communication-coordination-cooperation, integrated training and strategic implementation (Chapter 2, 3, 17).

Initial set-up (of socio-economic management or SEAM): [See Chapter 1, 5, 7 in Buono & Savall (2007)]

Innovation: Chapter 9.

Instable: Chapter 1.

Intangible investment (or immaterial or intellectual): Cost of creation of potential of an intangible nature (e.g., integrated training sessions, focus-group cost), should be considered as a profitable investment rather than a recurring expenditure in accounting (Chapter 1, 2, 4, 6, 8, 11, 12, 13, 15).

Intangible investment in/on human potential: Chapter 2, 4, 5, 6, 8, 11, 12, 13, 15.

Intangible investment on qualitative development of human potential: See *IIQDHP* (Chapter 1, 5, 15).

Integral diagnosis: An integral socio-economic diagnosis combines the *horizontal diagnosis* and the *vertical diagnosis* when the organization's workforce is less than 50 or 80 employees. The integral diagnosis takes an inventory of dysfunctions and hidden costs within all departments or perimeters, in small and medium organizations (Chapter 8).

Integral innovation: Chapter 1.

Integral performance: Chapter 3.

Integral quality: Quality of management, operations and products (goods and services), needed to satisfy the needs of internal and external actors (stakeholders) (Chapter 7).

Integrated corporate social responsibility: Chapter 11.

Integrated epistemology: [See Chapter 1 in Buono & Savall (2007)].

Integrated training manual: [See Chapter 1, 13, 15 in Buono & Savall (2007)].

Integrated training plan: Chapter 18.

Integrated training: Training carried out by an actor in the immediate environment (e.g., the hierarchical superior) involving an inductive pedagogical contribution to local work situations and capitalizing on expertise acquired through experience by explicitly capturing it in an integrated training manual (Chapter 2, 9, 15, 17, 18).

Integration of standards: Chapter 1.

Integration phase (or process): Chapter 2.

Integration: Chapter 3, 4, 10, 11.

Interaction: Dynamic process that is constructed in iterative fashion through mutual influences exerted by actors on one another. These influences cause modifications of operations and socio-economic performance. These combined modifications enable actors to pass from operational State X to a new operational State X (Chapter 3, 4, 6, 7, 8, 9, 10, 12, 15, 16, 17).

Interactivity: Chapter 5.

Intercompany intervention (or action): In the multismall business Horivert, collaborative training in the implementation of SEAM tools is carried out in groups of four to six small enterprises (senior manager and two supervisors) [see Chapter 14 in Buono & Savall (2007)].

Interface: Critical zone between one or several groups, spaces or domains, which should be managed to ensure effective communication between them (Chapter 8, 11, 12, 13, 18).

Internal actor: Chapter 1, 17.

Internal and external (company) environment: Chapter 5.

Internal cohesion: See *cohesion* (Chapter 1, 2, 11, 16, 17, 18).

Internal environment: All active resources in the organization, e.g., human potential, actors, producers of activity and value-added (employees, owners or volunteers) (Chapter 3, 4, 13).

Internal interveners' role in ODC process: Chapter 1, 11, 13, 14.

Internal marketing: Term often employed to designate the techniques of information dissemination among the personnel concerning the life of the organization; also applied to in-depth, active listening (socio-economic diagnostic) and subsequent setting-up of innovative actions that respond to employees' actual expectations (socio-economic innovation project) [see Chapter 2, 18 in Buono & Savall (2007)].

Internal resources: Chapter 2, 5, 9, 15.

Internal stakeholders: Chapter 5

Internal training: Chapter 3.

Internal validation: Demonstrates the internal coherency of the links established between the different variables or hypotheses leading to the construction of a theory. [See Buono & Savall (2007)].

Internal/External Strategic Action Plan (IESAP): Specifies the enterprise's 3 to 5 year strategy, with regard to both key external actors (e.g., clients, suppliers) and key internal actors (e.g., from the CEO to workers). It is updated once a year to take into account change in the enterprise's relevant external and internal environments (Chapter 5, 11, 14).

Internal-client (or customer): SEAM considers personnel at all levels as clients whose needs for improved work life conditions should be satisfied (Chapter 2, 15).

Internal-external overall strategy: The boundary between the internal and the external sides of the company is porous. This is due to numerous permanent interactions between internal actors and external stakeholders. The socio-economic concept of strategy is holistic and includes simultaneous internal and external actions. (Chapter 14)

Internal-intervener (or consultant): Individual in the organization collaborating in the implementation of intervention actions. (Chapter 2, 3, 8, 11, 13, 14, 18)

Internalized cost: Cost generated by the external environment and imposed on the organization [see Buono & Savall (2007)].

Intervener-researcher: Person utilizing the results of his or her interventions to nourish research and scientific knowledge, to help to carry out further interventions (Chapter 3, 6, 8, 9, 15).

Intervention agreement: Contract negotiated by the external intervener with the enterprise that requests a socio-economic intervention. The contract specifies the precise intervention architecture, the number of persons involved, and the schedule of services to be provided [see Chapter 1, 4, 5 in Buono & Savall (2007)].

Intervention architecture: Horivert schema that shows the distribution of actors and intervention services [see Chapter 1, 6, 7, 11 in Buono & Savall (2007)].

Intervention impacts: Chapter 6.

Intervention-research: Concept of management research, which is close to "actionresearch," that implies the frequent presence of the researcher within the enterprise in order to ensure systematic observation of management situations under study. This epistemological option acknowledges that the researcher is clearly engaged in his or her research strategy and coconstructs knowledge with the actors "observed" (Chapter 6, 7, 9, 11, 12, 13, 15, 17).

Intracompany intervention (or intra-organizational): In the multi-small business Horivert, the socio-economic diagnostic and project, as well as the implementation of SEAM tools, are carried out inside each one of the four to six enterprises that make up the group (Chapter 11, 17).

Introducer: The person who introduces the external intervener into the client enterprise, but who does not have the power to negotiate the intervention (see *decider-payer*) [see Chapter 1 in Buono & Savall (2007)].

Investments: Chapter 11.

Involvement and cohesion of the actors: Chapter 1.

Isomorphism: structure nature and constant function of intangible or tangible objects, constant by nature and function, whatever the analysis level or the size. The socio-economic theory allows showing isomorphism in value generation or destruction at individual, team, company, and local, regional, national or international territory levels. It is thus the case for dysfunctions, hidden costs, hourly contribution to value-added on variable costs (HCVAVC), gross domestic profit (GDP), structures, behaviors: macro hidden costs or nano-GDP concepts illustrate this isomorphism (Chapter 1).

Itemized operations chart: Tool that breaks down an operation into stages. This tool serves as a medium for training, as a reminder, and for communication among actors who take part in the operation [see Buono & Savall (2007)].

Know-how transfer: See *engineering transfer* (Chapter 8)

Knowledge creation: creation is a human specific capability that the so-called intelligent machines do not have because they contain stocks of virtual knowledge incorporated by human in the technology, see *living knowledge* (Chapter 1).

Labor value theory: Chapter 5.

Learning process: Chapter 18.

Learning-by-doing: In Aristotle's perspective, thought and action are indivisible. Each one involves simultaneously the other one, as well as speaking and human breathing. In economics, Arrow brought to light the importance of the action learning process (Chapter 1).

Living knowledge: Epistemological concept of the socio-economic theory that distinguishes (a) the virtual knowledge, hoarded in human brains and different supports such like books or: printed, filmed or digitized media, considered as potential of knowledge, (b) from the living knowledge that is created by human interaction, which generates actions and performance creation. The living knowledge is a direct source of performance, contrary to virtual knowledge that requires a transformation into living knowledge by interaction between actors (Chapter 1).

Macro-dysfunction: dysfunction (gap between expected and actual functioning) of social and economic activity at local, regional, or national territory level. Just as in a company, these dysfunctions caused by negative interactions between structures and behaviors of households, companies, organizations, public administrations and institutions of a given territory, such as: high level of unemployment, unfilled positions in an industry, delivery delays and defects of a public building (Chapter 1).

Macro-economic theory of the two production factors: Chapter 2

Macro-hidden cost: Measurement at a territory level (local, regional, or national) of hidden costs generated by a macro-dysfunction and supported by different actors: households, organizations, public administrations, such as the destroyed value of prescribed medicines purchased and not consumed in France (Chapter 1, 5).

Maintenance phase (or actions): Follows the socio-economic management set-up and in-depth intervention phases; consists in regularly restoring good practices (Chapter 3, 8, 11).

Management control decentralization: The development of economic performance, based on the conversion of hidden costs into value-added, is facilitated by decentralization of management control. This consists in sharing the economic steering activities among the management controllers and the operation managers, who assume a management self-control role (Chapter 2)

Management control: Chapter 6

Management tool: Dynamic tools that mobilize human potential and stimulate internal actor behavior and, at times, external actor behavior (Chapter 3, 4, 6, 8, 9, 12, 13, 17, 18).

Management tool axis: See *(SEAM) three key forces of change* [see Chapter 1, 11 in Buono & Savall (2007)].

Managerial and entrepreneurial abstentionism: Chapter 5.

Managerial cohesion: Chapter 15.

Manual of integrated training: Chapter 2

Market of standards and norms: Chapter 1.

Material investment versus intangible investment profitability: Chapter 1, 2, 4, 5, 6, 8, 11, 12.

Mediator: One of the three fundamental functions of the intervener in the socioeconomic intervention method. It entails developing cooperation among actors to build teamwork [See Chapter 11 in Buono & Savall (2007)].

Mental structures: Sustainable characteristic of internal organizational mindsets: management style instilled by the top-management, dominant conceptions affecting managers' behaviors and decisions, staff mindset and social atmosphere. (Chapter 16)

Meso-socio-economic approach: Chapter 17.

Meta socio-economic theory: Chapter 1.

Metamorphosis: Progressive, radical and sustainable transformation of an organization's operations, performances, structures and actor behaviors (Chapter 9, 14).

Metascript: [See Chapter 1, 9 in Buono & Savall (2007)].

Methodologist: One of the three fundamental functions of SEAM interveners: methodological and pedagogical support to actors so that they might discover by themselves or invent their own solutions [see Chapter 14 in Buono & Savall (2007)].

Method-product: Part of the selling method for intangible products (example: consultancy), corresponding to an effective technique (e.g., diagnostic, project, assessment and collaborative training are all method-products of socio-economic intervention) (Chapter 8).

Micro-project: Chapter 4

Mini-diagnosis: [See Chapter 14 in Buono & Savall (2007)].

Mirror-effect: Chapter 3, 4, 7, 11, 12, 14, 15.

Misunderstanding: Category of dysfunctions related to incomprehension on the part of actors concerning strategic choices or procedures. The solution is found in clarifying and communicating, rather than transforming (Chapter 11, 17).

Multi-skills: Chapter 2.

Multi-Small Business Horivert (or Multi-SMEs): Scaled-down Horivert process applied to a group of four to six small enterprises to reduce the intervention cost and to stimulate emulation amongst them (Chapter 11, 17).

Negotiation phase (or process): Preliminary, complimentary phase of socio-economic intervention that aims to make potential client organizations understand socio-economic management and the rigorous nature of its intervention methodology (Chapter 6, 8).

Negotiation: Contradictory dialogue engaged between actors to arrive at an agreement that combines the compatible interests of the parties, through a dialectical game that is ultimately positive (win-win) (Chapter 3, 6, 7, 8, 11, 12, 13, 18).

New role of interveners: directivity to get rapid results: Chapter 1, 8, 12, 13.

Non dit (unvoiced comments): The second constituent of the expert opinion that finalizes the diagnosis. The intervener reports major dysfunctions he or she perceived, but that were not mentioned by actors during the diagnosis interviews (Chapter 17).

Noncreation of potential: One of the six components of hidden costs, namely a possible or planned investment of an intangible nature that was never carried through [see Chapter 1, 11, 16, 17 in Buono & Savall (2007)].

Noncreation of value: Chapter 7.

Nonproduct: [See Chapter 1 in Buono & Savall (2007)].

Nonproduction: [See Chapter 1, 11, 12, 14, 16, 17 in Buono & Savall (2007)].

Non-profit: Chapter 11

Non-quality: One of the five indicators of hidden costs corresponding to quality defects or lack of quality [see Chapter 1, 2, 11, 13, 15, 16 in Buono & Savall (2007)].

Non-sales: Chapter 11.

Objective-product: Major issues pointed out by the decider-payer during the negotiation phase preceding the intervention. They constitute the explicit goals that serve as references throughout the entire process (Chapter 18).

OMSP (Objective-Method-Service-Product) tool: Synthetic tool summing up objective-products, method-products and service-products which constitute the specification manual at the center of the intervention agreement [see Chapter 11, 11 in Buono & Savall (2007)].

Operation Scheduling Grid (OSG): Chapter 4, 10, 11.

Opportunity costs: The opportunity costs constitute with historical costs the two categories of dysfunction hidden costs. When dysfunction effect represents a shortfall in earnings; margin or turnover losses, current or prospective; it entails opportunity costs. We distinguish three components of opportunity costs: *nonproduction, noncreation of potential* and *risk* (Chapter 11).

Organizational biology metaphor: Chapter 2.

Organizational learning: Chapter 8.

Organizational pathologies: Considering that organizations are living beings considerate as a living being in the socio-economic theory, the dysfunctions are taken as pathologies. They cause functioning pains, loss of resources, dissatisfaction and call treatments: improvement actions (Chapter 1).

Orthofunctioning: Functioning desired by the organization's internal and external actors. Orthofunctioning is a relative notion, a flexible reference that admits a certain degree of variability over time. It is useful for defining grosso modo the direction of progress actions for the enterprise (Chapter 1).

Overall economic performance: Chapter 3.

Overcharges: Chapter 1, 11.

Overconsumption: Component of the cost of certain dysfunctions corresponding to the quantity of products or services over-employed resulting from the regulation of dysfunctions [see Chapter 1, 8, 11, 12 in Buono & Savall (2007)].

Overtime: Time in excess of a set limit. Component of the cost of certain dysfunctions corresponding to the time spent in regulating dysfunctions (Chapter 2, 10).

Participative (and structured) management: Chapter 5, 13, 14, 18.

Performance evaluation: Chapter 5.

Periodic assessment of HCVAVC : economic creation source: Chapter 2.

Periodic resurgence (of dysfunctions and hidden costs): Chapter 1.

Periodically negotiable activity contract (PNAC): Management tool that formally states the priority objectives and the means made available for attaining them, involving every employee in the enterprise (including workers and office employees), based on a biannual personal dialogue with the employee's direct hierarchical superior (Chapter 2, 8, 9, 11, 12, 13, 17, 18).

Personal (or personalized) assistance: Every collective collaborative-training session in the "clusters" is followed by a one-on-one interview with every manager and senior manager to help him or her adjust SEAM tools to his or her own personal function (Chapter 8, 11, 12, 13).

Personnel (staff) turnover: Chapter 7, 14.

Pertinent environment: [See Chapter 1 in Buono & Savall (2007)].

Physical working conditions: Chapter 1.

Piloting (method; structure; resources): Refers to piloting acts that expend human energy, piloting team cooperation and immaterial management tools (Chapter 2, 3, 7, 8, 10, 12, 13, 14, 15.

Piloting logbook (or tools): Chapter 1, 2, 4, 14, 18.

Pivotal ideas (idées forces): Family or group of key-ideas. It is a key-idea of a higher generic level (Chapter 12).

Planning and scheduling (practice): Chapter 11.

Plenary executive committee (or plenary steering committee): See **steering group** (Chapter 18).

Plenary group: [See Chapter 1, 6, 11 in Buono & Savall (2007)].

Policy decision-making process: Chapter 4.

Policy-decision axis: [See Chapter 11 in Buono & Savall (2007)].

Poorly executed tasks: One of the deep causes of numerous dysfunctions corresponding to neglected tasks, tasks not carried out, executed behind schedule or lacking quality [see Chapter 13, 14 in Buono & Savall (2007)].

Porosity: Chapter 5.

Positive externalities: Chapter 2.

Priority action plan (PAP): A coordinated inventory of actions to be accomplished within a period of six months to attain priority strategic objectives, once priorities have been defined and tested for feasibility. These actions are partly generators of dysfunctions (current project on the external environment) and partly reducers of dysfunctions (action on the internal environment) (Chapter 7, 8, 9, 11, 14, 17, 18).

Pro-activity (pro-active strategy): characteristics of actions that anticipates events, without waiting for reacting to environmental signals. The pro-active strategy is based on innovation, differentiation even diversification: it avoids disadvantages due to the imitation strategies of the competition. (Chapter 2, 8)

Production function (economics concept): See chapter 2.

Productivity: Capacity to produce material and immaterial goods appreciated by actors, clients or users for a given period (Chapter 1, 2, 4, 5, 6, 7, 9, 10, 11, 12, 13, 14, 15, 17, 18)

Professional behavior: Chapter 1.

Progressive spiral: A continuous process of cumulative improvement. (Chapter 14)

Project baskets: Chapter 14.

Project group: See *focus group* (Chapter 2, 5, 15, 18).

Project leader (or manager): Hierarchical leader in charge of conducting the improvement process of socio-economic performances in his or her team, the CEO, department head or workshop head, depending on the situation (Chapter 2, 4).

Project management: Chapter 1, 9.

Project phase: Chapter 2, 9.

Project: See *socio-economic project* (Chapter 3, 5, 6, 7, 9, 10, 11, 12, 13, 14, 15, 16, 17).

Provisional intervention schedule: [See Chapter 11 in Buono & Savall (2007)].

Proximity management (or supervising management or managers): The proximity management concept considers that the immediate (or direct) hierarchical superior plays an important role in good working conditions, daily communications and development of competency among his or her co-team members, due to direct and frequent interaction with them (Chapter 5, 7, 8, 11, 13, 14, 15, 18).

Psycho-social risks: Chapter 3.

Public resources: Chapter 17.

Public vs private (change): Chapter 2, 17.

qQFi analysis: see *qualimetrics* (Chapter 1).

qQFi evaluation: Chapter 6, 7.

Qualimetrics (evaluation or methodology): Chapter 3, 4, 6, 7.

Qualitative development of human potential (QDHP): Chapter 5.

Qualitative diagnosis: All dysfunctions expressed during a horizontal diagnostic or during the qualitative part of a vertical diagnostic (Chapter 8, 11, 12).

Qualitative investment in human potential: Chapter 15.

Qualitative model: Chapter 1.

Qualitative, quantitative and financial (qQfi) Evaluation: Evaluation combining qualitative and quantitative and financial assessment and measures (Chapter 4).

Quality of collective work environment: Chapter 1

Quotes: Chapter 4.

Rationality: Chapter 8.

Recycling hidden costs into value added creation: Chapter 2, 11, 18.

Reducing costs: Chapter 2.

Regressive spiral: A continuously-amplified negative process [see Buono & Savall (2007)].

Regulation of dysfunctions: Chapter 15.

Regulation time: Chapter 2.

Regulation: Chapter 5, 9, 10, 14.

Resistance to change: Chapter 8.

Resolution chart: A tool filled out during a meeting and distributed immediately afterwards to all participants, providing responsibility for and encouraging action steps (Chapter 8, 11, 13).

Resources: The organization's physical and human means, material and immaterial, utilized in company activities and applied to its products (goods or services) (Chapter 4, 6, 7, 8, 10, 12, 13, 14, 17, 18).

Results assessment: [See Chapter 1, 10 in Buono & Savall (2007)].

Risk: Chapter 4, 8, 9, 10, 13, 15, 18.

Root causes (of dysfunctions): Deep, primary causes of dysfunctions of which actors are rarely conscious; they are revealed in the non dit (unvoiced comments) constituent of the expert opinion (Chapter 4, 8, 10, 14).

Rooting phase (or process or approach) of socio-economic management (or of SEAM intervention): Chapter 3.

Scheduling: Designing a precise activity program for all actors in cooperation with their partners; also an activity piloting indicator (Chapter 7, 8, 10, 13).

Scientific consultancy: Advice to organizations based on scientific knowledge drawn from experimentation; it is also a rigorous method of management research (intervention-research) [see Chapter 1, 2 in Buono & Savall (2007)].

Scientific observation: Chapter 6.

SEAM: Chapter 1, 2, 3, 7, 8, 11, 13, 14, 16, 17, 18.

SEAM diagnosis: Chapter 13.

SEAM implementation: Chapter 2.

SEAM in-depth training: Chapter 11.

SEAM intervention (process): Chapter 2, 3, 7, 16, 17.

SEAM maintenance: Chapter 1, 3, 8, 11, 14, 18.

SEAM model: Chapter 1.

SEAM set–up (phase): [See Chapter 1 in Buono & Savall (2007)].

SEAM star: Chapter 3.

SEAM (management) tools: Chapter 17.

SEAMES® software (or SEAM Expert system software (SEGESE®): Expert system developed by ISEOR that processes over 3,500 types of dysfunctions identified in 1,200 organizations in 34 countries through SEAM interventions (Chapter 2, 3).

(SEAM) three key forces of change: The socio-economic intervention method consecutively follows three axes: improvement-process axis, management-tool axis and policy-decision axis (Chapter 3).

(SEAM) trihedral: See *(SEAM) three key forces of change* (Chapter 3).

Security-management: [See Chapter 15 in Buono & Savall (2007)].

Self-analysis of time grid: A simple tool enabling an actor to become conscious of the ineffective and inefficient structure of his or her use of time, which causes professional-life quality and under-performance problems (Chapter 14).

Self-analysis of time: [See Chapter 1, 13 in Buono & Savall (2007)].

Self-management control: The operation managers assume two assignments, in connection with the management controllers: accurate and concrete analysis of the budgetary gaps through extrafinancial indicators, and the implementation of concrete corrective actions, affecting the gaps root causes (Chapter 2).

Service-product: Actions requiring competency on the part of interveners or actors in application of a "method-product" of the OMSP tool [see Chapter 1, 4, 11 in Buono & Savall (2007)].

Set-up phase: See *initial set-up* and *(SEAM) set-up (phase)* [see Chapter 1, 7, 17 in Buono & Savall (2007)].

Short term (ST)- Long term (LT) balance: Chapter 4, 8, 13.

Short, medium and long term survival and development: See *survival and development* [see Chapter 1 in Buono & Savall (2007)].

Small vs large hidden costs level: Chapter 2, 12.

Social and economic efficiency: Chapter 4.

Social cohesion: Chapter 5.

Social performance: Multiple sources, notably of a psycho-physio-sociological nature, of satisfaction for actors, clients or producers of the organization in their professional life (Chapter 1, 3, 6, 7, 8, 11, 12, 15, 17).

Social value: Chapter 5.

Socially Responsible Capitalism (SRC): Chapter 4, 5.

Socio-economic (innovation) project (group): Chapter 2, 18.

Socio-economic (innovation) project: Chapter 9.

Socio-economic (sustainable) performance: Combines social performance and economic performance, the development of one based on the development of the other, neither being exclusively attained to the detriment of the other (Chapter 2, 4, 6, 10, 13, 14, 18).

Socio-economic accompaniment: Chapter 7.

Socio-economic analysis: Chapter 16, 17.

Socio-economic approach to management (SEAM): see *socio-economic management* (Chapter 3, 17).

Socio-economic approach to management control: See *socio-economic management control* (Chapter 4).

Socio-economic benefits: Chapter 11.

Socio-economic competitiveness: Capacity to withstand economic competition from the market without weighing too heavily on the social component (Chapter 17).

Socio-economic development actions: Chapter 1.

Socio-economic diagnosis or diagnostic (phase): Diagnostic of dysfunctions in an organization and their destruction of the value-added (hidden costs) they cause (Chapter 4, 7, 11, 13, 14, 15, 16, 17, 18).

Socio-economic engineering (of change): Chapter 15, 17.

Socio-economic evaluation: Stage of the socio-economic innovation process that involves evaluating impacts of the implemented improvement actions on the social performance and economic performance of the organization and its actors [see Chapter 1, 5 in Buono & Savall (2007)].

Socio-economic framework: Chapter 5, 16.

Socio-economic general management (for CEOs): Chapter 1, 2, 3, 7, 8, 11, 12, 13, 14, 15, 18)

Socio-economic HR Management: Chapters 11, 14, 18.

Socio-economic indicators: Chapter 2.

Socio-economic information system: Chapter 4, 6, 10.

Socio-economic innovation process (or action): Enables change to be progressively assimilated during the experimentation phase, notably through the diagnostic of the enterprise's dysfunctions; the innovation project includes improvement actions for both social and economic performance, their implementation and the evaluation of obtained results. See also socio-economic project (Chapter 9, 11).

Socio-economic intervention axes: See (*SEAM) trihedral* (Chapter 7, 9).

Socio-economic intervention: Simultaneously engaging actions within an enterprise on all its structures and human behaviors, by intervening in the six domains of dysfunctions. The enterprise's operations are thus dealt with as a whole, in order to facilitate the emergence of sustainable, effective and innovative solutions (Chapter 3, 6, 7, 9, 11, 13, 14, 15, 16, 17).

Socio-economic intervention-research: Chapter 13, 16, 18.

Socio-economic management (SEAM): Increased participation and dynamism on the part of the enterprise's or organization's entire personnel and by the development of all human know-how and competency, in the strategic pursuit of both improved social (qualitative) and economic (quantitative) performance, the benefits of which are more or less distributed among internal and external actors (stakeholders) (Chapter 2, 3, 4, 7, 9, 17, 18).

Socio-economic management control: Piloting of the organization's short-, medium-, and long-term economic and social performance through qualitative, quantitative and financial evaluation of visible and hidden costs and performance. It contains a self-control component carried out by operational personnel and an external control component carried out by management control specialists (Chapter 1, 4, 6, 7, 10, 13, 14).

Socio-economic management tools: Chapter 2, 7, 11, 14, 17, 18.

Socio-economic marketing (and sales): Chapter 1, 7, 8, 11, 12, 13, 14, 16, 17.

Socio-economic operation management: Chapter 2, 7, 10, 13, 14, 16, 17.

Socio-economic organization: Chapter 7, 10, 12, 14, 15, 16.

Socio-economic productivity: Chapter 1, 5, 15.

Socio-economic project (phase): Second stage of the socio-economic innovation process. The goal is to seek solution baskets (improvement actions) that respond to dysfunction baskets. A socio-economic project is an ensemble of socio-economic innovation actions (Chapter 14, 17).

Socio-economic prosperity: Chapter 3.

Socio-economic research and development (R&D): R&D function opened to the other departments of the organization, achieving its mission of products & technologies innovation, in close cooperation with the marketing department, the sales force, the technologic and competition vigilance and production. (Chapter 7)

Socio-economic strategic vigilance: Shared function among the different departments and the different levels of responsibility of the company. The people part-time responsible for doing permanent vigilance constitute a network of decentralized and synchronized sensors, which are more effective and responsive than a strategic vigilance specialized department (Chapter 4, 5, 8, 13, 14)

Socio-economic strategy: [See Chapter 1, 7 in Buono & Savall (2007)].

Socio-economic theory (of organizations): An original theory experimented in X,XXX enterprises and organizations, developed by combining knowledge from the social and economic sciences in order to improve sustainable performance (Chapter 1, 2, 5, 6, 7, 9, 10, 16).

Socio-economic transorganizational intervention: Chapter 17.

Socio-economic value: Chapter 5.

Spiral: Chapter 4.

Staff turnover: see *personal turnover* (Chapter 2).

Stakeholders: Chapter 1.

Steering committee (or group): Chapter 7, 8, 11.

Steering indicators logbook: Chapter 13.

Stimulating information system: See *HISOFIS* (Chapter 1).

Strategic activity list (or nomenclature): Chapter 4.

Strategic alert indicators: Indicators that make it possible to detect the probable critical state of an organization within a timespan of 3 to 5 years [see Buono & Savall (2007), *op.cit.*].

Strategic alignment: See chapter 10.

Strategic ambition: Distance separating an organization's current strategic situation and its intended strategic situation; it may be dependent on or independent of the organization's current strategic force (see chapters 2, 11, 15).

Strategic autonomy: See chapter 18.

Strategic development: Sustainable effort that focuses on medium- and long-term objectives without maximizing nor sacrificing short-term results [See Buono & Savall (2007)].

Strategic energy: Intangible resource enabling actors to develop their strategic force and capacity to transform their strategic positioning (Chapter 4).

Strategic force: Capacity of an enterprise to transform material and intangible resources into activities that enable the enterprise to improve its strategic situation, namely its capacity for survival-development and its power to negotiate with its internal and external environment (stakeholders) (Chapter 17).

Strategic gear: Chapter 18.

Strategic implementation: Concrete actions to attain the organization's strategic objectives, broken down and discussed at every hierarchical level, in a synchronized, transversal effort uniting various internal and external partners. It involves explicitly defining coherent strategic objectives and scheduling the necessary means to accomplish them (e.g., material, human, intangible) (Chapter 8, 9, 13, 15, 17).

Strategic interactivity: [See Chapter 1 in Buono & Savall (2007)].

Strategic keys of success: Chapter 11.

Strategic management tools: Chapter 11.

Strategic management: Chapter 2.

Strategic objectives: Explicit, recognized objectives that the organization wants to attain within X to X years, in order to guarantee its survival-development (Chapter 5, 11).

Strategic patience: [See Chapter 2 in Buono & Savall (2007)].

Strategic performance: Chapter 1, 4.

Strategic piloting indicators: See *strategic piloting logbook* (Chapter 3, 4).

Strategic piloting logbook: A tool composed of qualitative, quantitative and financial indicators enabling efficient communication-coordination-cooperation among the members of the management team, enabling them to accomplish decisive actions in operational and strategic activities (Chapter 4).

Strategic piloting: Includes implementation and application of the strategy decided upon by the senior management, as well as evaluation of differentials between obtained results and projected objectives, through a heuristic process of "intelligent groping" (Chapter 5, 12, 14, 17).

Strategic pro-activity: See *pro-activity* (Chapter 15).

Strategic project: Chapter 15, 17.

Strategic situation: Chapter 11.

Strategic threat: A particular state of uncertainty among internal company actors caused by change in the external environment and to a lesser degree in the internal environment, with the subsequent possibility of the organization's partial or total disappearance, or the irreversible obsolescence of an actor's current job (Chapter 3)

Strategic variable: An aspect of the internal or external environment, economic or social in nature, to be taken into account in the strategic analysis when preparing a strategic decision and its implementation [see Buono & Savall (2007)].

Strategic vigilance (or intelligence): See ***vigilance*** (Chapter 4, 5).

Strategic warning: Chapter 2.

Structure: Relatively stable elements of an organization permitting actors to carry out their activities, interacting with their behaviors and their competencies (Chapter 3, 4, 8, 9, 10, 13, 15, 17).

Submission: Chapter 2.

Successive iterations: Chapter 5.

Superstructure (organizational): A visible and relatively stable component of the organization (Chapter 2).

Survival and development (capacity): Sustainable state of short-, medium- and long-term survival; the development component facilitates the medium and long-term survival of an organization (Chapter 2, 3).

Survival: Chapter 3, 8, 12,.

Sustainable (Corporate) Social Responsibility: Chapter 1.

Sustainable (global or integral) performance: Socio-economic performance that can be evaluated or appreciated by the principal stakeholders (Chapter 3, 6).

Sustainable (overall) performance: the current definition of organizational performance tends to become wider, taking into account its contribution to the different stakeholders and to the ecological environment. Since its origin, the socio-economic theory proposes a richer concept of performance, which incorporates short, medium and long term social and economic performance, as well as the externalities. (Chapter 3, 5, 6, 12, 17)

Sustainable autonomy: Chapter 5.

Sustainable change process: Chapter 8.

Sustainable development: Chapter 6, 7, 14.

Sustainable economic performance: Chapter 2.

Sustainable effectiveness and efficiency: Chapter 4, 5.

Sustainable prosperity: Chapter 3.

Sustainable socio-economic performance: Chapter 18.

Synchronization: Coordination in real time or within a very short interval. Synchronization aims to ensure compatibility between activities and decisions of the organization's various entities, divisions departments, units, teams and individuals in view of achieving the objectives and goals of that organization. It is one of the three efficiency factors for strategic and operational piloting of organizations and their performances (see ***HISOFIS*** and ***clean-up***). It is one of the main sources of reduced dysfunctions and hidden costs (Chapter 1, 8, 11, 15, 18).

Synchronized decentralization: Transferring the initiative of the decisive act to the responsibility level where its implementation will be launched, while setting up game rules (communication-coordination-cooperation) that ensure its compatibility with actions from other zones of responsibility and with the strategic piloting of the entire organization (Chapter 4, 5, 8, 11, 13, 14, 15, 17, 18).

Tangible and intangible investment policy: Chapter 11.

Task group: Chapter 8.

Taylorism-Fayolism-Weberism virus (or TFW virus) infection level: Chapter 1, 18.

Technology development: Chapter 10.

(Territorial) extension (phase): In large enterprises, this second phase enhances the first socio-economic management set-up phase by extending and applying it to additional departments or plants [See Chapter 1 in Buono & Savall (2007)].

Tetranormalization: Chapter 1, 5, 8, 12, 15, 16, 17.

TFW virus (Taylorism, Fayolism, Weberism): Concept suggested by Savall & Zardet, which characterized "the" mixed theory built by the engineers Taylor, Fayol and the sociologist Weber, late 19th and early 20th centuries, based on 3 principles: maximization of position and function specialization, dichotomy between conception and production activities, depersonalization of organizational processes, procedures and functioning rules. The numerous applications of the socio-economic theory have illustrated the anachronistic feature of those principles applied in economic, social, and institutional contexts which were/are radically different with regard to the time of their conception. Those stubborn principles are root-cause for more than 50% of the dysfunctions and hidden costs (Chapter 1, 2, 4, 9, 10, 18)

Theater of SEAM: SEAM considers a management situation as a "theater piece," metaphorically speaking [see Chapter 1, 9 in Buono & Savall (2007)].

Theory of two equivalent factors (capital & labor): Chapter 2.

Therapist: One of the three fundamental functions of SEAM interveners. It consists in producing mirror-effects through active-listening of company actors [see Chapter 14 in Buono & Savall (2007)].

Three key forces of change: See *(SEAM) three key forces of change* or *(SEAM) trihedral* [see Chapter 1 in Buono & Savall (2007)].

Three strategic ratios: Chapter 1.

Time management: Temporal organization of work that cultivates automatic reflexes of activity planning and scheduling: prevention time, regulation time, preparation time, execution time, control time, improvement time, development time and strategic piloting time (Chapter 2, 3, 7, 9, 11, 12, 13, 15, 17)

Transorganizational (socio-economic) intervention: Chapter 17.

Trihedral model: Chapters 3, 4.

Unvoiced comments: See *non dit (unvoiced comments)* (Chapter 8, 14).

Value creation: Chapter 5.

Value-added: The very goal and raison d'être of an organization (private or public), useful to its societal environment. It is measured by company accounts: the sales figure or revenue minus purchases and other external expenditures (Chapter 3, 4, 11, 14, 15).

Variable cost depending on strategic choices: Chapter 4.

VAVC (Value-added on variable cost): Chapter 4.

Vertical action: In the Horivert intervention process, this action involves every department, its entire hierarchical line of command from the CEO to shopfloor (line) personnel (Chapter 15, 18).

Vertical diagnosis: Inventory of dysfunctions expressed by all department actors, calculation of hidden costs with the cooperation of management, and analysis of competency grids for all actors (Chapter 14, 15, 18).

Vertical project: Concrete project of actions on the dysfunctions discovered during the vertical diagnostic; developed by the focus group and piloted by management with the assistance of line personnel in task groups (Chapter 7, 14, 15).

Vertical synchronization: Chapter 18.

Very Small Enterprise (VSE): Chapter 2.

Vigilance: Active surveillance of the organization's internal and external environment to extract information useful for the efficient strategic and operational piloting of the organization (Chapter 8, 12).

Visibility: The property of an object, action, decision, information item, material or intangible good, as well as a phenomenon of being perceivable by the actors. Visibility influences representation, comprehension, behavior and relevance of decisions (Chapter 7).

Vital sales function: Socio-economic theory places the exchange of resources among actors at the center of human and social activity; the socio-economic intervention develops the sales function among all actors of the organization, public or private, commercial or nonprofit (Chapter 7).

Warning indicators: Chapter 5.

Work accidents: See *industrial injuries* [see Chapter 1 in Buono & Savall (2007)].

Work organization: Includes the distribution of missions, functions, operations and tasks, their more or less specialized assignment to internal actors, entities and individuals, and the rules governing the relationships among them (Chapter 2, 7, 9, 10, 13, 15, 17).

Working conditions: Both physical working conditions (e.g., workspace, annoyances from the physical environment, physical or mental strain of the work, security) and the technological conditions and constraints of the work (e.g., equipment, tools available) (Chapter 2, 7, 9, 10, 15, 17).

ABOUT THE CONTRIBUTORS

Emmanuel Beck is an associate professor at EUGINOV business school, Institut d'Administration des Entreprises, University Jean-Moulin Lyon 3. He is also a researcher at ISEOR. He heads the "Social Audit" Master's program. His research focuses on SEAM and interculturality. In the 1980s, he was hired as international controller manager of a French company. He holds a PhD in management sciences from the University of Lyon.

Marc Bonnet is professor of Management at EUGINOV Business School, IAE Lyon, University Jean Moulin Lyon 3, and deputy manager of the ISEOR Research Center. His research in the field of Socio-Economic Approach to Management, based on the Qualimetrics Intervention-Research methodology, has been mainly carried out in industrial companies. With ISEOR colleagues, he has published articles in journals such as *Journal of Organizational Change Management, International Journal of Action-Research, Organizational Development Journal, Society and Business Review,* and *Organizational Research Methods*. Prior to the two chapters in this book, he has also co-authored five book chapters in the RMC series.

Daniel Bonnet is a consultant in change management. He is also an associate researcher at the Institute of Socio-Economics of Companies and of Organizations (ISEOR). His research and experimentations are designed to understand the tensions in change management and organizational transformation within organizations. He holds a PhD in Management Sciences.

Céline Broggio is an associate professor in Geography at the Department of Geography and Planning of the University Jean Moulin Lyon 3, France. She is associated with the ISEOR Research Center. Her research is centered on strategic planning and local development management.

Anthony F. Buono, RMC series editor, is professor of Management and Sociology and founding coordinator of the Alliance for Ethics and Social Responsibility at Bentley University, which he directed from 2003 through 2013. He is also a former Chair of Bentley's Management Department. Tony's interests include organizational change, inter-organizational strategies, management consulting, and ethics and corporate social responsibility. He has written or edited seventeen books including *The Human Side of Mergers and Acquisitions* (Jossey-Bass, 1989, Beard Books, 2003), *A Primer on Organizational Behavior* (Wiley, 7th ed., 2008), and *Exploring the Professional Identity of Management Consultants* (Information Age Publishing, 2013). His articles and book review essays have appeared in numerous journals, including *Academy of Management Learning & Education*, *Across the Board*, *Administrative Science Quarterly*, and *Human Relations*. Tony holds a PhD with a concentration in Industrial and Organizational Sociology from Boston College.

Laurent Cappelletti is chair professor of Management Control at the Conservatoire National des Arts et *Métiers, University of Paris, where he is the director of the executive training programs and researcher at the* LIRSA center. He is also Program Director at the ISEOR Research Center in Lyon. In 2005 and 2009, he received with Florence Noguera and Richard Baker, the Academy of Management "Best Paper Award" (Management Consulting Division) for his work on human capital and the socio-economic management control system. His research is focused on human potential and the improvement of socio-economic performance in companies and organizations, particularly in public services and small- and medium-sized businesses. He holds a PhD in management sciences from the University of Lyon.

Frantz Datry is a program director at the ISEOR Research Center. He has been an intervener-researcher of Management Sciences since 1999. His research focuses on SEAM, strategic change management, management control, and socio-economic performance in companies and organizations. He holds a PhD in Management sciences from the Institut d'Administration des Entreprises, University Jean Moulin Lyon 3.

Miguel Delattre is an assistant professor at EUGINOV business school, IAE Lyon, University of Jean Moulin. He is the director of the Master's

Program in the field of organizational development. He is also an intervener-researcher at ISEOR Research Center. For over 20 years, he has carried out longitudinal intervention-research projects in a variety of companies and organizations. His current research focuses on the contribution of social performance to sustainable economic performance of companies and organizations, and the contribution of human potential development to organizational performance. He is highly involved in several academic associations, including the French association of HRM (AGRH), ADERSE (Academic Association of Corporate Social Responsibility), and the Academy of Management. He holds a PhD in Management Sciences.

Gérard Desmaison was a senior executive at Nabisco/Danone (Belin Biscuits), ACCOR (Lenôtre, Carlson-Wagonlit), and Ferrero (International Headquarters) implementing SEAM for over 35 years. He is now a consultant at +PHOR and a researcher at ISEOR Research Center. His research focuses on SEAM, management methods, corporate social responsibility (CSR), human potential. He published many conference papers. He holds a HEC Certified Coach (member of ICF) and does coaching, training and conferences for executive and project managers. He is a member of Atelier Du Dirigeant Durable (A3D), a think tank focused on the reconciliation of "economic" and "human" in organizations, ADERSE (Association for the Development and the Education of the CSR), and 36000 Rebonds (French ONG in charge to coach entrepreneurs after a bankruptcy). He holds a PhD in Management Sciences.

Cécile Ennajem teaches management control at the Institut d'Administration des Entreprises, University Jean Moulin Lyon3. She is also in charge of the accounting and management control department of the ISEOR Research Center. Her research is focused on management control and the improvement of socio-economic performance in companies and organizations. She holds a PhD in Management Sciences from Institut d'Administration des Entreprises, University Jean Moulin Lyon 3.

Guillaume Fernandez is an intervener-researcher at the ISEOR Research Center. His research interests are SEAM, corporate social responsibility, and management control, especially within non-profit organizations. He holds a PhD in Management sciences from the Institut d'Administration des Entreprises, University Jean Moulin Lyon 3.

Pierre François is a PhD student in SEAM at the Institut d'Administration des Entreprises, University Jean Moulin Lyon 3. He is also an intervener-researcher at ISEOR. His research is focused on differentiation strategies and the improvement of socio-economic performance in companies and organizations. He holds a Master degree in Consulting Engineering Management and Socio-Economic Management Research.

Robert P. Gephart, Jr. is professor of Strategic Management and Organization at the University of Alberta School of Business. His research has appeared in several journals including *Administrative Science Quarterly, Academy of Management Journal, Journal of Management, Organization Studies,* and *Organizational Research Methods*. He is the author of *Ethnostatistics: Qualitative Foundations for Quantitative Research* and a co-editor of *Postmodern Management and Organization Theory* published by Sage Publications. Dr. Gephart's current research interests are ethnostatistics, temporalities in risk sensemaking, and organizational change management using the SEAM approach. He received his PhD from the University of British Columbia.

Françoise Goter is an associate professor at EUGINOV business school, Institut d'Administration des Entreprises, University Jean Moulin Lyon 3. She is also an intervener- researcher at the ISEOR Research Center. She heads the "Team and Quality" Master's program. Her research is focused on the improvement of socio-economic performance in private enterprises and public services. She holds a PhD in management sciences from the University of Lyon.

Nouria Harbi is a member of the research staff at ERIC Laboratory, University Lumière Lyon 2. She joined the ISEOR research center, where she has worked on SEAM information systems. She is currently working on the security of decisional information system and modeling datawarehouse. She received a master degree in computer sciences and holds a PhD from INSA Lyon.

Isabelle Horvath has been a researcher and teacher at ISEOR since 2007. Her research focuses on change management in the arts and culture industry and on the artist-manager concept. She is also interested in strategic management of territories and has started a research on creative neighborhoods as a possible lever for social and economic development.

Nathalie Krief is an associate professor of Management at EUGINOV business school, Institut d'Administration des Entreprises, University Jean Moulin Lyon 3, and a researcher at ISEOR. She heads the General Bachelor's program in "Team Management, Quality and Sustainable Development" and the Master's program "Management of Public Organizations and Decentralized Administrations." Her research focuses on hospital management and public services, with an emphasis on strategic change management in that sector. She holds a PhD in Management Sciences from the University of Lyon.

R. Murray Lindsay is the former dean of the Faculty of Management and professor of Accounting at the University of Lethbridge. Dr. Lindsay's current research interests in management accounting lie in several areas, especially relevant to practice including performance management and how management control systems must change to foster employee empowerment and innovation. His research in this area has earned him an award from the International Federation of Accountants. More recently, his research has begun to examine the role of management control systems in facilitating strategic adaptation and why transformational change needs to be socially constructed. Since 2003, Dr. Lindsay has been a perennial presenter in performance management in the Certified Management Accountants of Canada (CMA Canada) Executive and CFO professional development programs. He was the President of the Management Accounting Section of the American Accounting Association in 2013-14 and is currently a member of the editorial board of *Contemporary Accounting Research*.

Rickie A. Moore is an associate professor in Entrepreneurship and associate dean of International Executive Programs at EM Lyon Business School, where he teaches, conducts research and publishes in the fields of entrepreneurship, firm performance, and management consulting, mainly at the graduate and executive levels. Former Chair of the Management Consulting Division of the Academy of Management, Rickie has also served on the Executive Committee of the Entrepreneurship Division. With extensive corporate experience at a global level, he has been assisting and advising corporate executives and entrepreneurs for over a decade and has won a number of national and international awards. Rickie holds a PhD. He has carried out his doctoral and post-doctoral research within ISEOR.

Florence Noguera is a professor of Management Sciences at the University Paul Valéry Montpellier. She is also the treasurer of the French Human Resources Academy (AGRH). She leads the Executive leadership MBA program and the Management DBA program. Her research focuses on measuring HRM performance and normalization in service and public companies. She published a hundred of papers in French and International conferences, such as AGRH, Academy of Management, IFSAM, and American Accounting Academy. She mostly teaches HRM-oriented courses. She holds a PhD in Management Sciences and an agregation title from Université Panthéon-Assas, Paris 2.

Michel Péron is an emeritus professor at the University of Paris III Sorbonne Nouvelle. He is also a researcher at the ISEOR and CERVEPAS research centers. His research interests lie in cross-cultural management, corporate ethics and the history of economic ideas. He received his PhD from the University of Lyon.

Renaud Petit is an associate professor at the University of Franche-Comté. He holds a PhD in management sciences; he has been an intervener-researcher at ISEOR for 15 years. His research interests are focused on the development of the attractiveness and loyalty of junior employees in organizations and companies, as well as the development of the socioeconomic performance of healthcare and not for profit organizations.

Xavier Pierre is currently associate researcher at the ISEOR Research Center, and teaches at the University of Lyon. His research focuses on managing the implementation of territorial strategies and inter-organizational cooperation, and he has published extensively in these areas of work. He is an active scientific consultant in both public and private sectors. Xavier is the author of the book *Institutional Piloting of Inter-organizational Cooperation: The Implementation of Territorial Strategies* (*Éditions* Universitaires Européennes, 2011). He holds a PhD in management sciences from the Conservatoire National des Arts et *Métiers* (CNAM, Paris).

Andry Rasolofoarisoa is currently involved in several scientific consulting intervention-researches, aimed at helping leaders and organizations improve performance and their development. He has worked for more than 4 years as a scholar-practitioner at ISEOR, combining the best of academia with practical business management. He is an innovative, multilingual, goal-driven leader with hands-on operations, business diagnoses and project management expertise that has helped increase the economic performance of several public and non-profit organizations. He holds a Master's degree in Management Consulting from the University of Lyon in 2012. Andry is now a PhD student in Management Sciences at the University of Lyon (France). His research interest focuses on standards and regulations impacts on strategies and managerial practices.

Maïté Rateau is a PhD student in Management Sciences. She studied at the Institut d'Administration des Entreprises, University Jean Moulin Lyon 3. She is now an intervener-researcher at ISEOR where she has carried out several intervention-researches. Her research is mainly focused on the sales performance steering by the non-sales managers in social and medico-social organizations.

Alexis Roche is an associate professor of Management Sciences at EUGI-NOV business school, Institut d'Administration des Entreprises, University Jean Moulin Lyon 3. He works with Professors Henri Savall and Véronique Zardet at the ISEOR Research Center. He leads intervention-research programs in industrial organizations, service companies and medico-social associations. His research is focused on human resources, with an emphasis on recognition, reward, equity, meaning of work and the improvement of socio-economic performance in companies and organizations. He holds a PhD in management sciences from the University of Lyon.

Samantha Rose is an intervener-researcher at ISEOR where she participates in several socio-economic interventions in various organizations. She is also a PhD student in Management sciences at the Institut d'Administration des Entreprises, University jean Moulin Lyon 3. Her research is mainly focused on the demonstration of elitism in organizations.

Thibault Ruat is an intervener-researcher at ISEOR, where he has carried out various interventions since 2012, particularly in the building firms and architectural industry. His research interests are SEAM, cooperation practices, strategic management, prime contractor, and qualimetrics methodology. He has presented research papers in a number of international conferences. In 2014, he presented his first research results at the second SEAM conference in the US (Minneapolis, MN). He also teaches management, audit and quality at the University of Lyon to undergraduate students. He is currently a doctoral student at the Institut d'Administration des Entreprises, University Jean Moulin Lyon 3.

Guy Saint-Léger is an associate researcher at ISEOR. His research and publications focus on organizational transformation in relation to the implementation and use of integrated systems. Beyond his teaching activities in public universities and private business schools, he held management positions for ten years in various industrial groups. Since 1990, his consulting activities have allowed him to participate in the realization of thirty ERP projects in the industry and the service sectors. He holds a PhD in Management Science (2005) and an accreditation to supervise research (2012) from the University of Lyon 3.

Jérémy Clément Salmeron is a doctoral student in management sciences at EUGINOV business school, IAE Lyon, Jean Moulin University. He is also an intervener-researcher at ISEOR where he has carried out various intervention-researches since 2012, especially in service industry. His research focuses on innovation processes and management methods that merge exploration and exploitation outputs. He also teaches leadership and quality management to graduate and undergraduate students.

Amandine Savall is an intervener-researcher at the ISEOR research center, where she has carried out various interventions in European and American companies. She teaches at the graduate, undergraduate, and doctoral levels at IAE Lyon business school. Her research interests are SEAM, management consulting, management control, family businesses, and international management, using the qualimetrics methodology. Amandine was awarded the best doctoral student paper from the Management Consulting Division (Academy of Management Annual Meeting, August 2014, Philadelphia). She has co-authored the book *Becoming Agile* (in press, Jossey-Bass) with Christopher Worley, Véronique Zardet, and Marc Bonnet. She has also coordinated two books edited by Tony Buono and Henri Savall, in the Research in Management Consulting Series (Information Age Publishing). She holds a PhD with a concentration in International Management and SEAM from Conservatoire National des Arts et **Métiers in Paris.**

Henri Savall, co-editor of the volume, is an emeritus orofessor at the Institut d'Administration des Entreprises, University Jean Moulin Lyon, where he is the founder of the EUGINOV Centre (École Universitaire de Gestion Innovante) and the Socio-Economic Management Master's program. He is the founder and president of the ISEOR Research Center. Professor Savall has a multidisciplinary education and his fields of interest include accounting, finance, political science, linguistics, economics, and economic history. His current research interests are socioeconomic theory, strategic management, qualimetric methodology, and tetranormalization. His research methodology is referred to as "intervention research" and "qualimetrics" as it goes beyond traditional action research. Henri (along with Professor Véronique Zardet) has been awarded the famous Rossi Award by the Academy of Moral and Political Sciences (Institut de France) for their work on the integration of social variables into business strategy. He is the founder and the editor of the *Recherches en Sciences de Gestion – Management Sciences – Ciencias de Gestión* (Journal of Administrative Science), Paris and Lyon.

Patrick Tabchoury is a scholar-practitioner in the field of Management Sciences, and an adjunct professor at University of Balamand and the Lebanese University. He is also the co-director with Marc Bonnet of the DBA program at University of Balamand and University of Lyon 3. As an associate researcher at the ISEOR Research Center, his research and consulting interests focus on organizational change in the field of healthcare especially in the MENA region where he made many intervention-researches. Among his publications, he has several book chapters and articles focused on qualimetrics research and the Socio-Economic Approach to Management. He holds a PhD in management sciences from University of Lyon 3.

Olivier Voyant is an associate professor in Management Sciences at EUGI-NOV business school, IAE Lyon School of Management, University Jean Moulin Lyon 3. He is a Master's Program Director at the EUGINOV (University School for Innovative Management) and a Program Director at the ISEOR Research Center. For 24 years, he has participated in many intervention-researches within companies as well as public and private organizations. His research on strategic management demonstrated that space and time should be taken into account when driving change and developing an organization in order to meet the increasing long-term challenges of external environment.

Véronique Zardet is professor of Management Sciences at EUGINOV Business School, Institut d'Administration des Entreprises, University Jean Moulin Lyon3, where she is the director of the EUGINOV Center (*École* Universitaire de Gestion Innovante) and director, along with Professor Henri Savall, the founder, of the ISEOR Research Center. She heads the "Research in Socio-Economic Management" Master's program. She holds two PhDs in management sciences from the University of Lyon. In 2001, she received with Henri Savall the Rossi Award from the Academy of Moral and Political Sciences (Institute of France) for their work on the integration of social variables into business strategies. Her research is focused on strategic change management and the improvement of socio-economic performance in companies and organizations, particularly in public services and health industry. She is a deputy editor of *Recherches en Sciences de Gestion-Management Sciences-Ciencias de Gestión* Journal.

CPSIA information can be obtained
at www.ICGtesting.com
Printed in the USA
LVHW01s1448151217
559797LV00005B/69/P